ANCHORS

ANCHORS

*Brokaw, Jennings, Rather
and the Evening News*

by Robert Goldberg
and
Gerald Jay Goldberg

A Birch Lane Press Book
Published by Carol Publishing Group

A Birch Lane Press Book
Published by Carol Publishing Group

Editorial Offices   Sales & Distribution Offices
600 Madison Avenue   120 Enterprise Avenue
New York, NY 10022   Secaucus, NJ 07094

In Canada: Musson Book Company
A division of General Publishing Co. Limited
Don Mills, Ontario

Manufactured in the United States of America

5   4   3   2   1

Library of Congress Cataloging-in-Publication Data

Goldberg, Robert
        Anchors : Brokaw, Jennings. Rather and the evening news / by
    Robert and Gerald Jay Goldberg.
          p.   cm.
    "A Birch Lane Press book."
    Includes bibliography and index.
    ISBN 1-55972-019-0
        1. Brokaw, Tom. 2. Jennings, Peter, 1938-   . 3. Rather, Dan.
    4. Television journalists--United States--Biography. 5. Television
    broadcasting--Political aspects--United States. I. Goldberg, Gerald
    Jay. II. Title.
    PN4871.G6   1990
    070.1'95--dc20   90-40480
                                                              CIP

For Nancy and Colleen with love

Contents

Preface

They could be members of the family, their faces are so familiar to us. The aggressive Dan, who fronts the CBS cameras like a heavyweight with hard, determined eyes and punches out the news. Likeable Tom with his easy smile and colloquial style, the gray-haired choirboy eager to win our approval for NBC. And urbane Peter of the receding hairline and flashy breast-pocket foulard, ABC's spit-and-polish wing commander, clipping his words as they quick-march past us with military precision. Who doesn't know Rather, Brokaw and Jennings? Collectively, these three top journalists who anchor the national evening news are among the most influential media figures in the country. Small wonder the networks are willing to pay them big bucks, a combined total of well over $8 million annually, when each night over forty million viewers tune in to watch them.

For these many Americans, the three anchors are more than just journalists. They are suprajournalists, with a higher public recognition factor than many of the politicians and statesmen who figure in their stories. Try to elude them by fleeing your television set for a pueblo in Taos or an igloo in Fairbanks and it's more than likely you'll find Dan or Peter or Tom already in residence. As reporters on assignment, the three of them have had their cover blown, and inevitably they become part of the stories they're tracking. As stars, they're accustomed to it. Their high visibility has a purpose: The networks use the modern anchors not only to report the news, but to sell it as well—to market their programs. It goes with the system.

Whether or not the cult of personality is good for television news, the networks' system provides Jennings, Rather and Brokaw with three of the best jobs in journalism. If the networks use them as bellwethers, all three are more than repaid in terms of prestige, influence, money and control. And then, too, there's the satisfaction of covering the major stories.

Even in a dull year, making news programs is a complex high wire act. But in a remarkable news year such as 1989, when historic developments occurred at fast-forward speed, the news business took on an added excitement and importance. Planes crashed, and so did coup attempts. Hurricane Hugo rattled the East Coast, and an earthquake rattled the West. Meanwhile the Exxon Valdez spill, global warming and acid rain raised the specter of environmental self-destruction, rattling just about everyone coast to coast.

Democracy flowered in China, only to be brutally crushed in the bloody massacre in Tiananmen Square. But halfway around the world, democracy sprang up again. Dictators Honecker and Ceausescu were overthrown, and Communist Party rule was ousted in Poland, Czecho-slovakia, Hungary and Romania. Even the USSR held open elections for the first time. And, as if the year were in danger of closing without a final exclamation point, the U.S. Army invaded Panama in December, and deposed the "Panamanian pineapple," the pock-marked "maximum leader," General Manuel Noriega.

From San Francisco to Sioux City, from Tiananmen Square to East Berlin, from Poland to Panama, 1989 proved to be volatile and unpredictable—without a doubt the most significant news year in the four decades since television has become a household item. And it was television news that brought the stories home. Who can forget the powerful images? A lone Chinese student holding off a line of tanks. Millions of Czechs taking to the street, singing their national anthem. Jubilant Germans swinging pickaxes at the Berlin Wall. Although polished photographs later appeared in many magazines, it was the sometimes blurred, sometimes shaky television pictures of these events, shown on network news the same day they occurred, that had, in photo critic Andy Grundberg's words, "an emotional immediacy that still burns in the mind."

In the middle of all this violent history and fast-breaking news, the network anchors, Dan Rather of CBS, Peter Jennings of ABC and Tom Brokaw of NBC, donned the trench coat of their office, and took to the streets of the world. Rather was in China, interviewing the students who massed in Tiananmen Square. Brokaw was in Germany, at the opening of the Berlin Wall. Jennings was in Hungary. And at year's end, all three were in Malta and going head to head in their coverage of the summit, each trying to outdo the others, to score a beat and up their ratings, as Presidents Bush and Gorbachev met to shape the face of the future.

Are they competitive? "Hey," says Jack Chesnutt, domestic producer for NBC's "Nightly News," "that's why we're in the news business and not the short story business. We want to get the story first, best. Of course we want that borne out in the ratings." Competition is the heart of the trade. Newsmen like to call themselves "adrenaline junkies." They compare putting together an evening's newscast five seconds before air time with "changing the fan belt on a car going ninety miles an hour."

The kind of people who get ahead in this business are driven, deadline-oriented workaholics—the sort who don't complain about being out on the road and missing Thanksgiving dinner, the type who value career over Christmas at home with the kiddies. "To say we're obsessed is overstating it," says Dan Rather, "but just barely." Veteran electronic journalists have been known to talk about their calling as "a paramilitary brotherhood." And to be a general, to get to the top, is the most competitive of all.

The story of Brokaw, Jennings and Rather and their rise to the top of network news is the focus of this book. In part, it's the story of the year-long battle they fought in 1989 in the war of the ratings. It's also the story of the teams they gathered around them, and the day-to-day issues they faced in putting together their nightly broadcasts. To understand these three competitive men, you have to understand the business they work in, and know, too, that they have gotten to the peak of their profession just as the whole damn mountain has started to shake.

New York, June 1990

ANCHORS

CHAPTER ONE

San Francisco:
The Earthquake

At 5:04 PM, Pacific time, the ground began to shake. It was a low freight train of a rumble, gathering speed and intensity as it rolled along the San Andreas fault towards San Francisco. From the Marina district to the Castro, from the financial center to the Haight, bookcases toppled over, windows cracked, chunks of plaster and stone began to crumble. Out at Candlestick Park, where the third game of the 1989 World Series was just about to start, lead-off batter Rickey Henderson never quite made it to the plate. As the seats began to shake, and the stadium began to undulate with the force of the 6.9 earthquake, the crowd went absolutely still. Then, as if a natural disaster were just one more spectator sport, 60,000 fans started to cheer. And all around the ballpark, those with portable "Watchman" sets flipped on their TVs to look at themselves on the news.

Three thousand miles away, John Terenzio, then a senior producer with ABC News, was having dinner in a New York restaurant before his nightly commute back to Old Greenwich, Connecticut. The broadcast of "World News Tonight" had gone off without a hitch that evening, and it felt good to relax.

Walking by the bar on his way to the bathroom, he looked up at the TV set mounted on the wall and stopped. "Holy shit!" he said. "Are you serious?" There was baseball commissioner Fay Vincent talking, and there, from the Goodyear blimp, were shots of the Oakland Bay Bridge. It looked devastated, the top roadway collapsed onto the bottom. Ted Koppel, who had been in the Washington bureau preparing his regular "Nightline" broadcast, was filling in commentary as the ABC news organization scrambled.

That evening, Terenzio never made it home. Jumping into a cab, he raced across town to West 66th Street and the crowded newsroom of "World News Tonight." Within an hour, he was heading west, being driven across the George Washington Bridge to New Jersey's Teterboro Airport.

Four planes left that night. As the first Lear jet took off at 12:30 AM, it was crammed with the members of ABC's special "SWAT Team," the small, hand-picked, high-powered group it takes to put the broadcast on live from anywhere on the globe: the bearded Terenzio, who as live "site" producer is responsible for picking the location for the broadcast, and getting it on the air; Stu Schutzman, the veteran who crafts the primary taped piece that leads the broadcast; the bespectacled Dennis Dunlavey, who was functioning as chief editorial coordinator overseeing the writing of the "pages" (the introductory scripts); and at the center, the anchor of the team, Peter Jennings.

Up in the front right-hand seat of the Lear, Peter Jennings removed his raincoat and stretched out his 6'1" frame. Reaching down, he picked up his briefcase and swung it onto his lap. It wasn't the sleek attaché case one might have expected from the cosmopolitan Jennings, not an attaché case at all, in fact, but an old faded yellow-orange box of a briefcase, frayed along the top, the leather peeling. It was the same serviceable box that had carried his notes around the globe for the past twenty years, still bearing the press tags from the Reagan-Gorbachev summit in Moscow. His tie loosened, the anchorman was talking with the team of producers on the plane.

For those who know him only from the news each evening, this off-the-air Jennings would be a surprise. Most people expect him to be as crisp and polished as his upper-crust Canadian diction and his well-tailored clothes. But not the producers he works with. They'll tell you that Peter Jennings, clothes horse that he is, is a man who always has a shirttail loose somewhere, a man whose cheeks scrunch up and whose face turns bright pink when he laughs. And he still gets a good guffaw out of the prank he pulled on *The New York Times*, after he had made a best-dressed list and the paper called to ask who his London tailor was. "Mr. Marks and Mr. Spencer," he responded, customizing the name of the low-rent London Department store. The memory still cracks him up. "They printed that straight-faced," he chuckles. "I laughed like hell when I read it."

His colleagues will also tell you that Jennings isn't just a man with a sly schoolboy sense of fun. He's a hard taskmaster, an editor with little patience for sloppy work. He's a person of strong enthusiasms, forever trying to catch up, to plunge into the next adventure, always with the vague feeling that he might be missing something.

In the air over Pennsylvania, crammed together in the tiny Lear, Jennings and his producers were firing questions at each other, questions for which they had no real answers: Where should they land? How bad was the damage? From what location should Jennings deliver his reports—what background would sum up the message of the disaster? Jennings asked for the latest information on the quake. Picking up the plane's phone, one of the producers tried to reach the news desk in New York. All he could get was static.

Finally, they decided to catch a nap. Three producers, jammed together on the tiny rear bench, tried to get comfortable. Jennings, up front, stretched out his large frame. Sleep was to be a precious commodity in the coming days and hours, and no one needed it more than the anchor, who would be the on-air face of the tragedy.

Three-and-a-half hours later, the jet touched down in Salina, Kansas, for a refueling stop. Although the ABC team was halfway across the country, they still didn't know exactly where they were headed. As the plane was being gassed up, Terenzio put in a phone call to the Los Angeles desk, and was given instructions: "Oakland Airport is shut down. Land in San Jose. Helicopters will be waiting to ferry you to Oakland."

But once up in the air, it became clear that the Lear's pilots were getting other information. They were hearing that the Oakland International Airport was open. Talking it over with the pilots, Jennings and his team decided to head for Oakland and take their chances.

When the ABC plane began its descent for the final approach into Oakland International, it was 5:30 AM, Pacific time (8:30 AM Eastern).

On the phone in the Lear, Terenzio had at last gotten a call through to New York. His big question: When would Jennings have to go on the air live with a special report from the Bay Area? Jeff Gralnick, head of special reports (the live news briefs that interrupt regularly scheduled broadcasts) was making the decision. His ruling: air time would be four hours later—9:00 AM local time (noon on the East Coast).

In the pre-dawn hours at Oakland Airport, Peter Jennings got out of the Lear, and headed for the lounge in the Butler Aviation terminal. He could just make out the two choppers waiting for them across the airport. With only four hours until airtime, he was eager to get aloft, to survey the damage and get a sense of the scope of the story. He and Stu Schutzman had to put together a piece for "World News Tonight" by the end of the day.

Waiting for first light, Jennings, Dunlavey, Schutzman and Terenzio were talking, trying to come to a decision. They finally agreed that as soon as the sun was up, the anchor and his story producer would take off in one of the helicopters for a reconnaissance mission. Terenzio and Dunlavey, meanwhile, would go to the Oakland Coliseum where the ABC trailers, set up for the World Series, still had intact phone lines with the East Coast. It was Jennings' responsibility to be back on the ground forty-five minutes before his special report went on the air.

By 7:00 AM, Terenzio was at the Oakland Coliseum, and on the telephone. It was 10:00 on the East Coast, and time for the news division's daily ritual, the morning conference call. Senior management in New York and all the bureaus around the country were linked up, discussing the day's coverage. The hottest story, of course, was San Francisco. It was so hot, in fact, that vice president of news coverage Bob Murphy wanted to get Jennings on the air right away.

"Right away?" said Terenzio, incredulous. "Jeez, you said you didn't need him till 9:00 Pacific."

"Yeah," Murphy said, "but we think we're first. Brokaw and Rather are still up in the air."

It was clear that the order was coming from Roone Arledge, the impulsive head of ABC News. Arledge wanted his anchorman on the air first. He wanted ABC to "own" the story.

Arledge's reaction was predictable. Today, in the competitive world of news, live coverage has become the key; there is no substitute for being on the spot with your anchor, and being there *first*. The networks call it a "pop," or "waving the flag." Like Neil Armstrong on the moon, like Columbus in the Bahamas, ABC, CBS and NBC all want to plant their banner on uncharted territory, and claim the turf for their own. All this flag-waving frequently has little to do with the quality of the coverage; a "pop," as the name indicates, is only a brief report from the spot. But to arrive first on the scene and win the footrace, to blanket the area and be perceived as "owning" the story, these are the ways that network news divisions currently chalk up their "wins."

At the Oakland Airport, Jennings and Schutzman were watching the last pieces of camera equipment being loaded into their helicopter when the call came through from Arledge, frantically trying to reach the anchor before he took off. Luck was on Arledge's side. Within minutes, the helicopter was unloaded again, and Jennings was on his way to ABC's only live camera position, the cameras and the satellite dish that had been commandeered from World Series coverage and set up near the collapsed Nimitz Freeway (U.S. 880) in Oakland.

Rolling by van to the live site, Jennings flipped on the local news, then turned to talk in concentrated snatches with the driver, a cameraman from the L.A. bureau who knew the area. Along the way, they picked up the local papers. The rest of the trip was made in silence, as Jennings hurriedly scanned the headlines, the articles, the pictures.

Although they got lost en route, Jennings was at the camera position in a much shorter time than he had expected, describing the scene with reporter Greg Dobbs: "Hello, this is Peter Jennings reporting live from Oakland..." he began, and sketched out the devastation near the collapsed roadway. And only a few minutes later, Jennings was off. "A pretty good report for nobody knowing anything," Schutzman would later say.

Terenzio got back on the phone with the head of special reports, Jeff Gralnick. The report was a success. They were first; they had won. In fact, it was such a success that Gralnick wanted another pop in an hour.

That was when Peter Jennings started to get annoyed. "Look," he said, his voice rising with exasperation, "I can't go out and report my story for 'World News Tonight' if I have to go on the air every ten seconds with special reports." Gralnick huddled with Arledge in New York, and within minutes they were back to Terenzio. "Okay," said Gralnick, "release him for 'World News Tonight.'"

By 9:30 AM Pacific, Jennings and Schutzman were finally getting their aerial look at the city, hovering over the smoldering ruins at the

Marina. This wasn't their first encounter with the raw force of an earthquake. When the massive 7.6 aftershock hit Mexico City, the affable, bearded Schutzman had been jolted from sleep in his hotel room, the walls shaking, the windows rattling, the bed doing a crazy tango before it half dumped him on the floor. He had had no time for safety precautions then, no time to remember to stand under the arch of a doorway. There was only time to be scared as hell. Outside, cars were smashing into each other, horns exploding into the air. "Frankly," says Schutzman, "we thought we were going to die."

When Jennings joined Schutzman on the scene the next day, he found that although 16th century churches, ironically, had not fared badly, modern government buildings, even hospitals, had turned into instant rubble. Mexico City had been flattened.

But here in San Francisco, the mood seemed amazingly tranquil over the Presidio and the Golden Gate Bridge. "We were very surprised," recalls Schutzman, "because except for the Bay Bridge and the freeway, San Francisco looked absolutely normal. It was sunny, hazy, a nice day, and downtown looked untouched."

While Jennings and Schutzman peered down at the city, Terenzio and Dunlavey were trying to get another kind of view, one that would give the ABC audience a feeling of the tragedy. "The question is," Terenzio asked himself, "where do you place Peter? Where does he deliver the news from? You want a shot that has 'the look.' You want something that says it all. It has to be the best picture. You should start with your very best picture."

At the live camera position near the Nimitz Freeway collapse, Terenzio surveyed the two tiers of road that had pancaked one atop the other. Local authorities were saying that more than two hundred people had been killed there when the old concrete roadway gave way and crushed the drivers on the lower level. It was the hardest-hit spot in the Bay Area, the core of the disaster.

Looking over the rubble, Terenzio shook his head. "I hate it," he said. "As a picture, you can't really understand it. What is this? It says destruction, but it's not articulate destruction. You can't tell one highway's on top of the other. It's no good."

In fact, that had been exactly the problem with ABC's coverage the night before. True, the network had clearly beaten everyone to the punch with riveting ground and blimp coverage (thanks to the World Series), plus commentary by both sportscaster Al Michaels in San

Francisco and Ted Koppel in Washington, all while Dan Rather was just starting to roll up his sleeves and NBC was still searching for Tom Brokaw. But ABC had clearly been broadcasting pictures without any idea of what they meant, and this stretch of the Nimitz Freeway, the deadliest real estate in the quake, had aired repeatedly before Koppel belatedly realized that it was not a one-level highway, but a two-level sandwich of destruction.

Walking around the area, Terenzio, the "site" producer, and Dunlavey, the chief editorial coordinator, were searching for other angles on the collapsed roadway. "We were looking for high shots. You're always looking for high shots." Calling on landlords of neighboring buildings, they began clambering up ladders, examining rooftops, trying to find a vista and getting more and more discouraged with the options available. Meanwhile, time was going by: 11:30, 12:00, 12:30. "The show is on in three hours," Terenzio said. "We gotta pull the ripcord. We gotta get out of here. We gotta get back to San Francisco."

Terenzio and Dunlavey took off for the ABC bureau, located in local affiliate KGO's headquarters in downtown San Francisco, near the Embarcadero area. Meanwhile, in their helicopter, Jennings and Schutzman were already hovering over the building that housed the bureau, trying to land in the parking lot next door. They had been trying for over an hour, circling and circling while they awaited permission to land. In fact, they had been forced to return to Oakland once for fuel, and the situation didn't look much better the second time out. "We could see the bureau," Schutzman recalls. "It was right there, but we couldn't land." San Francisco authorities are careful about helicopters touching down in the city at the best of times, and this certainly wasn't the best of times.

As they hovered above the city, circling past the nearby Coit Tower and the collapsed Oakland Bay Bridge, Schutzman and Jennings looked at their watches and exchanged glances. "Getting a little dicey," Jennings yelled, his penetrating voice cutting through the engine noise. When they finally received permission to land, it was just past noon on the West Coast, but after 3:00 PM in New York, little more than three hours to the evening broadcast.

Over the next few days, transportation would be a nightmare for all the news teams covering San Francisco. Roads were blocked, traffic gridlocked. But for Jennings and ABC, transportation was also an embarrassment. "In San Francisco," said the anchor, "some smart aleck desk assistant who thought he was doing the right thing hiring cars for us—he got us limos, white stretch limos." Jennings' eyebrows lifted skyward. "I called up and said change it, get me a truck, anything. But we were stuck. So we showed up on the site of a tragedy in white limos. We got roasted for that."

For Dunlavey and Terenzio, slowly making their way towards the San Francisco bureau, the stretch limos turned out to have an unexpected advantage. Snarled in traffic, and desperate to find a location for the day's broadcast, they switched on the limo's TV, flipping around the dial to scan the local stations' live coverage. Sure enough, they saw two sites that looked possible, both in the Marina district, the old Victorian section down by Fisherman's Wharf. Both were multi-story wood frame gingerbread houses that had crumbled during the earthquake.

In the meantime, another drama was being played out, a technological drama. One of the major victims of the quake had been San Francisco's power system. Local affiliate KGO, running on an emergency power generator, was having a hard enough time getting out its own broadcast, let alone trying to service the national news show. That left ABC casting around to find an alternative way to broadcast.

The big question was: How could they get the signal from San Francisco up to the satellite and down to New York (where it would be mixed together with the rest of the show: the music, the graphics, the other stories coming in from all over the world) and then sent back out across the nation as "World News Tonight"?

This was a new age kind of problem. Twenty years before, the pictures in the field were shot on film, not videotape, film that needed time for processing and developing before it could be put on the air. Even after the introduction of video in the mid-1970s (which like the home VCR variety could be rewound and played as soon as it was shot), it was still difficult to send images live. Only six to eight years ago, with the invention and widespread use of satellite "uplinks" (often housed in large U-Haul type trucks), did the networks burst into the modern age. Now they could easily bring their audience an entire news show live from anywhere on earth.

Just such a satellite "uplink" truck was rolling north from Los Angeles, speeding along U.S. 101. But when Dunlavey and Terenzio arrived at the bureau, they heard the bad news: the vehicle had busted an axle. Broken down on the freeway between L.A. and San Francisco, it would never arrive in time for the broadcast. Half a million dollars of high-tech equipment was sitting useless by the side of the road. There was a second truck, a backup dispatched from Salt Lake City and given the site address in the Marina, but no one knew if it would get there in time.

It was now 1:30 PM—two hours before airtime. Inside the San Francisco bureau on Front Street, Peter Jennings ran both hands through his thinning hair and peered over the top of the Ben Franklin half-glasses that perched on the tip of his nose. He and Stu Schutzman had been going over the footage for the taped piece that would lead the broadcast that night.

Picking up his pen, Jennings began leafing through the written copy, making broad blue deletion marks as he went. Paragraph by paragraph, his pen darted over the pages. And as he skimmed through the copy, he read aloud, checking the words for cadence. "There are horrible scars all over the landscape...and in people's lives...." He paused and repeated "and in people's lives," shifting the emphasis, trying to feel the rhythm of the words. "By first light," he continued, "we could see from the air that last night's fire, made worse by leaking gas, had been very well contained...." He stopped, then read on. "From the air the next day, you can see the people in San Francisco fared the best in places they instinctively fear the most—skyscrapers."

All around him in the San Francisco bureau, the scene was frenzied, over two hundred people crammed into three little offices. "It was wall-to-wall people," recalls Schutzman—so jammed, in fact, that video tape editing had to be done out in the KGO garage. "Every time a truck started up," Schutzman says, "we had to go back inside because of the fumes."

As always in these fast-breaking situations, telephones were at a premium. On the line with executive producer Paul Friedman, Jennings discussed the other stories on the show. When he finished, he turned to Dennis Dunlavey, and went over the "tell" items, the no-picture stories the anchor simply reads each night. Lastly, he strode over to ask Terenzio how they were doing on a location. "Well," said the senior producer, "Our Salt Lake City truck hasn't been able to get into the Marina district. It's closed off. We have a backup location on the roof of KGO here, set up in case, but it's not great, and frankly,

KGO is having so many problems, we're gonna be screwed if we depend on them...."

Just then, the phone rang, a call from the Salt Lake City truck. Turned away from the first Marina site, it had managed to sneak into the second. "They bullshitted their way in!" Terenzio exulted. "God is smiling on us!"

In front of the half-collapsed buildings in the Marina district, it was chaos. Police, firemen—blue uniforms, red uniforms, no uniforms at all—were running around yelling confusing, often conflicting orders. The area was cordoned off. The area was not cordoned off. The area was *about to be* cordoned off.

Up on a balcony in one of the teetering buildings, a man could be seen removing his belongings from an apartment. Terenzio had a brainstorm: Could they broadcast from there? Yelling up, Terenzio explained who he was and what he needed.

But as he climbed up the decimated stairway, he saw how precarious the situation was: the building in shambles, no electricity and worst of all, the balcony too narrow to get a good shot of Jennings. Looking at his watch, Terenzio muttered to himself: "This is getting wild." It was going on 2:30 PM, 5:30 in New York, just over an hour till air. Terenzio put in a call to Dunlavey, with a message for executive producer Paul Friedman. "Look," he said. "We can do it from in front of the building here, but we run the risk that they may start knocking the building down. You might not be able to hear Peter. They might even move us out. Who knows?" The word came back from Friedman, "We've got an anchor in Washington if we need—Ted can do it—so we'll go with it."

Terenzio went to huddle with the technical team. "All right," he said, "we're gonna try to anchor out of here." The technicians got back to their work, setting up the wires and cables connecting the anchor site—cameras, monitors, headsets—with the satellite truck, and from there on to New York.

Meanwhile, Terenzio tried to make friends with the fire lieutenant who was in charge of the building. "I'm busy here," snapped the overworked fireman. "These buildings are dangerous. I can't guarantee I won't tear them down. When our equipment shows up, they're coming down."

At 3:00 Pacific, a half-hour before the broadcast, Terenzio was on the headset with ABC director Charlie Heinz in New York, hooked up via satellite. "How does this shot look, Charlie?" he asked, as Heinz set up the framings.

Fifteen minutes to airtime, and Peter Jennings showed up. He'd been polishing the scripts with Dunlavey. Terenzio grabbed the anchor by the arm and explained the situation. The fire lieutenant might pull the buildings behind him down at any moment. "You gotta speak to him," the producer said desperately.

Terenzio had already talked the fireman's ear off, explaining how this was the national news—broadcast live to almost fifteen million people—not just a local reporter doing a brief "stand-up." The fireman seemed harried and more than a little uncertain about how an evening news broadcast was being done live in the middle of the afternoon. He was not inclined to cooperate.

But then Jennings appeared and turned on the anchor magic. "We need your help," he intoned, giving the official an earnest glance. It was more than just charm; it was anchorman's charm, star power mixed with the aura of weighty men doing weighty things. "We're going to be going live to millions of people." The fire lieutenant softened slightly.

"How long is your show on for?" he asked.

"Thirty minutes."

"Okay," he said grudgingly. "I'm going to rig the building now. But I won't pull it down until four o'clock."

Elated, Jennings and Terenzio thanked the lieutenant, and headed over to the anchor site. And, when everything was looking fine with just seven minutes to air, who should show up but the San Francisco police.

"Just what are you doing here?" they demanded. "This area is absolutely off limits. You'll have to leave."

"Leave? But we have permission from the fire department."

"The fire department's not in charge here," said the men in blue. "We are."

Terenzio sprinted over to the fire lieutenant.

"I beg of you," he panted, "talk to these guys, tell them it's okay."

With the firemen and the police still haggling over jurisdiction, the final countdown began and, at exactly 3:30, the show went on the air, the opening voice-over announcing: "From ABC, this is 'World News Tonight with Peter Jennings,' reporting tonight from San Francisco."

"Tonight, in fact," Jennings began, "from the badly damaged

Marina District of San Francisco, but the good news is this...." He gestured back at the destruction behind him. "Despite what you see going on behind me—they're taking down a building in the Marina District because it's a threat to public safety—despite that, San Francisco is still standing. All along the San Andreas fault, years of anticipation and years of preparation have paid off for the most part. The worst news is this: In one location, on the Oakland side of the San Francisco Bay, more than two hundred and fifty people may have died, and they may have died in part because of government neglect."

Over on the Oakland side, standing near that very same pancaked stretch of roadway, at exactly that moment, Dan Rather, with a small team of his own, was busy describing the damage for his television audience.

And elsewhere in San Francisco, Tom Brokaw was running through a similar unhappy litany of earthquake events.

Later, after all the rest of the day's news had been covered from the East Coast—the lift-off of the space shuttle Atlantis, the resignation of East Germany leader Erich Honecker—ABC director Charlie Heinz switched live back to the Marina.

"One final note from here in San Francisco," Jennings concluded. "It's not the most original thing to say, but earthquakes always remind us how fragile man is. Nature just reaches up and grabs us by the throat. We'll be back later this evening for an hour special on the earthquake here in California....I'm Peter Jennings. We'll see you then. Good night for now from San Francisco."

Fifteen minutes after the broadcast had finished, the San Francisco fire department began to tear down the building. But the evening wasn't over for the news team. Going on thirty-six hours straight, they now had to face their biggest challenge, a one-hour news special at 7:00 PM (10:00 Eastern).

Tired but wired, Jennings headed back to the bureau to work on the writing with Dunlavey and Schutzman. Meanwhile, Terenzio was facing a new problem. It had turned dark. He ordered a generator truck from the World Series equipment, and fifteen minutes before seven, ABC had an extra stroke of luck, a City of San Francisco light truck showed up to aid in the removal of debris. In short order, Jennings' anchor site was lit up like the Cotton Bowl. Of course, the noisy, heavy machinery was still at work, but New York indicated they could hear Jennings just fine.

Coming on the air, Jennings obviously felt comfortable, though by this time he and the others were running only on heavy doses of adrenaline and coffee. "Good evening. From a city that is trying to recover its balance," he said in his clipped, polished, wry delivery. "Earthquakes don't have names like hurricanes do, but people will not forget this one in a hurry...."

As Jennings launched into his special, a fire rescue team was searching through the rubble for survivors. And by the end of the second segment in his broadcast, the team came out bearing first one dead body, then a second on stretchers. Charlotte Taylor (the blonde, soigné, middle-aged woman who travels around the globe doing Jennings' makeup) tapped on Terenzio's arm. "John, see that guy?" she pointed. A lone figure blackened by soot, was striding down the street. "That's the guy that went in and found the bodies." Terenzio raced over. "Yeah," said the rescue worker. "We found the two bodies, one male, one female, in their mid-thirties. It was kinda sad, actually. I found them with their arms wrapped around each other."

Terenzio dashed back just as the show was going into a commercial break. "Peter, Peter—you gotta use this," he said. The teleprompter was cued up to another piece of copy, a teaser for an upcoming live interview with Vice President Dan Quayle. But the Vice President was put on hold as Jennings ad-libbed, "If I appear to be shouting at you it's because there's a generator going behind me and they have indeed found, in that building, within the last couple of minutes, what they anticipated to find, not one but two other casualties of this earthquake of '89 in San Francisco...."

As the two dead, mangled bodies were carried away from the wreckage, the rescue workers, in sorrow and frustration, took off their helmets and threw them into the heaped rubble.

By the next day, ABC's location in the Marina would become everybody's live location—from CNN to NBC to the locals—and the rubble would be everybody's rubble, the media rubble. ABC had had a good day. They had gotten lucky.

But a short way across town, fate was not so kind to Tom Brokaw and NBC News. Right before their special that evening, everything seemed to go wrong. Their generator died, leaving them with only minimal lighting to illuminate the anchor, but not his background. Then the police moved them off their spot. Brokaw was finally stuck in front of a police car, and all the audience could make out was the flashing red light. It was only the luck of the draw, but then ABC News had been coming up with good luck, and NBC News bad, for much of the preceding year.

When the earthquake had struck the night before, Tom Brokaw had been off at a dinner party at writer Calvin Trillin's home. Many television journalists carry beepers. (Around New York, they joke that only three types of people have beepers: doctors, drug dealers and TV journalists.) When they don't, they leave a phone number where they can be reached. Brokaw had left a phone number that night, but in the confusion no one was quite sure where it was.

Compounding the problem was the slow overall response of the NBC staff. And to make matters still worse, NBC's local affiliate in San Francisco was having major technical problems that evening. Completing this comedy of errors, there was no real crisis team back in New York at the network's headquarters, no system in place to handle such a fast-breaking mega-story. After regular working hours, there were only a few junior personnel on duty. In the end, NBC went on the air with pictures about fifty minutes later than ABC or CBS. As for Brokaw himself, he didn't get on the air until the next morning.

As if to compensate for their poor showing, NBC continued their coverage much further into the night than either of their competitors, well after 12:30 AM. But in the ultra-competitive, ultra-fast world of today's news, fifty minutes is an eternity, and NBC was stunned. "I was brought in to improve NBC's news coverage," said the new director of their news desk, Donald Browne. "This has been a humbling experience."

Over at CBS that first night, Dan Rather took off his coat, rolled up his shirtsleeves, and almost singlehandedly managed to get CBS on the air. His performance was measured, even cautious, as he continually reminded viewers how natural calamities and their death tolls tend to get exaggerated. It was a strong performance from the man who has been on the scene of so many tragedies that he might be called the "master of disaster."

For CBS, San Francisco wasn't the defeat it was for NBC. But it wasn't a "win" either. Nothing could diminish the fact that ABC had been first on the scene, that ABC had all the best pictures and that ABC had provided the most thorough coverage. In a very competitive framework, it was a clear ABC win.

Over the next three days, Peter Jennings would move his anchor site from the devastated Marina block to locations of recovery and repair, and finally across town, on the last day, to San Francisco's classic beauty shot, the Golden Gate Bridge. "The shot we show on the news each night is important," Jennings said. "We wanted to send a message to America that this town was not devastated, that it was well on the way to recovery."

Of course, in the end, the image America had come away with was the devastation of the first twenty-four hours. In the rush to be there live, in the rush to establish a presence and to show what was happening, all three networks had emphasized the spectacular—the cracks, the destruction, the fires. In fact, over two hundred people didn't die in the quake. Only fifty-nine did.

If a network is going to stay on the air for hours, and do one special after another, it has to show something. But in most of San Francisco and Oakland, the damage was minimal. Not much had happened, just a little shaking. A few broken windows, however, don't make for exciting TV. Dead bodies and blazing buildings do. And so, on all the networks, the sheer volume of the coverage tended to distort the picture somewhat, and San Francisco came out of the week a double loser: once by earthquake, and once by television.

But there is no question who the winner was: ABC and its anchorman, Peter Jennings.

CHAPTER TWO

The Competition

Back in the sixties and early seventies, America came home from work each night, sat down at the dinner table, and flipped on Huntley-Brinkley or Walter Cronkite. Almost eighty percent of TV viewers made network news-watching a nightly ritual. For CBS, NBC and to a lesser extent ABC, it was as if a genteel arrangement existed, a sort of old boys' club neatly divvying up the profits, which were huge.

The first hint of trouble came in the mid-seventies when Thornton Bradshaw, the chairman of RCA, put together a study group to consider the future of broadcasting. Looking into their crystal balls, his panel of Cassandras came up with the gloomy news that by the end of the 1980s, the networks' audience was due for a plunge. Unfortunately for the networks, Bradshaw's group of experts turned out to be right.

By 1981, the audience of the major network news programs began to fall off, dropping to seventy percent, sixty percent and, most recently, thudding out at fifty-seven percent. In 1989, a year of political, economic and seismological upheaval, television's three major networks felt some significant tremors of their own. With their viewership shrinking—limiting what advertisers could be charged—CBS, NBC and ABC suffered a painful late-20th-century adjustment.

The stakes for them were enormous. By the middle of 1989 every thirty seconds of network news time sold to commercials was worth about $50,000; with six minutes available in a half-hour newscast, one night's work by Tom or Dan or Peter could bring in $600,000 a week, or more than $150 million a year. A great deal of money was in the balance as the audience changed its viewing habits.

Why the change? Simply put, there were more options available in the eighties. First of all, there were more broadcast channels. Anyone who didn't feel like being depressed by the body of Colonel Higgins swinging at the end of a terrorist's noose could try reruns of "Three's Company." Then, too, there was cable to watch. Even more channels, even more choices, even more reruns. (In the seventies, it was a rare house that had cable. But by the end of the eighties, more than half of TV households had it.)

And then there was competition of a direct kind from cable, newsgathering competition from Ted Turner's CNN and its sidekick Headline News. During the 1980s, these cable newscasts developed from the "Chicken Noodle Network" into legitimate threats to the major networks, with a nearly equal breadth of international coverage, and most important of all, a round-the-clock delivery system offering twenty-four hour access. Viewers could tune in the news at any hour of the day or night to suit themselves, not just at 6:30 or 7:00 PM. It was the ideal way to present the news, and it made CNN truly useful. "When I want the news," President Bush was quoted as saying, "I do just what everyone else does. I turn on CNN." The networks, of course, were shocked.

A final factor eating into network popularity was the radical shift that occurred at the local affiliate stations. (Each network is a loosely connected group of more than two hundred privately owned affiliate stations across the country.) Given the new satellite technology, any station with half a million dollars to spare could now buy a satellite truck of its own, and thereby broadcast from anywhere on the globe. Previously, local news was in fact local: cops, fires, murders—the evening lineup governed by the credo, "If it bleeds, it leads." Only network news was national and international. Today, it's sometimes difficult to tell the two apart. Local newsmen show up at the White House, even at the Berlin Wall. And regardless of whether it's Eastern Europe or Panama or any other big story that they're watching, by the time viewers get to the network news after the local newscast, they often feel as if they're seeing reruns.

Affiliate stations have also become more independent. Whereas once they saw themselves as the poor relatives of the networks, begging cup in hand, that's hardly the case now. "Whoa! Wait a minute!" they cry. "We're the big-money profit centers, not those guys in New York. The networks should do our bidding, not vice versa." (A local affiliate owns all the advertising time on its own local news; from network news it makes very little. The network, for its part, makes money by selling its affiliates primetime programming and through its outright ownership of seven or eight local affiliate stations.)

In the early eighties, the newly enlightened affiliates discovered that they could make more money airing "Wheel of Fortune" than the news. "Any news program that goes up against 'Jeopardy' gets its ass handed to it," said Tony Malara, president of CBS Affiliate Relations. And so, the affiliates kicked the network news out of its sacrosanct 7:00 PM slot to 6:30 or, even worse, as in San Francisco, to 5:30, which meant still fewer viewers. The network news was on, but no one was home.

All of these changes hit the networks right where it hurt, in their money belts. As a result, the once genteel competition for ratings became downright cutthroat during the past decade as CBS, NBC and ABC scrambled to hold on to their dwindling audience. "The competition is brutal," announced former CBS News president Van Gordon Sauter, taking stock of the situation. "There's everything out there but mustard gas."

The key element in this competition was the Nielsens, the well-known weekly TV ratings system by A.C. Nielsen Company. Breaking down the viewing audience with an arcane system of points (1 point = 921,000 households with television) and share (the percentage of the total TV audience watching any one show), the Nielsens had since early television days tabulated these diary-based figures, which then served as the basis for determining advertising rates. But as the competition heated up, these ratings took on a life of their own, becoming a weekly scorecard in a big-money game. Every Tuesday, the results appeared on network computers like something from Oz. "We used to never even know when the Nielsens came out," says Richard Cohen, a former CBS producer. "Now people live from Tuesday to Tuesday."

Just how accurate are these Nielsens? No one knows. In 1987, after several network complaints that the figures were unrealistic, Nielsen came up with its People Meter, a push-button system similar to a TV remote control unit, rather than a diary. Recently, the networks complained again. By 1991, Nielsen promises it will introduce a passive People Meter, a sort of electronic Big Brother that will automatically keep an eye on what's being watched, removing that tricky, unpredictable human element altogether.

In spite of the fact that no one is sure just how precise the Nielsen numbers are, they are nonetheless a myth that everyone has agreed to accept. Dick Wald, senior vice president of ABC News, says, "I emphatically believe that the Nielsens represent a necessary mythology that the business couldn't do without. Those are the only rules. We have to live with them."

And by the late 1980s, the Nielsen numbers had become even more significant for network news divisions because their bosses had changed. The new owners—Capital Cities for ABC, Larry Tisch's Loews for CBS, and General Electric for NBC—were big corporations, and corporations believe in numbers as the measure of performance. Though they all claimed to respect news, what they really wanted was to be number one.

As 1988 ended, the battle to be number one was heating up. Only fractions of percentage points separated the three evening newscasts: CBS and Dan Rather were first at 12.1 points and 22 percent share; ABC and Peter Jennings were second at 11.4/21 percent; NBC and Tom Brokaw were third at 11.2/21 percent. This kind of close, toe-treading competition had little precedent in the television news business. Through the sixties, Huntley-Brinkley had dominated. Reuven Frank, executive producer of that NBC newscast, claimed that in those years NBC News was so far ahead in the ratings, it was a one-horse race. In the seventies, Walter Cronkite at CBS had a clear lock on the decade.

But by the end of the 1970s and the dawn of the eighties, everything had changed. Roone Arledge was named president of ABC's News Division in 1977, introducing the era of the million-dollar anchor and changing the look of network news with his glitzy production techniques. Then in 1981, Walter Cronkite none-too-willingly stepped down. What followed was a free-for-all. Throughout the mid-eighties, Rather, Brokaw and Jennings all had their crack at first place, although Rather's "Evening News" was most often on top. For CBS, ABC and NBC, the evening news had become a wide open three-horse race.

Much to everyone's chagrin, as the results got closer, the corporate owners of the networks began to become more obsessed with the Nielsen numbers. And they weren't the only ones. Newspapers across the country started to act like racing forms, printing the weekly results as if they were from Santa Anita or Aqueduct. Victories were hailed; losers criticized. "CBS on Top!" exulted headlines, and champagne corks popped at corporate headquarters. "NBC Falls!" groaned the press, and GE tried to find a sunbeam in the demographics.

But smiles were as rare as Kennedy half-dollars when midway through the season, NBC's "Nightly News" discovered itself still in third place. One of the network's producers frankly admitted, "You go through a very involved process of justifying yourself in a year when you're in third, when you think your work qualifies you to be number one." Not that the corporate bosses call anyone up and say, "You're third. Close down that bureau, and forget about covering Berlin. It's too expensive." For this one NBC staffer, it's much more a matter of professional pride and self-image, as if the Nielsen were actually measuring quality rather than size.

In an atmosphere where the competition was so close and the results so carefully watched, any minor change came to be seen as affecting the ratings, and even something as insignificant as Dan Rather donning a sweater became worthy of extended press comment and studious reflection—some pro, some comic. In this climate, as books and articles about the news business started appearing everywhere, TV newsmen began to close ranks. By the mid-eighties, the free-wheeling television newsrooms had begun to settle into bureaucratic middle age. Throughout the business, there developed a close-lipped, institutional paranoia, a cover-your-ass mentality.

"Look," says Tom Brokaw irritably, "we are constantly under the magnifying glass." And he doesn't like it. "Almost anything we do these days turns up a negative for us. What it does is feed a certain grist mill around here." He speaks of taking a critic to lunch and telling him that the open-door policy is over. "We are allowing you guys to come in and open our arteries, and you're describing it as in the public interest, and it ain't. It's in your interest and not ours. I believe that very strongly." And at the networks, Brokaw is clearly not alone in his belief.

Under increasing corporate pressure to make their investment pay off, network news divisions have apparently become as sensitive to their own interests as to the public's. Perhaps even a tad more so.

Hence they are circling the wagons and keeping their heads down. Except for politics and politicians, it's hard to imagine another business so concerned about what the public thinks, but so set on keeping it at bay. Their siege mentality is strange for a group of people whose job it is to interview others. Network public relations departments now seem to be set up to forestall relations and to keep the public out. To journalists familiar with Washington, the networks have started to feel like the Nixon White House. "Everyone's scared to talk," says one former CBS producer. "There's a paranoia around the newsrooms."

In the midst of the instability that has accompanied the corporate takeovers of the networks—the management shuffles and reshuffles, the executives hired and fired, the correspondents ping-ponged from network to network—the only constant through the greater part of the 1980s has been the presence of the anchors. As star journalists, Brokaw, Jennings and Rather have been paid huge salaries and kept in place for a reason. They are the identifiable "faces" of the networks' news divisions, their so-called "living logos."

But if the anchors remained fixed in the eighties, all around them the rules of the business were changing, sometimes subtly, sometimes dramatically. Brokaw, Jennings and Rather were faced with a host of compelling questions. How, for example, would they handle the corporate takeovers, and what would these takeovers mean for their newscasts? Would the new penny pinching, let's-make-news-profitable attitude weaken their ability to cover events? How would they cope with the sophisticated technology that has made simulations and re-creations possible? What about the threat of info-tainment, the perceived need to make news entertaining as well as informative? How would they adapt to the recent trend of putting anchors on the road, and the pressures to broadcast live? And, finally, what would the future of network news hold for them? Faced with such concerns, any anchor could be excused for regarding his peaceful nightly interlude in front of millions of viewers—a grand total of about six minutes—as fun.

RATINGS: As 1989 began, the ratings stood at:

1st. Rather   ("CBS Evening News")—13.5/23 [12,204,000]

2nd. Jennings (ABC's "World News Tonight")—12.3/21 [11,119,200]

3rd. Brokaw   ("NBC Nightly News")—11.6/20 [10,486,400]

N.B. The first figure is rating points; multiplied by 904,000*, it indicates the number of American households watching the program. So, for example, CBS's 13.5 means that 12,204,000 households were tuned in to Dan Rather. We've included the number of households in brackets at the end of each line.

The second figure is share, the percentage of all households watching TV in a given week that were tuned to the program. CBS's 23 share means that 23 percent of all TVs on were tuned to Rather.

How many people were actually viewing? Nielsen cautions against any sweeping generalizations, but one may obtain a broad estimate by multiplying households by about 1.4 or 1.5. In other words, each household is considered to have about a person and a half watching.

By this imprecise formula, CBS's 13.5 rating, which is equal to 12,204,000 households, multiplies out to around 17,695,800 viewers. ABC's 12.3 is equal to 11,119,200 households, and 16,122,840 viewers. And NBC's 11.6 is equal to 10,486,400 households, and 15,205,280 viewers. By comparison, *The Wall Street Journal*, with the biggest daily circulation of any newspaper in America, sells just under 2,000,000 copies.

*(In September 1989, this figure changed to 921,000.)

CHAPTER THREE

Tom Brokaw: Small Town, Big City

It was early evening at 30 Rockefeller Plaza, NBC headquarters in the heart of Manhattan. Strolling on stage, Tom Brokaw gave a tired smile as the "Late Night with David Letterman" audience burst into applause. Only 5:00, and he still had to do his "Nightly News" right after the taping. Frankly, Brokaw looked bushed. He looked as if he was badly in need of the vacation he was about to begin. Letterman asked where he was going.

"Yankton, South Dakota. I lived there when I was in high school."

"It must have been ideal for a kid," said Letterman, deadpanning sincerity.

Brokaw brightened and leaned forward. "It was wonderful! It was a wonderfully Tom Sawyer kind of boyhood!"

In southeast South Dakota, the land is tabletop flat and seems to go on forever as you drive south toward Yankton, the sky a heart-stopping stretch of blue. Corn and soybeans pack the fields. There's Gayville, "the hay capital of the world!" Just outside of Yankton on I-29 a sign declares it: THE TOWN FOR ALL SEASONS. In this very neighborhood, Smutty Bear and his tribe of Yankton Sioux once ruled the roost. Another marker boasts of 12,011 folks inside the city limits, but the clean streets appear almost empty.

Six years ago, Yankton merchants hungering for a few more customers created River Boat Days, a weekend-long August celebration, to attract summer visitors. This centennial year of South Dakota statehood, 1989, Tom Brokaw is the Grand Marshal of the parade, their own local boy who has made very good indeed.

The Saturday morning of the parade, the 19th, there are about one hundred floats in all. Not to mention the antique cars, the horses, the high-stepping banner twirlers in their short pleated skirts flashing creamy suntanned legs. Right behind the Yankton High School Band comes the Grand Marshal, perched on top of the back seat of a white convertible and waving good naturedly at the crowd of several thousand that line the parade route.

Smiling from behind expensive shades, Brokaw—his blue sport shirt topped by a tan bush jacket that looks very much like the one he wore only a few months before in the streets of Beijing—seems to be enjoying himself thoroughly. And still to come are the mud volleyball games, the water skiing competition and the big high school class reunion.

Beside him, his wife Meredith, the former Miss South Dakota, her dark hair crowned by a white beret, bestows her smiles royally. The kids sitting on the curb with cans of pop wave back. The sky looks as if it might rain any minute, but it doesn't. The music is spirited, though not always easy to identify.

When the parade is over, Brokaw generously signs autographs and tells one of his admirers, "You know I often think of people on Main Street in Yankton when I'm interviewing world leaders. What would they want to know?"

In fact, just before interviewing Gorbachev in Moscow, Brokaw recalls standing on the red carpet in the great hall of the Kremlin and thinking, "How am I going to make small talk with him? Then I remembered that he came from a small town too in a largely agricultural area. I told him I came from the Great Plains and that I've been out in a combine. He had, too. And that was a real connection between us."

It's perfectly clear that Yankton means a great deal to the successful anchorman, but why it does is not quite so obvious. For as a young man, oddly enough, Tom Brokaw longed desperately to get out of town.

The Brokaw family arrived in Yankton in 1955. Tom, the eldest of the three boys, was fifteen at the time and about to begin his sophomore year in high school. Born in the small community of Webster, the nearest place in the northeast part of the state that had a hospital, Tom actually lived about sixteen miles away in a still smaller town called Bristol. The family owned the old Brokaw Hotel, a failing three-story bed and board run largely by his aunts.

Tom's parents, Anthony and Jean Brokaw, were poor, hard-working people with a growing family to support and no future in Bristol. They headed west to Igloo, South Dakota—a smidgen of a town that made Bristol look like the big city—where Anthony got a job at the U.S. Government's munitions depot. One of Tom's earliest memories is living with his family in two large rooms on the second floor of a white frame house. There he'd spend cold winter afternoons lofting a rolled-up sock toward the space above the door frame and imagining it was the final seconds of the South Dakota "B" basketball championship, his team behind by a point, and Brokaw had the ball.

"The crowd is on its feet. You can't hear yourself think. Ten seconds. Brokaw moves to the top of the key. Five seconds! He gives a little head fake, jumps, shoots! It's GOOD! The rolled-up sock went in every time. My teammates never failed to carry me off the floor. The little blonde girl who coolly ignored my overtures during second grade alphabet recital by now realized what a fool she had been. It was all I asked in life."

After World War II, when the Missouri River Basin Project was authorized, workers were needed for the dams being built. It was around 1948-49 that Anthony moved his family to Pickstown and became maintenance foreman on the U.S. Corps of Engineers construction of the Fort Randall Dam. Around Pickstown, Anthony Brokaw was known as Red—a tough guy with red hair, a square jaw and an easy smile—and was respected as a hard worker. Despite his gruff manner, he was, according to a former neighbor, "a very sweet man. I think his boys adored him." In order to make ends meet, Jean Brokaw took a job in the local post office. Hard work was something that young Tom learned about early. When Red found another job farther south on the Gavins Point Dam, the Brokaws moved to Yankton in time for Tom's second year of high school.

Yankton in 1955 was about the biggest place Tom Brokaw had ever seen, his new three-story, red brick high school of approximately 800 students the biggest school. "I was terribly intimidated," he readily admits. "I remember vividly the day that I first arrived down off Highway 50 and walked through the streets of Yankton to meet my father who was living with some friends before my family moved into town. And I thought it's not *possible* that I'm going to be able to live in a town this big."

After registering for the fall 1955 term at the high school, he wandered the halls, the classrooms, the gym, the study hall. "I thought it was the center of the universe," Brokaw recalls. Clearly awed by Yankton, the competitive teenager went out for basketball, football, track, and whatever else he could join in order to be accepted.

Not especially fleet of foot or, at 5'11" and 162 pounds, physically overwhelming, Tom is remembered today by his football coach, Don Allan, as a good second-string quarterback who was smart and could throw the ball. Allan would not hesitate to use him in the last ten or fifteen seconds of any game in which they were leading by at least two touchdowns. The team's first string quarterback was the 6'3" behemoth Bill Whisler, who had a rocket arm and would go on to glory at the University of Iowa and in the Canadian Football League. Bill Whisler also had a cute cheerleader girlfriend named Meredith Auld. There is a glamour in such people, as F. Scott Fitzgerald knew, and Brokaw seems to have fallen under their spell.

WELCOME TO THE YANKTON HIGH SCHOOL ALL-SCHOOL REUNION announces the sign in Memorial Park. Picnic tables are lined up end to end and crowded with people eating from paper plates. The smell of hamburgers mingles with fresh-cut grass. The day that had started out threatening rain now sees the sun break through. A small stage with a lectern has been set up and beside it sits a band of eight men, mostly elderly, dressed in curious uniforms with epaulets, feathers and silver helmets. They play oom-pah-pah music, heavy on the bass drum and tuba. It's the sort of band whose last gig might have been playing in rural Italy for a Bertolucci movie.

Tom Brokaw, still in dark shades but dressed now in a white tennis shirt, blue shorts and running shoes, is busy signing autographs for anyone who asks. He looks like a movie star.

From the lectern, the head of the alumni association, Celia Minor, calls him up for an award. She tells the attentive crowd, "Those of us who remember Tom during his high school career, and the extensive preparation he used to do for the classes in which he participated, thought that maybe he needed this. We're going to call it the 'First Annual Alumni Fly-by-the-Seat-of-Your-Pants Award.' " From a paper bag, she presents him with a large pair of red suspenders.

"Oh how nice!" he says dryly. Nevertheless, Brokaw immediately tries to hook them on.

Then Meredith Brokaw is called to the microphone to receive the "First Annual Yankton High School Lost and Found Award." The head of the alumni association reveals that "during her sophomore year, thirty-three years ago, Meredith forgot to pick up her 1956 annual." Her audience laughs and so does Meredith. "I know what you're all wondering," Celia Minor goes on. "Did Tom write in the annual?"

Leaning into the microphone, Brokaw quips, "The same thing he wrote to all the other girls in the class of 1956."

Celia Minor ignores him. "The answer to your question is yes. And I know that Tom and Meredith would want me to share with all of you what Tom wrote in the 1956 annual." She opens the book.

No longer indifferent, Tom peeks anxiously at the page to see what it was he had actually said. "Come on...Did I tell her I loved her too? I don't remember."

People in the audience seem to be enjoying the super-smooth anchorman's obvious discomfort.

"It says: 'Meredith, Hope you have the best success always. You have a wonderful start. Let's make the class of '56-'57 one to be remembered for its accomplishments. Luck to you, Tom Brokaw.' "

Clearly, even after a year, this was still very much the new boy in town. If Tom Brokaw was eyeing Bill Whisler's girlfriend, he was doing so from a most respectful distance. The formality of Tom's relationship to Meredith was striking. But also striking was his rather clever insinuation that in the future they might have common goals, might in fact become collaborators in some outstanding joint venture to the greater glory of Yankton High. Even then Brokaw was a smooth operator.

In 1956-57 crewcuts were as common in Republican Yankton as I LIKE IKE buttons. Like the rest of his high school teammates, Brokaw wore his hair cropped close to the scalp. And where Meredith Auld was concerned—his brown watchful eyes locked on her every bouncing, leaping, irresistible cheer—he played his cards close to the vest. One day before football practice, Coach Allan recalls, Tom was chatting with the star of the team, "Barney" Whisler, and casually asked if he had kissed Meredith after their last date.

"I never got around to that," admitted the big guy uncomfortably. "We were talking about something else." Yankton's Number Two quarterback said nothing, but it would have been hard for Coach Allan to miss the look on his face. There was still hope!

If his sophomore year was a success, Brokaw's junior year proved still better. There were winning seasons for the football, basketball and track teams. There was a part for him in the junior play alongside Meredith. And then, like the maraschino cherry atop an ice cream sundae—with Breyer's ice cream, his favorite, of course—came Tom's selection as one of the eight outstanding boys chosen to represent Yankton High School at Boys' State.

The goal of this annual nationwide program, sponsored by the American Legion, is to help to develop an understanding of the way the American political system works. A crucial part of the five-day experience is the political campaign the boys wage, climaxing in the election of a mock state government from among four hundred of South Dakota's best and brightest.

"From the word 'go,' Tom was going to be governor," Coach Allan, who accompanied the Yankton delegation, recalls. "It wasn't an accidental thing. We kind of schooled them a little bit. We said if you want to be active politically, you have to be involved. Your name has to become known. Remember, you've only got five days." But even Allan was astonished to see young Tom get up at the very first meal and address the crowd.

"My name is Tom Brokaw," he told them in his rich, smooth, full-throated baritone, and then went on to make an announcement that wasn't terribly important. But then it didn't have to be. At dinner the next night, Tom again got up and did the same thing. "Who is that Brokaw?" people began asking. With the same sure political instinct that would later serve him so well as he climbed the NBC corporate ladder, Brokaw had slyly placed his name on the ballot.

His campaign manager was a bright young man named Bob Legvold from Sioux Falls. Impressed with the energetic Brokaw whom he had only just met, Legvold helped to plan his gubernatorial campaign with a strategy that consisted largely of Tom saying, "Now I want you all to stand." And when the assembled throng of four hundred rose, he said, "Now I want you all to sit." And they sat. At this point, Legvold leaped to his feet and announced, "Now, you see? *That's* the kind of leadership we want. We want a man who tells you what to do and gets it done."

Brokaw's campaign style was marked by prankish humor and personal charm, qualities that his friends say still characterize the fifty-year-old anchor. When the ballots were counted, Tom Brokaw was declared governor of Boys' State and Bob Legvold his lieutenant governor. Today, Legvold is head of Columbia University's Harriman Institute of Advanced Russian Studies and, ironically, a consultant to Brokaw's ABC competitor, Peter Jennings. ("Peter asked me first," says Legvold.)

On Friday morning, the last day of the mock political convention, Joe Foss, the reknowned World War II naval air hero and governor of South Dakota, put in an appearance and met the newly-elected seventeen-year-old governor of Boys' State. Tom was bowled over. It was the closest he had ever come to the people who lived in *Life* magazine. During those early years, *Life* and television were his twin picture windows on the world beyond Yankton. Seeing Governor Foss and young Brokaw together, both good-looking in an All-American sort of way, someone had the bright idea of arranging for them to team up on Herb Shriner's popular television comedy-quiz show, "Two for the Money." They appeared in New York on August 3, 1957, paired as the Two Governors from South Dakota. Shriner's questions were lobs. "Name as many trees as you can that begin with the letter B." The two governors cleaned up, winning $1,225.

Glimpsed for the first time, New York may, as some writers tell us, seem to be filled with "the first wild promise of all the mystery and the beauty in the world." The South Dakota "rube," as he called himself, was wide-eyed. Staying on for a few extra days in the city, he took in the Grayline tour, Carnegie Hall, Ebbets Field. He returned home a minor celebrity. On an inside page of the *Yankton Daily Press and Dakotan*, there appeared a small picture of the two governors and a three-inch story of their television success.

The Brokaws were not a wealthy family. Today when asked why his mother worked in the Pickstown Post Office, Brokaw says with astonishing innocence, "She liked working." He seems to have no idea that in those days it was rare, indeed, for a married woman to work outside the home. True, Eugenia Brokaw had been a South Dakota farm girl and knew *how* to work, but she did so, as one of her close friends remembers, because she *had* to work. "Times were hard and they needed the money." When the family moved to the small clapboard house on Mulberry Street in Yankton, Jean continued to work, finding a job in a local shoe store. In addition to Tom, her eldest, she had William and Michael, three young boys to clothe and feed. Her husband's salary during those early days was not much.

Tom, himself, was soon working after school. "I think he always worked," says a former neighbor. "He worked in high school and he worked in college." In town, he got a part-time job at Hanny's, a local clothing store. In the summer, he worked out at the dam as a guide, writing his own tour description.

It was in 1955 that a new local radio station opened in Yankton. KYNT, independently owned and operating at a modest 250 watts, was located downtown on West Third Street. Tom applied for a job and got it. When asked why KYNT was willing to hire the young inexperienced Brokaw, Darold Loecker, who sold advertising for the station and would later become its manager, said, "Tom was easy to hire. He had a great personality. Even in those days he had a certain charisma about him that people liked."

In his senior yearbook, Brokaw listed his hobbies as dancing and records. Ninety percent of what he did at KYNT was disk jockeying, spinning his favorite Fats Domino and Elvis records through the night and, during the summer months, in the mornings. In the summer, he would generally open up the station at about 5:15 AM. Despite what Loecker called Tom's "nocturnal tendencies," he was usually dependable.

Often, however, Loecker would catch the fledgling broadcaster napping at the turntable when he came in at 6:15 AM, a long-playing record filling the air waves. Tom never seemed to get enough sleep in those days. According to Loecker, "He spent a lot of evenings out. You know he's a handsome fellow, and he always was, and it didn't take him too long to find a date."

With his custom-cut silvery salt-and-pepper hair and dark glasses, Tom Brokaw, the featured speaker at the all-class Yankton High School reunion picnic, looks like a million bucks. Or more precisely $2.8 million, his annual salary as anchor of NBC's "Nightly News." During this weekend visit to Yankton, Brokaw and his wife are staying at an expensive resort on nearby Lake Lewis and Clark, lavishly entertaining a group of old friends, out by the dam his father helped to build.

Pacing back and forth with microphone in hand in front of the hundreds of alumni and friends seated on beach chairs and benches, Brokaw works the crowd like a carney pitchman bringing everyone in ur ler the tent with shared memories of nine-cent movies at the Moon Theater and the fun that came afterwards at the Tastee Treet Drive Inn. He reminisces about favorite teachers. "Was there ever a better one than Al Halsted, who could take you into a physics lab and make it all come true?" And Ambrose Schenk, his debate teacher. "An exceptional man," declares Brokaw flatly, and heads in the audience nod their agreement. Then with typical self-deprecating humor, Brokaw adds, "He taught even me to walk and think at the same time." Roars of laughter fill the park.

On February 6th, one of the coldest days of 1989 (and coincidentally Tom Brokaw's birthday), there was a telephoned bomb threat, the third in a series of bomb threats, received by the principal's office at Yankton High School. "It wasn't funny," said one of the students who had to rush out into the sub-zero cold. "At least they let us get our coats, but it's still cold." When they caught the caller, he claimed that it was only a joke.

For young people growing up in Yankton, there is an enormous boredom factor that even Brokaw, with his rose-colored memories of the place, is willing, on occasion, to acknowledge. With characteristic irony, he points out: "One of the advantages of a South Dakota childhood is that there is so little around you intellectually that you reach out for broader sources of material."

But Brokaw's reach did not always exceed his grasp. Self-described as a goof-off in high school, he admits, "I got away with a lot. I pushed the edge of the envelope." There were the memorable drinking bouts, the fights. "We used to run wild on the river, didn't we?" says Jerry Huntley, the bartender at Boomer's, when waxing lyrical about the good old days with the visiting anchorman. He still marvels at the weird things they did.

Take, for example, the visit to Deadwood with its legendary reputation as "the wildest, the wickedest, the most flamboyant mining town on the American frontier." It was, of course, easier to sow one's wild oats out of town, but the best the boys could do in the way of decadence was get drunk and then literally dry out in a local laundromat.

Brokaw remembers, "I think I still hold the record in downtown Deadwood for riding the dryers for the most revolutions. I'd be inside the dryer with a friend on the outside holding the door so I didn't bake to death. It drew a large crowd. And as the gendarmes arrived at the front door, we ran out the bathroom window."

Small wonder that Brokaw left town as soon as he graduated high school. If not for Meredith, he might have gone even sooner.

Looking back, Tom Brokaw loved Yankton High School. So what if Ron Soulek was elected senior class president and Arickara Chief, and the best Tom could do was merely to be nominated. So what if Barney Whisler received All-American nominations and a football scholarship to the University of Iowa while all he received was admission to the school's freshman class. As he told his reunion audience, he loved Yankton High because it was a great equalizer.

"And even though my father worked out at the dam," he told them, "I knew a girl in town whose father was a doctor and she lived in a big brick house up on Eighth Street, and we were all treated the same. By everyone. It was part of the family. It didn't make any difference whether you lived in East Yankton or on West Eighth Street, whether you lived on a farm or whether you were the sons and daughters of professional people or laborers or whatever you were. You were all treated the same way in that high school."

There were many in the audience who remembered that the big brick house up on Eighth Street belonged to Meredith's father, the well-to-do Dr. Merritt Auld. Himself the son of a doctor, Merritt Auld was a major mover and shaker in Yankton who, like his father before him, owned farmland and local real estate. He was a member of the state school board, president of the local school board. His friends were the town's prominent bankers and businessmen. Yankton High School may well have been an enclave of democratic egalitarian ideals, but if the town of Yankton was intimidating to the newcomer whose father worked at the dam, one can only imagine how the people who lived in the big house on West Eighth Street seemed to him.

Brokaw's comments suggest that he has a retrospective need— perhaps born of a former have-not's sensitivity—to sentimentalize Yankton into a classless society. It isn't and wasn't. Although charm, energy, good looks and talent would eventually win him access to the big house, he was plainly not born into it. But like Fitzgerald's Gatsby, he was an enormously likeable and ambitious young man who refused to be disqualified by accidents of birth and fortune and, in order to realize his dream, "sprang from his Platonic conception of himself."

It was perfectly clear to Coach Allan that "Tom was infatuated with Meredith. I never saw anybody so taken with a young woman." Although Tom began to date her in their junior year, Meredith had other boyfriends besides the shy Barney Whisler and the lovesick Brokaw. "She dated a lot of different fellows," Marjorie Gross, a friend of the family, remembers. "She was very popular. A beautiful girl. Striking! Meredith has her mother's beautiful blue eyes. And black, lovely blue-black hair. Very attractive. I don't think Tom had the inside track with her at all. But I think he was pretty persistent."

Following graduation, however, they each went their separate ways, Meredith to Cottey College, a tiny two-year liberal arts school in Missouri, and Tom to the University of Iowa. He didn't do well that first year away from home. Brokaw describes what happened to him in this fashion:

"I had always been able to prevail, I suppose, by putting in a minimum amount of work and having a very good time and getting good marks. And I got down there in a much tougher environment and I just didn't. I was so bedazzled by the social environment and all these teriffic-looking girls from Chicago and other places that I kind of fell off the track."

Leaving Iowa by mutual agreement, the prodigal returned home somewhat chastened. He tried to pick up the pieces of his life by enrolling at the University of South Dakota in nearby Vermillion. To help support himself, he got a job delivering the Saturday news at WNEX, the CBS affiliate in Yankton where Lawrence Welk headed up the house band. He liked WNEX and worked there for most of that year. Then he was fired.

"I think it was a friend was getting married," he says, his eyes narrowing as he squints into the past trying to recall, "and I asked my boss for permission to go to the guy's wedding. And he said okay. So I went to the wedding. And when I came back, a big storm had blown up and some guy at the station had a double duty. So I was relieved of my job."

In retrospect, Brokaw can call it a useful experience, teaching him the importance of being on the spot when news is breaking. At the time, it hurt. His academic career at USD was also not going well. Following the suggestion of Professor Farber—his avuncular adviser at the university—that he get "all the wine, women, and song out of his system," Brokaw in 1960 once again dropped out of school. Farber recalls, a forgiving twinkle in his eye, "I was not impressed at the time with his interest in doing any considerable amount of reading."

Brokaw took a job at a little radio station in Marshall, a town of about six thousand in Southwest Minnesota, where he worked the four to midnight shift. He and the owner of the station were soon at each other's throats—his irascible boss even locking away the hungry young man's cold cuts in the refrigerator—and in less than a week Brokaw was at the Marshall City line, hitchhiking back to South Dakota.

Meredith had also returned to South Dakota. She had come home because of an unlikely twist of fate that involved the Yankton County Republican Party. In the summer of 1959, the Yankton GOP had been in serious need of money and its Treasurer, the banker Norman Gross, had had a bright idea. What better fund raiser than a Miss Yankton Beauty Pageant?

Gross encouraged Meredith, who was home for the summer after her first year at Cottey College in Missouri, to enter the competition. Meredith did and, much to her surprise, won. Next came the state contest. Marjorie Gross recalls, "I can still see us all sitting around and our saying, well, for that competition she really needed to be in South Dakota because of appearances. The next day, it was decided she'd come back and go to the University instead of going back to Cottey." Before Meredith fully grasped what was happening, she was on her way to Hot Springs, South Dakota, as Yankton's candidate for the title of Miss South Dakota.

Brokaw, who was working for KYNT at the time, was eager to interview her and made banker Gross promise to call him just as soon as the winner was announced. "Boy don't you forget, Mr. Gross," he reminded him, "because I really want to know how it comes out. I'll be at the station."

Gross's wife, Marjorie, recalls that as soon as Meredith was declared 1959's Miss South Dakota, her husband called Tom and brought Meredith to the phone. "Well, Tom was so excited that when he finished interviewing her, he thought his mike was off and told her that he loved her. But the mike was *on*, and it went all over town. And then of course EVERYBODY in town heard that Tom Brokaw loved Meredith Auld."

The transition from high school to whatever comes next is difficult for any young person, but it proved to be especially painful for Brokaw. "I went through a two-year period in which I lost all the points of my compass," he readily admits. "I learned a lot about myself in the course of that. About what you have to do with your life." Instrumental in helping him find out, as he tells the story, was Meredith. She sent him a "Dear Tom" letter that he has never forgotten. She was disappointed in him. She was disappointed in the sort of things that she had heard he was doing. She saw no future for their relationship. Brokaw still remembers how incredibly shocked he felt.

"Can you believe this?" he asked a mutual friend, showing him the letter. The friend could and said so. "I think she's right on every point." It was, claims Brokaw, enough to cause him to clean up his act. "Everybody had great expectations that I would go off and whip the world," he recalls, as if after high school he, too, had been a believer. "And I did fall off the track."

To get back on the track, Brokaw applied for readmission to the University of South Dakota, and it was granted. He was especially interested in his political science courses such as Professor Farber's classes on state and local Government. He loved to get into heated discussions of controversial topics but, according to a friend from that time, he had a smooth way "of getting involved in a discussion that everybody came out a winner." If he didn't do as well as Farber thought he should, he nevertheless certainly did improve. Farber attributed Brokaw's less-than-stellar academic performance to his long working hours—first on radio, then, in his senior year, at KTIV, NBC's affiliate in Sioux City, Iowa, where for the first time he appeared on television.

One day on campus, Tom ran into Meredith. She was pleased to see that things were going better for him. "Listen," she said, "let's have a cup of coffee and I'll tell you what I *really* think." They began dating again, and on Sundays when he worked for KTIV, she drove down with him to Sioux City. After he finished the evening newscast, they would go out for a late dinner. There was a quiet place where they loved to eat in South Sioux City. Soon they were talking of their plans and dreams after graduation, and Tom asked her to marry him. Meredith was in love. Things were exciting with Tom. He was fun to be with. He had a lot of energy. He was a doer. "I think she sensed *that*," says Marjorie Gross. "I know she told her mother that life would be *exciting* with Tom."

On the second floor of the old Yankton County Court House, a red brick building with three Roman columns placed incongruously out front in a provincial effort to suggest major doings, is the office of the

Registrar of Deeds. On August 15, 1962 the twenty-two-year-old Thomas John Brokaw and the twenty-one-year-old Meredith Lynn Auld climbed the rickety stairs and took out a marriage license. "M-e-r-e," Meredith corrected the clerk's spelling, and the clerk changed the i to e.

The wedding took place on Friday, August 17 at 7:00 PM at Christ Church Episcopal. Though Tom had been brought up in the less affluent Congregational Church, attending the small Congregational Sunday School in Pickstown, he deferred to the Aulds' high-church preference. The Aulds were, according to Marjorie Gross, "*very very devout Episcopalians.*"

A double-ring, flower-bedecked ceremony, the wedding and the champagne-drenched reception at the Hillcrest Country Club that followed were attended by over three hundred guests. Meredith was a cloud of organza and lace, a white gardenia in her hand. Though Tom in his tuxedo may have felt as uncomfortable as Huck Finn, the ex-governor of Boys' State and the former Miss South Dakota were a stunning All-American couple. And Brokaw had done something that even Jay Gatsby had failed to do: He had married the girl of his dreams. Their honeymoon was two nights in South Sioux City at the Flamingo Motel.

Although no one had (as in *The Graduate*) come up to Tom at the wedding and whispered, "plastics," he soon received a different tip about his future. "UPI," he was advised. It seemed as if everyone who counted in television network news in the early sixties had a background in print journalism. "Go off and get a job with UPI." But Brokaw had other ideas. "That's not what I want to do," he thought. "I like television. I like working with the tools of television. I like the craft of television. I think I'll see if I can't be a good reporter within television."

It was clear that no matter what Tom finally decided, he and Meredith would not remain in Yankton. "I think they always knew that. I don't think they ever intended to stay," said a friend of the family who attended their wedding. "We export our very best commodity in this area."

The newlyweds left almost immediately for Nebraska and Tom's first job at KMTV, the NBC affiliate television station in Omaha. "They initially offered me $90 a week, and I turned them down after having begged for the job." Brokaw is still astonished at his rashness.

"But I was the first college graduate in my family, just married, with a doctor father-in-law a bit unsure about his new son-in-law's future. I needed $100. They finally agreed on the condition that I never be given a raise. And I never was."

In the shadow of the wealthy Dr. Auld's doubts about him, his new son-in-law would have to run faster, stretch out his arms farther in order to win the approval of the people who lived in the big house up on the hill.

Six days a week, Brokaw worked the early morning shift, covering whatever they asked him to cover: murders, farm news, scandals, strikes. KMTV was a small station and he learned to do everything from shooting and editing film, to writing his scripts, to putting on his own makeup. It was a valuable apprenticeship in television news, and this in a year when, for the first time in history, more people were getting their news from television than newspapers.

The next year, 1964, the World's Fair opened in Queens and millions came to New York to see the future. The Brokaws joined the crowds strolling past the Monorail, the Unisphere, the Pool of Industry. Afterwards, they headed across town to visit the NBC studios at Rockefeller Center where the "Today" show broadcast from a street-level, glass-walled studio. Dave Garroway, the host of "Today," was one of Brokaw's heroes. Though he had never met Garroway, Brokaw regularly filled in five minutes of local news for "Today" watchers back in Omaha. It was too good an opportunity for him to miss.

He recalls, "I came and stood outside the "Today" show windows and held up a sign with Meredith that said: WATCH "TODAY" IN OMAHA WITH TOM BROKAW AT 7:25 and 8:25. And they put it on the air." The memory still makes him smile. "I thought that was going to be my one moment in the sunshine of network television."

After three years in Omaha, Brokaw in 1965 was offered the opportunity of an anchor's slot at the NBC affiliate in Atlanta, WSVB-TV, and he grabbed it. NBC had 203 affiliates in those days but, according to Reuven Frank, who would become president of NBC News in a few years, most of them were no good. Atlanta, however, was very good indeed. "We were very weak in the South," Frank acknowledges, "so we would rely very heavily on Atlanta."

The story of the hour in the South was the civil rights movement. On

March 20, President Johnson had ordered troops to protect the freedom marchers in Alabama. Racial violence in the South was as common as grits. Brokaw's arrival in Georgia coincided with the growing struggle for racial equality, and it was the major story he covered while there. His pieces, on occasion, even received national exposure on the "Huntley-Brinkley Report." As a result, people at network headquarters in New York began to take notice of him.

In less than a year, the Brokaws were packing their bags and again en route, this time to Los Angeles. There Tom would work for KNBC-TV, one of the network's major owned and operated stations, where he was both reporter and anchor of the 11:00 PM news. It was clearly an important stepping stone for the ambitious, twenty-six-year-old Brokaw. If he did well in LA, he might even look forward to a job one day at the network level. Anything seemed possible.

Brokaw, who knew nothing about California beyond the popular clichés, worked "like a horse" in Los Angeles to bring himself up to speed. Rising before dawn, he covered such political events as the California gubernatorial campaign of 1966 in which actor Ronald Reagan defeated incumbent governor Edmund G."Pat" Brown. Brokaw worked so hard, in fact, that he was dubbed by KNBC producer (later executive producer of "NBC Nightly News") Steve Friedman: "Duncan the Wonder Horse."

His reports on the anti-war movement, the murder of Robert Kennedy, and the 1971 Sylmar earthquake helped to establish his reputation as a solid journalist. Richard Threlkeld, who was network correspondent in CBS's Los Angeles bureau at the time, went head to head with Brokaw on a number of stories. One concerned several Mexican children in Tijuana who had become desperately ill after consuming food made from flour laced with rat poison. Both reporters raced to the border. "I thought going in that he was just a pretty face," Threlkeld admits.

But by the time Threlkeld had located the hospital where the kids were being treated and found that the press was barred from entry, Brokaw had already arrived and had his pictures in the can. "He totally beat me out that day," Threlkeld says. "I developed an enormous respect for him after that."

And as anchor, Brokaw was attractive in that blow-dried style so dear to local broadcasters. Who cared if, as a news reader, he often stumbled over certain letters? So what if he had a heartland accent? If he lacked the verve and charisma of KNBC's early evening news anchor, Tom Snyder, he had earnestness and sincerity. Despite his youth, you could trust Brokaw.

Los Angeles smoothed away Brokaw's rough edges like a pumice stone. He now wore his hair fashionably long and expensively styled. His fingernails were manicured. His clothes were Beverly Hills. He had always had the ability to get on well with people who counted, but now his job gave him access to flocks of them. He was attracted to celebrities, and they seemed to find him charming. In addition to the Hollywood stars and political powers whom he and Meredith frequently entertained, he also courted wealthy industrialists such as steel magnate Norton Simon and Arco president Thornton Bradshaw. A former NBC colleague describes Brokaw as knowing important people everywhere, as being "very plugged in."

Recalling a visit from his parents, Jean and Red, Brokaw admits, "When I would drop names and talk big, my father looked at me with a great deal of skepticism." It was a Yankton reality check, a Midwestern caveat against uppityness.

The Brokaws loved California. Two of their three daughters were born there. And in their peripatetic life since marriage they had lived there longer than any other place. It was an out-of-doors existence— skiing, hiking, swimming, tennis—and Tom and Meredith thrived on it. They decided to put down roots and build a house in fashionable Malibu. Tom's friend, Norton Simon, loaned them his own Malibu beach house to stay in during the construction. Simon was a little like his own father. Brokaw describes him as "a tough guy for a lot of people to communicate with, and I sometimes serve—" he hesitates, searching for just the right term, "I sometimes serve as a communications broker for him."

Simon was genuinely fond of young Brokaw, so fond in fact that he appointed him to the board of directors of his Pasadena museum. A distinguished world-class collection, the Norton Simon Museum is particularly strong in old masters and the works of Picasso and Matisse. At the time, Brokaw's taste in modern art was Oscar Howe, a local favorite in Vermillion, South Dakota, who painted slick American Indians in primary colors, and one of whose paintings had been given to Meredith Brokaw by her parents. Though Brokaw may have known little about old masters and next to nothing about modern art, he was, as all who knew him then attest, handsome, attractive, ingratiating and extremely likeable. Clearly, he had all the right credentials.

Meanwhile, Brokaw's work went well. He was asked by the network in April, 1971, to anchor an edition of their monthly primetime news magazine, "First Tuesday." The following year at the Democratic National Convention, he distinguished himself in covering the large California delegation, and caught the eye of the newly appointed anchor of NBC's "Nightly News," John Chancellor. And so in 1973, when the network was searching desperately for a reporter to rival CBS's Dan Rather in covering the White House beat, Brokaw was suggested.

Dick Wald, the president of NBC News at the time, flew to the West Coast to look him over. Brokaw took him to a vegetarian restaurant called the Aware Inn, one of those health food places in Los Angeles with plants hanging down from the ceiling—the foliage dense as the Mato Grosso—and sprouts sprinkled on everything. And then, according to Wald, "this nice young man started talking California politics, the national economy, the environmental movement, and so on, and it was apparent that here was not just someone who was good on the air, but a fellow with a good head on his shoulders."

The Brokaws never even had time to move into their new L.A. house. No sooner was the place finished then it had to be sold, and they were on their way to Washington. The erstwhile political science major from the little department at USD was off to watch the government operate close-up from the privileged position of a White House correspondent, one of the most important beats the network has to offer. In spite of the fact that the new job required a hefty pay cut (KNBC had promised him $100,000 if he remained in Los Angeles, whereas his Washington salary as a network correspondent was $65,000) it was an offer he couldn't refuse.

The White House press corps is an aggressive and motley mix of print and electronic journalists from all over the world. It includes some of the best in the business. As the new boy on the block, and only thirty-three at that, Brokaw had to prove himself. There were many tough old campaigners in the corps—their motto, never give a competitor an even break. They dismissed Brokaw at first sight, writing him off, the way Threlkeld did initially, as just another "pretty face." It was as if the sincere, wide-eyed Charlie Brown had just stepped into the ring with Rambo. If NBC's experienced Richard Valeriani was coming up short against CBS's dynamo at the White

House, Dan Rather, what could they expect from this replacement, a local anchor who had gotten his start in Armpit, South Dakota? Even at NBC, there were those who doubted.

John Chancellor was not one of them. He had seen what Brokaw was capable of doing at the '72 Democratic Convention. Yet the White House was another matter, especially given the Byzantine ways of the Nixon administration. If Brokaw needed to be put on notice about the intrigue and hypocrisy he was up against, the laminated sign that John Chancellor still keeps on an end table in his NBC office should have alerted him:

To John Scali from Charles Colson, November 5, 1971.

I suggest that you call the networks today regarding the unemployment story. You told me this was one we could rely on to give us a fair break. Chancellor's performance you should rerun. It's scandalous—yellow, scabby journalism which as you know is pretty scandalous, yellow and scabby. We should not bother to call him. We should break his goddamn nose. But it's our fault because we rely upon the integrity of news broadcasters of which there isn't any.

Printed directly beneath this is another note dated less than two months later, December 15, 1971:

Dear John,

Patty and I enjoyed greatly Barbara's and your hospitality. It was a delightful evening fron start to finish. We were almost finished trying to find our way home and we look forward to a chance to reciprocate once we are a little better settled in our new house. Thanks again for a delightful time. Best personal regards,

Sincerely,

Charles W. Colson, Special Counsel to the President

Treading softly in the corridors of power, where he was soon very much at home, Brokaw kept his eyes open and was not afraid to ask questions. He was sufficiently confident in himself as a journalist that he preferred appearing uninformed to being stupid. According to *The Washington Post*'s Bob Woodward, he didn't pretend to understand everything when he began, but he learned fast and was good at his job. "A reporter's reporter," Woodward called him.

Ann Compton, his ABC competition at the White House, was similarly impressed. In an interview in *TV Guide*, she said, "Tom always asked good questions at briefings. He always had a good angle on something that everybody else had missed."

The White House journalist who would be the most influential on Brokaw was Peter Lisagor, who wrote for the *Chicago Daily News*. They became close friends, and once a week, they had lunch together at the Federal City Club. Brokaw calls Lisagor "the single most impressive journalist I'll ever know."

Brokaw plainly grew in the job. He was working harder than ever now because he loved the political action in the capital. And almost every night he was on the air, seen by millions along the network, including his friends and family in Yankton.

When Bill Farber, his old political science professor visited him in Washington, he was impressed by how much his former "very average" student had matured. "As the world opened up to him, Tom saw the importance of the need to know. He told me that he now always had a book on his lampstand near the bed, and he liked to read before going to bed. And he suggested books for me to read, and from time to time he even sent me one he thought I should be reading."

Nightly, the pool of light from his bedside lamp revealed a Brokaw who, at last, had become the serious student he never was in college.

If during his first fifteen months in Washington he never overtook Dan Rather's popularity in covering the Watergate scandal, he did attract a sizable following of his own. Though there were viewers who found him dull and unconvincing, some preferred his calm restraint to Rather's electricity.

In an interview he gave to *Mother Jones* magazine, Brokaw described his journalistic style this way. "I think that my job is to stay calm at the center and point out [what is] wrong, not become histrionic about it."

While Dan Rather was a Jeremiah, damning the corruption and incredulous at its scope, Brokaw was offering viewers a different message, a reassuring message about the resilience of our system of government. Dick Wald, the President of NBC News, and others in top management there liked Brokaw's style and marked him down as a definite comer.

In April 1974, when Frank McGee, the co-host of NBC's successful morning show "Today," died of bone cancer, NBC executives quickly sought a replacement. They considered about a dozen different men for the job and Tom Brokaw was one of them, coming to New York for a week-long audition. Co-host Barbara Walters liked Jim Hartz, a Midwesterner with a good deal of boyish charm not unlike Brokaw's, and NBC management agreed. They signed him up for $250 thousand. Even for that enormous salary, Brokaw had refused to read commercials, which he felt would compromise his journalistic standing and seemed to be a requirement for the job.

Back in Washington, Brokaw was asked by his anchor, John Chancellor, to join him in January 1975 in a live one-hour interview with Nixon's successor, Gerald R. Ford. Though he didn't ask the new president if it was true that he couldn't walk and chew gum at the same time, Brokaw did raise the issue of Ford's qualifications for the job.

Brokaw is so smooth that he can make even a lead bagel like this seem digestible. His wife calls him the most confrontational man she has ever met, but if he is, he seems so unthreatening, so attentive, so polite, so ready to smile that he can usually get away with it. On the other hand, can somebody so cute be taken seriously? Can we trust a "button" nose?

Charm and good looks may have helped to thrust Brokaw into the limelight, but he is dismissive of them. Perhaps having traded in charm for so long and seen doors fly open to him, he has come to distrust both it and himself. No wonder he wants to be prized solely for his ability or, like the young woman in the poem by Yeats, "for myself alone and not my yellow hair."

Brokaw puts it this way: "I have always been very protective of my image. Partly it was a necessity, because of the way I look. I have always been determined that people would realize there was more to me than just cosmetics. I have always been conscious of wanting to be taken seriously as a journalist."

If some in journalism rated Brokaw a lightweight, NBC News took him *very* seriously. They invited him to do news specials, they assigned him to fill the "Nightly News" anchor desk on weekends, and they bestowed on him the journalistic plum of being a floor reporter at both 1976 National Conventions. Brokaw was part of the

NBC convention team that included John Chancellor, David Brinkley, Catherine Mackin and Tom Pettit. It was, he told an interviewer, "something I've always wanted to do, like a kid wanting to grow up and play second base for the Yankees."

Jimmy Carter won the White House in 1976, and Tom Brokaw, after three heady seasons of network reporting from Washington, decided to give it up. Barbara Walters had left the "Today" show for ABC, and NBC's top management, desperate to find a replacement, let Brokaw write his own ticket. He would not have to read commercials. He could take an active part in the behind-the-scenes, long-range planning for the program. And if he wanted to, he could even read the morning news. All this plus a lavish five-year contract about which Brokaw would later say, "I've made more money in the past five years than I thought possible." His starting salary was approximately $350,000. On August 30, 1976, Tom Brokaw went before the cameras for the first time as the new host of "Today."

The program—a news, weather, and chat show that had long been a leader in its time slot from 7:00 to 9:00 AM—had fallen on hard times. At that hour in the morning, it had never had a huge audience, but it had always been popular. In fact, since the days of Dave Garroway and the telegenic chimp, J. Fred Muggs—"Today's" heroic period—it had usually been a moneymaker. But ABC's "Good Morning America" was now serious competition, and "Today" was in trouble. Under its new thirty-one-year-old executive producer, Paul Friedman (who years later would move to ABC and become Peter Jennings' exicutive producer on "World News Tonight"), "Today" had instantly plunged to an all-time rating's low of 2.7. Brokaw was determined to turn things around.

The 5:00 AM wake-up call for his new job didn't faze him at all. Though the early-to-bed routine inevitably played havoc with his family and social life, Brokaw had long been accustomed to early hours since his days back at KYNT in Yankton. His radio work had also prepared him for something else. If his speech difficulties with semivowels are painfully obvious, less well known is his ability to ad-lib, judged by those who have worked with him as phenomenal. John Terenzio, who recently became executive producer of NBC's "Weekend Nightly News," said, "I was amazed at how smooth he is in improvising."

Brokaw himself attributes his skill to his training at KYNT. "I would have to go out with live microphones," he recalls, his brown eyes twinkling at the memory. "I think it helped me later in life. You know how to fill time. Ad-libbing."

In order to take advantage of Brokaw's skill and to eliminate some of his initial stiffness as well as the program's predictability, Friedman abbreviated his scripts. Interviews with authors, politicians and celebrities from the entertainment and sports fields were conducted from notes. Then he and Brokaw began searching for a co-host. They screened two hundred and seventeen applicants from whom they selected a group of semifinalists that included Linda Ellerbee, Catherine Mackin, Kelly Lange, Betty Rollin and Jane Pauley.

They chose, of course, Jane, an Indiana girl who had been working in television in Chicago. Though a local critic there had accused her of having "the IQ of a cantaloupe," Tom thought otherwise. He and Jane were an attractive, fresh-faced, Midwestern pair who looked as if a few years back they might have been found at the fraternity sock hop, the sorority tea.

With the help of a supporting cast that included Gene Shalit, their all-purpose critic and mustache, and Willard Scott, the rotund and rubescent weather man with his passion for food and female centenarians, "Today" rose from the ashes to top the competition.

Brokaw, as host of "Today," attempted to blend information with entertainment. He interviewed an enormous range of people from Walter Mondale, Jimmy Carter, and the Soviet Ambassador to the United States, Anatoly Dobrynin, to Burt Reynolds and Charlene Tilton, one of the stars of TV's "Dallas."

"I've tried to put her name out of my mind," Brokaw admits. He apparently had no idea who she was and, even worse, didn't really care. The interview was a disaster. "I can't do this for the rest of my life," he decided.

"Jane always figures that the day I made up my mind to leave, Steve Lawrence and Eydie Gorme were on. And Eydie gave me a big wet kiss on the air. And my discomfort showed through. It was hard to turn from that and get back to some serious matter."

After five years he had had enough. It was time to move on. A number of developments had occurred that were about to radically change his life. Brokaw had felt all along that "the long curve of my career was always serious journalism. The 'Today' show was kind of a left turn."

During Brokaw's final program as host of "Today," the President of the United States, Ronald Reagan, put in an appearance to say goodbye and, "Good luck in the new work schedule." And then the orbicular Scott, his weatherman pal, backed by the full chorus of the University of Maryland, hymned him away to glory, singing,

> You're leaving "Today,"
> And we've got the blues,
> But we'll see you nightly
> On NBC News.

RATINGS: Week ending January 27th

1st. Rather ("CBS Evening News")—11.6/20 [10,486,400]

1st. Brokaw ("NBC Nightly News")—11.6/20 [10,486,400]

3rd. Jennings (ABC's "World News Tonight")—11.5/20 [10,396,000]

N.B. Once again, the figure in brackets indicates households watching. Multiply by 1.45 for the approximate number of total viewers.

CHAPTER FOUR

From Readers to Rathers

With his multimillion dollar contract in hand identifying Tom Brokaw as co-anchor of NBC's "Nightly News," the newly-crowned high prince of electronic journalism, from tiny Yankton, SD, ascended to the network anchor chair. In its own way a more valuable piece of furniture than any antique Chippendale, this remarkable seat—one of only three in the entire country today—carries with it influence, prestige, power, money and fame. Its lucky occupants have more minutes on national television each week than any sitcom hero, and a unique opportunity to help set the national agenda on a wide range of issues from the drug war to airline safety, from health problems to education. It is, in short, a very big deal. But it was not always so.

During World War II, TV-land was harder to find than butter and gasoline. Though television had been introduced to the general public at the 1939 World's Fair, few sets were then available. In the dark early days of the war, with Hitler overrunning Europe, it was the warm embrace of radio—not television—that held America together. After dinner, families across the country, eager for reassuring news, sat down around their Zeniths, Emersons and Atwater Kents to listen to President Roosevelt's fireside chats. And when war actually came to America in 1941, it arrived by radio.

"*This*," and half-a-heartbeat later, "is London." It was Edward R.

Murrow reporting for CBS News, broadcasting from a rooftop somewhere near Victoria Station with German bombs falling all around him. There he was, splendidly defying the odds to bring us the war in Europe. His gaze hooded against the dazzling flares and beacons, Murrow described the flashing antiaircraft shells dotting the midnight sky as the Battle of Britain unfolded before his eyes, our ears.

In the course of the war, Murrow was to assemble an extraordinary supporting cast of first-rate CBS correspondents, including Eric Sevareid, Howard K. Smith, Charles Collingwood, David Schoenbrun, Daniel Schorr, Richard C. Hottelet and Larry LeSueur. A poll taken in 1945 at the end of the war by the National Opinion Research Center reported that 61 percent of those interviewed said they got most of their news from radio, with only 35 percent preferring newspapers.

In the years immediately following the war, television sets began to appear at local taverns as a lure to entice thirsty lovers of boxing and baseball. Joe Louis on the screen filled bar stools and cash registers. Soon afterwards, private households acquired television sets, and the pressure for improved programming brought about swift changes at the networks. If television news began in 1944 with Paul Alley's brief NBC newsbreaks, it really didn't start in earnest until four years later, when on August 15, 1948, CBS launched its first nightly news service.

The selection of Douglas Edwards for the role of television newscaster was the idea of CBS president Frank Stanton. Edwards had a large, potentially translatable, midday radio audience and what Stanton regarded as a warm, telegenic personality. Radio had taught Stanton the saleability of personality.

But Edwards was reluctant to take the job. It was then customary for radio correspondents to receive a share of the fees from broadcast sponsors, and Edwards earned a lot of money. Stanton decided to allow him to continue to do his radio broadcasts and offered him twice his salary. Television, he implied, was the future. Edwards preferred the present, but seeing that he had no choice, he took the job.

Murrow had never had a very high estimate of Edwards' ability, and Edwards' decision to switch to television merely confirmed his opinion. Howard K. Smith recalls that "we felt it was kind of unmanly to go on TV and perform, just as it was in an earlier era somehow unmanly for a newspaperman to go on radio."

Murrow distrusted the show business aspect of television—the makeup, the cameras, the lights—and he had his doubts, too, about whether it would ever be the equal of radio for reporting serious news. Eventually, he would prove that television could be just as effective in his famous "See It Now" series of documentaries.

Though Edwards had a background in journalism, he was chosen for his job because of his appearance, his manner, his ability to read a teleprompter and, when necessary, ad-lib. As those who remember Murrow's later television appearances hosting the celebrity interview program "Person to Person" will confirm, the veteran reporter apparently had little skill at ad-libbing and was notoriously uncomfortable as he chain smoked in front of the cameras. Even his questions had to be read from a script. Given Murrow's discomfort, it's no surprise that this most celebrated of newsmen never became an anchor.

Initially, the "CBS News with Douglas Edwards" had no sponsors. The newscast proved valuable to Stanton because the Federal Communications Commission looked kindly upon news as a public service when it came time for the network to renew its three-year license. Back then, news wasn't expected to pay the bills. CBS made its money elsewhere. Edwards' program was produced in tiny, cramped, airless quarters high above Grand Central Station, and broadcast from a converted German singing club called Liederkranz Hall in midtown Manhattan. Everything about the early history of TV news suggests that its pioneer newscasters, producers, and technicians were making it up as they went along.

By his second year on television, Edwards had attracted a sponsor. On April 7, 1949, his fifteen-minute, black-and-white broadcast airing at 7:30 PM, opened with the voice of an announcer declaring, "Olds brings you the news. Your Oldsmobile dealer *presents* the 'CBS News with Douglas Edwards.'" This was followed by a cheerfully upbeat advertisement for "the new thrill, that new futuramic Oldsmobile with the new rocket engine." Only after that did Edwards finally appear.

He had a young "choirboy" look, slicked-back dark hair and a big radio voice. "Good evening, everybody. Here's the news picture tonight." And the news picture that night was, quite typically, very short on pictures. The broadcast was in fact a radio broadcast televised. Read almost exclusively by Edwards, it had no reports from correspondents around the world because there were no TV correspondents around the world. The program was a low-budget operation, and the quality of its news made that fact perfectly obvious. The lead story of the night was a scintillating report on the government announcement of a new farm program calling for subsidies and price supports for food products. Edwards droned on as charts and graphs appeared on screen. Then followed a segment on the Army Day Parade, which resembled a newsreel. Only fifteen minutes long, the broadcast seemed interminable.

As a personality, Edwards was obviously important to CBS, and to his new sponsor Oldsmobile, but Edwards' visibility proved to be modest at best. No one cared about his annual compensation, his love life, his antics off the screen. He was little more than a news reader.

It was in February 1949 that NBC began its own competing evening newscast which ran from 7:45 to 8:00 PM with that sartorial dandy, the breezy and boutonniered John Cameron Swayze. Right from its inception, his broadcast—the "Camel News Caravan"—had a sponsor. The cigarette company made it blatantly clear to Swayze that the one cardinal sin he was to avoid at all costs was any hint that a law-abiding citizen might enjoy a good cigar. Only Winston Churchill, allegedly, was exempt from this proscription.

The set for the broadcast was a stage with a desk on which were a few books, an ash tray and, of course, a pack of Camels constantly in camera range. On the shelf behind Swayze stood a teletype machine. Like Edwards' program, his, too, was a "rip and read" affair—with stories directly from the wire services' teletype—though the pace was somewhat brisker. The graphics were primitive, with occasional stick-figure drawings. Because the film had to be flown by propeller-driven aircraft, it often seemed dated by the time it finally arrived. Toward the end of each broadcast, Swayze would abruptly announce to his viewers, "Now let's go hopscotching the world for headlines!" He would then quickmarch through a list of headlines gleaned from the wire services, and all without benefit of pictures. "And that's the story folks," he'd conclude. "Glad we could get together."

And then there was ABC, known at the time as the "Almost Broadcasting Company." Born out of NBC's rib, it came into existence in 1942 when the government in a well-publicized antitrust action, directed NBC to divest itself of one of its two radio networks, the Red and the Blue. The Blue became the American Broadcasting Company. By the mid-1950s, it still had only about a fourth as many affiliates as NBC. Not surprisingly, it wasn't until 1953, some four years after the other two networks already had evening television newscasts, that ABC asked John Daly to begin its televised news coverage.

Daly, a senior correspondent for CBS radio during World War II, had joined ABC in 1949. Because the network was so woefully underfinanced and understaffed, Daly was stretched to the breaking point as vice president for news, special events and public affairs, including sports. In addition to his work on the evening news, he also broadcast the conventions, the elections and news commentary as well. His budget for the evening newscast was so small that an office party might shoot it for a week. Daly, wonderfully calm in a crisis (as amply demonstrated in his subsequent seventeen years as host of the popular quiz show, "What's My Line?"), was often tested in the crucible of the newscast's repeated equipment failures.

The next year, 1954, Daly was given the go-ahead to cover live from gavel to gavel the Army-McCarthy hearings in Washington. ABC, with its weak daytime programming, had significantly less to lose than the two senior networks which had decided against continuous live coverage. It was still a daring decision, and it was to pay off handsomely for Daly and ABC, attracting national attention and thousands of new viewers. ABC's emergence as a serious contender in the news business is generally traced back to this pivotal event.

For the political conventions of 1956, NBC decided to team up two new faces to handle the coverage: David Brinkley and Chet Huntley. Brinkley had been working out of Washington for the Swayze broadcast. His partner, the good-looking, forty-five-year-old Huntley, whose resemblance to movie star Burt Lancaster would in no way impede his television career, had a news program in Los Angeles for the local ABC station there. With his solid journalistic background and serious manner, Huntley proved an excellent foil for the boyish and slightly irreverent Brinkley of the ironic look and lop-sided grin. In short order, Swayze—who according to some viewers had overstayed his welcome and, in the process, fallen behind Edwards in the ratings—had been replaced by Chet and David.

It was on October 29, 1956, that executive producer Reuven Frank debuted with his "Huntley-Brinkley Report." At first, neither the ratings nor the total absence of commercial support seemed reassuring. The numbers, in fact, were terrible. Though his anchors remained unfazed, Frank began to have stomach pains. "I went to a doctor," he recalls, "and he said quit your job." Eventually, in the fall of 1959, the program did obtain full sponsorship, becoming the "Texaco Huntley-Brinkley Report." And by 1960, the newscast finally began to dominate the ratings.

As Huntley-Brinkley remained on top for the next five years, Frank's stomach problems disappeared. He delighted in the team assembled with NBC president Robert Kintner's help. He delighted in the fact that his program had the largest news audience ever assembled. "The only one I can think of that was larger were the people gathered around loudspeakers in the squares of Chinese villages. It was larger than any British national newspaper. Anything. We put that little thing on the end of the broadcast that said, 'More get their news from the "Huntley-Brinkley Report" than any other news...in the free world.' I hated using 'free world,' but as I said the Chinese... We reached more families than *Pravda*. We must have reached twenty million households."

Asked if Huntley and Brinkley became celebrities, Frank instantly replies, "Oh yeah. Absolutely!" Their nightly sign-off, "Good-night, Chet!" "Good-night, David!" was plastered on billboards and buses all across the country. Television comedians could use it and be confident of instant recognition. They were so celebrated that at the Kennedy inaugural gala, Frank Sinatra and Milton Berle teamed up to sing in their honor some new lyrics to Sinatra's popular hit, "Love and Marriage":

> Huntley, Brinkley
> Huntley, Brinkley
> One is glum.
> The other twinkly.

If TV news men were becoming stars, it was in part because networks were promoting them more. The newscasters also spent more time on the air. On Labor Day, 1963, NBC and CBS doubled their broadcast time from fifteen to thirty minutes. As usual, ABC was once again bringing up the rear, the same position it would later occupy when the networks converted from black and white to color.

Then, too, in those halcyon days almost everyone who owned a television set watched the news. The total share of news watchers came to ninety-three percent, and more than a third of them watched Huntley-Brinkley.

The "Huntley-Brinkley Report" was so far ahead in the ratings that Reuven Frank—still cocky after all these years—didn't feel they had any competition at the other networks. Recently interviewing Douglas Edwards for an article he was doing on the fortieth anniversary of the first TV convention in '48, Frank and Edwards reminisced over lunch. Suddenly, Edwards put down his fork and asked with suspicion, "Is it true that you didn't even watch us?" Frank could hardly believe his ears. "Can you imagine that *still* rankling this guy? We went on the air in '56, and this was '88. Thirty-one plus years!" If Huntley and Brinkley didn't have to worry about Edwards, their competition was waiting in the wings.

In 1963, CBS, out of desperation, replaced Douglas Edwards with the mustached, pipe-smoking former host of the "CBS Morning Show," Walter Cronkite. Because of the Cronkite legend, it's hard today to imagine a time when Walter Cronkite wasn't "the most trusted man in America." But in his early years as anchor of the "CBS Evening News," he was at best an also-ran. Though Cronkite in 1963 may have beaten his competition in covering the assassination of President Kennedy—that national tragedy in which television came of age, binding the country together as radio had done at an earlier period—he was not yet first in the hearts of the viewers. Cronkite himself recalls one irate phone caller condemning the network for its bad taste in having "this Cronkite" who everybody knows "spent all his time in trying to 'get' the President," covering his death. A year later, while anchoring the CBS team at the Republican convention, Cronkite performed so poorly that Ed Murrow and Eric Sevareid were rushed into the anchor booth to help stanch the hemorrhaging in his ratings.

But by 1965, Cronkite had caught up to the "NBC Nightly News," and by 1968 he had surpassed it, taking over as undisputed champ. Through much of the next decade, he never looked back. Cronkite's "Evening News" aspired to include all the major stories of the day. It fancied itself the "broadcast of record." A former United Press reporter, Cronkite led a broadcast that tended to stress breaking news as opposed to feature stories. It also focused on Cronkite, as opposed to his excellent staff of correspondents. They accused him of being an air hog, of having a love affair with the camera. Amongst themselves, they called him "The Star." Ironically, though Cronkite saw himself as a hard-working, old-fashioned newsman, he was nonetheless responsible for fathering the "cult of personality" that he would later come to despise.

It was Cronkite to whom the word "anchor" was first applied. Borrowed from relay races and freshly re-minted for the 1952 political conventions by producer Don Hewitt (later head of "60 Minutes"), "anchor" was chosen to indicate that the person in the CBS news booth was the strongest member of the network's team.

"Cronkite!" Former CBS president Fred Friendly's large face lights up with pleasure. "Cronkite was the consummate anchor man. He looked like an anchor man. He seemed to have authority. He was avuncular. Everybody loved him, trusted him, believed in him. Nobody will ever have what Walter had. Marvelous fellow!" But if Friendly regards Cronkite as a better journalist than either Edwards or Swayze, he knows plenty of others who were better than Cronkite.

Now as then, the anchor still must be a solid journalist, but he needs performance skills and something else as well—electronic charisma. Media consultants have labeled it the "Q factor." Robert MacNeil of the "MacNeil-Lehrer Newshour" knew when he was working for NBC that he didn't have it. He would, alas, never make the grade as a Big-Three anchor. To be a Cronkite, you needed to be more than just a good journalist. You needed a face and voice and personality that riveted people. Anchors, according to MacNeil, are "*interesting* people to watch, whatever the mysterious qualities are that add up to the Q-rating. There's something real in that. Some people are more interesting to watch and listen to than others."

With his tremendous appeal, Cronkite and CBS News became one in the public mind. Like Huntley-Brinkley at NBC, Cronkite as anchor became the human face of CBS. For viewers, Cronkite gave his newscast its identity. Regardless of how bad the day's news might be, he was the familiar glue holding all the parts together. ABC's Dick Wald says, "The anchor is the equivalent of a newspaper format. And sending the anchor somewhere is like sending your newspaper there. Rarely does a single correspondent have that sort of identification."

Murrow certainly had viewer identification. But unlike Murrow— the newsman as foreign correspondent with intermittent reports—

Cronkite came down *nightly* from Olympus to give America thirty minutes of the Truth. Cronkite's power to influence his audience proved enormous because viewers trusted him implicitly. Few of them realized that he seldom wrote his own copy. In four memorable Vietnam reports that appeared on his regular evening broadcast in 1968, the cautious Cronkite, who had been pro-intervention in Vietnam, ultimately took an unequivocal stand against the war. Cronkite declared: "To say that we are closer to victory today is to believe, in the face of the evidence, the optimists who have been wrong in the past."

Lyndon Johnson, who had been watching the program at the White House that night, purportedly turned to George Christian, his press secretary, and said: "If I've lost Cronkite, I've lost the country."

Cronkite also had considerable power within CBS. But any anchor has the power (even Swayze or Edwards had it) not to read something. What Cronkite had in addition was the title of managing editor, and he was the first anchor to get it. Richard Salant, then president of CBS News, made the decision. Reuven Frank considers it to have been a bad idea, because "once Walter had the title, everybody wanted it." More important, the danger exists that the anchor as managing editor may well encroach on the domain of the executive producer, making editorial and assignment decisions. But in Cronkite's case he rarely exercised the powers that he had, or engaged in office politics or meddled in management. When his friend, CBS vice president Gordon Manning was fired, Cronkite made no attempt to intervene. He modestly assumed that he might be fired, too, if he did.

While Cronkite reigned at CBS and John Chancellor took over at NBC in 1971, becoming a solid second in the ratings and, on occasion, beating out Old Ironpants (as Cronkite was known) in special events coverage, ABC was still playing catch-up. In 1964, ABC hired a twenty-six-year-old Canadian, Peter Jennings, as anchor. A tall, brash, callow young man, the attractive Jennings had been plucked from the vine unripened, which even he soon had the good sense to realize. By 1967, he and ABC had both had enough, and the network sent him off to the Middle East to gain more experience. Two CBS alumni, Harry Reasoner and Howard K. Smith were brought in, and although they increased ABC's audience, the network was still firmly rooted in third place.

In an effort to improve ratings significantly, Fred Pierce, the president of ABC, offered Barbara Walters of NBC's "Today" show $1 million in 1976 to jump ship. Despite Walters' popularity, the offer was unprecedented, the sort of salary more often associated with show business than the news business. Walters' news experience hardly seemed to justify it. She was an interviewer of stars and celebrities, not a journalist. ABC was paying her for her own "star" quality. Pierce's coup was the beginning of the megabuck price war for anchor talent and, as an amusing footnote to the history of this male-dominated industry, it was a *woman* who started it all. Walter Cronkite's initial reaction to her million dollar contract was to groan. "All our efforts to hold television news aloof from show business had failed," he declared ruefully.

The co-anchor team of Walters and Reasoner marked the first time that a woman was regularly scheduled to appear as anchor on a weekly network newscast. But as it turned out, the Reasoner-Walters collaboration was short-lived, the chemistry between them proving bitterly acidic.

The year 1977 became a benchmark for network news. Technology was changing the face of the business, with video tape replacing film. Then too, a personnel shift—the appointment that year of Roone Arledge as head of ABC News—would herald two other pivotal changes: a revolution in the "look" of network news, and the coronation of the anchor. In a way, Arledge played a key role in the formation of all three of today's powerful anchors.

Arledge had made his career in television sports and was highly regarded as an innovative producer. Among other things, he introduced the instant replay into professional football. There were many, however, both in and out of ABC who had serious doubts about his understanding of broadcast news. The Arledge assignment seemed to be merely another indication that the network was turning news into entertainment.

Part of this fear may have been due to Arledge's personal style. Marlene Sanders, one of a small army of vice presidents at ABC at the time, recalls the group being summoned to meet the president of the news division at Montauk on the tip of Long Island. Typical of Arledge's lavish ways, he gave them the option of traveling by seaplane or limousine.

Sanders recalls, "My first glimpse of Arledge at the Montauk Inn revealed a short, pudgy man with . . . curly hair and aviator glasses. He was wearing a navy-blue-and-white polka-dot shortsleeved shirt, one he subsequently favored in the office as well, open to mid-chest. Around his neck he sported several gold medallions on chains."

Sanders seems to have taken a dim view of her new boss's get-up, feeling it inappropriate for the news business. Arledge couldn't have cared less. He was taking his cue from Zero Mostel in *The Producers*: "If you've got it, flaunt it."

But underneath his flashy exterior, Roone Arledge had a strong competitive streak. He had been a wrestler at Columbia University, and he still liked to win. Arledge was determined to lift ABC News out of the Nielsen basement.

The new ABC News president's first course of action was to dump the Reasoner-Walters broadcast, which was more like the strident sitcom, "The Bickersons," than the news. He replaced them with a troika of anchors. Two of the three—Peter Jennings and Frank Reynolds—were retreads, having formerly been ABC anchors. The third, Max Robinson, was a popular local newscaster in Washington, D.C., who would become the first black to anchor a network newscast. Arledge announced his plan with typical fanfare at a press conference at Manhattan's "21" Club, where he rechristened his newscast "The World News Tonight."

Turning the liability of his failure to attract a "star"—he had been unable to sign either Bill Moyers or Robert MacNeil—into a dubious asset, he transformed anchors into furniture. They were now "desks." Reynolds, based in Washington, would be at the national desk, Jennings in London at the international desk, and Robinson in Chicago would cover the domestic desk.

At an ABC affiliates meeting in May of 1977, Arledge announced, "I think the old concept of the anchor position is outdated and outmoded, and it can be changed. This doesn't mean we are going to eliminate anchor people, and it doesn't mean people are going to tune away from Walter Cronkite right away, because he's the best there is.... But we can offer an alternative, and I think we will. I think we will offer more coverage and better coverage, and more lively and more interesting coverage."

Despite Arledge's hands-on treament, his troika didn't always pull in the same direction. Nevertheless, by 1981 "The World News Tonight" had slowly, painfully overtaken NBC. The competition dismissed Arledge's multiple desks and zippy graphics—red slashes in the corner of the screen and eye-catching patterns (called "ka-ka" by those behind the scenes at ABC)—as nothing more than flash and trash. The aim of the new ABC president was to do all he could to distinguish "World News Tonight" from its older, stuffier competitors.

If ABC's "World News Tonight" needed more first-rate producers, writers and directors, what it lacked most of all was a star anchor in New York. In 1979, Dan Rather—at the time one of the four correspondents on CBS's popular "60 Minutes" and clearly possessing megawatt anchor potential —looked as if he were a likely candidate for the role. Arledge began to conduct a lengthy campaign to win him over.

CBS, for its part, was determined to hold on to Rather, whom they saw as a possible Cronkite replacement. The CBS counter-offer in all its particulars was a little less grand than ABC's, but it was munificent, more than $2 million a year. And this to a man who until then had been paid a "paltry" $300,000. Bill Leonard, the president of CBS News, had to swallow hard, but what truly stuck in his craw was having to give away the "managing editor" title, which he readily acknowledged "underscored the fact that the anchorman was in fact the boss of the 'Evening News' broadcast."

On March 6, 1981, at the conclusion of Cronkite's last broadcast, the veteran anchor gracefully signed off by saying, "This is but a transition, a passing of the baton." Using the relay team image, he handed the "Evening News" over to Rather, a newer, younger and much less experienced anchor.

Arledge, who had lost out, kept looking around for talent. Later that same year, he saw a possibility to get NBC's Tom Brokaw and proceeded to conduct what Brokaw describes as a "fairly intense courtship." The ABC News president appeared to be star struck. Obviously, despite his protestations about "outdated" anchors, Arledge never stopped believing in star power, in the simple truth that some people are more interesting to watch than others. Finally, Brokaw also turned Arledge down, but in the process he became anchor of NBC's "Nightly News" at a yearly salary of $1.8 million.

Eventually, in 1983, Arledge decided to put his money on an anchor already in the ABC stable, Peter Jennings, and to throw out the desks. Arledge would aggressively develop "World News Tonight," gathering together an impressive array of talent that would shape what many in the industry consider to be the "red hot center" of network news today.

But along the way, in his desperate desire to put ABC News in the big leagues, he had indirectly helped to establish three of the current anchors. Small wonder NBC's Brokaw calls him "the great Merlin of our business."

These days, the three anchors of the network evening news— Brokaw, Jennings and Rather—are without a doubt the stars of broadcast journalism. More Americans get their news of the world from them than from any other single source. Their "trustworthiness figures" are measured alongside those of presidents. They all receive multimillion dollar salaries. And within the networks, their power has increased tremendously over the years. Unlike a Huntley or a Brinkley or a Cronkite, today's anchor plays a much stronger role in management decisions. Each is the captain of a news division team with twenty to thirty worldwide bureaus, and between one thousand and fourteen hundred employees (including about one hundred correspondents, one hundred cameramen and two hundred producer-writers). Among other things, each anchor has a major voice in staff hiring and firing.

In addition, executive producers no longer control their own programs. Reuven Frank claims that he made all the decisions on the "Huntley-Brinkley Report," and in his nine years with Chet and David he only had one serious disagreement. In Frank's opinion, the balance of power between anchor and executive producer has shifted, and now the anchor has the controlling interest in the broadcast. "I don't know Rather," says Frank, "but knowing [CBS News executive producer Tom] Bettag I can't imagine that he'd stand up to the anchor. And between Brokaw and ["NBC Nightly News" executive producer Bill] Wheatley, Brokaw makes all the decisions he wants to and Wheatley makes all the rest."

Why all this power, why all these millions for mere journalists? After all, they were once simply news readers. In most foreign countries, anchors are still considered just news "presenters," no more worthy of interest than the newsprint that comes off on your hands. So why is today's anchor treated like a statesman? Why is he gawked at like a star? Perhaps it has something to do with the chicken and egg relationship between fame and promotion.

One leading TV anchor agent, Richard Leibner, who ought to know because he's made enough money on them, spoke of America's growing obsession with the rich and famous: "I date it to *People* becoming a mass media success. First there were movie stars, then rock stars, then the people-oriented magazines worked their way through sports stars and TV stars. And when they were all chewed up, they turned to TV journalists as stars. No form of communication has been left untouched. Today, news readers are stars."

But if the new crop of anchors had star potential, it took a lot of promotion to turn them into celebrities. First there were certain technical changes that occurred, like ex-CBS News president Van Gordon Sauter's development of the extra-closeup tight shot of Dan Rather. And then there were the expensive full-page ads, taken for all three in *The New York Times* and *Variety*, not to mention the additional minutes of on-air promotion throughout the day. Then there were the irregularly scheduled interviews and specials. To increase his visibility, Brokaw broadcast "NBC News Digests" from the World Series in 1986 and a chatty, sports-related interview with former President Reagan during the Super Bowl in January 1990. Jennings did news updates at half-time on "Monday Night Football." And Rather was constantly promoted on CBS radio and television for both the "Evening News" and "48 Hours," a weekly primetime broadcast that he hosts.

Why all this promotion? Because to many Americans, the three news shows are virtually indistinguishable. The networks all believe that more viewers will tune in for an "NBC Nightly News *with* Tom Brokaw" than for a faceless "NBC Nightly News." As in the movie business, a film with a star attracts more viewers than one without. CBS correspondent, Richard Threlkeld, puts it this way: "Research has shown that the reason people watch is because of personality. It's not a coincidence that the anchors' names are there on the show. Those personalities are crucial."

Ironically, the three are strikingly similar. They are all white, male, married, fathers with two or more children, wealthy, middle-aged (less than eight years separating the three of them), and Protestant. Their politics are confined to a narrow spectrum from centrist to center-left-liberal. All three are good-looking, energetic, ambitious, alert and enormously competitive. They are, needless to say, hardly representative of the majority of Americans.

"You ask me why the three anchormen look like brothers. That's because that's what the American people want," Fred Friendly observes. "That's the really corrupting force of television. Television is going to cause us to nominate candidates who look like the kind of people we want to be president—the anchor as president." Not represented by the trio are any minorities or women, although for the first time in 1989, women journalists like Diane Sawyer and Connie Chung became hot commodities in the network news competition, which may be a healthy sign for the future.

Aside from the personalities of the anchors, other differences between the programs seem to be relatively insignificant. ABC has its "American Agenda" and "Person of the Week," NBC has its "Assignment America" and "Spotlight," and CBS has its dramatic camera angles and standing Dan. But what really counts is that it's Dan (or Peter or Tom): standing, or squatting, or lying on his back. It's the anchor who wins the ratings, the anchor who sells the soap. Brokaw, Jennings and Rather sell the news the way Catherine Deneuve sells Chanel, Ricardo Montalban sells Chrysler, and Bill Cosby sells Jello. In the estimation of Bruce Northcott, president of Frank N. Magid Associates, a leading TV consulting group, "Ratings depend on two things: what your lead-in is and who is anchoring your broadcast. Viewers choose depending on whether they like Peter, Tom or Dan."

Today, the anchors are the most visible spokesmen for their entire network. As such, unlike their predecessors, they seem to feel that more demands are made on them.

Brokaw puts it this way: "When I came to work for NBC, Walter Cronkite, David [Brinkley], all those people were elder statesmen in a way. David could go to a town where there was an affiliate on private business to make a speech or see a friend, to make an appearance, to do something—and the same thing was true of Walter—and the affiliate would kind of pawn the court beseeching them for maybe a small audience. Now if I pass through Wichita, if I change planes, and I haven't told the affiliate that I'm there and can do some promos for him, a rocket arrives in the office of Affiliate Relations here."

It's the same with Jennings and Rather. One explanation is that the business has become much more competitive. Now they all have to record promotional material for network affiliates, meet with affiliate managers or news directors who happen to be in New York, pose for photographs for advertising campaigns, and dictate letters to station managers and viewers.

Trained as journalists, each of the anchors underestimated just how crucial it was to his job to be a celebrity, and how time-consuming it is. Peter Jennings says, "I never thought I'd have a job where I'd end up sitting down with people and talking about what I do for a living as much as I do." Part of their problem rests on the fact that the skills of a journalist are not identical with the skills of an anchor. And the pressures on them are as enormous as their compensation.

"I don't need this," Brokaw explodes, running out of patience with an interviewer. But of course, he *does*. A "mere" journalist is paid only a tiny fraction of what he makes. Anchors exist in a media context, and that's the primary reason they earn what they do.

"In the old days," Brokaw laments, "Chet or David or Walter could blow up at someone or they could come in and have a bad day or be impatient about something, or snap at somebody because they hadn't done their job well. Or they could be so consumed with other things they didn't have time to say hello to somebody. These days something like that happens, and it ends up in a column."

Rather seconds his view. "I knew that the magnifying glass on an anchor was much larger than anything I had experienced previously. But I underestimated it. Anybody coming into this job underestimates it. I don't care where he's been."

RATINGS: Week ending February 10th

1st. Rather   ("CBS Evening News")—12.0/21 [10,848,000]

2nd. Jennings (ABC's "World News Tonight")—11.0/19 [9,944,000]

3rd. Brokaw   ("NBC Nightly News")—10.9/19 [9,853,600]

CHAPTER FIVE

The Texas Scrapper

Born in Wharton, Texas on October 31, 1931, Dan Rather grew up believing, as a colleague would put it, "that he had to scratch his living out of the hard earth every day." He was a Depression Era child, the eldest son of a blue collar family. His father, Irwin "Rags" Rather, worked laying oil pipelines—hot, dusty work digging ditches under a blazing Texas sun. His mother, Byrl, worked for a while as a waitress at the Traveler's Hotel in Victoria, Texas.

When Dan Rather was only a year old, the family moved to Houston, to a run-down section known as The Heights. Today, the Heights is a ramshackle neighborhood, mostly Black and Hispanic. It's a part of town where the potholes don't get filled in, and the stores have signs: WE BUY ANYTHING OF VALUE. The address the Rathers moved to was on Prince Street, a royal name for what even then was a shabby block. Now it's an unhappy stretch where trailers are on cement blocks, where rusted Fords sit on front lawns, where paint flakes off houses and roofs sag under the weight of unpaid bills. On a wall covered with graffiti, there is a sign: STOP THE FASHOUS RULE.

Back in the 1930s, it wasn't quite so bad, but even then, recalls Dan Rather's younger brother Don, "it was never affluent." Don talks of a neighborhood of small but tidy wood frame houses, a neighborhood of "working people." It wasn't total poverty or destitution, but it wasn't the easiest place to grow up.

"There were parts of our neighborhood I guess you'd call tough," Don Rather recalls. "Put it this way, you had some choices to make. You had to walk a line. You could stay out of trouble, or you could go out and pop hubcaps."

But there were other influences in the neighborhood as well. There was the Baptist Church, that families from blocks around, including the Rathers, would walk to each Sunday. In fact, the ten-block zone in which they lived was a "dry" area. No alcohol could be bought or sold. There was the neighborhood park, where both brothers played football, their first love, in the city sports leagues. And there was the radio. The family would gather around to listen to big games, and country music, and Texas swing.

"You've got to remember," Dan Rather says, "I come from a time and place where if it wasn't written by Hank Williams, I didn't know it." He smiles and nods his head. "I can still remember dancing on the linoleum floor in the kitchen to the music of Bob Wills and his Texas Playboys."

In grade school, as some old friends remember it, the young Dan Rather would walk to school, and along the way he would create football games in his head. He'd call the play by play, making it up as he went along: "He fades back to pass...The rush is on...He gets the throw away.... Oh! And it's caught at the ten yard line!" Tackle by tackle, touchdown by touchdown, he would wile away the blocks.

At home, he was surrounded by newspapers. "My father was an impulsive subscriber," Rather notes in his autobiography, *The Camera Never Blinks*, "a voracious reader, and a man of sudden anger who would leap from his chair and cancel whichever newspaper had offended him. We went through every newspaper in town, the *Post*, the *Chronicle*, and the *Press*."

On the surface, his parents seemed an unlikely pair. His father was a tough manual laborer that some family friends remember for his "steely-eyed look," a man whose temper would flare up like a Texas twister and disappear as quickly. His mother, Byrl, was recalled as warm and gracious, a devout Baptist. But they were united in their common determination to improve their lot, for themselves and their children.

"It was a matter of looking to get ahead," brother Don recalls. "Dad was constantly reading, keeping up. And with Mom, it was never any question we would go to college, one way or another."

While Dan would inherit some characteristics from each of his parents—his mother's southwestern graciousness, his father's dark hair, dark eyes and short fuse—the dominant trait he would get from both of them was his drive, his single-minded determination, his raw hunger to get ahead. Dan Rather was a battler.

Of course, in his neighborhood, he needed to be. Anywhere in the Heights, you had to know how to operate your fists. And even grade school, as he would later recall, was a school of hard knocks:

"Remember when you were back in elementary school how the kids were always fighting? You know how it goes at that age—no self-respecting guy...would be without at least one fight a day. Fights and scuffles before school, at recess, during lunch and after school. That's the way it was when we were in elementary school.... Usually a new kid in school got initiated the very first day with a sound thrashing, designed just to kind of break the newcomer in."

Although the Heights didn't have that much to offer the energetic young Rather, it did have one thing—the pride of the neighborhood, Reagan High School. It was a good school, and when he wasn't in classes, Rather wrote about sports for the school paper, and played end on the football team.

Somehow, he had gotten the romantic notion that football would be his ticket to college. He would earn a football scholarship and go on from there to gridiron glory and a brilliant future of risk and radiance. In fact, he was a scrawny 150-pound kid, not all that fast and, frankly, not even that great a ball player. When he went up to Sam Houston State Teachers College, the school he had fixed on, the coach chuckled when he asked for a scholarship.

Nonetheless, in February 1950, he got on a Greyhound bus with his mother, and took the two-hour ride to Huntsville, Texas. To pay the $40 in enrollment and student fees, his mother went into town and cashed two of the family's precious $25 savings bonds, bought during the war, for less than face value. It was worth it. Her eldest boy was going to college!

As a college, Sam Houston State was far from Ivy League. With only about six buildings clustered up on "the Hill," the East Texas institution was lucky if it had 2,000 students. It was a small, easygoing school lost in the piney woods, a college whose major claim to fame was its mascot, Tripod, the three-legged mongrel pup. The students were farm boys and working class kids, the classes half vocational, half academic. Everybody knew everybody.

And soon everybody knew Dan Rather—a handsome guy, his black hair slicked back in a pompadour. He was, said school president Dr. Elliott Bowers, "ubiquitous." He was voted "Sam Houston's favorite" in 1952, and Junior Class President. He was a Caballero club member, raising money for the Red Cross and the USO. He emceed the "Press-Capades" show, and hosted the Bathing Revue, where lovely young co-eds vied for the crown of "Miss Sam Houston." He even won the beard-growing contest one year in "Frontier Days."

The one thing he couldn't win was a place on the football team. After getting knocked down and banged around by bigger, better, faster ball players, after scrapping and fighting to stay on the team, he finally had to give up his dream. But it was quickly replaced by another.

"Every afternoon, he'd come and talk with me," recalls Hugh Cunningham, who as a young teacher, was a one-man journalism department at Sam Houston State. "Dan hardly ever got in the scrimmages. I told him, 'You won't make the team, and if you did, you'd get killed.' "

Cunningham decided to take a chance on Rather, and the eager young man soon transferred his enthusiasm from football to journalism. Cunningham gave him a series of odd-jobs, like collecting statistics and doing PR work for the Lone Star Conference, to allow him to earn his way through school.

More than anything, of course, Rather was devoted to the paper, *The Houstonian*. "I worked on the paper with him one summer," recalls Norma Dell Jones, now executive director of Sam Houston's Alumni Association. "I was a mere reporter. But Dan always acted like it was for *The New York Times*."

While he and his buddy Cecil Tuck lived in an old barn just off campus, Rather would come in at all hours to the paper to work. Late into the night, he would wander the huge newsroom, pacing around the glass cage that served as the managing editor's office, fiddling with copy, changing layouts. "Dan Rather put in sixteen hour days," Hugh Cunningham recalls. "He had a girlfriend in the department. Poor thing! Any dates she had with him had to be in the newsroom."

"Yup," says Dr. Elliott Bowers, shaking his head in agreement. "He was a worker. He was Mr. Hustle." Working for the paper as a freshman and a sophomore, Rather convinced himself that he was simply going to work harder, put in more hours, and accomplish more than anyone else. It was the old work ethic. It was also sheer feistiness.

No one was going to get ahead of him in the race for editor of the twice-weekly *Houstonian*. "There's probably nobody more competitive than Dan Rather," Cunningham says. "This guy's just a human dynamo. Get in his way and he runs over you."

As it turned out, Rather was made editor of the paper, and not as a senior, the way tradition dictated, but as a junior. Writing his column, "The Editor's Beat," he sounded off on a variety of topics, from his summers spent working on oil rigs and digging ditches, to his used car, "the Thing," a singular vehicle with no window on the driver's side, and dense smoke billowing up through a hole in the floor.

In several of his columns, he sounded themes that would echo through his later life. Take the one called "Confidence in Washington, Sir?" Displaying a Texan's deep-seated distrust of big government, he wrote, "The thing that really makes me wonder about this confidence talk is the way all of Washington, from the janitors to the top brass, is grabbing for money and prominence. It seems a man is not a good politician any more unless he's a good thief."

Although Rather has become more of a centrist today, his populist sympathies were clear back then. In another column, he described his reasons for supporting Adlai Stevenson for President. "I'm madly for Adlai first and foremost because I'm a Democrat. I believe in the principles of the Democratic party and believe those principles have given this nation the most prosperous years. The party Stevenson represents brought this country from the doldrums of depression discontent to its feet and to victory in a struggle for freedom....The Democrats have long been the Workingman's party. Labor and people who sweat for a living have had more the last twenty years than ever before."

As a "true Texas Democrat," Rather blasted the effects of McCarthyism and Red-hunting in 1952: "Dean Carl W. Ackerman of Columbia University, says that with the McCarthy-type investigations comes 'the passing of individual, independent expression of opinion on controversial subjects....' These are words of wisdom from a man whose IQ and experience are considerably greater than McCarthy's. However, now that Dean Ackerman has spoken, it wouldn't be surprising at all to see McCarthy investigate him for 'Communist leanings.' That's the way said character operates. Frankly, we'll have to string along with Ackerman and the others who disapprove of McCarthy's ways. To us, his purpose does not justify his means.

Certainly it is true that Communists need to be uncovered in this country—in schools, in churches, wherever they may be. But a systematic, law-enforcing practice is needed."

And finally, in another column about the publication of a new, revised edition of the Bible, Rather revealed both the depths of his faith, and a down-home sentimental streak as wide as the Texas plains:

"The Bible should and does humble most people, myself included.... After reading it, I hesitate to call myself a journalist. For several years I had been telling myself that if I had anything to be proud of, it was in journalistic endeavors. But the Book has humbled even that bit of vanity now. Oh I had learned before that the Bible was the world's greatest book. But somehow or other, it never had the coronation of journalism as I knew it. Then comes the new revised edition.... Every chapter in this new printing is written in the language of today's newspapers.... You probably tried to read at least a few pages of Spillane's novels when they were the rage, so why miss the 'new' book? I guarantee you'll find it just as exciting, and much more hard-hitting. (It's a shame, Lord, but you have to sell some people that way.).... I might also add seriously that it should be required reading for embryo writers whose swelled heads have convinced them they are journalists."

More extraordinary than any writing Rather did was the sheer volume of work he was handling, the number of balls he had up in the air at once. Hugh Cunningham remembers Rather juggling his editorship with three or four jobs—from collecting sports statistics, to stringing for newspapers (providing results on the local St. Louis Browns farm club) and serving as a P.A. man.

Rather also knew how to parlay a minuscule opening into a full blown opportunity. Given the chore of gathering sports stats and results for the local radio station, the tiny K-SAM, Rather convinced the station manager to let him read the results on the air himself. Soon he was strapping on pole-climber spikes and shimmying up to a little box on top of a wooden telephone pole to announce the farm club ball games. It was a little catbird seat, a platform with no back walls, just a microphone and a view of the ball fields.

"He was very good at announcing even then," recalls Jack Nichols, who worked side by side with him at K-SAM. "He doesn't sound that much different today." The atmosphere at the station was very strict.

Ted Lott, the Baptist Pastor who ran K-SAM saw to that. But within that tiny three-room wooden shack near the school, on that 250-watt signal which barely carried to the Huntsville city line, Rather got the opportunity he prized. He announced football games—junior high, high school, college. He had an hour-long music show, spinning records as a DJ—anything but profane 45s like "In the Book." He wrote advertising copy for clients such as Dunlop Paints. He even broadcast a little news. And during the long night hours in the booth, he would sometimes sneak out back with a co-ed while the "Gospel Hour" was on, and make out.

"He was a Mister Everybody," Jack Nichols, his colleague at K-SAM, says. "He'd do whatever it took.... He wasn't necessarily an intellectual. He'd just do whatever it takes to get the job done." But two things were clear even then, Nichols says. First, he had a certain gift. He was always able to ad-lib. "Every morning we signed on with this taped prayer," Nichols recalls. "Well one morning, Dan came running in late and there wasn't time to get the tape and cue it up. So he just made up the prayer himself, off the top of his head."

And second, though the young Rather was only an average student, he had his eyes on the prize even then. "He used to say to me," recalls Nichols, attempting to capture something of the young man's earnestness, "'A person whose name is known nationally, in sports or whatever, that alone is quite a goal.' He had given it a lot of thought."

If Dan Rather was a young man in a hurry, back then he had his track shoes all laced up, and he was ready to go. Graduating from Sam Houston on a hot August night in 1953, he received his BA for secondary school teaching in only three and a half years.

Rather spent a six-month stint teaching freshman journalism, and then he joined the Marines. The Korean War had just sputtered out, and Rather put in only six months in the service. When the doctors discovered that he had contracted rheumatic fever as a boy, he was discharged.

"It was one of the least distinguished records in the military," he admits with a wry smile. But even that brief period made a mark on the young Rather. The discipline, the patriotism, the Marine Corps spirit, all would stick with him through his life. To this day, colleagues will say about Dan: "He's tough—he's a Marine." Those critics who would later blast Rather as a knee-jerk liberal do not understand this other side of him. "If you ever want to bring tears to Dan's eyes," says one CBS colleague, "put on a military parade, play taps, and bury a soldier."

Over the following summer, Rather did some part-time work at the *Houston Chronicle*, but newspapering was not his forte. He wasn't much of a speller, nor much of a writer, and so when the fall came around, and he was offered a job at the *Chronicle's* affiliated radio station KTRH, he snapped it up. This was the main chance, a 50,000 watt station, "the voice of the Golden Gulf Coast." Reporting on the streets of Houston—his beat covering everything from the police blotter to the mayor's desk—Rather attacked the job with his trademark energy.

"There were many nights," he would recall later, "when I wouldn't leave the station. To someone who doesn't know the business such zeal may seem incredible. It was real. And I enjoyed every second of it." By five in the morning, he was at work. He would do the morning news—the 7:00 to 9:00 AM slot for rush hour commuters—and keep working until 1:00 PM. Then he'd go out and report, and be back for the evening news.

As one of Dan Rather's oldest friends, Bill Johnston, recalls: "Dan was always at KTRH. I remember Sunday afternoon was one time there was no radio news, and he talked them into doing five-minute news slots at 5:00, 6:00 and 7:00. I thought, 'God damn, the guy's crazy—Sunday is your one day off.' "

When Bill, Dan and friends would make plans to get together over the weekend, or for an evening party, they always knew what to expect. "Dan would say, 'Y'all go on and start without me,' " Bill recalls. "Then an hour or so later, he'd call from the station with apologies, and say he just couldn't make it."

If Rather worked hard, there was a reason beyond his customary energy, and a growing addiction to the minute-by-minute excitement of the news business. Perhaps he felt he had something to prove to himself, and to his friends and family, who weren't quite sure this journalism was real work, let alone a career. His father, Rags, didn't get it at all at the beginning, and was quick to let his son know. Dan's good friend Bill was equally unsure at the time: "I thought if you weren't in sales or some kind of meat-and-potatoes field, you weren't working. I remember thinking, 'Journalism? That isn't a job!' "

But Rather made it a job. And, then, he had an extra reason to spend long hours at KTRH. There was a cute secretary there, Jean Goebel, and Rather had fallen in love with her, enchanted by her smile. She had an energy which matched his own. Not only was she cute, but dependable as well, a hard-headed woman who would look out for Dan.

In 1957 they got married, and are still married. As Dan has gone rushing around the globe, chasing his career, Jean has served as his touchstone. In whatever crises that have arisen, she has helped him and been his sounding board. Old friends describe her as a strong, smart woman, playing by the rules of her generation, who saw in Rather a man going places, and who decided, by the happiest combination of love and ambition, that they would make a great team.

Quickly jumping from radio to television, Rather was on his way up. KHOU, Houston's Channel 11, the CBS affiliate, was last in the ratings when they hired the young Rather as a reporter. Before long, the station's fortunes had changed and Rather's with it. He was appointed news director of Channel 11 as well as anchor of the station's 6:00 PM and 10:00 PM news. These radio and TV jobs through the mid and late fifties were the dues-paying years for Rather, the years in which he learned his trade.

Not only did he wear out a lot of shoes, he did a fair amount of experimenting, and his youthful inquisitiveness led him into dangerous regions. A profile in the *Ladies' Home Journal* discusses Rather's experience with drugs. "As a man who wants to see and hear and do everything, has he (Rather) smoked marijuana himself? Dan eyes his visitor for a full ten seconds. '...I obey the law,' he says carefully, then waving away the dodge, adds, 'I don't want to be coy with you. I have not smoked pot in this country. As a reporter—and I don't want to say that's the only context—I've tried everything. I can say, too, with confidence that I know a fair amount about LSD. I've never been a social user of any of these things, but my curiosity has carried me into a lot of interesting areas. As an example, in 1955 or '56 I had someone at the Houston Police Station shoot me with heroin so I could do a story about it. I came out understanding full well how one could be addicted to "smack" and quickly.' "

For KHOU, Rather covered a great many "Fuzz and Wuzz" stories—pieces on cops and corpses, the staples of local TV. Even back then, these stories brought up the ratings, and although the terminology is different today, the basic principle remains the same: flames, gunshots, blood, dead bodies—they all bring in viewers. But there was a difference down in the Southwest. You not only covered cops and robbers, you covered weather too.

In Houston, weather was more than just an amusing little coda to the news, more than just spring showers and fall's changing leaves. Weather in Texas was high drama: floods, hurricanes and tornadoes. Reporting the weather in Houston, you weren't just telling the audience about the temperature. You were telling them if their roofs were going to get ripped off their houses in the next hour.

Rather worked through many long nights talking hurricanes at KTRH, including Hurricane Audrey, which came barreling through Louisiana in 1957, and killed almost five hundred people. Disaster, ironically, always seemed to bring out the best in him. It was as if in crisis situations, when other people started shutting down, Dan Rather just amped up his intensity another notch and went to work. He was, and remains, a crisis performer, a "when the going gets tough" kind of guy.

Unquestionably, it was a disaster that propelled him to national attention. He calls himself "a child of the storm." When, on September 5, 1961, he came across a wire report from the U.S. Weather Bureau, noting a low pressure system in the Caribbean, moving across Mexico, he thought it might be something. His years of weather-watching convinced him that any storm that crosses land and then gets to build again over water, over the Gulf of Mexico, could be truly dangerous. The station management was skeptical. But two days later, by September 7, when the storm was upgraded to a hurricane, and named Carla, his bosses conceded he might be on to something. Rather wanted the KHOU team to cover the story out of Galveston, on the Coast, not out of Houston. He argued that the Weather Bureau had a weather-tracking radar scope in Galveston. KHOU's program and station managers, mindful of the expense involved in moving their mobile unit, weren't sure.

But Rather was adamant (as he recalled in his autobiography): "We ought to get down to Galveston, and we ought to throw everything we've got into this thing," he said. "If it lands anywhere on this coast, we'd be holding aces." By Friday, he had won his case, and by the end of the day, he and his team had moved down to Galveston.

Holed up in the Galveston Weather Bureau, Rather convinced officials to let him put the radar picture on the air. He argued that it was in the public interest, emphasizing the warning function of TV. Rather knew news, but he also knew something else. He understood high drama. Should the hurricane keep coming, the radar pictures would make for great television, pure and simple, and he would be just where he loved to be, at the center of a great story.

On Saturday night, KHOU broadcast live that Hurricane Carla was two hundred and fifty miles off the Texas coast, headed straight for Galveston. For the first time, TV was carrying live images of a hurricane. As Rather described it, Carla rose up from the bottom of the black radar screen first as a crescent, then a swirl. People around the studio gasped when they suddenly realized the true size of it. Four hundred miles across, with an eye of fifty miles, the hurricane blanketed a large part of the entire Gulf of Mexico.

Over the years, Dan Rather would become known for his "golden gut," his newsman's instincts, and although such stories tend to become myths, he would at several key points in his career be at exactly the right place at exactly the right time. Hurricane Carla was one of those times. By the next day, the Weather Bureau had ordered a mass evacuation. It was, Rather reported, the largest peacetime evacuation in U.S. history, more than 350,000 people.

When Carla hit land, just south of Galveston, early the next day, it caused millions of dollars of damage, howling up the coast, destroying building after building. But in all, only twelve people died. Rather and his team could feel justifiably proud in having saved many lives. It was also a hell of a story.

Rather's effectiveness—his thirty-six hours of continual updates during the peak of the storm, his calm in the middle of a catastrophe—impressed the CBS network management, who were keeping an eye on their affiliate's coverage. (Ironically, Roger Mudd, who would later be Rather's competitor to succeed Cronkite as anchorman, was also on the scene as the CBS network correspondent, reporting just ninety miles away in Victoria.) And in the weeks following the hurricane, as Rather slogged through hip-deep water to talk to marooned residents who wouldn't abandon their small shacks, Walter Cronkite spoke admiringly of Rather being "up to his ass in water moccasins." CBS management decided to offer the thirty-year-old Texan a prized correspondent's job. At first, he turned them down, still charged with his success on Carla, and reveling in KHOU's newfound status as the top local news station. But soon enough, he realized that the CBS offer was a big opportunity, and he grabbed it.

Arriving in New York in late February 1962, the brash reporter felt a little cowed. This was it, the big time—the home of Murrow, and Collingwood, and Sevareid. Sure, he was confident of his ability to report. He could out-report anyone. But Rather still had the sneaking suspicion he might be a country boy, just a little out of his league with all these East Coast sophisticates. "He knew he was going to the big city," recalls his friend Bill Johnston. "He knew he was competing with boys from Yale and Harvard. He knew he'd have to work twice as hard."

At the start, Rather was a little rough around the edges. Longtime colleague Peter Herford recalls the first time the Texan showed up at his home for dinner. "I'll never forget it," he says. "Dan walked in dressed to what he thought was the nines—a sky blue polyester suit, white socks and brown shoes." Even today Herford still chuckles at this vision of Rather. But one thing he and everyone else agree on. Rather was a quick learner, fast off the mark, a sponge soaking up everything he was told. Before long, he was wearing Savile Row suits.

"He hit the ground running, running about ninety miles an hour," Herford recalls. After less than two months in New York, Rather was sent back to Texas, to Dallas this time, to open CBS's southwestern bureau and serve as bureau chief, making a staggering $17,500 a year. It was quite a coup for the young correspondent. Determined to deserve it, he moved his family to Dallas, and almost immediately took to the road in search of big stories.

The major domestic story of the early 1960s, was the growing civil rights movement. It was an explosive period, when blacks fought against years of repressive Jim Crow laws, and the white South battled to keep things just as they were, even if it meant overturning school buses, shooting protestors or loosing attack dogs on crowds. Through 1962 and 1963, Rather traveled the South—Birmingham, Memphis, Jackson—covering what he would call the "domestic war story." He was there in Oxford when James Meredith came to integrate "Ol' Miss," and the town erupted in rioting.

Basically, reporters were considered a lower form of life by both sides of the struggle. Southern whites believed they were misguided, or Communist scum, or worse. They thought reporters were stirring up trouble. Blacks thought they weren't doing enough. In a race riot, blacks would beat journalists up for being white. Whites would beat them up because of their television equipment. It was a dangerous story, a story in which Rather more than once ducked bullets, and had sawed-off shotguns stuck in his ribs. But it was also the hottest story going. As he quite freely admitted, for him ambition outweighed danger.

"Ambitious? Wow!" says one CBS colleague of that time. Recalls another, Peter Herford, "Dan had been at CBS for two or three months, and I was in New York, and we'd often talk at 2:00 AM on the phone. Dan was putting in fifteen, sixteen hour days, and he *never* complained. Others bitched all the time, but Dan never did. Then one day he calls, and he sounds real down. I was curious. I asked him what was the matter. And he said 'Did you see the broadcast tonight?' Well, Walter Cronkite had this terrible trouble with names, and for some reason that night he called him *Don* Rather. Dan said: "'I've had lots of big stories. You'd think the guy would remember my name.'" Herford chuckles, "It was the first time I'd ever heard him complain."

Another colleague of those civil rights years notes, "Even back then, when we were on the road, he was looking at Cronkite, and he was determined that's who he would be. He knew where he was going even then. He had made up his mind. And he was going to get there by outworking everybody."

With so much time on the road, his family life suffered, as even Rather, when he is being frank, will admit. Wife and kids were temporarily forgotten in the excitement of the big story, and other excitements as well: "Look, he was young, ambitious, on top of a huge story that was changing the country," recalls one CBS colleague. "It was heady wine. He was handsome, he was on TV. He'd come into Birmingham, Alabama, and there'd be a young lady at the Hertz counter, or airline stewardesses, of which there were a number. But then again, he was no different from most of his colleagues, no different from ninety percent of the guys we knew."

Over the next decades, Rather would spend a lot of weeks on the road. He has described the cost he paid in his family life in one anecdote about his son, Danjack: "Who's that?" a friend of his son's once asked. "Oh," said his son, turning around, "that's Dan Rather."

Wherever the stories were the most explosive, he'd turn up, scrapping for his share of the news. But certainly few stories were bigger than one he stumbled onto accidently in 1963. In the middle of setting up a new CBS bureau in New Orleans, he was asked to coordinate coverage of President John F. Kennedy's trip through Texas.

Slightly annoyed because the work involved would distract him from the civil rights coverage he was trying to focus on, Rather nonetheless realized that his home state had little affection for the liberal President, and that conflict made good television. He set up the coverage and returned to his other duties.

In fact, as he tells it, it was only because of a last-minute, light, sidebar piece—on the 98th birthday of former Vice President John Nance Garner—that Rather was in Texas at all on the morning of November 22, 1963. When he finished filming the interview, he headed into the local newsroom, where he discovered they were one man short for the film drops along the President's motorcade route. It was the last position, just past an old brick warehouse, the Texas School Book Depository. Rather had nothing else to do, so he slung one of CBS's yellow "grapefruit" bags, used to carry film, over his shoulder, and headed off for the position.

A little before 12:30, he was standing there, just thirty yards beyond the infamous grassy knoll, when he saw the President's limousine speed past, taking the wrong turnoff, going way too fast. Rather never heard the shots, but he could see that the motorcade was in complete confusion. He took off on the run, and when he came to the grassy knoll, everyone was running around screaming, the place in an uproar. Rather sprinted back to the station, dashing into the still-calm newsroom, turning on the police band radios. Overhearing a mention of Parkland Hospital, he dialed furiously, badgering switchboard operators, doctors, whoever was on hand there for information. "I'm a reporter!" he shouted. "Dan Rather, CBS. Don't hang up on me!" And the story emerged: the President had been shot. The President was dead. CBS got the story out first, perhaps before it had been thoroughly double-checked, but luck was on their side that day.

Breaking news is a business that thrives on tragedy, and throughout that long tragic weekend, as Lee Harvey Oswald was captured, and later shot, Rather and the CBS team were all over the story in what became one of the textbook examples of broadcast journalism. Few will forget seeing Walter Cronkite take off his glasses and announce in a choked voice that the President was dead. And few will forget Rather's dogged coverage, his icy determination.

"What most people went through on the weekend of the assassination, I went through two or three weeks later," Rather recalled, in a taped interview with *American Focus*. "A trained reporter can do this. If you're trained to be a boxer, even if you're hurt, you learn to cover it up, not to show when you're hurt. The professionalism takes over.... I spent three days weeping two or three weeks later."

Many consider that long weekend the turning point in Rather's career. It was certainly one of them. A crisis had brought him to CBS, and another crisis had stamped him a star. And when Lyndon Baines Johnson took over the Presidency, Dan Rather was assigned to the White House to cover him.

Most people around CBS, and outside, believed that Rather would have a special rapport with LBJ, a Texas mafia kind of relationship. In some ways, they were right. There was a psychological similarity between the two men. Both were Texas leaguers, each, in his own way, strong, driven, slightly larger than life. It is startling when reading Rather's descriptions of LBJ in his autobiography, to notice how well so many of the words apply to Rather himself:

"He was never an easy man to label. His critics were never quite sure if he was a liberal or a conservative or just ambitious. In a way he was a Texas populist...It is a pity, I always felt, that he never convinced himself that Austin was as good as Boston.... [And, quoting David Halberstam] He was a man of stunning force, drive, and intelligence and of equally stunning insecurity. His enormous accomplishments never dimmed the hidden fears which had propelled him in the first place."

But if they shared a Texas background, there was in fact, very little rapport between Rather and Johnson. Rather always felt that he was being manipulated by LBJ, just like everyone else. And as for Johnson, a scrawled note, found in the LBJ Library, sums up his feelings about the correspondent. Handwritten on a memo from Press Secretary George Reedy to LBJ, dated February 1965, outlining Dan Rather's request to come to the White House and film the President's assistants at work was this scrawled response: "This man [Rather] and CBS...out to get us any way they can. Tell them...these men are workers, not actors."

On at least one occasion Johnson called CBS president Frank

Stanton to complain about Rather, and at more than one press conference indicated his displeasure by not recognizing the correspondent. One memorable time, LBJ blasted Rather face to face:

"You did a good job down there in Texas and then you got up here to the big time, and the first thing you've done is fallen in with all these Eastern people...Well, you've made the biggest mistake of your life. The best thing about you is that you're all Texan, and I'm all Texan, and what you're doing now, playing Easterner, is a phony and I know it's a phony and you better get it right."

If Rather was going after LBJ and the news, he was also pursuing his career full-tilt. Colleagues remember one time when Rather, as White House correspondent, followed LBJ to Germany. If there was anyone more ambitious than Rather, according to a number of them, it was fellow Texan and fellow CBS correspondent Daniel Schorr. Schorr, as a European-based correspondent, knew Germany. He knew the layout. He knew where LBJ was going. He figured out the key stories, and how he could get his film to New York before anyone else. And while Rather ran around with the White House press corps, Schorr stole the story right out from under Rather's nose and got it to New York first.

"When Dan found out what had happened," recalls one ex-CBS staffer, "he blew into the Bonn office. He almost blasted the door off its hinges. He was white with rage, literally livid. He wagged his finger in Schorr's face, and he shouted, 'You fucking son of a bitch. You ever try that again and I will goddamn kill you!" The message, says the staffer, was crystal clear: "You don't step on Rather's turf. Then again, Schorr was exactly the same. Both of them would run over their mother to get a story, to get it on the air."

By 1965, that ambition had been rewarded with a key foreign posting to London. Rather himself was not so thrilled with the assignment. He viewed London as a "backwater." But CBS News in those days had a clear system of picking out hot prospects, and grooming them. In Rather's case, the grooming was both literal and figurative. He was lucky enough to have two of the great CBS correspondents as mentors—in London, Charles Collingwood, and later in Washington, Eric Sevareid. The line around CBS was that "Collingwood taught him how to dress. Sevareid taught him how to think."

It was from Collingwood that Rather picked up his taste for Savile Row suits and Borsalino hats. From both men, he acquired a certain polish. But when it came to stories, he was still the same hard-nosed reporter, and by mid-1965, technology made London a logical hub from which to cover international hot spots. Soon he was ducking tank shells near the Indian-Pakistani border, treading gingerly through Athens at the beginning of the Greek Civil War, and feeling the tension as armed Red Chinese soldiers gathered along the Natula Pass, 14,000 feet up in the Himalayas.

Throughout this period, the story Rather really wanted to get his hands on was Vietnam, even though both his boss, Fred Friendly, and his wife Jean, had tried to argue him out of it. Danger didn't dissuade him. In a big story, it was almost an aphrodisiac. Finally, his boss and his wife reluctantly gave in to his insistence, and by the end of 1965, he was on his way to Saigon.

He arrived as the story became huge, just as the U.S. built up its military presence from 50,000 to 500,000. Rather was part of a rotating CBS team that included, among others, Morley Safer, Bernard Kalb, Peter Kallisher, Bill Stout and occasionally Charles Collingwood. "What a crew!" says Peter Herford, then Saigon bureau manager. "Kallisher had the expertise....Safer was untouchable as a reporter—no matter where he went, something would happen....And Rather, Rather was the tiger. He was the war correspondent. He was the ex-Marine. He was out doing combat, and he couldn't get enough."

Lodging at the Caravelle Hotel in Saigon, Rather and his colleagues spent sixty to seventy percent of their time in the field. Rather often shipped back footage via courier, in order to stay longer in the field. Others, like Kallisher, or Kalb, were usually Herford's choice for political stories. "But when the shit hit the fan," he recalls, "you sent Rather."

One story several CBS veterans tell is of Rather's bravery. Together with a group of print reporters, Rather had gone to a pagoda in Da Nang under cover of darkness to talk to the militant anti-government Buddhist monks. As they were doing their interviews, the pagoda was surrounded by government troops, with rifles drawn. Rather gathered the other reporters behind him, threw open the pagoda door, turned his TV lights on himself and yelled "Bao Chi, Bao Chi! (Press!)."

Holding up a white flag under the TV lights, he marched straight at the government guns, and past them, herding the other reporters to safety.

Rather had courage, but he wasn't reckless. He wasn't a cowboy. In addition to his caution, he also carried two types of protection with him as he went into the field. On occasion, he packed a gun. Several colleagues describe him as being "gung ho" about weapons. And almost always, he wore his lucky bush hat. When he left Vietnam near the end of 1966, he gave the hat to fellow correspondent Jack Laurence, who recalls that "the hat was always lucky for me, too."

Returning to the U.S., Rather was once again thrust into the spotlight by another kind of combat. At the 1968 Democratic Convention in Chicago, as the police in the streets waded into the ranks of the anti-war protestors with truncheons, and fired off tear gas, the scene inside, where Rather was part of Walter Cronkite's CBS convention floor team, was no less chaotic.

Trying to find out why a group of plain clothes, unidentified security men were giving a diminutive older Georgia delegate the bum's rush, Rather blocked their path and asked what was happening. Several beefy, crew-cut members of the group tried to shove him out of the way with forearms to the chest. They said they would arrest him if he didn't move. Rather didn't budge. "Take your hands off me!" he yelled. "Take your hands off me unless you intend to arrest me!" As they started to shoulder him out of the way, Rather dove past them like a fullback off tackle, trying to reach the Georgia delegate.

Suddenly, he came up short as a solid blow caught him square in the chest, and other strong-arm men dragged him backward to the floor. "Walter!" he called up to the CBS booth. "As you can see...." Then he went down. The CBS cameras caught the scuffle, and stayed with Rather as he bobbed up again, breathing hard but surprisingly unflustered. "The security people put me on the deck," he said. "I didn't do very well."

Cronkite, visibly shocked, said "I think we've got a bunch of thugs here, Dan."

To which Rather responded, "Don't worry about it Walter, I'll answer the bell."

It was a classic moment of TV journalism, another storm with Rather at the center. And perhaps as much as any moment in the tumultuous sixties, it capsulized the growing "us versus them," reporters versus the government schism, the pervasive questioning of authority that would become standard operating procedure for journalists by the early to mid-seventies. Once Washington reporters had been comfortable insiders, the boys in the club. Now, they demanded to know, "What's Tricky Dick up to?" And Rather was one of the most aggressive.

On his first meeting with H.R. Haldeman, Rather recalls in his autobiography, the President's chief of staff fired at him: "You are a Lyndon Johnson, Texas liberal Democrat and we are going to be watching you." Over the next seven years, relations wouldn't get much more cordial.

"I always felt Dan took a bum rap," says Peter Sturtevant, who worked with Rather for three years in Washington. "He was just as tough on LBJ as he was on Nixon. He had a tough reporter's attitude. He was gonna dig as much as he could. He had this reputation of being a Nixon-hater. But he was just *real* aggressive."

Over the years, as Watergate unravelled and political divisions became more pronounced throughout the country in the early seventies, CBS took a lot of heat for their brash young correspondent. Frankly, Woodward and Bernstein and a number of other reporters were doing more to break the story, but Rather was much more visible, his TV presence more compelling. Right wingers focused their wrath on CBS, and tried to force owner William Paley to remove Rather from the White House beat. CBS, to its credit, stuck to its guns. And Rather? "His response was fairly typical," Sturtevant recalls. "Dan's a fighter. He fought back."

From Haldeman and Ehrlichman in the White House to loud-mouth critics in the street, Rather was fending them off on all sides. One little-known incident occurred in the early 1970s when he was in Georgia covering a speech that Nixon was giving at a local college. As Rather trailed after the President, some local cracker followed the reporter around all day, razzing him. Rather ignored the heckler. But when Nixon's speech was over and the story finished, the guy was still razzing him, louder than ever. Rather beckoned him over. Sticking his face squarely in the man's snoot, he said slowly, so there'd be no mistaking his message, "Fuck...off."

Afterwards, his producer asked him, "Don't you ever get tired of all this?"

Rather replied with a smile, "Beats working for a living." And for the son of a ditchdigger, it probably did.

Of course, a few of his more pugnacious moments have occurred on-camera. One of the most famous has become another classic bit of TV history. It occurred during a pre-packaged Nixon press conference in Houston, in March of 1974. Half Q & A session, half political rally to revive the flagging fortunes of Richard Nixon, the affair was packed by the Republican faithful. In this environment, Rather had assumed he wouldn't be called on. Even when he was, he thought it was the competition, NBC's Tom Brokaw, who had been pointed to first. Rising to ask his question, Rather, with his early-seventies sideburns and wide tie, announced, according to protocol: "Thank you, Mr. President. Dan Rather, CBS News." From the audience rose up a tide of applause, and almost immediately, an undercurrent of boos in response. "Mr. President," Rather tried to start. The commotion continued. "Mr...." Rather couldn't quite get into his question— about the House's role in investigating the President—because of the noise.

Nixon shot out, "Are you running for something?" As the crowd cracked up, Nixon flashed one of his rare smiles at his own bon mot. Rather smiled too, but as the applause started to build, he pursed his mouth and scratched his chin. In those fleeting seconds, there was enough time to think, and clearly what Dan Rather was thinking was, "I'm not going to stand here and take this crap."

"No sir, Mr. President," he shot back. "Are you?" Rather always downplays the incident, but it was absolutely characteristic of him, the Dan Rather who grew up in the Heights, Dan the street fighter. No one, not even a president, was going to yank his chain. It's impossible to imagine a Tom Brokaw or a Peter Jennings responding that way. Either one of them would, at most, have arched an eyebrow or murmured an ironic "Only a deadline, Mr. President."

Through the next years, through "CBS Reports" and "60 Minutes," this was the feisty, hard-charging Rather that the public came to know and admire. The match of Rather with "60 Minutes," and its muckraking focus and aggressive questioning style, seemed especially well-suited.

One typical "60 Minutes" muckraking piece was "Bum Steer." Dan Rather and his production team had discovered a company that was using a counterfeit "top grade" stamp on its beef. As he was being led around a meat packing plant, dressed in a white smock, he stopped between the hanging sides of beef, whipped the counterfeit stamp out of his pocket, and said, "Could you explain to me what this stamp is?"

His guide, the foreman, looked, did a doubletake, and turned ashen. "I think probably what you guys oughta do is leave." The camera zoomed in on him.

"I don't understand," said Rather.

"I don't think that's fair at all."

"I'm gonna give you the opportunity to tell me how you think it's unfair," Rather said, polite but tenacious.

The man walked off.

"May I get that back?" Rather called at the man's departing back.

"Where did you get it?"

"I got it," said Rather, his forefinger darting out accusingly, "from someone who told me that you use that to put a different type of stamp on meat than store buyers put on their own meat."

Rather stared at the man, his brawler's chin jutting out under the red "Beef" baseball cap, just daring him to tangle.

"Oh boy," the unhappy man mumbled. "What a disgusting deal...." He turned and walked off between the rows of beef, his head hanging down, well and truly defeated.

If Rather was a fighter on the screen, he was no less so off, especially when it came to his career. "A critical moment for me came in the late sixties," he once said, referring to the position of anchoring the CBS Sunday night news. It wasn't that he was eager for more money. Rather had even turned down an anchor role on the "CBS Morning News," saying he thought "being a reporter was a higher and better thing to do." Nonetheless, he had always had his eye on the evening news anchor chair.

He recalls, "I had covered Martin Luther King, civil rights, the Kennedy assassination, the Vietnam War, the White House—I thought I'd paid my dues. When an executive [Gordon Manning] pulled somebody out from pretty far down in the ranks [John Hart], I went to him and I said 'What's happening?' He said, 'I think you're a terrific reporter, but I don't think you'll ever make an anchorman.' Now rightly or wrongly, that's really the first time I'd thought about it."

Although Rather's comment may sound a little disingenuous, there's no getting around his fiercely felt response: "The second he said that to me, the competitive fire in me said 'Wait a minute—I don't like the idea that there's something maybe second class about me that you, sir, think I can't be an anchorperson. I hadn't thought about it, I hadn't worked on it, but you give me a shot, and I might make a pretty good anchor."

Eventually CBS did give him a crack at the weekend anchor position, and he shuttled back and forth from the White House office to the New York studio. But, as Rather tells it, it was the same scenario all over again, when it became clear that top CBS executives were heatedly discussing who would succeed Walter Cronkite:

"When I began to read in the papers that there's a race on and you Dan are in it, and you Dan are losing it, I said to myself, 'Wait a minute. I didn't know I was in a race, and if I'm in a race—I intend to win it."

RATINGS: Week ending February 24th

1st. Rather   ("CBS Evening News")—11.7/20 [10,576,800]

2nd. Jennings (ABC's "World News Tonight")—11.5/20 [10,396,000]

3rd. Brokaw   (NBC's "Nightly News")—11.0/20 [9,944,000]

CHAPTER SIX

Corporate Takeovers

W hat Rather, Brokaw and Jennings did not realize was that, as they raced to the top, the track itself was being sold out from under them. In the mid-1980s, CBS, ABC and NBC were being taken over by new owners, big powerhouse corporations. For these new bosses, news was neither a sacred calling nor a public service. It was simply one more way to make money, just like "The Cosby Show" or "Monday Night Football." This new "bottom-line" ownership would send shock waves rippling through the entire television news community.

At no point in its history had American TV news been treated in the same fashion as it had been in Britain or Canada or Europe, where it was considered a national obligation to keep the population informed. In America, home of capitalism, the networks had never been nationalized like the BBC, but were owned by stockholders. Nevertheless, William Paley and David Sarnoff, the original corporate owners, were men who knew communications. They had grown up in the business, and they were fascinated by it. If the news divisions did not make a profit, they were still prepared to look on them benevolently as "loss leaders" that more than made up in prestige and marquee-value what they failed to gain financially.

Longtime CBS chairman Paley was one of these media tycoons who never really worried when news didn't turn a profit. As "CBS Evening

News" executive producer Tom Bettag recalls: "There was a time when Paley was asked before the stockholders, 'How dare you lose six million dollars a year on news?' And Paley said, 'Because I *like* what that six million dollars buys me.' It bought him respectability. It bought him the ability to go before Congress and every time he got beat up on 'The Beverly Hillbillies' he'd say, 'Yeah, but I take a loss every year on Walter Cronkite. I do that as a public service.' It gave the corporation a sheen and a cachet." It also helped CBS get its broadcasting license renewed.

But in 1986, that attitude began to change. In January, the major media conglomerate Capital Cities bought ABC. In June, General Electric, the tenth largest industrial firm in the world, took over RCA, which owns NBC. And in September, Loews patriarch Laurence Tisch purchased CBS. Thus in the space of only nine months, America's three major TV networks were taken over by a new breed of corporate owner.

Why the sudden interest in the networks? For one simple reason: the TV business, specifically the TV station business, makes a lot of money, and back in the mid-1980s, the price of the networks' stock remained greatly undervalued. RCA, for example, was selling at almost one hundred percent below its true worth. In short, the networks had turned into a bargain, dangling like ripe fruit waiting to be plucked. "I think," says Natalie Hunter, chief financial officer of NBC News, "it was just a classic assets play in all three cases."

So for $3.5 billion Cap Cities acquired ABC, for $6.3 billion GE bought all of RCA, including NBC, and for $951 million, Larry Tisch acquired de facto control of CBS, a company whose assets were worth $5 to $10 billion. For many at the networks, and especially within the network news divisions, these buyouts were a nightmare, like some horrific scene out of the movie *Network*, where the Philistines, long on cash but short on taste and intelligence, start to call the shots. When Peter Jennings first heard about the purchase of ABC by Cap Cities, he recalls feeling "as if they were Nazis and we were occupied France."

At CBS, staffers felt somewhat more sanguine. Larry Tisch, after all, was one of their own, a member of the CBS board of directors, a "white knight" who had saved the network from the outside threat of the Dixie upstart, Ted Turner, "the mouth from the South." Who knew what the likes of Turner or Senator Jesse Helms might have done if they had gotten their hands on the company—mass layoffs, editorial meddling, the sale of its parts? So when Tisch bought up CBS stock, acquiring a controlling share of 24.9 percent of the company, everyone said they were relieved. Tisch promised no major shakeups. He swore that any changes he might make would be so small "you won't know it." As for the news division, he declared it would barely be affected at all by the new management.

Rather's news team breathed more easily. And yet, there were disturbing rumors floating around, rumors that Tisch was not really a champion of CBS, that he had cleverly taken advantage of a crisis and performed a friendly hostile takeover, that he was just as bad as the rest. CBS, the rumor went, had "replaced the Shah with the Ayatollah."

As it turned out, 1987 was a demoralizing year for all the network news teams. Soon after Tisch, and Cap Cities and GE started running the networks, they were clearly unhappy with the news divisions. Elsewhere, American corporations were entering a competitive era, a period of downsizing, of efficiency. The watchwords were "lean and mean." And the news divisions, once the pampered darlings of the networks, were seen as flabby and inefficient. They had no bottom-line discipline. It was simply a question of priorities. While the news divisions strove for top-notch journalism, no matter the cost, their new corporate masters were worried about price/earnings ratios, profit/loss statements. The journalists were thinking "Edward R. Murrow tradition"; the corporate types were thinking "fat and wasteful." The clash that came was inevitable.

An impartial observer, like Robert MacNeil, who had worked at Reuters and NBC, before moving to PBS's "MacNeil-Lehrer Report," had to admit that the networks' news progams had "profligate ways of spending which were really amazing." He recalled stories of the networks camping outside Bethesda Naval Hospital when President Reagan underwent an operation. Huge teams had been assembled, and hot catered meals were brought in. At each network bivouac, blackboards announced the menu of the day, and the networks vied with each other's gourmet cooking. The hungry print reporters wandered from camp to camp like impoverished refugees, looking for handouts.

MacNeil tells another story of the time the American hostages were released in 1981, and they came through Algiers. In this city of steep hills, the network production managers had literally commandeered all the available taxis for the entire duration of their coverage of the event, so that once again the print reporters, not to mention the rest of the population, were reduced to begging favors. According to Mac-Neil, "The networks' traditional way of dealing with anything was to throw as many bodies and as much equipment [and money] at any situation as they could, and then see what came out of it."

Even network employees had to admit the truth of this assessment. Crews were routinely booked for five days, "just in case," when only two days were necessary. Overtime costs were staggering. And news budgets at each of the networks had soared from about $80 million to about $300 million in just eight years. Tom Brokaw chuckles when he recalls the way NBC used to order up jets as if they were compact cars.

Obviously the wasteful ways had to be curtailed. The operations needed streamlining. Networks couldn't go on losing $75 million a year, as NBC News had when it bottomed out in 1984.

But when the corporate managers brought in their efficiency experts, it became clear that they had very little understanding of the business they were being called on to fix. In many instances, the experts were trying to quantify qualitative matters, and the results didn't make sense. At NBC, staffers started making jokes about management consultants McKinsey & Company.

"They were good on cash flow," domestic producer John Chesnutt said, "but they asked these bizarre questions. We were preparing a live piece one night on a snowstorm progressing along the East Coast, from Boston to Washington, and I asked Boston, 'What will your shot show—skyline, the Charles River?' They were standing over my shoulder and they said, 'Now why were you asking what they're going to show? Do you really get into that much detail?' And I said, 'This is television. These are *pictures* we're talking about.'"

The new corporate managers didn't have the sensitivity, the love of journalism that would cause a Dan Rather to say, "CBS News is not just another division of another corporation. We have a past, a responsibility." At the beginning of the writers' strike in 1987, one NABET (National Association of Broadcast Employees and Technicians) union member recalls being told by management, "Don't give me this crap about quality. What's it gonna cost?"

The pressure was on to reduce news budgets from over $300 million to under $250 million. "It's because of corporate turnover, same as at any corporation," said one well-known television agent. "They buy up companies, then slash to cover their debt. It's the same when K & K

[Kohlberg, Kravis and Roberts] bought RJR [RJR Nabisco], then sold off four of their companies. In news, the only way you can make real savings is through head cuts. It's a labor intensive business."

Over the next months, NBC and ABC, through early retirements, reassignments and layoffs dropped a large number of personnel. ABC proved the most sensitive. NBC News winnowed down its staff of 1,400 to 1,000 with a certain delicacy (e.g. early retirement benefits, etc.), considering that the division was losing thirty percent of its workers, and replacing its studio cameramen with robot cameras.

But at CBS, on March 13, 1987—"Black Friday"—the hatchet came down hard. In one fell swoop, more than two hundred of CBS News's 1,200 staffers were fired: producers, technicians, on-air correspondents. In the auto business, such layoffs might not be so unusual, but in the TV industry they are. It was the single largest firing ever at one of the most public of companies, and it stirred a massive outcry. Dubbed "the slaughter on 57th Street," the drama was played out all over the papers, and morale at CBS plummeted.

Producer Richard Cohen drafted an op-ed piece for *The New York Times*, signed by Dan Rather, that asked whether CBS was going "From Murrow to Mediocrity?" Condemning the layoffs, Cohen and Rather saw the danger that CBS News, under the Tisch regime, might "fall short of the quality and vision it once possessed." Rather and other stars like Diane Sawyer offered to take pay cuts if it would save jobs. Rather also kicked into a generous five-figure safety-net fund for the unemployed. But, as the disillusioned anchor would later say, "It took me a long time to understand that a corporation is not a family. It's a business."

Today, the news divisions of all three networks have become more streamlined. Profligate spending has been trimmed: "I guess we won't be taking the Lear jet any more," Tom Brokaw was told by one gloomy producer. And these days, strong, centralized assignment desks at all three networks (most recently NBC) mean that several in-house shows—for example, the "Nightly News" and "Today"—routinely share expenses and results on a big story such as the Berlin Wall or the Malta Summit. Some would argue that not much has been lost. "I don't think there's ever a hesitation on the big breaking news story," says NBC's Natalie Hunter. "Nobody ever checks. You just go and do it, no matter what it takes."

But in many ways, the new penny-pinching, bottom-line mentality is a terrible attitude for network news. Networks are now relying more and more on "one-man bands," that is, one overworked person, instead of two, to cope with both shooting the footage and recording the sound at the same time. Obviously, quality has to suffer. Then too, while the centralized assignment desk for all the news shows may lead to economies, it also results in less variety, less information and only one point of view, since all the programs end up sharing the results from just one reporter-cameraman team. Perhaps most important, bureaus have been cut. At CBS, Bonn, Warsaw, Bangkok and Seattle have all been pared down. And at NBC, even the Paris bureau is now just an answering machine.

John Chancellor, like many of his colleagues, fears that these cuts are not just fat, they're "down to the muscle." The real concern, as bureaus are trimmed or closed across America and throughout the world, is not necessarily that the networks won't be able to get pictures. They can always purchase pictures from a VisNews or a CNN, which is why networks are currently buying into these kinds of international companies. The concern is that *newsgathering* itself will suffer: because no one is actually on the scene, no one will know what the pictures *mean*. That's what Chancellor is worried about when he talks of "doing things with mirrors": giving the illusion of covering the world by buying footage from abroad, footage that is either worthless or potentially misleading, since no reporter is in place to analyze it.

"When I joined on," says ex-NBC newsman Ken Bode, "the Chicago bureau was forty people. It was the biggest run and gun operation. They covered anything that happened in the Midwest. Now it's three people. If the network heads are telling you that that hasn't had any effect—it's clear they don't know what they're talking about."

For an executive producer like CBS's Tom Bettag, "Budget pressures are everywhere." Each decision to cover or not cover a news story is not only a news decision, it's a dollars-and-cents decision: "Every time you decide to send somebody to Manila [from your Tokyo bureau] with a film crew and an editor and a producer and a correspondent and satellite time, it's a lot of money. The satellite time is a couple thousand dollars [for a half hour]. The rest is plane fare and hotels and food, and you hire on a driver. That's probably a six or seven thousand dollar decision." And, hypothetically speaking, if it turns out that the murdered American soldier, your reason for going, was killed by a jealous husband and not by Communist guerrillas, all that money is lost.

Under the corporate owners, news divisions are now *expected* to turn a profit. The news division is *supposed* to be a profit center. "I'm not looking for charity," Bettag says. "I'm not saying you have to do this because you owe it to people to lose money on the news....But we can't give a GE the kind of profits it requires of its divisions. We can make a profit, but we can't make a handsome profit, and I'm not sure we should."

When turning a profit becomes paramount, strange things start to happen. Stories in hard-to-get-to, faraway places get dropped. So, too, do important pieces that might bore viewers, hence lowering ratings, hence losing advertiser dollars. "They're not in the news business anymore," claims ex-CBS producer Richard Cohen. "They're in the corporate moneymaking business."

Cohen and others see this bottom-line emphasis as having a debilitating effect on the journalistic spirit: "News used to be a bunch of strong-minded people with authority problems. Now it's changed. People are more submissive, more willing to play corporate games."

CBS reporter Betsy Aaron agrees that big business has had a chilling effect on TV news: "After the corporate takeovers, when there were all those mass firings, it really frightened people. It had never happened before. Now we don't take as many chances [don't try risky stories that might not pan out], which is horrible for reporters and anchors. You *should* take chances. If you're worried about the mortgage, the kids, you won't be as good a reporter."

In the post-Paley era, staffers are running scared. Unsure of their jobs, unsure of when the axe might fall again, they often find themselves looking over their shoulders. Then too, they're confronted with a day-to-day stinginess, a cheapskate mentality, which many find depressing.

One CBS producer comments: "Ed Grebow [senior vice president of operations and administration, the financial head of CBS] has all these crazy schemes to save money. The latest is soap dispensers. They took liquid soap out of the bathrooms and put in sand soap, because it's cheaper. And then they raised the price of tampons. Five hundred percent! They've got to turn a profit, *even* on the tampons!"

Agents fume over the stinginess of the salaries, noting that NBC News is especially tough, with new president Michael Gartner "brought in to be pecuniary." What they don't mention is that newsmen and their agents, like pro ball players, have been raking in the money for quite a while: anchors receive $2 to $4 million a year, important senior correspondents $500,000 to $750,000, with even the average, run-of-the-mill correspondent getting around $150,000.

Today, there's an overall corporate paranoia surrounding matters financial. Take CBS's response to an article written for *The Wall Street Journal* on the superpower summit at Malta. In it, Robert Goldberg, the *Journal* TV critic, merely noted in passing that ABC and NBC each had around seventy people on the island, and that CBS had one hundred twenty. This brief mention in the middle of a long article apparently caused an uproar at CBS.

Executive producer Tom Bettag and director of special events coverage, Lane Venardos, were reportedly hauled across town to the corporate headquarters on Sixth Avenue ("Black Rock") to account to Ed Grebow and other top CBS officials. For the two of them, it was a very bad day at Black Rock. "Grebow gave the news division hell about how many people it had in Malta," says one CBS insider.

Formerly, if a news division had more people on the scene than its competition, it was commended for being committed to thorough coverage. But under the new corporate management, having more people on a story is considered to be merely profligate.

Tom Bettag admits, "After that article, we were called into financial meetings—literally three and four hour meetings with financial executives—and told, 'I read this in *The Wall Street Journal*'. They kept asking, 'You needed *this* many people?' And they demanded to know who had leaked the numbers.'"

Finally, someone figured out the obvious, namely, that in a foreign operation like Malta, every network puts up envelopes to serve as mailboxes for each of their staff members. Count the mailboxes, you're counting the staff.

"An edict went out," says a source at CBS. "We're never going to put envelopes up again. We've learned our lesson."

"That's the game everybody is into these days—having the fewest people," Bettag notes. "Then your executives can say, 'Isn't that wonderful? See how much leaner our shop is than the other two networks?'" No doubt this is why there's so much active disinformation being handed out by network news divisions nowadays. Instead of simply declining to talk about figures, which is certainly their right, executives will now lie just as frequently as they tell the truth. Of course, many businessmen lie when questioned by the press about difficult issues, but TV journalists, who think of themselves as members of the press too, once took some pride in being candid. Today they see themselves as members of a corporation.

"News executives have a hard time these days," says a CBS producer. "Is their job to cover the story or to look good—to look lean—to their corporate masters?" Several high-ranking people at CBS, for example, placed the costs for the China coverage at a little over $1 million. Yet according to a knowledgeable insider, the true costs were nearly double that, between $1.8 and $2 million.

Today, everyone in the three news divisions seems a little nervous about finances, a little gun-shy. A major week-long series on the environment at CBS, an important $5 to $7 million story ranging from Africa to Europe to the U.S., was cancelled to save money for the superpower summit coverage in Malta, and only a skeleton staff went to South Africa for Nelson Mandela's release.

Peter Jennings may argue, "I don't agree with all that about network news suffering because of less money. It's been overplayed." But he's in a more fortunate position than most, since Capital Cities, the corporation that took over ABC, has always been a *communications* conglomerate, and has, by all accounts, been much more sensitive to its news division. Certainly ABC has not had to go through the bloodletting and public trauma that CBS experienced, and the embarrassment of NBC.

The other major worry about corporate takeovers is that the parent corporation may try to influence the news. "Clearly," says CBS News executive producer Tom Bettag, "it's critical that the corporation have no say whatsoever in what goes on the evening news. It's critical that embarrassment to the corporation has no impact. We're in a very difficult, sensitive situation.... There are very real potentials for conflicts of interest between the needs of the corporation and the news division. Clearly the news division needs a layer of insulation."

Some experts, like Joan Konner, dean of the Columbia School of Journalism, assert that "the GE takeover of NBC is a conflict of interest [when it comes to stories about the defense industry or nuclear energy]. If it hasn't yet played out, it will." In practice, the danger has not been that General Electric, one of the largest industrial powers in the world, would turn NBC News into a propaganda machine to the greater glory of its lightbulbs. That kind of overt influence has simply not arisen. Instead, the influences have been more subtle, and are evident only from time to time. They can be seen in a hesitancy, a self-censorship on the part of reporters and producers, a "why-bother-with-that-story-it's-only-going-to-cause-hassles" attitude. The "Today" show, for instance, conveniently dropped a reporter's reference to faulty GE bolts used in airliners and missile silos.

On the other hand, when a plane crashed in Sioux City, Iowa, and a faulty GE engine was suspected, Brokaw's "Nightly News" reported the facts meticulously. In fact, the anchor seemed to bend over backwards to cite GE as if to prove his virtue. These days, NBC isn't likely to launch any major investigations of GE. But then again, as long as Jack Welch isn't picking up the telephone and ordering Tom Brokaw to kill stories, the news division and its paymaster are living in a workable, if uneasy, symbiosis.

As for the future, expect to see more changes as corporate imperatives continue to grind slowly on the news divisions. It is rumored that, in the nineties, one network might divest itself of its news business altogether—most likely NBC, under the leadership of GE's Jack Welch, regarded as "one of the world's most ruthless managers." While that rumor is probably not true, NBC News comptroller Natalie Hunter does admit, "I don't think you'll recognize NBC News in five years." Cuts totaling as much as forty percent of the staff are said to be in the offing there.

Meanwhile, at CBS, Larry Tisch began grumbling early in the year about business prospects for 1990 looking dreadful, even though he had just posted a remarkably strong 52 percent increase in first quarter net income. CBS employees were alerted to expect new rounds of firings, perhaps numbering in the dozens. This was followed by an ill-fated attempt to force CBS News to accept technicians from a general on-call pool. George Schweitzer, senior vice-president at CBS recently said, "Where efficiencies can be made, we are going to pursue them." Even if his grammar was a little muddled, his intention couldn't have been sharper.

These are the chills of the new corporate era. "Part of what's changed here," says Dan Rather, "is an acute awareness that every good and decent thing is constantly on the razor's edge of danger, and must be fought for minute by minute."

RATINGS: Week ending March 10th

1st.   Rather   ("CBS Evening News")—11.5/21 [10,396,000]

2nd. Jennings (ABC's "World News Tonight")—11.2/20 [10,124,800]

3rd.   Brokaw   ("NBC Nightly News")—10.2/19 [9,220,800]

The Jennings family on vacation in London (c. 1952): the teenage Peter, his father Charles, sister Sarah and mother Elizabeth. (Courtesy Sarah Jennings)

Tom Brokaw and Meredith Auld, newly elected Arickara attendants at Yankton High School, in Homecoming regalia. (Courtesy David Bitter, Yankton High School)

Brokaw played guard on his high school basketball team. He also won varsity letters in football and track (1958). (Courtesy David Bitter, Yankton High School)

Dan Rather, president of Sam Houston's Junior class, with other class officers (1953). (Courtesy Norma Dell Jones, Sam Houston State University)

Rather emcees the crowning of "Miss Sam Houston" (1953). (Courtesy Norma Dell Jones, Sam Houston State University)

Brokaw, the eighteen-year-old high school senior (1958). (Courtesy David Bitter, Yankton High School)

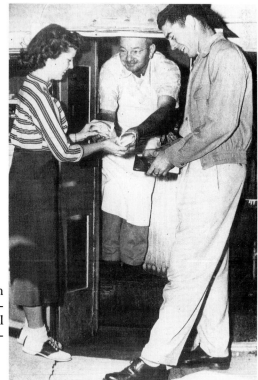

Rather, selected as one of "Sam Houston's Favorites" (1952 yearbook photo). (Courtesy Norma Dell Jones, Sam Houston State University)

Brokaw in his final year as host of the "Today" show, with regulars Gene Shalit, Jane Pauley and Willard Scott (1981). (Courtesy NBC)

Jennings in his first stint as anchor on "Peter Jennings with the News" (1966-1968). (Courtesy Capital Cities/ABC)

Rather being manhandled by security forces as he tries to discover why they're ousting a Georgia delegate from the Chicago Democratic convention (August 1968). (Courtesy UPI/Bettmann Newsphotos)

The Old Pro and the Young Aspirant: New anchor Jennings chats with Walter Cronkite at a New York cocktail party for Canada's CBC (c. 1967). (Courtesy Sarah Jennings)

Jennings reporting from Vietnam (c. 1967). (Courtesy Capital Cities/ABC)

Brokaw interviewing Rabbi David Hartman and Palestinian leader Sari Nusseibah for his documentary on Israel "6 Days Plus 20; A Dream Is Dying" (1987). (Courtesy NBC)

Rather confronts Richard Nixon in his first news conference as chief executive (January 1969). (Courtesy UPI/Bettmann Newsphotos)

ennings with Gerald Ford . . .

and Jimmy Carter. (Courtesy Capital Cities/ABC)

Brokaw in the first one-on-one U.S. TV interview with Mikhail Gorbachev (May 1988) . . .

and at the White House with George and Barbara Bush (February 1990). (Courtesy NBC)

CHAPTER SEVEN

On the Set with Brokaw

In the 1930s, perhaps nothing more aptly captured corporate power in America than the RCA building at 30 Rockefeller Plaza, its lobby, according to one architecture critic, "pulsing with the energy of capitalism." Today, the letters surmounting the slender gray shaft that rises dramatically in stepped thrusts from the plaza below are GE.

On any normal working day between 9:15 and 9:30 AM, Tom Brokaw can be seen being dropped off in front of 30 Rock. He strides to one of its revolving doors and into the impressive art deco lobby with its huge Jose Maria Sert murals. Hurrying past the guard desk to the bank of elevators, he goes up to NBC News on the third floor. Off a long carpeted hallway, his office is just beyond that of his executive producer, Bill Wheatley (replaced in May 1990 by Steve Friedman). The hall is dotted with the desks of secretaries. Brokaw's secretary, Geri Jansen, sits at the end of the line.

On this Friday late in March, it's still early morning but Brokaw is already at his desk, seated before two huge Rolodex wheels, working the phones. Though not denying the glamour of his job, he's quick to point out that being an anchor is much more labor intensive than most people realize. Above his desk, the book shelf is heavy with reference works such as the *World Almanac*, the *Washington Introduction Dictionary*, the *Almanac of American Politics 1986*, and *A New*

113

Dictionary of Quotations. There is also a small box of baseball cards. Prior to leaving for Havana to cover the meeting between Castro and Gorbachev, Brokaw is preparing for his trip by talking to specialists in the field of Soviet studies.

His jacket off, he works in his shirtsleeves, his collar open at the neck. He is wearing a blue silk tie and maroon suspenders over his blue striped shirt. Clothes look good on him, and his appear to be in the Paul Stuart mode and expensive. His hair is rumpled and grayer than it looks on television. Also unlike his television image are the glasses he wears. Several more pairs are on the desk beside his coffee mug, which bears the legend, "Litchfield County Times." Brokaw owns a large country house and a million dollars worth of land in the town of Cornwall, in what has been called the "toniest county" in Connecticut.

If his desk, tucked away in a corner, is cluttered with the anchor's immediate concerns, the rest of his comfortable office is filled with remnants from his past, including a "Light Roadster" All-Star bicycle. Looking oddly out of place amidst the modern couch and chairs is a strange, ornate, old-fashioned wooden rocker with the head of a woman carved just below each armrest. "My father used to fix up old furniture," Brokaw explains. "This was his work."

Behind the glass-fronted bookcase along one wall are autographed photos from old friends Muhammed Ali and Nancy Reagan. Tommy Lasorda, a pal from his Los Angeles days, has written, "To Tom, the greatest news reporter in America. You and the Dodgers are both great." On a lower shelf, a small burlap bag of peanuts commemorates the time in December 1976, when Brokaw, then host of the "Today" show, went down to Plains, Georgia, to interview the newly elected Jimmy Carter. On the wall near his desk are pictures of him interviewing Ronald Reagan and Mikhail Gorbachev.

The most striking photo of all is a huge, poster-sized image of a tombstone that hangs over Brokaw's desk. Inscribed on it is the name CHRISTIAN SUNRISE and the dates 1833-1916. Brokaw took it himself. "When I was growing up in South Dakota," he says, "we used to go sledding on Sunrise Hill, and I always thought it had to do with the sunrise. Then I found that tombstone and realized it was named after Christian Sunrise, a local Indian."

You won't see a photo of Brokaw with Peter Jennings and Dan Rather in the office, but despite their differences in background and temperament, all three are friendly. "Peter and I are pals," Brokaw says. "It's genuine, and it goes back a long way, and there's a *real* affection. And Dan and I are friends. We've known each other a long time. It's just that the personal relationship is not as close as it is with Peter. I mean, Peter and I have conversations in which I tease him and he teases me. That kind of thing."

The pictures of his family are all over the office. His wife, Meredith, has a smile that just won't quit. There she is with their three daughters camping, backpacking, skiing, climbing. The woman seems inexhaustible. In her spare time, Meredith is also a successful businesswoman, the owner of a popular chain of four Penny Whistle toy stores in New York, not to mention the author of three books for parents on the feeding and entertaining of children. On occasion, she even plays tennis with Dan Rather's wife, Jean. As for Tom, he's a jogger, a kayaker and a rock climber. The entire Brokaw family seems to have a fondness for outdoor life and energy to burn.

When he arrived at his office that morning, Brokaw already had a good idea of what the major stories would be that night. He and his principal producers are hooked up at home to a main computer through which they have access to the wire services. In addition, he had already looked through *The New York Times, The Washington Post* and *The Wall Street Journal.*

"Oh sure," he says, "today is easy." The lead most likely will be the environmental disaster in Alaska, the Exxon Valdez oil spill. Then there'll be a story from Rob Bazell about cold fusion and something from Ed Rabel in Cuba. Generally, the tentative lineup won't be set until Bill Wheatley and his top producers get together at 10:15 AM, a meeting Brokaw sits in on from time to time. But this week Wheatley is on vacation, the anchor recalls. Subbing for him is the senior producer of the "Nightly News," Cheryl Gould.

During the actual newscast at NBC, the executive producer is on the set while the senior producer is in the control room speaking into Brokaw's ear. But today Cheryl Gould has the responsibility of putting the show together. The one thing she hates about the executive producer's job is constantly having to tell people no, but it goes with the title. Gould is athletic, tanned and trim. "I'm an aeroboholic," she confesses. Her blonde, permed hair is shoulder length, her earrings long and funky. Wearing a short, gray-green dress with a large black belt, she might be going to a party. Around her wrist, a matchbox-size sports car. Then she taps a button and, *voilà!*, a watch. Everything about Gould seems to be an event.

Already that morning, Gould attended the brief 9:30 AM executive meeting with the president of the news division, Michael Gartner, and vice presidents Tom Ross and Joe Angotti, as well as the executive producers of "Nightly News," the "Today" show, "Sunrise" and "Meet the Press." Then at about 9:45, she chaired the regularly scheduled conference call with all the domestic bureaus of the network. At that time, the bureaus passed along to Gould their "offerings," or suggestions of pieces for "Nightly." At 10:15, Gould is in the conference room with five of the newscast's producers and Brokaw, the anchor impatiently twirling his glasses by the stem as he listens to the discussion. He seems to be thinking about the half dozen other things he has to take care of before leaving for Havana.

By the early afternoon, the pace of the day begins to quicken perceptibly. In Bill Wheatley's office beneath a poster for the Seoul Olympics, Cheryl Gould is listening to "Nightly" correspondent Bill Schechner plead his case for a piece about an Asian woman who just became a naturalized citizen. A modern Betsy Ross, she sews American flags by hand and makes a business of it. It's the sort of cute, offbeat, heart-tugging story that Schechner seems to specialize in, and Brokaw loves. Though Schechner insists that it run that night, Gould has another "closer" in mind. She's already committed herself to a piece by Mike Leonard. In the current period of tight budgets and reduced resources, "Nightly" has had to go to other NBC programs to get more correspondents for this sort of closing story.

"We had to fight to get Mike Leonard from 'Today,' " she explains to Schechner. "If his piece doesn't run tonight, we can't use it."

"But my story isn't as good if you have to say, 'Last week she became a citizen,' " Schechner argues. "This is a news program after all.... Maybe if we added in, 'And she's about to be indicted for running a white slavery ring.' "

Cheryl smiles. "That would do it. No, we really have to do the Leonard piece. We sent him up to Wisconsin—"

"Are we back to doing the ponderous closers? Or is it still the lighter stuff?"

"No, it's a mix," she says.

After the disgruntled Schechner leaves, Gould says, "I just hate this part of the job, disappointing people. I'd love it if someone would say to me, 'Yeah, you're up against it.' We had to work out this intricate deal with 'Today' to get Leonard. And he did this piece on this kid breaking the record for consecutive days fishing in a small town in Wisconsin. We *have* to do it, cause by next week he might have stopped."

The phone rings. It's Schechner calling to apologize. He's feeling guilty. All afternoon the phone continues to ring, and people are coming in with questions, problems, demands. Everything seems to flow into the acting-executive producer's office: by foot, by phone, by memo, by computer.

Ed Deitch, the head newswriter, comes in with a question about the Armenian earthquake story. He's writing an introduction for Brokaw. In white shirt and gray slacks, he looks like a young banker.

Gould glances up from the desk. "You want twenty-five seconds for Armenia?"

"It'd be nice."

She sighs. "All right, I'll try."

Hard on his heels comes Jack Chesnutt, domestic producer for "Nightly." He's a pleasantly rumpled man, about forty, in a tweed coat with brown elbow patches and corduroy pants. He has a mustache, clear horn-rimmed glasses, a thoughtful air. Right now he's thinking about the lineup for the evening newscast, and asks Cheryl what the time situation is.

"We're running heavy," she tells him.

"So what should we nuke?"

She and Chesnutt look over the list.

He says, "I guess it's goodbye Jensen."

"Can Tom summarize?" she asks.

"Sure. It's a blip." Then he tells her that they've already begun seeing ecological damage to the animals in the Alaskan oil spill. "We'll go with the animals first. Then we'll get into such things as was the pilot drinking."

She wants to know how much time he'll need. "Will 2:15 be sufficient?"

"We'll have to crimp it to bring it in at 2:20."

"So that'll be Lewis, Cochran, Stern, Cuba and fish," says Gould, ticking off the lineup so far. The phone rings. The voice at the other end tells her that Brokaw is on the set doing a promo for Leonard's fishing piece that evening. Putting down the phone, Gould rolls her eyes as if wondering who's in charge here anyway. But she knows very well who's in charge, as does everyone else at the "Nightly News." "God," she says, "I hadn't even said that was definite yet."

Just down the hall from Gould, past Tom Brokaw's office, are the newsroom and the studio placed side by side. Brokaw is seated at the round anchor desk in the center of the studio, completing the promo. "...Tonight, on 'NBC Nightly News,'" he says, gazing into the camera. His copy scrolls by on a teleprompter, an electronic box that sits just below the camera. The words are reflected up on the lens so that when Brokaw looks into the camera, he's actually reading. The curve of the lens prevents viewers from seeing the words; only the anchor sees them.

Finishing up, Brokaw strolls back towards the newsroom, which is subdivided into rows of individual booths, each with its own computer, its own mini-monitor. The first row is reserved for Brokaw, Wheatley and Gould. Facing them on the wall are ten numbered TV screens, and nine small clocks labeled Moscow, Tel Aviv, Paris, London, GMT (Greenwich Mean Time), New York, Managua, Seoul and Tokyo.

Brokaw takes a seat, and starts twirling his glasses again. He doesn't care for the way the newsroom and the set have been linked. "Unfortunately, they built it totally backwards. They decided to do a newsroom first and then add a set on to that. The two ideas are conflicting. It doesn't work. We know that. Frankly it's an aggravation." Brokaw feels that the set doesn't look contemporary. It looks like an add-on to something else. He also finds it hard to have visiting people join him there for interviews. But his special ire is reserved for the three computerized cameras that NBC alone uses, the ones they've dubbed "Larry, Curly and Moe," the ones that have attacked Connie Chung and taken chunks out of the anchor desk. Brokaw sneers at the very thought of them: "Those robotic cameras are a pain in the ass!"

The headline on the wall in Jack Chesnutt's booth says, JUST CALL HIM JACK. Brokaw peers over Jack's booth to see how the Exxon Valdez stories are coming. This is a topic of special interest to him. Brokaw is not just an avid outdoorsman, whose vacations are often spent in the wild, hiking, camping and climbing. He's also an active environmentalist, a member of the Nature Conservancy and the Sierra Club. Later in the year, the anchor would attend the Global Warming Conference in Sundance, Idaho, hosted by his friend Robert Redford. This interest in environmental issues is often reflected in "Nightly," especially in the "Assignment America" section.

But right now, the Exxon Valdez disaster is on everyone's mind, even David Letterman's. Throughout the newsroom, a number of the staffers have tuned the dial on their monitors to watch the David Letterman show being taped. It's a Letterman Top Ten list, and they've turned up the sound to listen. He's giving the top ten reasons that the Exxon tanker crashed. "Number 10," he says. "It swerved to avoid an oncoming Eastern jet." The newsroom cracks up.

"Shana," Chesnutt shouts, "can you turn that down?" He is on the phone to George Lewis in Alaska. "Are we still following the same game plan?" he asks. "We lead with oily animals. Then follow with people getting pissed off. Are you going to have scientists talking about the long-term effects, and that kinda stuff?"

Chesnutt listens to his reply and says, "Okay. Then from that to the Exxon news conference. The graphic would come there. How about the cleanup? Can we see some of that? And make sure to tell us that the weather has not been helpful. Will that be toward the top or after the Exxon conference?"

After telling him what he wants, Chesnutt says, "You'll have between 2:15 and 2:30. By the way, do we have the FBI guy from Anchorage?"

Senior producer Cheryl Gould comes hurrying into the newsroom. "Let's do a lineup, guys....Hello, it's run-down time.... Let's go kids!"

"If I were paid by the ulcer today," says Chesnutt, as he hangs up the phone, "I'd be a rich man."

It's four o'clock, and Wheatley's office is crowded with people. They're seated on chairs, on the floor, perched on the banquette, standing in the doorway. All of them are holding yellow legal-size pads. Cheryl Gould is seated behind the desk. She calls this "dictation time from the executive producer," or "the sermon on the mount." It's when they begin in earnest to, as Gould describes it, "squeeze a lot into a small bag."

"Is George [Lewis] happy with 2:20?" she asks Chesnutt.

"I've limited the scope of his story," he replies.

Deitch chimes in, "Here's the answer. Put the Exxon piece in with the closer. It's about fishing, too, isn't it? Let's have tougher alcohol standards for people on boats."

The entire meeting is a little like a briefing of pilots before a mission, a mixed bag of jokes and tension.

Gould says, "We've got that piece about Bush, and one about the environment. Bush works better in the [White House correspondent John] Cochran piece. We sure don't want him in both pieces. He fits better in the Cochran."

Deitch tells her that the Cochran lead-in he's writing for Brokaw can include some of that material.

"All right," she says, "that'll make more time for the intro to Cochran." She picks up her lineup on which the first item listed on the broadcast is TB (Intro) for twenty seconds. "Okay, here we go. Tom for twenty [seconds]. Into Lewis on the spill for 2:20. Then a twenty intro and Cochran on refuge for two minutes. Sandy," she calls to news editor Sandy Polster, "make sure Tom knows."

The shape of the evening news at all three networks is essentially the same—a five act play with four intermissions for commercials. Each act averages about four minutes in length. Though viewers may not require a recess after so short a period—even given their alleged notoriously limited attention span—the networks most certainly do. Currently receiving about $100,000 a minute for the use of their commercial time, the networks have to regard these intermissions as the pause that refreshes. But for the majority of Americans, who get their news of the world only from network television, all that's left of their half-hour of information after promotions for Advil, Maalox and Metamucil is a mere twenty-two minutes. And the lineup meeting is about cramming as much as they can into those twenty-two minutes.

The second act, Gould announces, will open with a Washington story about the Iran-Contra affair. "Then Pentagon scandal and into thirty [seconds] for the Chicago mayor's race: two minutes. S&L's for fifteen and put the stocks bumper there. Segment three, earthquake and intro for thirty-five to [Ed] Rabel in Cuba for 2:30. Can do, Marc?" she asks. "Marc?"

Marc Kusnetz, the foreign producer, who's helping out with domestic news tonight as well, says, "Oh sure, we can make it happen."

When the meeting is over, when they've finished talking about the time for each piece and the stills they'll need for over Brokaw's shoulder, everyone goes out the door joking about how Donald Trump has been forced to up his bid for the Eastern shuttle to $365 million. Eastern didn't know that he wanted the planes, too. The sound of laughter fills the hall.

Gould leans back and sighs. "Now all the disciples go out. They call the correspondents and start begging them to cut time out of their pieces. I get a fifteen minute breather now. Then I go out and talk to all the people who want more time."

In the news room, science reporter Robert Bazell's fusion piece is coming in by satellite. Everyone flips to Channel 22 to watch. News editor Sandy Polster, bald and bearded with wire rim glasses, watches the piece and, seeing Cheryl enter, stalks over to her with an unhappy expression on his face. "It's awful wordy," he says. "Real long." She tells him to see what he can do. Getting Bazell on the phone, Polster says, "You don't need to go into that much detail."

Meanwhile, producer Dave McCormick announces to the newsroom that the first part of George Lewis' piece is coming in by satellite from Alaska on Channel 14. Tom Brokaw, who's been at his desk typing away furiously at the introductions that he'll read in the opening and closing segments, glances over his glasses and flips on 14. He seems to like what he sees.

He types in a few last words, then hands the copy to be edited to Jack Chesnutt, in the next booth over. Brokaw stands, hikes up his pants and, obviously pleased at having finished, rubs his tummy contentedly.

"So, is Geri [Jansen] coming to Cuba?" Marc Kusnetz asks.

"She doesn't have a visa," Brokaw says.

Jack Chesnutt interupts with a suggestion about the anchor's copy. "Why don't you just say Valdez deliveries are running at half the normal...?"

"Why? Are we long?" Brokaw asks. "It must be because we got Kusnetz involved with domestic," he adds, riding his friend. "Okay," he tells Chesnutt, "I'll tighten that up." He goes back to his computer and gets at it. There are only eleven minutes left to air time, but they stretch before the focused anchor like 660 seconds.

The control room is situated down the hallway from the well-lighted newsroom with its electric hum of activity and across from the maintenance shop. Above the door, the red ON AIR sign is lit. Unlike the comfortable, high tech ABC control room, this place has a cluttered, run-down, makeshift feel to it. The two-tier arrangement is the same at all three networks, though in this case the chairs in the two rows are fewer and wooden. Despite the peeling paint on the ceiling, the electronic equipment seems to be first rate. Taped haphazardly to the walls are pictures of Xaviera Hollander, the Happy Hooker, the model Paulina, and a headline that says: ROBOT INVASION OF EVENING NEWS BEGINS AT NBC.

In the back row, John Holland fills in for Gould. He's just received the news that Trump has signed the deal to buy the shuttle from Eastern. Dressed casually in a purple shirt and khaki pants, Holland adjusts his tortoise-shell glasses and glances up at the clock. Only four minutes to air, and the Trump story is still being written. "Now I'm tense," Holland declares to no one in particular.

Up on the monitor, Tom Brokaw suddenly leaps into view and sits down in his anchor chair. He sips from a mug and looks over his script. Licking his fingertips, he turns the pages as a long-haired makeup man wearing a colorful vest puts on the anchor's makeup. Suddenly the rushed-through Eastern copy appears on yellow paper, and Brokaw goes over it. The stage manager helps him on with his jacket. Seated once again at the anchor desk, Brokaw checks himself over in a small hand mirror. He pats down his hair, brushes off his shoulders, tightens his tie.

In the control room, the final ten-second ticktock before air is on, and the director kicks into gear. "Take one, cue. Take one—What the hell was that?" he asks. "Wipe it. Cue him...and fade...and take."

Everything is going smoothly, and Holland claps with pleasure as a picture of Richard Nixon comes on. "The one rule of news production," he says whimsically, "if you have Nixon, use him."

It's late in the third segment when an assistant pipes up, "Fifteen long."

"Kill the bumper," shouts the director, deciding to eliminate one of the five-second pieces that lead into commercial breaks.

"We did that."

"Kill the promo," he says, and takes a slug of Diet Coke.

The door of the control room opens and an assistant comes running in. "It's the American Institute of Physics, not Physicists," she shouts. Opening the fourth act, Brokaw is about to introduce Bazell's "Fusion Confusion" story. Holland gets to him over his IFB just in time to make the correction. (IFB stands for Interruptible Feedback. What it feeds back are voices from the control room. It's a one-way lifeline for the anchor, allowing a producer, as in this instance, to give him updated information, or a director to tell him which way to lean.)

Finally, the closer about Nate, the champion fishing kid, comes on. Brokaw, from the control room, can be seen watching the kid on his anchor desk monitor and cracking up. It's just the sort of soft piece he loves. As Mike Leonard finishes, Brokaw looks up into the camera. "What about it, Nate," he asks. "Want to trade jobs?"

"Hurry up Tom," mutters the director, looking up at the two clocks overhead, one analogue and one digital with an LED readout.

Brokaw finishes on the button at 18:59.

"Whew!" says the director.

Though NBC's main feed is at 6:30, its second feed—the 7:00 feed—goes to New York and Boston, and to Los Angeles for airing later that evening. Most of this second feed is simply a taped re-broadcast of the 6:30 program, except when segments are included live in order to update information or correct slip-ups in the first newscast. Tonight, Brokaw has only one or two small flubs to fix.

"Very nice," Holland says, when he's finished with his changes.

For the rest of the show, the anchor sits slumped in his chair, watching. As seen from the control room, the twin Brokaws are a weird pair, the one delivering the news crisply efficient, the other slumping passively in his chair, a typical couch potato like millions of his viewers.

No sooner is the second feed over at 7:30 than Brokaw is swiping at his face with a towel, trying to take off the makeup. "I don't know what it is," he says. "Maybe it's spring. But these days I wake up in the morning at 6:30, and I'm tired." And this from the man once described as the indefatigable Duncan, the Wonder Horse! "Meredith's father, a doctor, always said it's the ions, but I don't know."

Back in his office, Brokaw goes through some papers and packs up for the night. If he seems a little tired, he's had a long day. It's not just the broadcast, which he feels went pretty smoothly. "It's that I've been busy setting up the upcoming Cuba trip."

Though Brokaw's work is over, his day isn't. He's on his way to meet Meredith at a Broadway theater, and he's late. They have tickets to see Wendy Wasserstein's comedy, *The Heidi Chronicles*. Brokaw enjoys the theater. Quickly straightening up his desk top, he flips off the light, closes the door, and hurries downstairs in quest of a couple of hours of make-believe and a few laughs.

RATINGS: Week ending March 31st

1st. Rather ("CBS Evening News")—10.6/21 [9,582,400]

2nd. Jennings (ABC's "World News Tonight")—10.4/20 [9,401,600]

3rd. Brokaw ("NBC Nightly News")—9.4/19 [8,497,600]

CHAPTER EIGHT

The Education of Peter Jennings

On the wall of Peter Jennings' office is a framed newspaper clipping, now yellowing with age. The logo reads *Evening Telegram*, Toronto 1935. The picture shows a distinguished, British-looking gentleman, leaning forward over a desk cluttered with paper. And the copy states: "Presenting Charles Jennings, announcer de luxe. Mr. Jennings has a natural cultured voice that lends color to any programme on which he may appear."

Any story about Peter Jennings, journalist, must begin with his father Charles, for the younger Jennings, unlike Dan Rather and Tom Brokaw, inherited his father's profession. "The family business?" muses Jennings. "Very much so. It was almost automatic in my case. My father was a very large presence in the family, and he was a very large presence in the business....So I think it was natural—if your father is a doctor you may become a doctor because your house is cluttered with stethoscopes."

Charles Jennings was a shy, reserved man with a mischievous sense of humor. He had gone to the right school in Canada: Trinity College at the University of Toronto. Although he eventually dropped out of the University, he retained the aura of an intellectual, a reader. Professionally, he had always wanted to become a newspaperman, a Hildy Johnson from *The Front Page*. But, according to one account at the time, as he was walking down the street on his way to apply for a job at the *Toronto Daily Star*, he stopped in at the local radio station. These were the pioneering days of radio in Canada, and Jennings senior was blessed with a good voice. Quite by accident, he found a career.

When the Canadian Broadcasting Corporation was established in the mid-1930s—as Canada's first coast-to-coast radio hook-up modeled on the British BBC—Charles Jennings became its first voice, the voice of Canada. He read the news, and introduced a wide variety of cultural programming, from symphonies to operas. In time, he became known as the "Edward R. Murrow of Canada," although by World War II, he had already moved upstairs in the CBC bureaucracy, and it was Lorne Greene ("Bonanza") who covered the war. Jennings senior was primarily an announcer, very infrequently a reporter in the field.

In the late 1930s, as the Jennings family legend has it, Charles received a letter from the United States, from the National Broadcasting Company. They offered him a lot of money to come down to New York for their Texaco Opera program. He would be the announcer for the Metropolitan Opera. Charles Jennings accepted the job, and the night before he left, his friends gathered together to give him a big drunken farewell dinner. The next day found him on a train headed for New York. When the train arrived at the border, U.S. immigration authorities boarded. In those days, there were strict immigration procedures, and the officers began subjecting the travelers to a third-degree quizzing.

In short order (either because he lacked the requisite papers or because he wouldn't sit still for the lengthy interrogation), Jennings was put off the train, and found himself out on the platform waiting for the return express to Toronto. And before his friends' hangovers had worn off, he was back at his old CBC job, which annoyed them no little bit since they had just seen him off. "Oh well," Jennings said, "I didn't want to go down there anyway."

The anecdote is a family joke all the Jennings love to tell, and it's made all the more ironic by the father-son linkage. Twenty-five years later, son Peter would make the same journey, and he would make it past the border in a big way. Born in Toronto on July 29, 1938, Peter Charles Archibald Ewart Jennings grew up in a privileged household. By the time Peter was born, his father was known across Canada. In fact, a year later, the elder Jennings traveled with King George VI, the first British monarch to visit Canada, as he made his royal tour by train.

If his father's side of the family was solidly middle class (Peter's grandfather was a builder of veterans' housing), his mother's side was society—as society as Canada got—and money. The family was slightly shocked when their Elizabeth married a radio announcer. They were, after all, among the original investors in Massey-Harris, now Massey-Ferguson, an agricultural machinery business that numbered among Canada's biggest firms. Massey-Harris made tractors. It also made money, hand over fist.

Growing up in this solid Scottish-Canadian Protestant household, Peter Jennings and his sister Sarah, younger by three years, never lacked for anything. Although it would be an overstatement to call the family aristocratic, especially in down-to-earth Canada, and while they certainly weren't rich (the money all belonged to the grandparents), Peter and Sarah had a pampered childhood, a childhood of riding lessons, cricket, and all the right schools.

But more important than any financial grounding was the cultural background they received. From their earliest years, young Peter and Sarah remember a house filled with strange and exotic people. Sarah Jennings recalls, "It was just after the war, and there was this flood of DPs, displaced persons from Europe. They were writers, intellectuals, musicians." At the time, Charles Jennings had advanced from being an announcer to become the head of programming for the CBC, and the DPs came through looking for work on his programs.

"Our home was always filled with the most talented and interesting and eccentric group of people," Sarah Jennings says. "There were obscure French horn players, dancers, the people who started Canada's national opera company and the National Ballet." It was a household like the one Henry James talks about growing up in, a house filled with artists and musicians and statesmen, a wonderful environment for a child.

No wonder then that his father's profession always seemed intriguing to the young Jennings. Before he was even a teen, Peter was taken outside one day and given his first broadcasting lesson. Pointing upward, Charles Jennings asked his son to describe the sky. It wasn't easy for the young man. Other times, Peter would accompany his father into the studio.

And Friday evenings, for a special treat, when Charles Jennings sat up in the plush red "announce booth" at Massey Hall, and introduced the Toronto Symphony to listeners across Canada, young Peter was allowed to sit in the booth next to his father if he remained extra-quiet. Perhaps it wasn't magical, but it was close. "It did seem like something of a passport," recalls Jennings, looking back down the years, "a passport to an even more interesting world."

Peter himself got a temporary visa to this world at the age of nine. His father was off on a UNESCO trip when CBC approached Elizabeth Jennings and explained that they wanted a child to host a Saturday morning radio show for kids. Could Peter do it? And so "Peter's Program" was born. With a weekly paycheck of five dollars, young Peter went on the air each Saturday and played songs that his equally young listeners requested. The most requested tune for the junior DJ was "The Teddy Bear's Picnic."

But when Jennings senior finally returned from abroad, he was furious. The CBC executive set a high moral standard, and "Peter's Program" struck him as the worst form of nepotism. He made Peter give back the money he had received, and was going to shut down the show when his staffers argued him out of it, explaining that the program was already successful. He grudgingly acquiesced and, to add insult to injury, Peter got so much kiddy fan mail over the next weeks that Charles and Elizabeth had to spend hours answering it.

A portrait of Peter Jennings at twelve, off to board at Trinity College School—the same upper-crust establishment that his grandfather had attended—would have shown a precocious young man, more than a little good looking, more than a little athletic, and more than a little full of himself. Things came easy for young Jennings, and he liked it that way. He was a spoiled first child who preferred comic books to school books. Frequently, he would sneak off to smoke cigarettes. "What," his mother would ask, "is going to become of Pete?"

At Trinity, Jennings showed a real flair for cricket. Unfortunately, he didn't show much of a flair for school work. Bored by the academics, he ignored the classrooms and concentrated on the playing fields. And in no time at all, Trinity's headmaster, a friend of the family, talked to Charles and Elizabeth Jennings. "Look," he said, "this is a great waste of your money and our time." And so, after ninth grade, Jennings was sent down from Trinity. He began tenth grade at a public high school in Ottawa, where he was tremendously popular with the other students, but he was no more popular with the teachers than he had been at Trinity. Before the year was up, he had dropped out again.

By the time he was seventeen, Peter Jennings had acquired social poise, a certain lazy sophistication, a string of girlfriends and a natural athletic grace that extended from hockey to skiing. What he had not acquired was an education. It was a lack that meant little to Jennings at the time, but as he grew older, it would come to be more and more important to him, until it was practically an obsession.

In the meantime, his father had problems of his own. As head of programming for both radio and the newly developed CBC national TV chain, he had been forced to move his family to Ottawa when the CBC transferred its offices there. It was a move the elder Jennings had bitterly opposed. Ottawa was the seat of Canada's national government, and he feared that placing the national broadcasting system right next door was a sure-fire recipe for political pressure, not to mention the lost contact with Toronto, the artistic center of English-speaking Canada.

Charles Jennings felt certain that an Ottawa-based CBC would degenerate from a strong, independent national service into a stale, compromised voice of the government. And when the CBC took on a president more fascinated by technology than programming, he was especially depressed. But although he lost many battles, he kept fighting for his ideals over the next fifteen to twenty years.

That unwavering toughness would become a model for both his children. "Our father never compromised his values," Sarah Jennings recalls. "He never ran with the herd. He remained this pale beacon for the importance of public broadcasting." Over the years, though, the struggle wore him out, and although still a vice president of the CBC, and one of its leading voices, he remained in the minority of boardroom votes, and unhappily turned his attention to becoming a country squire and a keeper of dogs. "For us," says Sarah Jennings, "our father was this idealistic figure, this image to emulate. But he paid a high price. He died at sixty-five of internal problems. He was just worn out."

Young Peter, at seventeen, wanted nothing more than to go into broadcasting. His father dissuaded him, and sent him off to work as a teller at a bank run by friends of the family. Banking, at the time, was a job that accepted black sheep sons, provided they were nicely dressed and well behaved, and Jennings was soon ensconced at the Toronto branch of the Royal Bank of Canada, cashing checks and adding figures. Although he's still proud of his figures—the gracefully turned 2s, the forceful 7s— Jennings' years as a teller didn't add up to much beyond a first crack at independence and freedom, and an up-close look at the "scores of good-looking women" who worked in his building.

But professionally, as time went by, he stuck with his original dream, a broadcasting career. So at twenty, Jennings auditioned for the CBC. There was no denying the talent of the young man. The audition proved a success. There was only one problem. The CBC rules against nepotism, put in place by his father among others, meant that Peter Jennings couldn't be hired. Understandably aggrieved, Jennings asked his dad, "What the hell am I going to do?" And Charles Jennings, understanding the inequity of the situation, called up another old broadcasting associate, Jack Radford, who ran CFJR, a small private station in Brockville, Ontario.

Brockville was a tiny town set on the flat, wooded land by the St. Lawrence Seaway, beautifully green and pristine in summer, harsh and bleak in the clutch of winter. It wasn't much of a town, and CFJR wasn't much of a station. In fact, its signal was so weak, according to Jennings, that it could barely be heard on the outskirts of town. But for Peter Jennings, CFJR was a big break. In this tiny little station, he was an announcer-operator. On his shift he had to do all the on-air work, and most of the off-air work too, running around and flipping switches. He was, in short, a one-man radio band, hosting everything from the news to the late night "Moods and Music" to a Saturday-morning gospel hour. Spinning records, he would sign on "Good evening, it's your old DJ, PJ."

By 1960, Jennings was working for the northern service of the CBC, getting up at three in the morning to broadcast to the Eskimos: "Every day," he recalls, "I used to do the farm broadcast. The farmers had to have the prices. The CBC was committed to that then. My father gave me that strong sense of public service."

In 1961, his radio dues paid, Jennings made the jump to television. He began work at CJOH, Channel 13 in Ottawa, one of the first private television stations in a country where the air waves were dominated by public broadcasting. There Jennings got the TV utility-man experience equivalent to his earlier radio job on CFJR. He handled everything from news to variety shows.

One time, he was called upon to sing the "Miss Canada" song at the national beauty pageant. The memory still makes Jennings smile. "The only reason I sang it was because Gordon MacRae, who was the guest star, was loaded and couldn't do it." And so Jennings was transformed into a crooner. Hauled up on stage, he was put under the spotlight. "We found her at last," he sang, "the fairest girl in Canada...."

Then too, he hosted "Club 13," a TV dance party for kids. Turning the stacks of wax like a Canadian Dick Clark, Jennings watched over teens screaming to the tunes of Roy Orbison and others. But if the show had a great beat, Jennings couldn't dance to it. He was greatly relieved when

CJOH was made part of the first national private TV chain, CTV, and he was offered the job of first Parliament Hill reporter, and then appointed co-anchor of the national newscast. Peter Jennings had arrived.

"Dad was terribly proud of Peter when he became the anchor of CTV," Sarah Jennings remembers. "He had been such a difficult teenager. Dad had despaired he was going to make something of himself." At last, Peter and Charles Jennings could talk to each other on a professional level. (Sarah was working in the business too, first with the BBC, then as a prominent cultural correspondent for CBC radio.) Peter, so lazy and dilettantish as a teen, had finally begun to live up to his father.

But it was in these early years of success that his lack of formal education began to nag at Jennings. Whenever academics came up in conversation, he tried to change the subject. "I suppressed it," he recalls. "I didn't admit to it for a very long time." Actually, he used to say that he had attended Carleton University in Ottawa. This was not an utter lie: He had in fact gone to Carleton's night school for a couple of weeks. But trying to juggle night school and a full-time TV career turned out to be "a total disaster." And so Jennings quit, more upset than ever by his academic failures. "Ohhhh!" he told one journalist, "I was desperately embarrassed about it for almost twenty years. Oh, yes. Oh, yes."

For all that, Jennings' on-air work was well received, and when ABC Correspondent John Scali followed Secretary of State Dean Rusk to Ottawa for an economic conference, he saw Jennings and his co-anchor Baden Langton on CTV. Scali called down to Elmer Lower, the president of ABC News: "There's these two guys up here doing a Huntley-Brinkley number," he said, "and they're pretty good." Jennings and Langton had a certain smoothness, a certain authority, and when Lower and his associates obtained a videotape, they thought both had possibilities. Both were invited to New York and eventually offered jobs.

In August 1964, Peter Jennings packed up his bags and his hopes, and, with his new wife Valerie Godsoe (a Canadian TV researcher), set off for New York, making the journey his father never completed. But it wasn't exactly as if he had arrived at the big time. ABC in those days was a pale shadow of its two competitors, CBS and NBC. Journalists, even ABC staffers themselves, called it "a bush league operation." ABC, as previously indicated, was known around town as the "Also-ran Broadcasting Company," or the "Almost Broadcasting Company."

One anecdote illustrates why. When President Kennedy was shot in November of 1963, NBC and CBS were all over the story. They had whole teams of correspondents, including CBS's Dan Rather and NBC's Robert MacNeil, on the scene. Not ABC. Junior employee Betsy Aaron, now a CBS reporter, had to run downtown and pull ABC News president Elmer Lower out of the New York Athletic Club pool where he was swimming. Lower decided immediately to dispatch a team to Dallas. There was just one problem. It was Friday afternoon, and all the banks had closed for the weekend. ABC was such a small-potatoes operation that no one had any money to send the reporters to Dallas.

Finally, ABC staffers ran across the street to McGlade's, their regular bar and hangout, and asked bartender Paddy McGlade if he could advance them $15,000 or $20,000. And it was with this booze money— straight out of the bar's safe—that ABC was able to cover the assassination of the President. "It was only fair," recalls Lower. "Paddy was making enough money off our barflies."

Arriving just in time to observe the political conventions, Jennings was dispatched to the South for six months, to cover the hot story of the time, civil rights. "He hadn't done much reporting in Canada," Lower says. "He had been bound to the studio. So this was pretty exciting for him, being chased by some rednecks and deputy sheriffs down in Mississippi."

Executive vice president Jessie Zousmer had set up a career track for Jennings, a track that would give him five years in New York, five in Washington, ten overseas, then back to the U.S. It was a long-range game plan designed to create the consummate reporter. But it never got implemented.

By early 1965, Peter Jennings, only twenty-six years old, was brought back to New York and made ABC's news anchor. "I was made anchor for all the wrong reasons," recalls Jennings. "We were a very small news organization at the time and we were struggling." Deep in third place in the ratings, ABC cast around for a new look. First, Lower tried to lure ace reporter Charles Collingwood away from CBS. But when CBS owner William Paley sweet-talked Collingwood out of leaving, and when no other options were available, ABC management looked in-house. And their gaze fell on the new boy, Jennings.

"I thought Peter Jennings didn't have great experience," Lower said, "but he came from a broadcasting family. He had a good personality on screen. And ABC had a primetime schedule that 'played young,' the eighteen to forty-nine bracket, and advertisers like that. So our theory was, if primetime plays young, maybe our newscaster should play young too. That was our gamble."

"That's it," says Jennings. "I think somebody at the network said, 'We're doing pretty well with "Gidget" and "Gadget" and all those youth programs. Let's try it in the news division!' And I was the youngest guy around with my hair and my teeth who could string two words together, and they said 'Okay—you be the anchorman.' It was pretty much as simple as that."

Of course, the risk for ABC in using an inexperienced Jennings was a lot smaller than it would have been for CBS or NBC. No one at that time referred to three network news shows. They talked of two-and-a-half. If CBS and NBC had gone to a thirty-minute newscast on Labor Day of 1963, ABC still had a fifteen-minute broadcast, and would for another two and a half years. What Jennings inherited was half the news program of his competitors.

Then again, he was half the newsman. The painfully inexperienced twenty-six-year-old was going head-to-head with Walter Cronkite at CBS, and the redoubtable Huntley-Brinkley team at NBC. He was barely in their league.

"I once had to show up at a luncheon with Huntley-Brinkley and Cronkite at the Waldorf," he can now joke on TV. "I was up on this big dais, with hundreds of people in the audience. And some guy in the audience got up and said, 'You guys in TV are just in show business.' Huntley said, 'Now hold it! My only concession to show business is that I stop in the makeup room every day and have these bags under my eyes painted out.' And Cronkite said, 'Yeah, Jennings stops in and has them painted *on*....' I look back on it now to see how unbelievably unqualified I was then."

Peter Jennings would read the ABC evening news for three years, through the end of 1967. He sat at a rounded desk in the middle of a wraparound set, a huge oval screen over his right shoulder. He would be introduced: "Peter Jennings with the news, a fifteen-minute summary of the day's events." In black and white, with his lean, trim look and his slicked-back hair, Jennings appeared to be the image of one of those urbane cigarette smokers in an advertisement, or perhaps a James Bond type. He looked more like a male model than a journalist.

His colleagues in ABC's news division thought so too, and although Jennings would log some miles traveling to Vietnam, to Newfoundland, to Santa Domingo, and to India to interview Indira Gandhi, he was still dismissed in-house as "Stanley Stunning" or "Peter Pretty." They snickered at him behind his back, and isolated him from decision making. Looking back, Jennings comments: "My greatest weakness, aside from my youthful arrogance, was that I really didn't know anything about America." Determined to keep his Canadian identity, Jennings would say "shed-yule" for schedule and "bean" for been. His aides had to write out "LOOTENANT" in the teleprompter to remind him of the correct pronunciation. And when it came to covering LBJ's inauguration in Washington, while his ad-libbing was smooth, he managed before the end of the broadcast to wedge his foot in his mouth by identifying the U.S. Marines' hymn as "Anchors Away."

"Peter didn't really know much about the U.S.," Elmer Lower recalls. "We needed a good fast writer who knew the U.S." Enter Sid Kline, a rewrite man from the New York *Daily News*. An old-time reporter— green eyeshade and all—Kline had worked the beats, from arson to murder. "Kline is a writing fool," said Lower. "Give him a noun and a verb and he'll go."

The newspaperman became Jennings' principal writer. What the anchor didn't know was that Kline had also been hired to keep him out of trouble. Kline remembers that executive VP Jessie Zousmer came to him and said, "Help that boy. Back him up. Give him guidance." The newspaperman became Jennings' guardian angel and, in time, his close friend as well. He would come to visit Jennings and his wife, Valerie Godsoe, in their Upper East Side apartment. Jennings would drive up to Woodstock to visit the Kline family.

"Jennings had everything you needed," Kline says. "He was bright, he was handsome, he was talented. There was no humility in that man, no false modesty. He was on his way and he knew it." But as both Kline and Jennings eventually had to admit, the anchor was just a little too green for the job, a little too young. What other network news anchor would hop on his bike and cycle to work across Central Park? For all his talent, Jennings' callowness showed through, and the viewers and the critics didn't go for it. "I tried very hard to sell Peter Jennings," Elmer Lower remembers. "But he was faulted in many places for his lack of experience. The hardest sell was to the magazine and newspaper writers. They just wouldn't buy him."

In the meantime, Jennings himself was getting restless. He felt chained to the anchor desk: "I just got bored with it. It just got *very, very* tedious coming to work and doing something every day for which you really weren't qualified and didn't have an enormous amount of input."

And so at the end of 1967, just before Jennings would probably have been fired, he walked into Elmer Lower's office and resigned the anchor position. He wanted to get back in the field. Lower, who was coming to the same conclusion, had to agree. "The most important quality for a good anchor is credibility," he said. "Peter needed some wrinkles in his face. He needed to get dirtied up a bit." And so began what sister Sarah would later call "the education of Peter Jennings."

With a mixture of chagrin and relief, Jennings took to the road. At first, he was assigned to the U.S., covering George Wallace and Eugene McCarthy on the '68 election trail. Along the line, he reported on a wide range of social ills, from campuses in turmoil to environmental issues. "I was wandering around the country," he recalls. "I'd close my eyes, put my finger on a map, and go to that place to handle the next story on the rotation." He chuckles. "I covered crime in Brigham, Utah, which hadn't seen a crime in fifty years. I covered blacks from Aberdeen, Idaho, which hadn't seen a black ever."

But just as soon as he could, he headed overseas. He had had the bug for foreign coverage for a while, ever since covering the 1967 Arab-Israeli conflict, the "Six Day War." It was that assignment, in fact, that had convinced him to leave the anchor chair. In 1969, Jennings was sent to the Rome bureau as number two man under fellow Canadian Barrie Dunsmore. By the end of the year, he had moved to Beirut, Lebanon, and had become the first U.S. TV reporter based full-time in the Arab world, opening America's first permanent television bureau there. For the next six years, an "ecstatically happy" Jennings lived and breathed the Middle East.

Beirut in 1969 was a delightful playground in the Mediterranean, not the hellhole it would later become. Known as the Paris, or more often, the Switzerland of the Middle East, Beirut was a town of cafes and palm trees, of belly dancers and Chanel dresses. As a city, it was a monument to the sybaritic life-style: rich Levantine traders with gold Rolexes, gentle Mediterranean breezes blowing across well-tended golf courses. Lebanon was never to be a major power in the Arab world. It was more an R&R stop for Syrians, Egyptians, Saudis. In spite of that, or perhaps because of it, this neutral center grew into an impromptu Arab capital, the center of the Middle East. "Sooner or later," recalls ABC's John Cooley, "anyone of importance would show up in Beirut. It was a sea of rumors, of information and disinformation."

Beirut was, in short, the perfect billet for a journalist. Setting up shop in a suite of rooms on the twelfth floor of the Gefinor building— a modern office structure overlooking the center of Beirut near the American University Hospital—Jennings quite literally mapped out his future. Realizing that ABC had no other correspondent east of the Mediterranean, one of the very first things he did was to get out a large map and start calculating how far it was to various places. He drew circles—one hour from Beirut by plane, two hours from Beirut by plane. He began conditioning the New York desk: "Jennings is only three hours away from there—put him on a plane." And he ended up owning almost every story between Israel and Hong Kong, and a fair share more.

With a team partially recruited from the local American University of Beirut (including Charlie Glass and Bill Blakemore, both of whom would become ABC correspondents and close friends of the reporter), Jennings began flying off to cover breaking stories everywhere from Nigeria to Calcutta to the Kingdom of Hunza, on the Chinese border. "We were always barging in and out of countries," Blakemore says. "We were always on planes going back and forth...We were commandeering jeeps all the time, talking our way through roadblocks, hiring taxis in the middle of some desert." Jennings reveled in the excitement. "For six years," he recalls, "we never stopped."

One of the most harrowing trips for the thirty-three-year-old Jennings occurred in 1971, when he flew off to cover the India-Pakistan war, the war for Bangladesh. "The Bangladesh story had a terrible impact on him," Sarah Jennings remembers. "He was young. It was exotic. But then, traveling up river by boat, he saw how people lived along the river, begging for food. There was just no food anywhere. That made a deep impression on him. He was shocked."

Bangladesh would expose Jennings to a world of great cruelty, a world the privileged young man had never really experienced. Bill Blakemore remembers hiking into East Pakistan with Jennings and a guerrilla leader. "Someone was coming up the road with a prisoner, and this macho soldier said, 'Oh look, a collaborator!' He cocked his rifle. He was going to execute him. And all of us turned around, lowered our cameras, and walked away. We wanted to make sure no one would be killed just for our audience. I've always been proud of that moment."

If stories like Bangladesh were eye-openers, they also represented an education in another way. During the sixties and seventies, TV foreign coverage was a business referred to as "shoot and ship." Operating with great freedom, foreign correspondents would wander the globe, cover their assigned story, and send off their footage and recorded commentary by airplane back to New York. Out in the field with few international hookups, they were on their own, free to make their own mistakes and learn from them. In fact, these years were a period of great learning for Jennings. He calls them "the most significant time for me."

Colleagues started to notice something about their Beirut bureau chief. He was always reading—books, magazines, newspaper articles. He was trying to catch up. Back in his teens, he couldn't wait to get rid of his books. Now he was riveted to them, almost as if trying to make up for lost time.

Though only an apprentice at history, economics and politics, Jennings had already mastered the techniques of broadcasting. Out on the road, he had, colleagues recall, a breezy generosity, an eagerness to learn and a willingness to share what he knew.

Bill Blakemore recalls, "I'll never forget the day Peter taught me how to do a radio spot. We were out covering the Bangladesh War. I came back from a day with the Indian Army, watching their tanks. I had this academic background. I tend to take a while to get my thoughts organized. Well, Peter was rushing around, and he said, 'Okay, I'll come back later.' A half an hour later, he came back and said, 'Let's go!' I said, 'I haven't fed my piece yet.' And he said 'What?! No, no, no!' He sat down at the typewriter, put a sheet of paper in, and asked me 'Where did you go?' I told him, and he typed a sentence. 'What did you see?' I told him. Another sentence. 'And why did you go?' I told him, and he typed out a few more sentences. He ripped it out of the typewriter, and he said, 'There's your spot. Feed it. Let's go.'"

Although Jennings would eventually cover the world—he has now, he estimates, visited over ninety countries—it was of course the Middle East that he came to know best, during those years he was based in Beirut. Reporting the news of the Arab world, he developed a passion for the Middle East, a passion he still feels. He traveled to every country in the region, and interviewed leaders who had seldom if ever been seen by an American TV audience: Syria's Assad, Egypt's Sadat, the PLO's Arafat, even the Ayatollah Khomeini when he was still living in exile in Paris. His was the first TV team allowed to wander freely through Saudi Arabia.

"He had great contacts in the Arab world," recalls ex-ABC News president Elmer Lower. "On one trip, I met Jennings in Jordan. He knew everybody in the Jordanian government. King Hussein. Everybody. The crown prince lent us his helicopter for the visit."

Getting up at nine, Jennings would walk out the front door of his seaside apartment, go for a swim in the Mediterranean, and walk up the hill to his office by eleven. There was a Middle East Airlines agency right downstairs in the building, and Cairo was only forty-five minutes away by plane, Amman, Jordan an hour. Israel was a mere forty-five minute drive. Jennings and his team could go for lunch anywhere in the Arab world and be back by three. And on any given Sunday, he might pop over to Damascus and wander around a seouk.

His infatuation with the Middle East extended to a young photographer he had met in Beirut, Anouchka Malouf. Jennings' marriage to his first wife Valerie had fallen apart back in New York. "They were both very young and erratic," his sister says.

But Anouchka—Annie—was something else altogether. Vivacious, cosmopolitan, sophisticated and startlingly attractive, she was also a typically Lebanese blend—an Arab woman, schooled in Switzerland, fluent in French, English and Arabic. Annie, who went to the stylish Paris fashion houses each year to buy her clothes, was as continental as could be. And yet her father was an important Arab businessman who had been forced out of Egypt when Nassar came in, and her mother was a Syrian. To this day her grandparents live in Cairo. Through Annie, Jennings was immersed in the local community in a much deeper way than most journalists. "She was a great asset in exposing him to the region," Sarah Jennings says. "She helped introduce Peter to Anwar Sadat."

Peter had married the attractive Annie by 1974, and whenever he wasn't on the road, they would often host hordes of visiting professors, journalists and politicians in their seaside apartment. It was a social time, a time when Jennings did more than just cover the Arab story. He lived it. He was married to it. And in his own way, he sometimes laughs, he made a small contribution back to the Arab cause. "I used to have this small rubber boat, with a Johnson outboard motor. Well one day, it was stolen. I always figured it became the Palestinian navy."

Over those years, Jennings acquired a detailed knowledge of—and a fascination with—the Arab world. Some Israeli and Jewish-American leaders feel that this makes the anchor a less-than-impartial journalist today when he discusses the Middle East. They argue that his bias is strongly pro-Arab.

His sister, Sarah Jennings, argues otherwise: "Peter saw a lot in the Middle East. It had an important effect on him. And because he lived there, he inevitably got closer to the Arab world. But when we were growing up in Toronto, we were the only Gentiles in a Jewish neighborhood. We were adopted by the synagogue for holidays. Rabbi Abraham Feinberg lived right across the street. Peter and I have always thought of ourselves as half-Jewish."

Slightly weary of his beat by late 1972, Jennings leaped at the opportunity for a change of pace when Roone Arledge, then head of ABC Sports, called and asked him if he'd like to cover the various international news stories arising out of that year's Olympics in Munich. "Roone said 'How would you like to spend two nice weeks in beautiful Bavaria,'" Jennings recalls. "I went there to escape the Middle East."

Little did he know that the Middle East was following him. When a group of Palestinian terrorists, members of the Black September group, charged into Building 31 in the Olympic Village on September 5 and seized eleven Israeli athletes, Peter Jennings was the only reporter left in the Olympic Village. The Italian athletes in the building right across from the captured Building 31 hid Jennings in their bathroom when everyone was supposed to clear out. As the interminable twelve-hour hostage drama dragged on, Jennings was out on their balcony, looking right in the window of the Palestinians and Israelis, and reporting back via a high-tech Telefunken walkie-talkie. And Jennings not only had the position, he had the expertise. He knew what Black September was all about. He knew their goals and their grievances. He had been in Jordan in 1970 when the Palestinians were dispossessed and turned to terrorism.

About a week later, Peter Jennings, looking natty in that early seventies' style—blue double-breasted blazer with big gold buttons, mod longish hair covering his ears and curling in back—strolled on a hilltop near the Olympic Stadium, and summed up the tragedy for viewers:

"When the Olympic Games opened on August 26, it was really one of those magnificent days. Athletes from 122 nations marched in, the Olympic torch was lighted... and we embarked on what rapidly became known as the games of serenity....And then it all happened. The morning of September 5 will unquestionably be remembered as perhaps the most infamous day of the modern Olympic Games."

The footage rolled to show Building 31, the Olympic Village, the Palestinian leader in his white cap (later identified as Abu Nidal), the long tense hours of waiting, and finally the tragedy at the airport when police marksmen opened fire, Nidal escaped, and the nine remaining hostages were killed. Jennings summed up with a startling revelation: "The Munich police were not on their own. There was a special squad of Israelis in place—the Germans followed their advice to the letter." This reporting would win ABC many awards.

In the fall of 1973, Jennings, while off covering a story in the Karakorum mountains between China and Pakistan, was forced to return to his base because of a broken camera. In remote Gilgit, Pakistan, he got a desperate call from New York: "There's a goddamn war going on," the voice roared down the line. "Get your ass back."

The Arabs had launched a blitz attack on the Israelis, and the Yom Kippur War had begun. Dashing off to the airport, Jennings and his camera crew climbed aboard a plane that Pan Am had held for them, and set off for the Middle East. But there was a problem. The ABC team couldn't get into Egypt. In the end, Jennings entered Syria illegally, and was thrown into a Syrian jail for a few hours.

Released, Jennings tried to make his way to the front lines along with several print reporters. The Syrian Defense Minister said no. But Jennings and the others finally convinced him. The Syrians were so disorganized, they didn't even have a military censor.

"You just have to set up a military censor," Jennings explained. "That's the way it's always done." Eventually, he and the other reporters took matters into their own hands and set up their own censor, which was enough to satisfy the Syrians, and he rubberstamped their reports.

There were a number of incidents of courage in Jennings' reporting of this Arab-Israeli conflict, such as the time he climbed up on a rooftop in Damascus to report on an Israeli raid. But for Jennings, the

'73 war didn't compare with his most harrowing reporting experiences, the bullets whizzing overhead back when he was a young anchor and reporting on the revolution in Santo Domingo, or the war in Vietnam. From those days on, Jennings has laughingly referred to himself as a "devout coward."

"I'm not at all heroic," he'll say. When the shooting starts, he makes no secret of it, "I get down behind a rock."

From their offices in central Beirut, Jennings and his ABC colleagues could observe the opening rounds of fire as the Lebanese civil war began to escalate in the mid-seventies. They could poke their cameras out their twelfth floor window and report the main story, while the bullets flew back and forth between Christians and Moslems. With the beginning of one more war, Jennings after six years in Beirut decided that he had had enough of the Middle East. It was time for a change.

In 1975, Jennings convinced ABC management to bring him back to the U.S. as Washington correspondent and anchor for "AM America," the forerunner of "Good Morning America." For eleven months, Jennings delivered the news between Bill Beutel and Stephanie Edwards' happy talk. For eleven months, he reported from the U.S. capital. And after eleven months, he was sick of the whole thing: "I couldn't stand Washington. There was too much pack journalism, too many photo ops. And I found the studio suffocating." Fundamentally miscast in the role, Jennings found the experience to be a complete fiasco. So, too, did his wife Annie, coming from the Middle East to the capital's cliques. Washington was an unhappy posting for both of them, and for their marriage. And as soon as he could, Jennings and Ted Koppel got together and, as Jennings puts it, "connived" to get George Watson back from London to Washington, and himself to London.

By 1977, Jennings was installed in London with the title "Chief Correspondent." For the Anglophile Jennings, who had first visited the city on summer holidays in 1952, the return was something of a homecoming. It was what Jennings would often call his "dream job," in a wonderful city. And he would celebrate for the next six years.

"Britain has seen nothing like it since 1953," he reported on June 7, 1977. "It is Jubilee Day here in London, a day of celebration for twenty-five years on the throne for Queen Elizabeth." As an elaborately ornate gilded carriage rolled down the Mall, the camera cut to the correspondent, dressed in a light blue suit, seated in an armchair in front of a red curtain and a golden picture frame. "I'm Peter Jennings, and my colleague Hilary Brown and I are terribly pleased you've been able to join us...."

And even if he had to cover slightly silly events from slightly cheesy sets, Jennings loved his job. It had flexibility. It had clout, permitting him to span the globe as the chief foreign reporter for a major U.S. news organization. There was only one thing that could make it better, and that happened the following year, in 1978. Jennings, though still posted in London and covering foreign stories, was named co-anchor of the ABC evening news.

"Roone Arledge came up with that idea of the three-anchor system because we didn't have a star, a Cronkite," Jennings recalls. The troika included Washington-based Frank Reynolds and Chicago-based Max Robinson. "Arledge was diffusing the anchor as a central character. At any point, any two of the anchors could be out working as a reporter. From my point of view, it was ideal."

Based in London, Jennings might find himself anywhere on the globe on a given evening. For many weeks, on and off, he was in Iran. Having done the first TV interview with the Ayatollah Khomeini when he was in exile in Paris, Jennings actually accompanied the Ayatollah when he returned to Iran. For much of the flight back, he was sitting in the seat next to Khomeini. The whole time, he says, "I was thinking we're all going to be shot out of the sky. And if the Shah had been smart, that's what he would have done."

What happened after they landed didn't come as a huge shock to Jennings. "I had been in Iran back in the Shah's time, in 1970 and '71. You could see the rot. You could see the shape of the future of Iran. When the Revolution occurred, most of us who had been there—as opposed to Jimmy Carter just going to the Shah's party—were less than surprised. The revolution itself was a very happy time, uplifting for journalists. Then came the hostage-taking and the mood in the country began to shift."

Jennings would wake up in the middle of the night, go out and find one of the students or professional thugs called the "revolutionary guard" and bring him back into the Iranian television center. His interviews with these Iranians would go out live to either "World News Tonight" or Ted Koppel's series of special reports ("America Held Hostage"), which eventually grew into "Nightline."

Although the days after the hostages were seized were filled with tension, Jennings recalls Iran as "an easy place to be a correspondent. They didn't hate us. They wanted us to get the story out." Asserting his Canadian citizenship, Jennings avoided many hassles, but eventually, as he recalls, a large part of the press corps began walking around with Maple Leafs in their buttonholes. Jennings would occasionally go to lunch at the house of his friend Ken Taylor, the Canadian ambassador. All the time they were eating, the few hostages who had escaped and were being sheltered by Taylor were hiding upstairs. Jennings never knew.

By mid-1980, the atmosphere in Iran had become scary, even for neutral journalists. The reporter's instinct was to cover the scene, but even reporters were fair targets. "When the Shah was being moved," Jennings recalls, "I remember screaming down the phone lines to the States, 'You move the Shah, you fuckers, and it's gonna be us next.'"

If the story in Iran was exhilarating and tumultuous, so too was Jennings' personal life. His second marriage, much like his first, was falling apart. Jennings says, "Annie and I married shortly after the time my dad died. We both look back on it as a mistake." But many of his friends and relatives think back fondly on them as a couple. She was delightful; they were happy together. "It just went wrong," recalls his ABC friend John Cooley. "Most foreign correspondents' marriages don't survive."

Around the London office, Jennings was known as a charmer, a flirt, a ladies' man. With one marriage behind him, one on the rocks and all sorts of affairs notched up, he was called "the Prince of Araby."

When pretty Kati Marton, former ABC Bonn bureau chief, was dispatched to the London office, her colleague Lynn Sherr told her, "Whatever you do, don't get involved with Jennings." All the same, intrigued by the dashing foreign correspondent, Kati decided to wear a kilt into the office. For a Scotsman like Jennings, the slim, dark-haired beauty all decked out in a kilt was like a red cape waved at a bull. Before they had even been introduced, Jennings walked up to Marton, and announced that her kilt pin was one inch too high. And, with scarcely a pause, he knelt down and refastened it.

On their first date, they went to a mediocre Portugese ballet performance. As they walked out at intermission, Jennings and Marton were already talking about what it would be like to have children. By their second date, they were seriously contemplating marriage. In 1979, they were married. By 1982, they had two children, a daughter, Elizabeth, and a son, Christopher.

But if life in London was idyllic for Jennings, both personally and professionally, things were less than perfect for his two co-anchors. Max Robinson felt particularly out-of-sorts, Jennings recalls. The first black network anchorman, Robinson would later charge ABC with racism, with not giving him a fair third of the news. Jennings and others at ABC felt that Robinson, just up from a local anchor role in Chicago, lacked the reporting experience to get the most out of his national anchor role. "Max was reluctant and anxious to take on America as a beat," Jennings says.

Three months into their troika arrangement, as the three anchors were each jockeying for position in their new roles, a dinner was held for the triumvirate.

"It became known as the 'Last Supper,'" says Jennings. "There was angst on the table. It was all about how these three medium-sized gorillas could work together."

Jennings suggested that since Frank Reynolds was the most senior and the most respected, he should take the lead anchor role, and that Jennings and Robinson should spend more time on the road, which was what Jennings wanted anyway. Eventually, an uneasy truce was worked out, but the three-anchor format was never really balanced. Viewers felt confused, as if they were jumping all over the globe, and they found it hard to keep straight who was saying what about what. In the meantime, for all his declarations about the troika as a new wave in news, Roone Arledge kept furiously hunting for a "real" anchor, an undeniable star to headline his broadcast.

In January of 1981, when "World News Tonight" slipped into first place in the weekly ratings, it had more to do with Arledge's flashy production techniques and glitzy graphics than it did with his non-anchor anchors. Nonetheless, Arledge was elated. He sent Jennings a case of champagne. Jennings thought the celebration was a little premature, and teasing Arledge, sent back the champagne with a note saying that the wine wasn't vintage. It was just as well. Only two weeks later the program was back in last place.

And then suddenly, in the middle of 1983, Frank Reynolds became sick. Roone Arledge and Dick Wald flew over to London to convince

Jennings that he had to fill in for the ailing Reynolds until he got better. In July of 1983, not without trepidations, Peter Jennings boarded a plane at Heathrow Airport bound for the home office. Sixteen years after leaving the ABC anchor desk, he was returning once again to his old job.

RATINGS: Week ending April 14th.

1st. Jennings (ABC's "World News Tonight")—10.2/21 [9,220,800]

2nd. Rather   ("CBS Evening News")—10.0/21 [9,040,000]

3rd. Brokaw   ("NBC Nightly News")—9.3/19 [8,407,200]

CHAPTER NINE

China Bulletin

With its gleaming facade and its stately pillars, the Capital Cities/ABC building at 47 West 66th Street looks like a temple of broadcasting—maybe a little garish, maybe a little heavy on the marble and chrome, but with a brash, opulent splendor that speaks of the big money and the high-tech flash of late-20th-century communications. It's the kind of place in which you'd expect to find media moguls, especially when you step around the handyman gingerly buffing the polished pink-granite exterior, and enter the triumphant red and green marble entrance hall, its ceiling soaring heavenward. Like many of the buildings in this Upper West Side area (just across from Lincoln Center), this one was built where a stable for Central Park horses once stood. Today, of course, this sleek structure stables something else altogether.

Up on the third floor, at the end of a long corridor and through a heavy glass door is the newsroom that serves as the studio for "World News Tonight." It's a large, wide-open space that sprawls to accommodate four clusters of desks (foreign/domestic/morning/northeast plus satellite). At the near end is Peter Jennings' anchor desk, the size of a small swimming pool.

Like its counterpart at CBS, this newsroom stretches two stories high. From the glassed-in second story, correspondents' offices open onto corridors that look down on the action. Both broadcasting set and workspace, the newsroom is brilliantly illuminated by fluorescent fixtures and theatrical lamps. It's a clean, well-lighted place, this dramatic newsroom. Staffers call it "The Bubble."

On a Friday in May, 11:00 AM is normally a quiet time on the set, a time when the morning conference of producers has ended, and the technicians and cameramen are straggling in. But today, there's an unusual hubbub on the floor. Everyone seems to be either holding a phone or typing something into a computer or both. Bob Murphy, vice president of TV news coverage, comes charging out of his office, the one in the corner with the glowing Mercator world map on the wall. "We've got a crisis on our hands," the bearded Murphy says, his square, compact rugby-player's frame bristling with energy. "It's the China situation."

Across the floor, at the satellite desk, someone is shouting, "Do we have a bird or don't we?" He doesn't seem satisfied with the answer he gets from the other end. From the foreign desk, Wes Downs calls, "Are they going into the square?" Troops have been sighted heading toward the center of Beijing.

Ringing the floor just below the second-story balcony are TV monitors, 28 monitors in all, identified as WCBS-TV, WNBC-TV, WABC-TV, CNN. On CNN, Chinese Prime Minister Li Peng is being seen via CCTV (Chinese Television). He's telling his countrymen that he will take all reasonable measures to restore public order. It's a major announcement, just one step away from martial law. Though the pictures are only fair, the people on the floor keep glancing up at the CNN screen to see what's going on. All the other monitors are showing game shows.

Suddenly, Peter Jennings comes striding in. He seems absorbed, focused. He pulls off his jacket, and sits down at the anchor desk. Glancing up, he notes what CNN is showing. Then he turns back to his desk, and leafs through the papers in front of him. Milt Weiss, the bearded, balding writer in a canary yellow shirt, comes by to confer with him. "So far," says Jennings, "the only source we have on Zhao Ziyang being under house arrest is the students." He needs another confirmation and more information for the special bulletin. Jennings shakes his head and says, "I hope we wait until something happens in the square." The square is Tiananmen Square in the heart of Beijing where at that very minute, hundreds of thousands of students and workers are massing.

Behind one of the three Ikegami cameras that point toward the anchor desk, Morris Mann, a thirty-year veteran cameraman is peering through his viewfinder, looking at Peter Jennings. A gray-haired man in a green cardigan sweater, Mann has a pen sticking out of his shirt pocket. His official title is Field Engineer and the pen in the pocket is the techie's badge of honor. Looking into the viewfinder, he sees a rectangle inked in on the glass in the upper right corner. The rectangle shows where the Quantel (the little graphic story headings that often perch over the anchor's left shoulder) will go.

Also walking around in the darkened space behind the cameras is Joey Durden, a young woman wearing a headset. Durden is the stage manager for the "World News This Morning" show. Because of the emergency and the special report coming up, she has stayed late to fill in.

Jennings, taking a break from looking at his notes, puts his IFB ear piece in place. It connects him with the control room two stories below. Under the desk, in addition to cables, is the volume control for the ear piece. And up on top of the desk is a tiny microphone, flush with the surface and half the size of a domino.

Waiting for the special report to begin, Jennings starts to fiddle with his copy, banging away on the typewriter at the end of his desk. Sitting there under the lights in his immaculate white shirt with gleaming cufflinks and his crisp red-striped tie, he looks as if he were awakened too early or hasn't slept all night. Paul Friedman, his executive producer, stops by briefly, and Peter nods without looking up from his typewriter. Friedman is nattily turned out in a broker-blue pin stripe, perfect for Wall Street. The producer turns and goes into Bob Murphy's office to discuss what's worrying him. Coming out a few seconds later, he's saying, "They're going to pull the plug on everybody anyway." But Bob Murphy doesn't think so. He doesn't think that China is going to cut satellite transmission, at least, not for a while.

Near the foreign desk, Elyse Weiner, who handles news briefs, is trying to get something down on paper. She's having some trouble. She bites her lip and tries again.

The clock on the wall says 11:22. There are clocks all over the newsroom. White faced clocks, desk clocks, everything but cuckoo clocks; against the far wall red digital clocks report the time in Chicago, Denver, LA, Hong Kong, Beirut, Mexico City, Moscow and Beijing. In Beijing the time is twenty-two minutes after midnight. Whatever the hour, it's eight minutes to airtime.

Up at the anchor desk, a makeup man with a very red face is doing Peter. He works from a compact and lightly dabs at the anchor's forehead, then his cheeks. He moves about Jennings carefully, keeping his distance as if he doesn't know quite what to expect. He ordinarily works on "Good Morning America" and clearly is not accustomed to being in the ring with the champ. Jennings' normal makeup person, Charlotte Taylor, has yet to arrive.

It's 11:28 and the makeup man is dabbing as fast as he can. Suddenly a cry goes up, "CBS is on!" Up on the WCBS-TV monitor, the screen declares CBS SPECIAL REPORT. There's Dan Rather in Beijing and he's got the news: Chinese Prime Minister Li Peng has just addressed his nation. Everyone in the ABC newsroom freezes. For a few seconds, they stand immobile, staring at the monitor as if a video spell has been cast on them. And in a way it has. CBS has beaten them out of the blocks on this story.

Peter jumps up and quickly tosses the wire from his IFB over his shoulder. Milt Weiss comes over and helps him on with his dark blue jacket. The jaunty red foulard in the anchor's breast pocket hints at carefree doings at the yacht club. But Jennings is a picture of concentration, grimly studying the copy on his desk. Out of camera range to Jennings' left, at a small desk that sits next to his own, Milt Weiss is furiously making notes. Peter leans down to his right and quickly pulls out a tissue from the Kleenex box tucked away underneath a little wooden table, and brushes at his nose distractedly.

Suddenly the stagelights go on and Tom King, the regular stage manager for "World News Tonight" appears from nowhere with his headset on, and Joey Durden is gone. King is as cool as an Indy 500 starter. He runs his hand through his hair to instruct the anchor what to do and Peter pats down his own thinning locks. Over Jennings' head all the theatrical lamps are burning except for a few with the name "Diane" taped to them. They're to be used, no doubt, for an anchor named Sawyer, to give her that golden girl glow. Looking into the monitors facing him to see how he's being photographed, Peter subtly shifts his position in his chair. He's framed up nicely, a huge simplified map his backdrop, above his head a sign that reads ABC NEWS NEW YORK, the word NEWS in ABC blue.

Seconds to airtime. King straightens his shoulders, nods, and starts the countdown: "Five, four, three, two..." He points to Peter, and they're on the air.

"We'll bring you up to date," says Peter Jennings. "Li Peng is addressing the nation...." On the monitor in front of him there's a video of Li Peng giving his speech, the video that America is seeing while Jennings provides the voice-over narration. Off-camera, Jennings adjusts his tie nervously, tightening the knot, and once again pats down his hair. "Troops have been sighted on the way to the Square," he reports. "We have been told by our sources that Communist Party leader Zhao Ziyang has offered his resignation, but it was not accepted. The hunger strikers in Tiananmen Square have refused to leave. The city," he says, "is rampant with rumors."

He probably means "rife," but under the circumstances he's doing fine. He seems even calmer than his stage manager behind the camera whose eyes never leave him. Jennings notes some of the rumors flooding the city and concludes his special report with a final one: "Li Peng may be declaring martial law...."

As soon as he's off the air, Peter looks into the camera and shouts "Pat! Where's Pat?!" He's upset. The last rumor he reported was a late-breaking piece of information that he got through his IFB from a producer in the control room. "Where did you get the martial law from?" he demands to know. Jennings is agitated.

If there's an answer in this ghostly conversation, only Jennings can hear it. And what he hears isn't making him happy. Peter Jennings is not only a reporter but a senior editor as well, and he wants to be damn careful about his sources when the subject is martial law.

"Do you want some coffee?" Tom King asks him. King has to ask several times before he finally gets an answer. Peter isn't interested in coffee. He has other things on his mind right now. Up on the CNN monitor, the demonstrators are chanting slogans and waving banners. The student leaders are being interviewed. Jennings glances up at the screen, more than a little annoyed. Halfway around the world in China, a major story is developing, and here he is watching it unfold from West 66th Street.

RATINGS: Week ending April 28th

1st. Rather   ("CBS Evening News")—9.8/21 [8,859,200]

1st. Jennings (ABC's "World News Tonight")—9.8/21 [8,859,200]

3rd. Brokaw   ("NBC Nightly News")—8.7/19 [7,864,800]

CHAPTER TEN

Anchors Away

Recently, TV journalism has undergone a major shift. Today, there's a new emphasis on foreign coverage. The startling events of the past year, in places as far-flung as Beijing and Berlin, have certainly played a huge role in this development. But there has also been a new *style* evolving. Call it "anchors away."

For as long as anyone in the news business can remember, foreign news had always been considered a loser. Study after study commissioned by the networks seemed to confirm it: Americans wanted to know about America.

Add to that the dubious reputation Americans have long held for being bad at geography. *Especially* international geography. High school students have been known to misplace whole continents. For many young marrieds, Armenia is harder to find than an apartment. Talk about Bandung or Bandra to someone in Peoria and his eyes glaze over, his brain shifts into park.

But if this lack of world interest is to some extent a reality, it is also partly a myth. The myth is exploited by cost-conscious network executives who know how much cheaper it is to cover events in New Jersey than in Bangladesh. It's not that a major foreign story won't be covered by the network. The issue is whether it will be covered by a three-sentence in-studio synopsis or by a team of reporters on the scene.

Dan Rather, describing the bottom-line mentality of management today, says: "As with any commodity, the game is to buy low and sell high. Foreign news is expensive. Buy low. Buy domestic. News from and about other countries is the most expensive news to gather.... The 'news-is-only-a-commodity' brokers hire consultants to tell them what they want to hear. They take polls indicating that Americans say their first interest is local news, then national news. International comes in last....I believe those arguments are a misleading mixture of half-truths and no truths."

If foreign news is expensive, nothing is more expensive than sending the anchor himself on the road, with his standard traveling entourage of fifty to one hundred reporters, producers, cameramen and technicians. But about two years ago, Rather, Jennings and Brokaw began regularly uprooting themselves from their studio settings in order to broadcast live from locations around the globe.

This change actually started in earnest near the end of 1988, with CBS's summit coverage from Moscow (including their prize-winning series of reports from the USSR entitled, "Inside the Kremlin"). In early January 1989, CBS and ABC sent their anchors to Emperor Hirohito's funeral in Japan. Covering diverse aspects of Japanese society, Rather and Jennings presented a rich tapesty of information to their viewers. Although NBC's Brokaw was also on the scene, he arrived in Tokyo late and left early, remaining for only a brief two-day stay. Asked if the brevity of his visit was an economy measure, NBC News's comptroller, Natalie Hunter, says, "Sure it was. Economics doesn't control the news, but it does control the way it's presented."

The way it was presented by NBC in Japan was with a minimum of contextual information. ABC, on the other hand, gave American viewers not only the funeral of the Emperor, but also a portrait of life in contemporary Japan, including a lesson on how to do business Japanese style. But it was CBS that really excelled, skillfully using this only marginally interesting event as an occasion for a wide-ranging, in-depth look at the Japanese people and culture, as well as at the effect of Japan's powerhouse economy on the international market.

Executive producer Tom Bettag, who had lived in Japan as a Fulbright scholar, first convinced Dan Rather, then the management of CBS, of the importance of the story. Rather says, "We felt that Japan's emergence as an economic superpower and the dawn of a whole new era in U.S.-Japanese relations was an under-reported, not very well understood story. And we faulted ourselves for that. When the Emperor died, we said to ourselves, and to our top management, this is the time." And with both Rather and Charles Kuralt there, along with the rest of their correspondents, CBS gave an impressive mix of the hard and soft sides of the news.

The live transmissions used by all three networks from Japan were nothing new. The capacity to do these live "remotes," as they are called, has been in existence for over two decades, although for years it was infrequently used, mostly for conventions and space shots. But within the past two years a new idea has been percolating at the networks: There's nothing like getting the feel of a place, and nothing does that better than having an anchor on the scene.

From the Kremlin to Japan to Cuba to China to Eastern Europe to San Francisco then back to Eastern Europe and finally to Malta for the Superpower Summit, the anchors were almost constantly on the move last year. Jennings, Rather and Brokaw got out of their suits, and put on their trench coats, their safari jackets, the beige battle gear of the foreign correspondent.

Peter Jennings over the past several years has been on the road one hundred and fifty nights, in seventy-five cities, according to senior producer Steve Tello, who's in charge of getting Jennings on the air from all these different locations. But recently, the pace has become more frenetic than ever. "Today it's *double* what we were doing five years ago," says Tello. "Hell, he's made six trips to Europe since April!"

NBC's William Wheatley makes similar claims for Brokaw. "In the past four and a half years we've broadcast from forty cities—with more than a dozen cities this past year. These days, people are beginning to *expect* us to go."

For the three newsmen who had become the network anchors, this "on the road" coverage came as an unanticipated and exciting change in their regular routines. Though they had won the top jobs in journalism, they had no longer been able to do the thing they loved best, reporting from the field. Instead, they were "anchored" to a chair. For Rather, Jennings and Brokaw, this new mobile anchor role was a dream come true.

Not so for some critics. *The Nation* issued this blast: "How about a vow from Rather, Jennings and Brokaw to stop traveling to foreign captials to read teleprompters while dressed in trenchcoats, as though they are at the scene actually to report a story?" Comedians cracked jokes about President Bush racing after the three anchors around the globe. And even Peter Jennings had to admit the downside of these international expeditions: "There's nothing more asinine...than to stand in the middle of Tiananmen Square or the shipyards of Gdansk and say, 'On the stock market today.' It's ridiculous."

But as Jennings and his colleagues know, there are several splendid reasons to take the anchor on the road. The first is strictly promotional. Anchors have more star power than correspondents. As Jennings acknowledges, "When the anchor goes, you draw attention to a story."

There are also reasons that have nothing to do with advertising or viewership, and everything to do with the way these foreign stories are appreciated. Though some critics may claim that the three anchors are not acting as "real reporters," their complaints are beside the point. Anchors on the scene serve other functions: They can transform material that might otherwise seem remote or inaccessible into something more vivid, more immediate.

Take Dan Rather's broadcasts from China. The sight of a million Chinese faces in Tiananmen Square was overwhelming. But seeing Dan Rather plunging through that throng, shaking hands, talking, listening intently was a revelation. Suddenly we had a sense of scale. We were in the story.

A week or two after Rather returned, NBC sent Tom Brokaw to Beijing. To many it seemed as if NBC was closing the barn door after the horses had gone. With the government crackdown, news was hard to come by, interviews with frightened citizens even harder and, as it turned out, Brokaw failed to gather much additional information. But he did do something else. He put us back in the scene.

Mounting rickety, undersized bikes, one of which was equipped with a hidden camera, Brokaw and his cameraman rode through the blood-stained streets of Beijing and brought us footage of the forbidding city. The images weren't much in the way of news, and the hidden camera was more than a little gimmicky. Yet as he pedaled and wobbled, so frail and vulnerable on that beat-up bike, Tom Brokaw showed us something important about Beijing: the tension, the uncertainty, the paranoia under martial law. Tom Brokaw endangered made for good TV. And it *was* news, a different kind of news but still important. It gave viewers the feeling of a city occupied by its own troops.

There's a psychological reason why anchors function so effectively in these dramatic situations. Foreign correspondents are less familiar to us. They tell us stories from a distance, from somewhere "out there." The TV audience is quite simply closer (visually and emotionally) to Dan and Peter and Tom. They've spent more time with them. They know them better. NBC's George Lewis, CBS's Bob Simon and ABC's Jackie Judd did skillful reporting from China. But it was Dan Rather, and later Tom Brokaw, who gave the story that extra bit of visceral impact, catching us up more intensely in it. Through their presence, they brought the story home

Curiously, as Brokaw, Rather and Jennings have developed into "stars," the audience has begun to see them almost as familiar characters in an ongoing drama. And according to the basic conventions of TV drama, "regulars" should be placed in new situations, new locales, each week. That's why a traveling anchor, with a string of adventures, feels "right."

Then there's the "tonnage" factor. When one of the anchors goes into the field, his network's news organization gears up to turn out more stories in more depth from that location. Insiders call it "throw weight" or "tonnage," and the financial and organizational motivations for it are obvious. If the network is going to spend lots of money (often more than $1 million a trip) to bring over its star attraction plus supporting cast, it wants to get the most bang for its buck. In addition, everyone in the "shop" (the news organization) has his or her attention focused on that location. So America gets stories, lots of stories, the stories behind the story. There are mini-documentaries on the people, the history, the politics, the mood. This is the most interesting type of coverage, not just facts but texture.

Finally, with major events happening from Iran to Central America, and with a new globalism on the rise (Europe 1992, Gorbachev's "one European homeland"), network news has an obligation to give U.S. audiences an international perspective. And contrary to conventional wisdom, in-depth international coverage makes for great viewing. It's more exotic, more colorful and much more compelling to consider big issues (East-West relations, the crumbling of Communism), not trivial ones (ghost towns, indoor wall climbing and roller coasters).

Of course such coverage is expensive. And the downside was shown at Cuba's communist summit, when everyone showed up and, beyond the bare fact of the Gorbachev-Castro meeting, there was almost no news worth reporting. Nevertheless, the network anchor must continue to go—and with greater frequency—where major stories are breaking. For when the anchors get out of the studio and into the world, they take their viewers with them. And by increasing their involvement and widening their horizons, they deepen and broaden ours.

Of course, anchors would have never left their studios had they not been driven out by network competition and aided by technological improvements. It was technology that made it possible to go on the road, to air a live broadcast from anywhere on earth. "We're much more capable of going to an unscheduled event live than five years ago," says ABC senior producer Steve Tello. "The technology has improved so greatly." There have been communications satellites orbiting the earth for thirty years (the first one, named "Echo," was launched August 1960), but uplinks were generally not available unless one went to the government station.

Peter Jennings recalls, "When I was on the road sub-anchoring, it was always touch and go. You shot your footage and you went to Polish TV in Warsaw. If they weren't in the mood, you didn't get on the air."

The flyaway satellite dish has changed all that. "The flyaway dishes are smaller," says Tello, "and they break down to fit into fifteen to twenty suitcases. They fit on commercial airplanes, even smaller planes." The technicians simply open the cases, reassemble the parts and, *voilà*!, a ready-built satellite uplink. "Five years ago, a trip abroad was very difficult to do," Tello adds. "Now with flyaway dishes and more satellites up there to bounce off, the news theater has become much more open."

Given this open and much larger stage, all three networks, of course, want to dominate it. Live international coverage has become the *sine qua non*, the latest measuring stick in a brutally competitive environment. Today when a story breaks anywhere on the planet, there is no substitute for the network news anchor being there live. Technology makes it possible. Competition makes it inevitable.

Says CBS executive producer Tom Bettag: "With the tightness of the competition between the three networks, in this intensely competitive environment, you use whatever technology is available to give yourself the edge." In other words, news is now a foot race between the anchors, a competition to see who can get there first. "It's becoming crazy, this compulsion to be there live, on the spot," says ABC's Washington correspondent, John McWethy.

From the anchor's point of view, Jennings sums up the competitive battle and his trips abroad this way. "There's more concentrated travel. We always would have gone to East Berlin for the 40th anniversary there. But we've been going in one week from Prague to Frankfurt to Rome to Malta, then on to Brussels and London. I said in my broadcast last week, 'Those of you who have seen the movie *If This Is Tuesday, It Must Be Belgium*, know what we're going through.'"

"Today," says NBC's Moscow correspondent Bob Abernethy, "one of the most important characteristics for an anchor is stamina. You have to be able to go to Prague, then go on to Rome on four hours sleep, and then get up and go on to Malta."

"Look at Peter," says McWethy, "The guy's been dragging his ass all over Europe. It's a killer."

RATINGS: Week ending May 19th

1st.   Jennings   (ABC's "World News Tonight")—9.4/21 [8,497,600]

2nd.   Rather   ("CBS Evening News")—9.2/20 [8,316,800]

3rd.   Brokaw   ("NBC Nightly News")—8.2/18 [7,412,800]

CHAPTER ELEVEN

Rather in Tiananmen Square

Thursday, May 11, 1989. At a gala black-tie dinner at the Grand Hyatt Hotel in midtown Manhattan, an elite crowd of international journalists had gathered. Amid the tinkling of wine glasses, Peter Jennings stepped up to the microphone to announce the winner of the Overseas Press Club's next award: for Best TV Spot News Reporting from Abroad, the "CBS Evening News" (Dan Rather and Tom Bettag), for its series of reports from the USSR entitled "Inside the Kremlin."

Cocking his head at the jaunty angle familiar to viewers of ABC's "World News Tonight," Jennings gave a little smile. "Dan Rather couldn't be here to accept the award this evening," he said. "Actually, Dan's flying off to China even as I speak." Jennings paused, and then gave his competitor a small jab. "Of course, Dan's missing the real story, right here in the Americas—the story of Panama."

ABC and NBC had passed up the China story. At executive news meetings, both networks had decided that the visit of General Secretary Mikhail Gorbachev to the world's most populous country was a non-starter for the evening news, even if it was the first meeting between the leaders of the two major Communist blocs since 1959. Certainly, it merited some air time, but was it worth sending the whole entourage over there? NBC thought not, for reasons both editorial and financial. ABC apparently just wasn't that wild about the story.

ABC senior vice president Dick Wald said, "The Chinese had already told us and the world that this was entirely a ceremonial visit....Our decision was that because it was just ceremonial, it was an occasion to look at China and the Chinese people. So we sent reporters to do that sort of thing, but we would not send the program."

Of course, Dan Rather and company almost didn't make it to China themselves. The bureaucracy at CBS had many reservations about the trip, the costs involved being high on their list. They had already laid out big money for the news division's Soviet visit, as well as its coverage of Japan.

Through 1988 and early 1989, recalls Dan Rather, "We talked about the changing face of Communism. You could smell it, you could feel it. You knew it was out there, you knew it was coming fast. It was the motif of our coverage. Wherever you turned inside the Communist bloc, Communism was viewed as politically obsolete, intellectually discredited, and its economic system was viewed as unmanageable."

First, Rather and his executive producer Tom Bettag had battled to send a larger than usual contingent to the USSR for the Bush-Gorbachev summit. According to the anchor, they were told by management, "This is impossible, given the current economic climate. We just can't do it. Even if you're right, we don't have money to do it."

After lengthy negotiations, Rather made CBS management a proposal: "We told them we'll take the money from someplace else, we believe in it so strongly. We have a budget for the broadcast. We'll take it out of our own hide, and wind up with the same figure."

Then, only a few months later, Rather and Bettag had returned with a new request, asking for a similarly large group to go to Japan to cover Emperor Hirohito's funeral. "Japan!" cried management. "What's that got to do with the changing face of Communism? A summit's one thing, but Japan?"

Bettag, Rather, and many at CBS felt a whole new era in U.S.-Japanese relations was dawning. Although the Asian manufacturing powerhouse had become a dominant figure on the global economic scene, it was still something of a mystery. As a former resident in Japan, Bettag was convinced that many Americans didn't really understand that country.

By this time, a new president of CBS News had come into the job, David Burke. At ABC, Burke had been Roone Arledge's assistant, and many there, like Dick Wald, considered him "tough-minded and pragmatic." This stern, no-nonsense approach led some CBS staffers to dub him "the Ice Prince."

But ironically, Rather believes that it was Burke who made the Japan coverage possible: "Frankly, if David Burke had not been in his first year, who knows what would have happened? That made it easier, because he was looking for something to score."

For Rather and CBS, the rich Japan coverage was unquestionably a score. With exemplary work by Charles Kuralt, Bob Simon, Susan Spencer and their other correspondents, it was contextual news at its finest. It was also extremely expensive, nearly $2.8 million, according to some informed CBS News sources.

Following President Bush on his way back to the U.S., the CBS team covered his brief visit to China. It was a Sunday in Beijing, and Rather and Bettag were relaxing around the hotel. The competing networks had already taken off, and the anchor and his executive producer were experiencing the typical feeling of backwash that follows the end of a Presidential voyage, or any big story: the adrenaline was wearing off, and the fatigue was setting in. But they were soon bored with just hanging around.

Having heard some vague rumors about a mounting sense of discontent in China, Rather and producer Harry Radliffe headed off into the Beijing streets to see what they could find. They had been told about the People's Purple Bamboo Park. There was a corner of the park where students and intellectuals—people who wanted to practice their English—would gather. Apparently groups were coming together in increasingly large numbers to talk about democracy and freedom. They decided to bring a camera to the park, to see if there wasn't a story in it for the "Sunday Evening News."

"We went over," Rather recalls, "and we hadn't been there five minutes when he looked at me, and I looked at him, and in that way that two people who played together for a long time know, we knew. We knew that what was happening below, was beginning to break through the surface. You could hear it, you could sense it. You just knew."

Rather stayed at that park the whole afternoon. For five hours, he listened. He filmed a piece for the "Sunday Evening News"—not much of a segment, even by Rather's own admission. But more important, he heard the Chinese talking: "It was all anyone was talking about, whether you talked to undergraduate students or professors, welders or philosophers—that economic reforms had raced too far ahead of political reforms."

On the flight home that evening, Rather and Bettag thought and plotted and schemed about how they could get back to China. "We talked about virtually nothing else the whole cross-Pacific trip. The changes were so incredible." En route, the plane broke down and was forced to land in Detroit. To fill the spare hours, they kept talking about China. How could they get back?

They knew this would be an extremely tough sell back at West 57th Street. After all, they had just spent nearly $3 million on Japan. And now China? How could they possibly convince David Burke, and more importantly, the overseer of the entire CBS operation, the bottom-line oriented Larry Tisch, to lay out even more money on this kind of gamble?

At that time, Burke, who had been at CBS for less than a year, was under heavy pressure to cut costs. Moreover, there was real resistance, even within the CBS News staff, to the idea of another trip. Not only had they just returned from a very expensive visit to Japan, they were already booked to follow George Bush when he went to meet with the NATO leaders. ("I've never known a NATO trip that amounted to anything," Rather would grumble, but they were already committed to this one.)

Rather and Bettag came up with a strategy: "There was some very good feedback about Japan, and we decided to build on it," Rather recalls. "It sounds pretty calculating because it was. We decided to let the good feeling from the Japan trip wash through the organization. Then we went in to David Burke."

Faced with financial burdens, Burke was not easily convinced, but Bettag kept coming back to him with variation after variation of his proposed China budget. He and Rather sensed that with sufficient prodding, Burke, in time, might go along. "Bettag is terrific. He has this tenacity," says Rather. "Tom's the supreme jaws. He just keeps hanging on."

Finally, Bettag and Rather convinced him. Charles Kuralt partly attributes the new president's decision to his willingness to be aggressive, a trait he had picked up in his years with ABC. "Burke decided to send a whole team of reporters over to China. He wanted to 'own' the story. That's something Roone Arledge [president of ABC News] used to do."

But if the decision was Burke's to make, the president of CBS News still had to go across town to Black Rock, the corporate headquarters on Sixth Avenue, to speak to his bosses—Larry Tisch and his number two, Jay Kriegel—to sell the plan. For while Burke controlled the purse strings for CBS News, the division was running way over budget, and needed more money.

When Burke took the China proposal to Tisch and Kriegel, he had to sell hard. Rather helped with the pitch. "I sold it at each stage," he says. Tisch went along with the plan, but according to sources, with a caveat. He'd write the checks if they went over budget *this* time, but come the next fiscal year, they'd get no such break. They would have to stick to budget, *no matter what*. That seemed fair enough to Burke. And as for Rather, given the green light, he was elated.

Money in hand, Bettag and special events director Lane Venardos dispatched four teams to China on April 18, a month before Rather was due. Included in this group of twenty-three were Bruce Morton, Susan Spencer and Bob Simon. They arrived the day of liberal Hu Yaobang's funeral, the day the student protests began in earnest. "Every morning we were getting calls from these guys saying, 'This is *amazing!*'" recalls Tom Bettag.

But up to the last minute, he and Rather wondered if they were making a mistake. The week they were scheduled to leave for China, the Panama story broke. Manuel Noriega had initiated the bloody beating of opposition vice-presidential candidate, Guillermo "Billy" Ford, and then had stolen the election. President Bush had ordered thousands of additional troops to the Central American state.

"It was a wrenching decision," Bettag remembers. "Should we hedge our bets and stay put in New York, so we could cover both Panama and China?"

"Right up to the last second, we were concerned," Rather admits. "That Panama thing really made us check our hole cards. We had made a big commitment. We had a heavy bet down, and nobody else had any bet down at all. I was concerned. We all knew what the stakes were. We all knew what the effect would be if we were wrong."

On Thursday, Rather and Bettag sat down one last time with David Burke. "I give Burke a lot of credit here," Rather says. "I've had my difficulties with him, any number of times, but Burke listened, he made a decision based on facts, and once he made it, he never wavered."

"We laid it all out for Burke," recalls Bettag. "He said, 'Look, by compromising, by staying in New York, you get nothing. Your gut tells you to go, so go with your gut.' He was unequivocal."

Flying to Beijing the long way around (not the westward route non-stop to Tokyo, but in slow eastward stages, with stops to get some sleep in Paris and New Delhi), Rather and Bettag had plenty of time to doubt the wisdom of their expedition to China. Calling in to New York from Paris, they heard that the Panama situation was heating up. In a later conversation, they learned that Jennings had ribbed them at the Overseas Press Club awards dinner, and they were anxious.

When they arrived in Beijing on Saturday morning, May 13, they paused only long enough to drop their bags at their hotel, the Shangri-la. The hotel was a strange place, its decor a surreal mix of East and West. In the lobby, Chinese musicians dressed in tuxedos played Brahms. The Shangri-la would serve as the base of operations for the CBS team of sixty to seventy. On the fifth floor, beds had been moved out of the rooms to create work spaces for tape editing equipment, assignment desks and correspondents writing rooms. In fact, there was even a control room. Down in the Pagoda Garden, a camera position for reporter stand-ups had been created. All in all, says Lane Venardos, "we built a studio from scratch at the Shangri-la."

The anchor and his executive producer headed directly for Tianan-men Square, where students were beginning to congregate in large numbers. There were so many people milling around that it was already hard to get into the area.

Tiananmen Square, that vast open space just in front of the Forbidden City, has long been considered the heart of Beijing, the heart of China. It was here that emperors handed down their edicts, here that Mao Zedong announced the triumph of his Communist revolution forty years earlier. And it was here that 100,000 students and hundreds of hunger strikers had massed to proclaim a new revolution, a revolution for democracy.

"When we got there, the student demonstrations had already started," Rather says. "Once we talked to the core leadership of students, once we felt the electricity, there wasn't any doubt it was a big story. Of course, we didn't know which direction it would go, or how big it would get. But we were absolutely sure that this was going to be a big story and that Deng and Gorbachev were the least of it."

That Monday night, as American viewers tuned in to CBS, they got their first glimpse of the story. "Gorbachev comes to China seeking to heal old wounds and neutralize America's strategic advantage in Asia," Rather began. "He is upstaged by striking students seeking to change the face of Communism....This is the CBS Evening News. Dan Rather reporting tonight from Tiananmen Gate in Beijing, China. Good evening."

Decked out in a beige safari jacket, Rather plunged through the square, and spoke to the demonstrators: "Getting to the center of the square means passing through an ocean of students, bicycles, loud speakers, slogan-chanting, singing and applause." So maybe Rather wasn't being 100 percent grammatical. But this was a blockbuster story, the kind that gets him all fired up, and for once his penchant for dramatic, emotional, even purple prose, seemed absolutely appropriate to the startling scene.

"Determination, not rage, is on the faces and in the voices. They defied a government order to be out of the square by the time Gorbachev arrived, and no one seemed afraid....Police were around in force; but instead of breaking up the crowds, they broke into patriotic song, and the students sang back." Like France's "La Marseillaise," it was music by which to bring down a government.

Over the next few days, the China story blossomed from news into history. Events would more than match Rather's extravagant language. ("After four days on hunger strike in this exposed, wind-swept area, students are dropping from exhaustion, some now are vowing to die if necessary.")

Charles Kuralt, on the scene to do stories on Chinese culture, art and nature, found he was covering another story entirely. "I've been in a lot of big crowds," said the chain-smoking Kuralt, "but I had never seen anything like that. There was this feeling of liberation, of a battle already won. I've never experienced joy on such a massive scale."

By Wednesday, the scale was truly awesome. Reporting from Tiananmen Square, Rather described how China's student protest had been transformed into a mass movement: "The world's largest public square has now become the scene of the biggest demonstration in the history of Communist China. It is Thursday morning here, the dawn of day six of a hunger strike for 3,000 students, but the whole character of the protest changed today, as scores of organized groups, including workers, poured in to join the rally. At its height, the crowd numbered more than a million....The government no longer even pretends to control this area."

If it was Thursday morning in China, it was still Wednesday evening back in the United States. Halfway around the globe, Beijing had a thirteen-hour time difference from New York. And that made for more than just difficult logistics; it created a brutally tough schedule, where sleep was caught in two-hour snatches.

"Working on the other side is always a real killer," says executive producer Tom Bettag. "What makes the days so long is that you're reporting all day long. You're shooting all day by daylight. And at the end of the day, the morning news is just coming on back home. Then you have to go back to the hotel rooms to screen and write and do all the scripting of material through the night, and have everything ready to feed by 6:00 in the morning, which is the evening news back home. In other words, you work all day, then you work all night."

Powered by the sheer excitement of witnessing major news unfolding, Rather and his crew were in action more or less around the clock. Out in Tiananmen Square, the CBS team was broadcasting from what it euphemistically termed a "mobile unit." It consisted of two vehicles: a flatbed truck and a ten-year-old beat-up Japanese panel truck, a Toyota that Rather termed "a reject from a demolition derby." The Toyota was stuffed with equipment it was never designed to handle. Jerry-rigged on top of the flatbed was a camera and a tripod at one end. Rather himself was broadcasting standing at the other end. After a few days, the top was so slippery that Rather's tech team built him a small platform out of wooden crates.

As the skies opened and rains began pouring down, Rather was at his position, on top of the crates. "In the streets," he was saying, "more than a million people were again flocking toward Tiananmen Square when, at 3:30 in the afternoon, a tremendous monsoon-type rain came down, completely out of season. Students talked about an old Chinese belief that violent weather in the heavens is a sign of great change to come on earth."

That was what Rather was saying on camera, but what he was thinking was something else altogether. "This whole set-up was so jerry-rigged, my great fear was that lightning was gonna hit and destroy the whole thing. There was a real possibility that somebody could be electrocuted with those wires."

As always in these productions, if the reporters were knocking themselves out, the unsung heroes were the technical staff: the cameramen, the soundmen, the guys who lay down the wires and set up the microwave "hops" that transmit video material from the remote location to the base (in this case from the square to the hotel). This technical staff was working twice as hard as anybody else.

"We were so consumed, and so shorthanded, everybody was driving themselves," says Rather. "This, money cannot buy. If someone invokes the union, forget it. These are not featherbedded things. You can't pay people to do the herculean work these guys were doing."

Brad Simpson, the cameraman on top of the Toyota, had been at his post for several days and nights running as the story unfolded, operating on the barest minimum of sleep. When the red light over his camera went on, and Rather launched into a live "insert" (one of the brief news updates that appeared throughout the day), the anchor saw his cameraman start to waver a little bit, rocking back and forth with exhaustion. And then, as Rather went on, talking live to the U.S. about China being the biggest story in the world, and Tiananmen Square the focus, he saw the cameraman collapse, just crumple onto the truck, almost taking the camera down with him. "Fortunately, he didn't fall off the darn truck," Rather says. The sound man quickly jumped up and steadied the camera, so all viewers in the U.S. saw was a tiny movement.

But the entire CBS team was a little shaky from time to time. With a wry smile, Rather recalls that toilet facilities were virtually non-existent around the square. "There were more than a million people. This is China. We're not talking about America, with McDonald's all over. You can relieve yourself up to a point, by going behind a post— that made the odor pretty strong—but eventually you have to go to the one big facility. Well, there was this guy on our team. I took him to that latrine. You have to imagine the scene. It was a huge tent, and inside the Chinese had dug slit trenches as far as the eye could see. Well, when he got inside, the combination of the tremendous smell and the shock of the scene, people squatting along trenches, and he just derricked, absolutely derricked. Frankly, he wasn't the only newsman to faint dead away."

Of course, Rather had more on his hands than fainting colleagues. At the beginning of the week, he had had a chance to do some reporting, talking to student leaders and new groups of workers who were joining the cause in the square. However, as the week wore on, he had less and less time to do any reporting.

Stationed at their remote unit in the Square, Rather told Bettag that he wanted to break away between tapings in order to talk to various student contacts. In the field, says Rather, he and his executive producer almost always stick together (unlike the other two networks, where the executive producers come into the field only part of the time, and spend the majority of time in the control room). According to Rather, he and Bettag are "joined at the hip in these situations." In response to his anchor's request, Bettag kept telling him, "Let me send somebody else to do that." Rather was definitely frustrated, fearing that his contacts wouldn't want to have anything to do with reporters they didn't know, but he accepted the fact that, at least in this instance, it was the executive producer's call.

This situation typifies the paradox of the network anchor's lot: While it is excellence as a reporter that often propels someone to the anchor job, when he gets there, he can no longer do what he once did best. The performance demands make the anchor an on-camera animal, seldom leaving time for more than a cursory survey of the scene, and certainly not enough time for an in-depth investigation.

"There is a point on a big breaking story, when you start doing every broadcast across the board—live cut-ins, '48 Hours,' all those extra broadcasts," Rather reflects. "At that point, you have to let loose. You have to loosen up on the responsibility of being the core of the editorial process, and shift over more into broadcast. The on-air work requires concentration. Dozens of people are knocking themselves out, and their effort isn't going to matter if you're not doing your job, not being coherent."

In most of the twenty-four-hour cycles that Rather and his team worked in China, he estimates they were doing up to a dozen different broadcasts. As the pace got even more frantic toward the end of the week, they did some forty-odd broadcasts (including cut-ins and brief spots for affiliates) in one twenty-four-hour cycle.

"Election night is this way to a degree, conventions are this way to a degree, but nothing prepares you for the pressure of this sort of situation," Rather says. "There's a lot of ad-libbing, because not everything can be written. You've got things in your notebook, things in your head. The most important thing is the story line. You have to think story line. Where are we in the story? This is where we were one hour ago, five minutes ago. This is where we are now, and where we're going. You have to make sure that the story line is clear.

"At the same time, you have to be talking to pictures—sometimes talking to pictures you've not seen. You've been told about them, but you haven't seen them. You're seeing them at the same time the audience is. But you have to give enough background and detail so the audience has some kind of perspective.

"And, at the same time, someone is talking to you in your ear about the next element you're going to, and indeed maybe talking to you in two ears. That is, one ear is plugged into New York, and New York is saying, you gotta cut away in thirty seconds, so you're counting down in your head—you've got this clock in your head—twenty seconds to go, fifteen. And in your other ear maybe you have the local contact, someone like Lane Venardos or Susie Zirinsky at the Shangri-la hotel.

"So, you're standing in front of this camera that's on top of this beat-up Toyota—standing on a platform built out of crates—and two people are talking, one in each ear, and you're talking to a picture which is on a monitor down here, and at the same time you've got a clock going in your head, and always in back of your mind is the story line. And what you're aware of is that all this work from all these people, everything depends on your being clear."

By this point, it was already quite obvious that China was a major story, but CBS (along with cable's CNN) had it all to themselves. "The others let us have a free-fire zone for the week," notes Tom Bettag.

Why, once it became clear that this was a major story, did ABC and NBC refuse to commit their anchors to it? ABC vice president Bob Murphy contends that by that time it was impossible to get an earth station into China to send images up to the satellite. The government was now forbidding it, and ABC would have been forced to depend on the good graces of the Chinese government TV station, an untenable situation.

But there was another reason that ABC's management advised against going. Senior vice president Dick Wald felt, "We'd just be catching up. The first person who starts running well with a story usually dominates it. You get the audience to understand that you are the news operation that has this thing best in hand. It's perfectly reasonable."

But many, including ABC's own anchor, Peter Jennings, didn't feel that it was reasonable at all. They thought the whole thing smacked of an unhealthy emphasis on competition: "To not be the first correspondent out the door to go to China was really profoundly offensive to me," Jennings said. "And I think that one of the reasons I didn't go was because we were all playing this [competitive] business—he's there and who's there and ... I think it was perfectly sensible not to go for the Gorbachev. But when the story began to break, [there was this feeling at ABC]—well, Rather's there and Jennings is coming after Rather, and where's Brokaw, and all that kind of stuff. Instead of the story."

By the end of the week, the story had turned spectacular. Friday, May 19, kicked off what Dan Rather would refer to in his broadcast that evening as "twenty-four riveting hours of roller coaster events and emotions." At 5:00 AM Friday morning, Premier Li Peng and Communist Party Chief Zhao Ziyang came to the square to talk with the hunger strikers. If this move was a concession on the part of the government, and if Zhao Ziyang would recommend a soft line toward the students, nonetheless the mood in the square began to change for the worse. The celebration gradually died, and a pall fell on the crowd. Many felt they had achieved everything they could. And many realized they'd better get the hell out of there. By late afternoon, it was clear that hard-line moves were being planned by the government. All demonstrations would be banned by midnight. The square was filled with rumors of army units on the move. Rather went on the air and described the situation this way:

"Midnight: The deadline passes. More reports and rumors of troop movements, many close by.

"12:30 AM: Premier Li Peng appears in radio and televison, speaking to an audience of top officials, and over loudspeakers to the crowds. He says anarchy and riots are threatening the state, threatening to wreck the economy. He blames it on a small group of conspirators trying to overthrow Communist rule. He declares a kind of martial law to put down the protest. Those listening on loudspeakers jeer and begin to chant, 'Li Peng come down! Li Peng come down!'

"2:00 AM: The army still hasn't arrived. Truckloads of strike supporters begin coming in again. The students dare to hope.

"4:00 AM: Reports increase that the army has tried to move closer, but has run into passive resistance from the students....

"By dawn's early light, the students were still there. They had won the night."

With the Saturday morning sunrise came a rising sense of optimism. The crowd in the square made way for a small military color guard that marched across the square and up to the flagpole placed in front of Mao's portrait. The students cheered, and sang the Chinese National Anthem as the flag was raised. At this point, Rather had been in the square twenty-four straight hours without sleep, running on pure adrenaline.

Though it was early Saturday morning in China, it was Friday night in New York, almost time to air the "CBS Evening News." Reporting live from Tiananmen Square, Dan Rather began: "Another night of living dangerously is over for the hunger strikers here in Tiananmen Square. They are still here. The army is not. Incredible! China's Communist Government hard-liners are finally in control of the government and the party, and they have called out the army in yet another desperate bid to break the back of the mass movement for freedom and democracy and reform. After weeks of government paralysis, while students took over the streets of Beijing and moved their protest into a national movement, soldiers are now massing to move against the protestors camped right here in the center of Beijing. The problem is the army has been massing for hours and is still not here.

"It's now Saturday morning in Beijing," Rather continued, "a week after the start of a hunger strike that threatened to bring down the government. There is a feeling of ecstasy in this square at the moment because the hunger strikers expected that the army would be here by now, and that they would be out. That hasn't happened. The square is filling back up again now with supporters. And the hunger strikers, their view is that the army is stymied, the pendulum is swinging back their way, and that again they have the government on the run."

That optimism would prevail for a while. But only a few hours after Rather signed off on the live news broadcast, the government made its first move. Rather, Bettag and their team were still in the square, still operating from their beat-up Toyota truck, when the helicopters came. "They sent the helicopters ostensibly for reconnaissance," Rather recalls, "but in fact it was a psychological move. You could hear them a hell of a long way away. It was like being back in Vietnam. You could hear them long before you could see them."

"The instant I saw them, I knew it was only a matter of time before they moved us out," says Rather. "Before that, I never thought they would, but the second they appeared, I thought it was only a matter of time.

"In the seconds you have to think, you think okay, they could strafe, they could land shock troops, they could tear gas. There are a lot of possibilities here. We had talked about it with our people. Many of them were experienced in battle situations." Rather himself, as mentioned earlier, had been a marine, if only briefly.

"We told our people, if there's tear gas, get down into the subway station—get down into the subway station because the gas won't penetrate down there. There'll also be some panic. So be careful. Stay close to the walls. Getting trampled is a real possibility in a crowd that size.

"We'd talked about some of these things, but in the seconds you have to review: Where are your people? Your equipment? How do you get them to the subway station?....It sounds so dramatic—but that's because it was. You just don't know what's going to happen."

As the camouflaged military helicopters came in that first time, they did none of the things Rather had feared. They simply circled around the square, past the Heroes Monument and the great Hall of the People, swooping low to inspire fear in the crowd, and then took off.

"We thought then it would be only a matter of time until they tried to cut off our broadcast," Rather recalls, "and by the second time the helicopters appeared, they had cut off the broadcast."

To understand what happened next, you have to visualize the electronic hook-up. Rather and his team were operating from Tiananmen Square out of their beat-up Toyota. The Japanese truck was loaded with equipment that would transmit audio and video via a microwave "hop" to a dish on top of a nearby hotel, where it would be relayed to their base camp at the Hotel Shangri-la. From there, the sound and pictures could be fed up to the satellite and back to New York. But nothing could be fed live out of China that didn't get to the satellite dish at the Shangri-la.

For Rather and his team in the square, the first indication of trouble came when the picture hook-up with the Shangri-la was cut. Someone was dismantling the microwave relay. Not too long after that, the audio was cut too.

As their link with their base camp was severed, the question Rather and his group faced: Was it worth it to stay, to keep taping on video, or should they try to head back to the hotel? "All the time, we didn't know what was gonna happen," Rather recalls. "And burning in your brain is the thought, the best pictures don't mean a thing unless you can get them out."

Uncertain when the troops would move against the square, the CBS team decided to keep video taping the scene, and send their tape by bicycle couriers back to the hotel. It was a long, difficult haul, with roadblocks and checkpoints along the way. Also, any ground troops coming towards the square would be coming from that direction.

Bettag and Rather huddled. "Here's the situation," Rather said. "It's only a matter of time. We're in a race against the clock. They cut us off here. We don't know when they'll cut us off at the Shangri-la. It's probably gonna be pretty soon. Plus, we can't even be sure the video tapes are getting back. We have no video communication, no audio communication—even the cellular phones aren't working. We have no contact with the Shangri-la."

Although he was having trouble making a call across town, Tom Bettag had ironically been able to get a call out on his cellular phone to CBS News president David Burke's home in Westchester only hours earlier. Chatting briefly, Bettag had convinced Burke that events were moving rapidly, and that they should put a special report on the air. But now, when they needed the phones, they were dead.

Not knowing how long it would take them to get back to the Shangri-la through the crowds of students and hordes of troops, Rather and Bettag decided they would shoot off some last video tape, and get the hell out of there.

Soon the two of them and several members of their team piled into a van and started back towards the Shangri-la. Once or twice, Bettag managed to get through on the cellular phones, for quick bursts of conversations, but contact was sketchy at best.

Their driver, a local blue-collar worker whose name the CBS crew would never quite get, had formed a bond with them early on, despite the fact that he spoke no English. Actually, he spoke one word of

English, "Hunter," the name of the action police drama that he enjoyed watching in translation on local TV. When they first met, he had flashed a smile at the sight of their TV equipment, and said "Hunter!"

Now, with tanks closing in, with checkpoints on the road, with troops everywhere, Rather and Bettag tried to convey some of the urgency that they felt about getting back to the hotel. Their driver gave a big smile, pointed to himself, gestured thumbs up, and once again said "Hunter!" Then taking off at top speed, he wove between the students and the workers, like a veteran stunt driver in a car chase. Rounding a corner and dodging the crowds in the streets, he slammed the van up over the curb, and went careening down the sidewalk.

Half out of control, he bounced off a Volkswagen, and skidded twenty-five feet down the sidewalk, not coming to a stop before he banged into a worker on a bicycle. Bike and rider went flying, but luckily, only the bike was mangled. The team checked him out, then sped off towards the hotel.

"When we got back to the hotel," Rather recalls, "we all bailed out of this van, which by then was a refugee from a junk heap, like a bunch of circus people."

Army units were already stationed outside the Shangri-la, and although none of them seemed to have any specific orders, large groups were milling around ominously, shouldering their rifles. Rather, Bettag and their crew dashed inside to the Pagoda Garden courtyard, where their basic broadcast position had been set up, looking for the CBS crew. Absolutely no one was there. In fact, there wasn't even a camera left in the courtyard.

Fearing the worst, they went sprinting up the five flights of stairs. Dashing down the corridor and rounding the corner, they stumbled onto a bizarre scene. In the dimly lit fifth floor hallway, in the middle of all sorts of equipment packing crates, Lane Venardos, director of Special Events coverage, a witty, rotund, Humpty-Dumpty figure, was locked in a tedious harangue with two ill-at-ease young Chinese bureaucrats in shirtsleeves.

"We've heard nothing from the foreign ministry," Venardos was saying. "We're authorized to be on the air until 0100 hours...."

Down the hall, Susan Spencer provided running voice-over commentary on the surreal scene outside her door. "The Chinese government has apparently decided to impose a news blackout on a situation over which it has no control....They have told us that all satellite transmissions must be stopped."

Spencer went on, "Unclear exactly what their rationale is, except that clearly the Chinese government is not too happy with the rest of the world seeing what the situation is here right now...."

"Do you have some identification?" Venardos demanded, launching into a stalling tactic. "I mean anybody could come here.... How do I know you're who you say you are?....We think turning off the satellite broadcast is a very serious prospect...."

Meanwhile, Susan Spencer updated the viewers: "I've just been told that another gentleman from CCTV is attempting to go into our control room and shut off our receivers while this discussion is going on," she cut in. "So if we suddenly go off the air, it won't be any mystery...."

All this drama was unrolling live in real time. It was, as Rather would later say, "a scene out of the theater of the absurd."

"Lane was holding the fort until somebody, almost anybody, could get there," Rather says. "My instinct was to stall them," recalls Vernardos. "I was just trying to keep going until Dan got back. I thought Dan would be a more effective negotiator than I was, in terms of expressing our concern and outrage."

Turning the corner, Rather and Bettag found themselves in the middle of these negotiations, which were being broadcast live at that very moment. Never one to shy away from a battle, Rather launched himself into the middle of the group, shaking hands with the Chinese, and simultaneously checking out the camera positions. Ironically, given the quintessential on-air beast that he is, he didn't at first realize that the cameras were doing anything more than simply taping the scene (instead of broadcasting live). Lane Venardos gave him a quick recap to bring him up to date: "These gentlemen are...here to tell us that we're being ordered off the air, in spite of our agreement with the Chinese foreign ministry which expires at 1:00 AM Sunday morning."

A little out of breath, Rather said, "Greetings to our colleagues, and I'm sorry that this is an awkward situation for you as it is for us." He was clinging with both hands to the face-saving diplomacy he had learned in over ten previous visits to China and the Far East. Then he launched into a recap of the ominous helicopter fly-bys, the frenzied twenty-five-minute drive back from the square.

As he described the scenes out in the street—martial law, students surrounding trucks and offering flowers to soldiers—powerful lights went on, illuminating Rather, his sporty blue polo shirt, his safari jacket. Bettag handed him a note saying "You're live."

Across America, a bright red "CBS News Special Report" sign flashed up on screens in living rooms from coast to coast, and this feisty debate suddenly appeared in the middle of CBS's 10:00 PM Friday show, "Dallas." Viewers expecting to see J.R. were suddenly confronted with a battle at once more mundane and more mythic— Dan Rather wrangling with two Chinese officials about his right to broadcast. It was a classic freedom of speech showdown between a reporter and a repressive government. On and off, it ran for a memorable half hour. Digging in his heels in order to keep open the communication lines between China and the outside world, Rather, with bulldog tenacity, held the bureaucrats at bay, never raising his voice, but never backing down either.

"At almost every intersection, there are crowds," Rather spoke into his hand-held microphone. "The army has engaged in tremendous restraint.... Where there hasn't been restraint is in this pulling the plug on our broadcast." He turned to CBS News China consultant and novelist Bette Bao Lord. "For those who find this hard to follow, welcome to the club."

Tom Bettag came to walk Rather into the control room, so they could keep sending out as much of the video as they had gathered. As he stepped away from the two Chinese officials, Rather said with a characteristic, though strangely involuted politeness: "Excuse me sir, to our Chinese bureaucratic friends who are here to try to shut us down."

When the fourth special report went on, a few minutes later, Rather and the two officials were now outside, behind the Shangri-la, standing by CBS's giant white satellite dish. The debate now centered around the CBS contract. Playing for time, the anchor demanded that the Chinese give him something in writing that would officially rescind the earlier contract.

In a strange, doppelganger situation, Rather was at once negotiating with the Chinese to stay on the air, and providing running play-by-play commentary of these negotiations for viewers as he went along. "We've been operating in good faith...." said Rather to the Chinese, then turned back to the viewers: "All this against the backdrop of

Deng Xiaoping and Li Peng trying to exert authority over the country, and it's clear that they simply couldn't take our coverage...They shut us down at Tiananmen Square and they're trying to shut us down here."

"They want to see our original contract," Lord informed him.

"This is a telex confirmation of the contract," said Rather, flourishing a document in his hand.

The Chinese launched in, and Bette Bao Lord translated: "They are not trying to stop our transmission....they would like to do this by another manner. After we film this, they will do it for us...."

Knowing that would mean the Chinese government would effectively take control of their broadcast, Rather gave a small smile, and kept going.

"Bette," he said, "It's very important to emphasize that we are guests in this country. We respect their country. We respect their government, but we have a written agreement. I hope they would understand that we have a written agreement with their government, and I respectfully hope that they would consider that....I would not feel comfortable ending the broadcast before I had something in writing."

Standing outside in the noonday sun, Rather and the Chinese continued their slow debate, neither side advancing, neither side giving an inch: "I respectfully protest as strongly as I can," Rather said through his translator Lord, "especially because he doesn't have anything in writing to break our agreement."

Meanwhile, there was a new piece of video to be relayed. It was the first scene of violence, demonstrators being beaten by police with nightsticks, students with blood on their faces and hands.

Then Rather was back on camera. "The government has issued a new decree for foreign journalists. They should not disseminate 'any information that would be harmful to the country,'" he declared ominously, just as the report came to an end. "And these gentlemen are in the process of trying to shut us down."

When the fifth special report of the night came on, and Tom Bettag gave Rather his cue, the drama took a new and final turn. "My instructions from CBS management are to follow your commands," Rather said to the Chinese bureaucrats with obvious chagrin. "If you give the command to my colleague, he will shut us down."

Turning back to the camera, Rather announced one last piece of video tape with his characteristic verbal flourish, half awkward, half elegaic, at the end: "These are final pictures of...considerable chaos in downtown Beijing. These are the last pictures we'll be showing to you through our own facilities. And if we're able to show any more at all, I know not when....This is Dan Rather, CBS News, Beijing."

And saying that, he turned to the heavyset technicican manning the satellite controls, who flipped the switch.

And then the screen went black.

But even when the Chinese government cut off the satellite transmissions from the Shangri-la, the show wasn't over. Later that night, Rather and his team headed back to Tiananmen Square. Here's how he tells the story:

"There was that night, after martial law was declared. It was the night after the government had ordered the troops to move on the square, only to be frustrated, humiliated by the opposition of the citizens of Beijing. We wanted to get our cameras into Tiananmen Square. Everyone piled into the car of the one driver willing to risk the trip at one o'clock in the morning. The government had declared a curfew, but the streets were full of people.

"They were pulling busses into the roadway, letting the air out of the tires. Guard rails and paving stones had been dragged into the streets. Each intersection we came to was filled with hundreds of people and thousands of bicycles lined up as if they could stop tanks. Citizens surrounded our car, making it impossible to move. The driver explained that we were journalists, American journalists. *Meiguo*. The crowd burst into applause. Fingers formed Vs. 'Okay Charlie.' The bicycles parted, and we moved to the next intersection to repeat the scene. *Meiguo*. Applause. When our camera crew got to the square, the students were dumbfounded.

'Where are you from?'

'*Meiguo*.'

A smile.

'Isn't it against the law for you to be here?'

'Isn't it against the law for *you* to be here?'

Another smile.

'They said foreign broadcasters were kicked out of the country.'

'No, we have not been kicked out. We cannot broadcast from here, but we can ship tape to Hong Kong or Tokyo and have it broadcast from there.'

A big smile.

'It is good that you are here,' said the students."

And for those students, even the ones who died on the bloody next night, crushed beneath the tank treads or shot by troops advancing on the northern perimeter of the square, it was good that Dan Rather and his CBS crew were there. Because as a consequence, their heroic deaths and their innocently idealistic message of political change had repercussions all around the globe, from Eastern Europe to Nicaragua. Maybe not as much impact or as much moneymaking potential as "Dallas," but still, impact all the same.

RATINGS: Week ending May 26th

1st.   Rather   ("CBS Evening News")—9.2/21 [8,316,800]

2nd. Jennings (ABC's "World News Tonight")—8.8/19 [7,955,200]

3rd. Brokaw   ("NBC Nightly News")—8.4/19 [7,593,600]

CHAPTER TWELVE

Upstairs, Downstairs at ABC

It's well after five o'clock on a late June afternoon, and in the control room at ABC, "World News Tonight" director C. Harper ("Charlie") Heinz is trying to solve the acid rain problem. The four-minute environmental piece by correspondent Ned Potter is a difficult mix of interviews, satellite pictures and complicated illustrations, and Heinz is busy touching up the photos, although the piece is a "future" and won't air till much later.

"Can we get a soft white top and bottom?" he asks the "Paintbox" editor via intercom. ("Paintbox" is the trade name of a device that is used to electronically alter a video picture.) And, as if by magic, the satellite image on the monitor in front of him suddenly acquires a frame, subtly altering the look of the photo. "All right," he says. "Lovely."

A heavy-set, white haired, white mustachioed, outgoing man with pinkish coloring and a comfortable belly, Charlie Heinz looks like a senior TWA transcontinental pilot, slightly avuncular and absolutely trustworthy. His eyes are clear, his style calming. He likes to talk, and there's a good deal of energy and enthusiasm in what he has to say. His flashy socks hint at something flamboyant just beneath the surface.

Up on the monitor, Potter is talking about trees dying. "I'll tell you what's dying," says Charlie matter-of-factly. "Everything in the cafete-

183

ria." A young production assistant seated behind him in the second row mutters softly, "Everything but the cockroaches."

Jokes aside, the dimly lit control room at ABC is calm, well ordered, high tech. Imagine an air traffic control tower, or the command deck of *Star Trek*'s "Enterprise," filled with sophisticated electronics and flashing lights, countless dials, chrome. Charlie Heinz faces a wall of more than fifty labeled monitors in assorted sizes. The large screen directly in front of him is the "Line" monitor, the monitor which shows exactly what the viewer at home is seeing. To its left is a screen labeled "Preview," which when broadcasting is used to show what will air next. It's a video on-deck circle. There are monitors to see what ABC's competition is up to, monitors for the Washington-New York fiber optic line, monitors just for credits or Chyrons (the name used for identifying captions made by a Chyron machine). And high on the wall are six screens numbered 52, 53, 54, 55, 56 and 57 that connect the control room to six crucial tape machines down below in the basement.

Just behind the control room and completely sealed off from it by a fixed glass window, is the audio room, a small space filled with state-of-the-art sound equipment. Inside, two guys are loafing around, eating pizza. The program goes on in twenty-four minutes and these fellows are stuffing their faces with pizza as if they have all the time in the world.

Which, by control room standards, they do. After all, nine out of ten tape pieces do not come in until between 5:45 and air time at 6:30, or even after 6:30. "In trying to get the story to be as up to date as possible, I think our deadline has moved as close to air as possible," Charlie Heinz says. "They're squeezing us a little further each time. So often, not every night but a lot of times, we'll be on the air with a lead story and a story in section three of the show hasn't yet started to be fed to us here in New York. And it may need some work once it gets to New York. It may need to be cut down, or have some graphics dropped in, or some tape from our archives added. In fact, it's not unusual to have the second half of a story still coming into our tape room while the top of that piece is going out to the country."

The telephones all over the control room now ring constantly. Charlie gets up and reaches for a ringing phone. "Who's on the gizmo?" he asks the caller. He glances at the clock on top of the monitor board. It says 6:13.41. Charlie takes a swig of coffee from his styrofoam cup. A young woman asks him, "Are we changing the font?"

"We're changing everything," says Charlie.

In front of him, a face appears on the screen. It looks like it belongs to a gypsy con artist. In reality it turns out to be Paul A. Bilzerian, chairman of the Singer Company. The government has just charged him with fraud. "B-I-L-Z-E-R-I-A-N." A production assistant spells out the name for Vanessa, the Chyron machine operator. She types in the identifying tag line that will appear under the image.

It's 6:17 when the word comes down. The lineup is running long. They'll have to kill the lengthy South Africa piece. With only thirteen minutes to go, an important news story that people have worked on all day is abruptly eliminated from the broadcast. "South Africa has gone away," says Charlie Heinz. "We're also dropping home sales and ethnic unrest."

Suddenly everybody in the room takes their seats and focuses on what they have to do. The easy chatting has disappeared as if it's a space shot and the bird is ready to fly. To Charlie's right, the associate director is marking the time. "Three and a half minutes," he calls. To his left and wearing a baseball cap, Gary Boyarsky, the technical director, silently fingers a dial.

Charlie, one of the few directors in the business who doesn't use a headset, glances down at the console in front of him. This is the communications nerve center of the broadcast. From here, Charlie can, for example, listen in to executive producer Paul Friedman's mike. If cameraman Morris Mann or stage manager Tom King have something to say, Charlie can hear them, too. And he can hear Peter Jennings even when his mike is closed. And most important, after years of experience, Heinz can tell which voice is which. "I think I'm comfortable with six voices at max," Charlie says. "But it's only because I know what to listen for."

Up on the wall on a number of screens including the Line monitor, Jennings is getting a finishing touch put on his makeup. Tom King helps him into his jacket. The anchor seems oblivious as he concentrates on the evening's script.

"Good afternoon, Peter," Charlie says softly, testing their connection.

Peter straightens his tie. He adjusts his mike, the wire of which goes under his jacket and down his back. "Hello boys and girls."

Paul Friedman, the executive producer, has come in and taken his seat in the second row. He leans forward intently and watches the Line monitor. Peter yawns nervously. He fusses with his tie. He yawns again. Paul Friedman and his two senior producers, Bob Roy and Dennis Dunlavey, all yawn together.

A voice says, "Milt's IFB [Interruptible Feedback] level is a little low."

Charlie says, "Put a quarter in the meter."

They correct the volume on Milt Weiss's IFB. Peter's writer sits just off camera to his left.

The associate director says, "Ten, nine, eight, seven, six, five, four, three, two, one. Hit it."

The program's logo fills the screen and a voice says, "From ABC, this is 'World News Tonight' with Peter Jennings."

Upstairs in the studio behind Camera number 3, cameraman Morris Mann gives viewers a deep shot of the ABC newsroom in New York with its simplified map of the world, its computers, its sprinkling of workers and then quickly zooms in on Peter who is about six feet away at the anchor desk. And across America about twelve million people stop what they're doing to see what Peter Jennings can tell them about their world.

"Good evening. We begin tonight with politics and money. The comedian Will Rogers once said...." Fifteen seconds later, he concludes with, "Here is ABC's Brit Hume."

"Take," orders Charlie, and Boyarsky, the technical director, punches a button. The image of Jennings is replaced by Brit Hume as the live camera at the White House is placed on Line. Hume is saying, "The President announced his plan as an attempt to end what he considers the corrupting influence of political action committees...." On the Preview monitor, Peter is yawning nervously. He puts his little finger in his mouth and watches Hume tell his story.

Jean Blake, Paul Friedman's blonde, good-looking secretary, comes rushing into the control room with an armful of papers that she hands out. The clock says it's already two minutes and seven seconds into the broadcast and they're just now getting final scripts!

On the Line monitor, Peter is telling viewers that Cokie Roberts on Capitol Hill has more on the story.

"It's been thirty-five years since the Republican House swept in on President Eisenhower's coattails," begins Cokie.

While she discusses campaign law changes, Peter, who has been busily working on his script, says without looking up, "Charlie, this next page will end on the word 'ethics.'"

"Okay," says Heinz coolly, without any hesitation. The script that Paul Friedman has only just been given is already old news. Heinz reshuffles his timings yet again to make sure the broadcast runs neither too short nor too long. This is the director's job, a split-second juggling act that requires an ability to anticipate trouble, especially when the elements of a single piece (video, sound bites, graphics, live plug-ins from correspondents) may be feeding from different machines, different floors, even different cities all at once, all having to be dropped in on the fly. Colleagues speak of directors as the "cowboys" of the profession. But the key, above all, is to remain calm.

"Everybody is so tightly connected, from the desk assistant on up through talent that if anybody stumbles along the line, cameraman or anybody else, the effect is felt all over," Heinz will say in a spare moment. "What makes it not as disastrous as it could be is that the recovery time on the part of all of us is incredible. Because there is always something that goes wrong."

"Take," says Charlie, and Peter comes on Line introducing a few foreign stories. The first one is a 1:15 piece by Dean Reynolds on eight more Palestinians being deported from Israel.

After that, Peter reappears and says, "Elsewhere, the leader of South Africa's ruling party calls it a new chapter in his country's history. The National Party today revealed a five-year plan which would share limited power with the country's black majority. It calls for a new constitution which would give blacks some political role. It rejects majority rule...and opponents call the proposal a 'New Label for old dogma.' ...In a moment...what Americans might learn from the Dutch about teenagers and birth control."

In the control room, Paul Friedman is angry and complains to those around him, "Just saying 'elsewhere' doesn't take the stink off this persistent link of South Africa and Israel."

"I did say 'elsewhere,'" says the anchor, who has picked up Friedman's remark on his IFB.

"Forget it, Peter," Friedman says, "you can't follow these conversations."

Peter laughs uncomfortably.

At 6:55, the final report of the broadcast is introduced. It's a ghost story by ABC's Charles Murphy from a tiny, former mining town called Bodie, California. It looks as if they're going to start mining operations again and "make a ghost out of the ghost town." Threatened by renewed mining, even the ghosts in Bodie might disappear. Having said that, the correspondent disappears from the screen, and a ghostly voice says, "Charles Murphy, ABC News, Bodie, California."

"Don't worry," ad-libs Peter. "I suspect he'll be back."

The control room howls as the closeout rolls. "From ABC, this has been 'World News Tonight' with Peter Jennings." And the broadcast is out at 6:28:26, just in time for the affiliates to pick up some loose change before the hour from their local one minute of commercials.

The second the broadcast is over, Peter has snatched up the phone on his anchor desk and is talking to Paul Friedman. Friedman says that they'll have to redo page twelve in the second (7:00) feed so that Peter can correct his flub in the U.S.S. Iowa story intro. He says, teasing Jennings, "We wouldn't have to do it if we had an anchorman who could read straight."

At 7:03, as the second feed unrolls, they're watching CBS in the control room. Senior producer Bob Roy leans over to Friedman. "It's interesting," he says, "that CBS led with the debt story."

At 7:05, Friedman gets a call and announces, "They're taking Marcos back into surgery again."

"He's going to die soon," Roy says. "They've taken out too many parts."

Friedman wants to know, "Does L.A. have an obit ready?"

"We could do a news piece and not an obit piece," suggests senior producer Dennis Dunlavey.

Friedman gets L.A. on the phone and explains about the deposed Philippine leader being near death. "Would you guys be in a position if he dies to handle it? Do you have a correspondent?"

Gary Shepard is available.

Charlie Heinz says, "I'd like to record a page that will feed out to the West Coast in case old Ferdie dies."

Peter says, "Okay, here we go."

* * *

A few weeks later, the scholarly-looking Rob Pattullo, a Harvard government grad who somehow has wound up an associate director in television news, is in an ABC elevator going down. Down beneath the well-lighted newsroom, down below the control room where his boss, the legendary Charlie Heinz holds forth directing traffic, way way down into the subterranean vaults of the building, he gets off on level-C and heads for the tape rooms.

Pattullo enters Tape 1, a cramped, noisy, smoky, windowless space with six large videotape machines, their reels spinning, their monitors going full blast. A dozen people are working inside. Motionless as statues, some watch the screens and adjust the dials, while others rush back and forth shouting at the top of their lungs. From down here, eighty percent of the evening's newscast will be fed up into the control room and then out across America.

If the crowd upstairs in the Bubble is, by and large, your basic bleached, clean cut and upwardly mobile gang, downstairs here in steerage it's more of a mixed bag. In addition to the young and serious Pattullo, the other person in charge of orchestrating Tape 1's controlled chaos this evening is the operations producer, Amy Katz.

Katz is a slim, dark-haired, thin-faced, wired woman in a long print dress and a Bohemian necklace of multicolored strands of beads. She seems to give off sparks even when sitting, which she doesn't do often. In perpetual motion, she works the phones, the tape machines, or the nearest ear with a no-nonsense, scatalogical bluntness. Then there are the raffish editors, like the olive-skinned Bobby, in sneakers and casual green tee shirt, a gold chain around his neck, a mustache on his lip, a stud in his ear. Or heavy-set Paul, his shirt hanging outside his pants because there's not much room inside for anything else but Paul. Or Raymond, of the scraggly beard, who might have done tuba for Sergeant Pepper.

Pattullo is working with Paul on the tape machines numbered 51 and 52, trying to get a long piece on clean air ready to roll in an hour. The "World News Tonight" has been a leader in discussing environmental issues, which the program usually covers in its "American Agenda" segment. This piece is the same Ned Potter story that Charlie Heinz had been working on more than three weeks ago. After all this time, if they can't finally put its multiple parts together tonight, it may be a future without a future. Right now, Pattullo isn't convinced that it's going to happen. "If this doesn't air tonight," he announces, "I'm going to kill myself."

Up on the monitor of 52 appears a face wearing a surgical mask and gown, and a voice booms out, "Doctors think 50,000 Americans a year die prematurely because of the fumes. That is why a new clean air bill is so urgent." The fumes in the room make it seem even more so.

Pattullo says, "That's a lot better than it was." He asks Wally, another editor, to check the edit.

"Caren," Katz calls across the room, having just picked up the ringing phone. "Washington's on three."

"What?" shouts associate producer Caren Zucker, who's working in the far corner.

"You want me to take it?" Katz shouts back, and she does.

Pattullo yells, "The edit work, Wally?" Wally nods.

Thus far in the day there have been three versions of the lineup, the listing of the stories that will probably be used for this evening's 6:30 PM broadcast, but the lineup is subject to sudden dramatic changes. "The rundown is best thought of as a useful fiction," Pattullo says. The last version appeared at 14:44 and contained a short-title list of the stories, their running time, the correspondents who did them, and where each will be originating from. All of today's material will be fed from either New York or Washington, even the piece on Britain's long, hot summer that is scheduled to conclude the program.

Tonight, Bettina Gregory's account of the crash of the United DC-10 in Sioux City, Iowa, will open the broadcast. Then comes John McWethy from Washington with 1:45 on new developments in the Felix Bloch spy case. It was McWethy who first broke the Bloch story last week. Then Bob Zelnick from the Pentagon for one minute and fifteen seconds, followed by Jim Wooten at the Capitol. Gary Shepard updates the Exxon Valdez oil-cleanup mess and Al Dale reports on the UAW vote at the Nissan plant in Tennessee and, if all goes well, then comes the Ned Potter piece for "American Agenda." Rounding out the program on a lighter note is Britain's unusually hot summer. It's a crowded slate.

In order to make it a bit less crowded, Paul Friedman has called Amy Katz and asked her to cut down Laurence's piece on the British heat wave. He's already notified London that he plans to "scrunch" it, and gives her the two cuts he'd like her to make.

"Cut them out completely? Okay, okay," she tells him, and slams down the receiver. It's only 5:50. No need to rush. There's plenty of time, forty minutes. But long before they hit air, she knows she'll be flying. "I need 54," she says, claiming the tape machine beside the two Rob Pattullo is working on. "Let's get going, Bobby," she tells the guy in the green tee shirt. "The boss called. He wants two things cut out of this." In one fluid movement, Bobby throws the tape on 54 and flips the switch. Taking a drag on his cigarette, he looks up at the monitor. The sign on the wall above his head says, "No Smoking."

"Can this be England? Cold, gray, damp, foggy old England? Transformed by some quirk of nature's mischief into warm, sunny, tropical England. It's already the warmest English summer in thirteen years...."

Katz adjusts her glasses and checks the stop watch in her hand. In front of 52 and 56 and 57, other hands are also holding stopwatches as they work. Except for the absence of fresh air down here, it could be the morning line at Belmont. "Bobby," she says, "do me a favor. Go back to that first lady. The lady in the bathing suit." He turns the dial and the lady in the bathing suit rushes back to the screen. Amy cuts eight seconds after the bathing suit and sixteen more a little further on. "So eight and sixteen," she jots down the numbers just to be sure. "It's 24. That'll bring it in on time at 2:01." She snatches up the phone and punches in Friedman's number on "The Rim" upstairs, to tell him that it's done. "Paul? Amy—"

"That's a buy!" Pattullo calls, finally satisfied with the Potter piece. He can hardly believe that the damn thing might actually make it this evening. He waits till Katz is off the phone and says, "I'm finished. We're going to dub it on 53." He already has two copies of Potter, but wants to protect himself by making still one more. After the amount of time and work that everyone has put in on this story, he doesn't want to have anything screw up now.

With less than thirty minutes to go before air, two new problems develop. The satellite feed from Atlanta is coming in with lots of static, and the feed from Valdez, Alaska, isn't coming in at all. Snatching up the phone, Katz calls Valdez.

"I'll call satellite," says Pattullo, and speaks to the satellite desk upstairs.

"What's satellite saying?" Katz demands.

Pattullo shouts at the top of his lungs, "SATELLITE SAYS, 'WE'RE DEALING WITH ALASKA. WE CAN'T TALK TO YOU NOW.'" Lowering his voice, he adds, "I'm on hold."

Katz says, "I'm going to call about Atlanta."

Still holding, Pattullo lifts his eyes skyward and says, "We're failing here."

"It's Amy Katz at 'World News,'" she calls into the phone, urgently. "We have two major problems that I really want you to help me with."

By the time the final lineup, printed at 6:07 PM on long pink sheets, comes through the door, the man upstairs, Paul Friedman, has delivered his edict: scrap Shepard's 1:20 Valdez story and replace it with a Peter

Jenning's twenty-second summary of the material. The Nissan story is still very much a go and scheduled to fill up 2:25 of the broadcast.

But now it's 6:14 and there's still static in the transmission of the Nissan story from Atlanta. "I'm getting real nervous," admits Katz, and picks up the phone to call their Atlanta bureau.

"Who's talking to Atlanta?" Pattullo wants to know.

"I am," Katz shouts. "I have Bill Henzel in my ear."

"Does Atlanta think there's a problem outgoing?" he asks.

"Tape!" Katz picks up the shrieking phone and puts it to her other ear. Paul Friedman is back on the line. He wants to know what's happening with the Nissan story. Handing Atlanta to John, an assistant, she tells the boss, "We've got a major crisis down here." They may not be able to get an ungarbled version of their Nissan story from Atlanta in time for the broadcast.

Pattullo yells, "Group W say's it's coming in like that. What does Atlanta say?"

"They're checking now," says John, loosening his tie.

Pattullo tells him, "I want them to take it back to the top. Let's get something going here."

John announces that Atlanta will be back to them in a few minutes.

"Okay," Pattullo says. "I'll give them a couple of minutes. About two!" He turns to Katz and says irritably, "Everybody is going to call in two minutes. That's like everybody's one edit away. Mother told me there'd be days like this."

All at once the phones begin ringing all around the room, howling like unattended babies. "Oh fuck!" cries Katz, who wants to call Paul Friedman upstairs on the Rim, "will somebody let me have a phone?"

The news from Group W is that the static problem is definitely originating in Atlanta. With ten minutes to go before air, Pattullo calls to the burly Raymond who's watching 54. "They're switching microwaves [setting up a new video transmission route at the last minute], Raymond. Doesn't that make your heart go pitty pat?"

In addition to being used in ovens, microwaves are also employed for short-range communication links. ABC obviously has a defective one somewhere along the line that needs to be replaced. Raymond turns on the Atlanta feed and, following a breathless half second of velvety silence, there again is the static and hiss.

"Shit!"

"Well," Katz demands furiously, "what's Atlanta doing to help?"

Pattullo tells her, "They switched microwave paths, and it's just as bad."

"WAAAAAAAHHHHH!" she wails, and raises her fists as if she's about to pound her desk into toothpicks.

Suddenly up on the monitor screen appear the numbers 5, 4, 3, 2, 1, accompanied by a series of limpidly clear signal beeps.

"There!" says Raymond. "Now—"

"Now they've switched paths," says Pattullo.

"Now it's working," Katz says. "Right?"

"Just outside of Nashville," correspondent Al Dale begins on tape, his rich baritone voice cured of electronic infection, all the scratchy static gone.

"Yeah, we've got it!" shouts an ecstatic Pattullo.

"—in the middle of rolling farmland a huge Nissan auto plant turns out more than a quarter of a million cars and trucks a year."

Katz grabs a phone. Before dialing the Rim, she calls to Raymond whose eyes are fixed on the monitor. "It's fine now Ray, right? It was a bad microwave?" Raymond nods without turning. "Hi," Katz reports upstairs, the relief showing in her voice, "now we're all right. It was a bad microwave. Okay. Thanks."

On the monitor, Al Dale is explaining, "But the billion dollar Japanese investment has become a battlefield. Twenty-four hundred of the plant workers are the prize—."

According to Pattullo, the last ten or fifteen minutes before air can get to be "a tragic situation." If the editing isn't finished or, equally bad, if Pattullo doesn't know which stories are on which of his six tape machines and the order in which they will flow, he's in big trouble. "I've got to get my ducks in a row," is the way he puts it. "Where am I going to play back my pieces from." Tonight he lines up Gregory on 54, Dale and Potter on 53, on 58 he'll roll the opening logo, on 54....

As Pattullo passes the information up to Charlie Heinz in the control room, Peter Jennings appears on several monitors. He quickly sits down at the anchor desk and begins to go over his script. It's 6:27. Behind him, the writer-producer Milt Weiss can be seen brushing off Jennings' jacket.

Over the speaker comes a calm resonant voice from the control room, "58, we'll get a start any moment."

"One minute! One minute!" cries Katz.

"On with the show," Paul says.

"Ten," announces the speaker, alerting everyone to the final ten seconds before air.

Pattullo counts them down and cries, "Hit it!"

The tympani rolls with preludial drama and over the opening graphic a commanding voice booms, "FROM ABC, THIS IS WORLD NEWS TONIGHT WITH PETER JENNINGS."

"Good evening," Jennings says, leaping into the news, "we begin tonight...."

After Gregory on the United plane crash and while the McWethy update on the Felix Bloch story is rolling, the control room calls down the next sequence of tape machines as if announcing commuter trains leaving Grand Central. "55 will be next. Shortly after that 58. Shortly after that 48 and 41 with the first commercials."

No sooner has McWethy finished than Jennings appears on screen to add something that's not in the lineup. "Just another note about the Bloch case, which was first revealed on this broadcast last Friday. In that first report, we simulated a transaction which our intelligence sources told us had taken place between Bloch and a known Soviet agent. We did not label that simulation as clearly or as quickly as we should have. It was a production error. We're sorry, and if anyone was misled we'll try to see that this doesn't happen again."

"In a moment," he concludes, "the United Auto Workers trying to unionize a Japanese car factory."

Above Katz's desk are three small monitors, like windows on a slot machine, tuned to NBC, CBS and ABC. On the three screens, Tom, Dan and Peter are going head to head. Above Peter's shoulder a box contains the word "Nissan." A few seconds later a similar "Nissan" box pops up over Tom's shoulder. If another Nissan box rolls up above Dan's, it's the jackpot. As it turns out, CBS doesn't get around to its Nissan story for a few minutes. Despite the world of news available, it's not at all uncommon to have all three newscasts airing the very same story, and doing so at the very same time.

But the particular environmental story that Ned Potter has written is not likely to be duplicated elsewhere. "Camelshump Mountain in Vermont," Potter begins, as the satellite pictures appear of the mountain top then and now. "The clouds that roll in here carry sulphur, lead, and more—" Pattullo keeps eyeing the monitor to make sure the four-minute story is actually all in one piece, and it seems to be.

By the time it's over and Potter is signing off, Pattullo looks as if a great burden has been lifted from him. Smiling, he turns to Raymond. "I thought it came together," he congratulates the editor. Pattullo can't quite believe it himself.

Raymond nods in agreement. "Yeah. Absolutely."

When Laurence's London heat wave has run its course and while Peter Jennings is saying goodnight, a voice from the control room upstairs thunders over the intercom. It's Charlie Heinz, delivering a benediction: "Thank you all very much. Excellent job!"

After the 7:00 feed, a group gathers around Amy Katz's desk to talk about Jennings' apology on the Felix Bloch simulation affair. One assistant mentions the articles in *The Washington Post* and *The Philadelphia Inquirer* that criticize ABC for its use of simulation. Katz says, "At the ten o'clock meeting Paul told us to be careful in the future about labeling."

In defense of ABC against its critics, Pattullo mentions the kind of thing NBC is planning to do on its new program, "Yesterday, Today and Tomorrow."

"That's dramatization, not simulation," Katz points out.

"Even worse," Pattullo says.

"But," says Caren Zucker, "that's not the evening news. It's prime-time. I don't think there's any place on the evening news for simulations." She is categorical, absolute, separating good and evil with the definitiveness of the Book of Genesis. For the first time that evening, there's a silence in the tape room.

RATINGS: Week ending June 30th

1st. Rather   ("CBS Evening News")—8.7/20 [7,864,800]

2nd. Jennings (ABC's "World News Tonight")—8.6/20 [7,774,400]

3rd. Brokaw   ("NBC Nightly News")—8.2/19 [7,412,800]

CHAPTER THIRTEEN

Simulations and Re-creations

The debate taking place in the ABC tape room that evening was just one of many across the country. It had grown out of one incident: In late July, the ABC investigative news team and reporter John McWethy learned that the FBI and the U.S. State Department were investigating Felix Bloch, formerly a senior diplomat at the U.S. embassy in Vienna, for allegedly passing secrets to the Soviets. It was a valuable scoop, perhaps even a major national story—so important, in fact, that in addition to Peter Jennings and Paul Friedman, even ABC News president Roone Arledge had gotten involved.

"I spent a large part of the day on the phone with the State Department, trying to verify facts," Arledge recalls. On certain facts, Arledge acceded to State Department requests. "We agreed not to report where the meeting took place. Instead of Paris, we said 'a European city.'"

Also left out, because of FBI concerns, was the fact that Bloch was potentially suicidal. But the meat of the story was strong, a major U.S. diplomat allegedly spying for the Soviets. And as Peter Jennings led off the program on Friday, July 21, he had every expectation that the Bloch exclusive would score just the kind of victory on which news organizations pride themselves. Instead, it turned out to be a fiasco.

"We begin with a harsh reminder that secrecy sells," Jennings opened that night. Viewers first saw generic black and white street scenes (shot for "Nightline"), complete with crosshairs and electronic time code, then a grainy, fuzzy image of Felix Bloch handing a briefcase to a Soviet agent. Only it wasn't Bloch, and it wasn't a Soviet agent. It was a simulation, a fake, complete with actors. Yet nowhere, as the image ran for ten seconds, was it labeled "simulation." John McWethy, watching on a monitor from his stand-up location at the State Department, spotted the error and frantically called the Washington control room. But it was too late. Only the second feed, for viewers who get ABC News at 7:00 PM, was correctly labeled.

Roone Arledge, leaving early for the weekend after a day on the phone, never even saw the actual broadcast. He had set his VCR to record, but he had been having problems with the machine, and that evening it didn't work. So it wasn't until Monday morning, arriving at the office, that he became aware of the brouhaha. ABC had aired contrived images about *alleged* facts—a double sin—and newspapers, magazines and pundits across the country were howling for blood. Former CBS News president Fred Friendly spoke of "a fraud perpetrated by ABC News."

The New York Times editorialized: "The fakery insulted viewers, ethics and journalism...[Bloch] has not been charged. Yet ABC has come close to convicting him; seeing the footage, an unwary viewer might think ABC had caught Mr. Bloch in the act....Doctoring the news threatens ABC's credibility and erodes public trust in journalism."

And former NBC News head Reuven Frank stated: "They now subscribe to the gospel of do anything for an audience. It's marvelous for drama. For news, it's lies."

In fact, the image wasn't a *lie* exactly. It was more a blunder, a stupid mistake. Originally, the picture of Bloch and the Soviet was supposed to have been an artist's drawing, like a courtroom sketch, or a cartoon, with "Spy vs. Spy" type figures. But on July 21, ABC's artists were tied up on other projects. So, with time passing rapidly that afternoon, the production staff in Washington, which is always having to cope with pictureless stories on government reports, turned to an alternate idea: Take a Polaroid of ABC staffers passing a brief case, then run it through the machinery known as a "Paintbox," which can electronically alter an image. In this case, the idea was to transform the picture into an obvious artist's rendition.

The Polaroid image *was* run through the Paintbox. Some edges *were* blurred. And the ABC staffer playing Bloch, who had a full head of hair, ended up like Kojak. But under deadline pressure, as the Washington staff crashed to make their 6:31 airtime, nothing more was changed. The image wasn't sufficiently distorted. And with an acting senior producer in charge in Washington who wasn't completely familiar with the operation, and a staff in New York that hadn't been alerted to the potential problem, and that didn't know that the Bloch footage wasn't real, a very realistic looking picture ended up going out on the air.

It was a comedy, or as Arledge put it, "a tragedy of errors." Not a deliberate deception at all, but as the ABC News chief later said, it was "a violation of every one of our standards." In the aftermath, ABC personnel received reprimand letters, and new guidelines were written to ensure that the president of ABC News himself, and not just a producer, would have to sign off on such decisions.

If the ABC incident ignited a firestorm of criticism, if it served, in Roone Arledge's words, as "a field day...for deposed ex-network news presidents, who, generally speaking, have nothing to do," if in short this tiny ten-second glitch got everyone monumentally upset, it was because the incident seemed to epitomize a trend. News programs had previously aspired to be pristine—showing actual footage or nothing at all—but in 1989, there was a new movement afoot, a movement towards playing fast and loose with the facts. The Bloch episode was a goof, but more and more news or "reality-based" programs (like "America's Most Wanted" and "A Current Affair") were, as a matter of course, purposely blurring the line between reality and drama by using re-creations.

What precisely are re-creations? The debate about them has been loud and messy and confused, but the facts are surprisingly simple. Television tells stories through pictures. The question is. What to do when there aren't any pictures? What if there's a story to tell, but no camera was present on the scene? Enter the reenactment.

Re-creations. Reconstructions. Reenactments. Simulations. They are all just different words for the same thing: faking it. If there's no actual footage, create your own (using technology, or more often, actors).

Proponents say that if a network has done all the reporting, if it has the facts, if all that's missing are the images, what's wrong with re-creating them? What's wrong with simply illustrating the facts that are known?

Opponents say that TV news has a unique contract with its viewers. By showing actual footage, TV news allows viewers themselves to be eyewitnesses to events. That's the contract. If you see it on the evening news, you know the events really happened. But with a re-creation, who knows? It's not so much that producers would utterly fabricate a whole story, although that could happen, but that, in a quest for extra drama or pizzazz, all sorts of subtle changes can creep in that distort the story. And then, how can anyone tell what's fact and what's fiction? These issues were widely debated through much of 1989. Some producers called re-creations "a natural step in broadcast news." Others called the notion a travesty.

Surprisingly, reenactments are nothing new. In the mid-1950s, Walter Cronkite had hosted a show called "You Are There." It was a history lesson as news program. Ranging back through the centuries, "You Are There" reconstructed events from the Boston Tea Party to the final hours of Joan of Arc. Actors playing Jesse James, John Dillinger, Amelia Earhart were interviewed by reporters. A hokey notion, entirely built around re-creations, but no one screamed with righteous indignation in those days.

Many producers in 1989, like NBC's Sid Feders, felt that reenactments were "an idea whose time has come." They looked at the ratings for shows like "America's Most Wanted," which re-constructed crimes using actors. They looked at the cheap costs of producing news versus the expenses of primetime entertainment programs, roughly twice as much. And they investigated the big-money success of primetime news shows like "60 Minutes." And so, in the fall of 1989, two news magazine programs, leaning heavily on recreations, were born, NBC's "Yesterday, Today and Tomorrow," and CBS's "Saturday Night With Connie Chung."

"Yesterday, Today and Tomorrow" ("YTT"), calling itself "an electronic time machine," went back to re-create the murder that led to the birth of fingerprinting, and the story of a young woman wrongly locked up in a mental institution. "Saturday Night," for its part, reconstructed the lives of a civil rights leader and a fourteen-year-old crack dealer. Actors portrayed everyone from Abbie Hoffman to hostage Terry Anderson.

An important distinction to bear in mind is that these programs were not the evening news. They were primetime, hour-long shows. "YTT" and "Saturday Night" were, however, being run, at least in part, by network news divisions. And for many critics, these programs constituted a corrupting influence on the whole news process. Despite ABC's glitch (or perhaps because of it), Roone Arledge lashed out at such programs, saying that re-creations "are very dangerous for a news division." "Saturday Night" was mocked as the only CBS News show with a casting director and auditions. And NBC's gimmicky "YTT" was blasted for having hosts who meandered from past to present to future, doomed to wander forever in some Twilight Zone between reality and fiction.

On "YTT," the line between actual footage and reconstruction was so blurred that at one screening, an NBC producer exclaimed, "What a good simulation! How did you set that up?," only to be told, "That's not simulated—that's real!" NBC staffers began to wonder whether there should also be identifying subtitles stating "This is real."

Around NBC, staff members took to calling the show "Yesterday and Today," because for this program, there would be no tomorrow. Faced with strong critical pressure and audience indifference, "YTT" was scrapped. By the end of the year, "Saturday Night," after internally deciding to ban re-constructions, still managed to limp along. Re-creations had been dealt a decisive setback.

These days the problem of what's actual footage and what's simulated has taken on an extra twist, because the technology now exists to alter video images electronically. Granted, the process is prohibitively expensive, but computers now can generate entirely new images or drastically rearrange old ones. Imagine: not only can President Bush's jacket be changed from blue to green, but he can be placed on the grassy knoll in Dallas, holding a rifle. The technology exists. The possibilities are endless, and scary. Like the field of medicine, with its test-tube babies, the technology of video has outpaced the accompanying ethics.

The whole debate stems from the terms of the contract—that what TV viewers see on the evening news did in fact happen exactly as presented. Which is why, in September of 1989, when the *New York Post* claimed that CBS had aired faked footage from Afghanistan in its 1984 segments on the "CBS Evening News" titled "Operation: Black Out," another major controversy erupted. The *Post* claimed freelance cameraman Mike Hoover's film of mujahadeen sabotaging high-tension electrical wires and later fleeing their villages had all been staged for the benefit of the camera. The real events had allegedly happened days earlier.

The *Post* pointed the finger squarely at Dan Rather: RATHER AIRED FAKE AFGHAN BATTLES screamed the headlines. Rather *had* aggressively pursued coverage of the Soviet/Afghan conflict ever since his days at "60 Minutes," when he had donned mountain garb and walked miles through Afghanistan's hill country to talk with the rebels. But just as then, when he was mockingly called "Gunga Dan," some of the accusations seemed mean-spirited and misguided. Rather thought Afghanistan was a big story, a poorly covered story—like Vietnam, the Soviet Union's unwinnable war. He pushed hard for more coverage. But no proof has ever been offered to show that he condoned or encouraged fakery. The *Post's* charge was, in short, a cheap shot.

The only grounds on which critics could legitimately attack Rather concerned his role as managing editor, or gate-keeper. If he was wearing the title of managing editor, then he would have to bear the responsibility for whatever happened on his show. As Peter Jennings said, "What gets put out there every evening has my stamp on it....Therefore, you take responsibility for what goes on the air. The audience doesn't blame McWethy for what goes wrong. They blame me."

In the end, Dan Rather, like Peter Jennings, was cleared. An internal investigation at CBS came to the conclusion that the charges of fakery were "simply not true." But since David Burke, the secretive CBS News head, never made the details public, viewers had to take Burke's word for it. Cameraman Mike Hoover later stated that the *Post's* two sources weren't even in Afghanistan at the time he was filming and declared himself the victim of "vicious infighting" between rival Afghan factions. Some who knew Hoover, however, were dubious.

The important lesson anchors Peter Jennings and Dan Rather had to draw from their respective contretemps in July and September/October of 1989—besides the fact that in any scandal they are the biggest targets— was that viewers are genuinely still concerned about the contract. The television news audience wants to be absolutely certain that what they're seeing really happened.

A brief postscript: recently, following an episode of "America's Most Wanted" in which a dangerous fugitive from the law was described, alert citizens seized and arrested the man whose face they recognized from the program. He turned out to be the actor who played the part.

RATINGS: Week ending July 21st

1st. Rather   ("CBS Evening News")—9.3/20 [8,407,200]

2nd. Jennings (ABC's "World News Tonight")—9.2/20 [8,316,800]

3rd. Brokaw   ("NBC Nightly News")—8.6/19 [7,774,400]

CHAPTER FOURTEEN

Crash and Burn at NBC

The crash of a Korean Air DC-10 with over two hundred passengers aboard is the lead story on the CBS 6:00 news this July morning. The crash occurred only three miles short of the Tripoli airport in Libya. It's much too early to determine cause, but there was heavy fog at the time of the accident and some indication of engine trouble from the plane. Early reports indicate that a number of people survived, including the pilot.

The first pictures that arrive in America are from the Libyan Press Service, JANA. Fed to New York via satellite from Eurovision, they begin to appear on NBC's "Sunrise" and "Today." It looks bad.

Earlier this morning as soon as the Foreign Desk at "NBC Nightly News" learned of the crash, Stephen Frazier, a young correspondent, was dispatched from the Rome bureau to cover the story. Given the six-hour difference between New York and Rome, Frazier missed the regular Alitalia flight that leaves every morning for Tripoli at 10:20. He quickly arranged to charter a plane to make the two-hour trip across the Mediterranean. He didn't quite know what to expect, or even if the Libyan authorities would let him anywhere near the crash site. But what counts for any reporter is to get there before the competition.

4:35 PM, New York time, and at NBC headquarters, Frank Shanbacker is pacing the halls. Shanbacker—"that's beautiful baker in German," he'll tell you—doesn't look anything like a baker. With his trim white beard and neatly combed blonde hair, the thin-faced, sensitive Shanbacker looks more like a professor of English (the subject of his Masters degree at NYU) than any roller of dough. But he dresses better than either baker or prof. Shanbacker began his career at the network in 1970 as an usher for the NBC Tours. It was in 1979, when Paul Greenberg took over as executive producer of the "Nightly News" (then featuring John Chancellor as anchor), that Shanbacker first joined the program's staff as a tape producer. Today, in addition to being a producer, Shanbacker is the tape production coordinator for "Nightly News" in New York.

All afternoon, Shanbacker reviews the satellite pictures relayed from Europe that continue to stream into NBC headquarters. They show the crash site and the survivors in nearby hospitals. From NBC's Tokyo bureau, he receives pictures of the Korean passengers' friends and family waiting for news back home. By late afternoon, he's collected five tape cassettes and using the time code printed on each video frame—thirty frames rush by in a second—as a reference point, he's logged in the principal images on a yellow legal pad. It's clear to Shanbacker that Steve Frazier may not make it back to Rome in time for the broadcast. Even if he does, he may arrive empty handed because of problems with the Libyan officials. With less than two hours to air, Shanbacker and "Nightly News" executive producer, Bill Wheatley, agree that they need a backup for their lead story. When the 4:55 lineup for the evening's program comes out, the decision has been made that the crash story will be handled by both Frazier from Rome and Stan Bernard in New York.

At 5:30, Bill Catalano—one of the nine full-time New York-based editors for the "Nightly News"—is sitting in EJ-3, a tiny room on the fourth floor of Rockefeller Center, reading the sports section of the paper. Although crowded with electronic editing equipment, Catalano's windowless cubicle seems as peaceful as a monk's cell. Occasionally he'll glance up at the silent monitor in front of him on which the Mets are struggling with Pittsburgh in the rain. The other monitors are all showing test patterns. Catalano has worked for NBC for sixteen years and has seen the change from film to tape:

"It was about 1976, and it happened gradually with maybe a five year overlap. Now with tape everything is speeded up."

But even with tape you can't wait forever, and there's only fifty-eight minutes to air time.

The phone rings. "Yeah," Catalano says into the receiver, "I'm getting ready to go nuts here. I've got a piece to go on air in less than an hour, and I still don't have anything." Catalano is accustomed to tight deadlines, but being this late with the lead story, thank goodness, doesn't happen every day. Across the hall, the sign above the door to another editing room might just as well be hanging over EJ-3. It reads "Mental Ward."

Suddenly, Frank Shanbacker is at Catalano's door. "I just got a call. Frazier's on his way back to Rome with material. He'll be there at 5:35. We should have it by six."

"How do we know that he's going to be back at 5:35?"

"We don't," says Shanbacker, running out.

Over the years, Catalano has proven that he can work under pressure. Both he and Tim Gibney are editors whom Shanbacker feels he can rely on in a tight spot, but Catalano doesn't particularly enjoy being squeezed. He would much prefer to have the time to use dissolves instead of harsh cuts, to make certain the audio is equalized, to allow for video gaps in the narration, and, above all, to make sure the over-all pacing of a story is to his liking. Even though this is the news and not "National Geographic Explorer," Catalano aims for work as seamless as glass. "Whenever you're crashing," he says, "there are a lot of things you'd want to change in the piece if you had time. But it gets there."

Out in the hallway, Shanbacker is pacing back and forth, checking his Casio digital watch. "Come on, come on," he mumbles. The phone rings and he lunges for it. "Thanks," he says to the caller, and hangs up. "Frazier's on the ground," Shanbacker reports. " He's about twenty minutes away from the bureau."

Twenty minutes later, just shy of 6:00 PM, the call comes in from Frazier. The correspondent is back at the Rome office, not a minute too soon. Only one problem. He doesn't have any footage. "He went all the way to Libya," says the annoyed Shanbacker, "and the only thing he came back with is a stand-upper. He's done some sort of ten or twenty second bridge on camera. That's all he was able to get." Shanbacker shakes his head. It's Shanbacker's guess that "they probably just let him land at the airport, and didn't let him go anywhere. That's what we were afraid of all day. They had permission to land and that was it."

It's 6:01. Twenty-nine minutes to air. The only reason nobody panics is that Stan Bernard is preparing a backup story and, as Catalano says, "Stan is fast." He'll be using the same pictures that have been coming in all day from Eurovision. But Bernard is still waiting for his piece to be approved by the Foreign Desk editor. Once he has the okay, he'll head for the recording booth down the hall and put his narration on tape. Then the rest is simply cutting the pictures to the track. As people at the networks say with admirable devil-may-care insouciance about most aspects of the television news business, "It's not brain surgery."

Shanbacker has made up his mind. Figuring that the Bernard story will probably be the "Nightly News" lead at 6:30, he's decided to let Bernard work with Catalano. For the 7:00 feed, he hopes to be able to use Frazier's Rome piece if, and it's a big if, he and Gibney can put the thing together in time.

An academic-looking, round faced, middle-aged man appears excitedly at the door with a script in his hand.

"Hi Stan," Shanbacker says. "Ready to track?"

"Ready," says Bernard, having received approval on his script. Shanbacker informs him that Frazier has arrived in the Rome bureau. "I know, I know," says Bernard, not waiting to hear any more as he hurries out the door on his way to the audio room.

Catalano, who up to this point has been merely biding his time, suddenly swings into action, swiveling around to his audio machine and punching in information with big-league concentration. The moment he hears Stan Bernard's voice on the mike, he snaps, "Give me a quick voice level."

"Let me catch my breath," gasps Bernard. "I've ...I've reordered some of the paragraphs," he explains, before he begins.

Another voice, Tim Gibney's, booms out from the speaker, informing Shanbacker that Frazier's material has arrived by satellite from Rome. "I've got the stand-upper, Frank."

"I've got to go," he tells Catalano, and racing out the door, hangs a ninety degree left and sprints down the hall to EJ-10, a somewhat larger windowless room where Tim Gibney sits before his bank of editing and audio machines, ready to "crash" the story for the deadline. Although he's been working for NBC News for twenty-seven years, Gibney—in his striped polo shirt and Reeboks—seems much younger than his long experience suggests. Only the half-glasses perched on the end of his nose hint at presbyopia and middle age. He began in 1961 as a film editor. "We were all film editors originally, most of us anyway." Then about eleven years ago NBC went to tape and everything accelerated. "It's a living," he says wryly, but it's clear he relishes the beat-the-deadline challenge. "Yeah," he shrugs, "I love it."

Shanbacker points to the cassettes on the table that contain all the pictures they have of the crash from Tripoli and the reaction to news of it back in Korea. "The tape that's going to have most of what we'll use, Tim, is 1. You should have 1, 2, 3, 4, 5."

He checks to see and nods. "Absolutely."

Shanbacker snatches up the ringing phone. "Yes, okay. We'll do our best."

Steven Frazier's stand-upper lasts only nineteen seconds and shows him in front of what looks to be a control tower, but there's no visual indication that it's in Tripoli. It could be a tower on the moon. Suddenly Frazier's voice is heard saying, "Go to the top. Three, Two, One. 'The fog in Tripoli was so thick rescuers had trouble seeing what they were hosing down. The plane hit the ground short of the runway and to the left, leaving a trail of small pieces as it ripped through two houses and parked cars. Most of the debris caught fire. Hundreds of rescuers rushed to help....They carried away dozens of survivors, including the pilot, who said he lost contact with the control tower fifteen minutes before the crash.'" Including the stand-up, the entire story that Frazier's narrated from Rome lasts only a minute and thirty seconds.

"All right," Shanbacker says. Checking the notes in which he's listed the time code of the principal video images he thinks he'll need, he tells Gibney that he wants cassette number 1, frame 06-05-11. The editor slams in the cassette and the tape whirls to 06-05-11. Out of the fog comes the tail of a plane with a South Korean flag painted on it. "That shot," says Shanbacker, indicating the picture that he wants. "But go ahead. There's a better, wider shot coming up. This one here. Yeah...." Frazier repeats, "They carried away dozens of survivors."

Shanbacker says, "Okay, now we definitely go to the bodies." He calls off another number, and Gibney sends the tape backwards into a paroxysm of high-pitched electronic gibberish. People appear and carry bodies out of the debris.

"There," Shanbacker says, "there's your basic stretcher shot." Frazier repeats, "Including the pilot who said he lost contact with the control tower fifteen minutes before the crash."

The large clock on the wall reads 6:17. A short white-haired staffer with glasses and a worried look comes in, and bending over between Gibney and Shanbacker, he asks softly, "You going to make it?"

Shanbacker says, "We'll try, Sandy. I can't guarantee it." Then turning to Gibney he says, "Now we go to the stand-upper."

Frazier's voice booms out, "But the cause of the crash isn't clear yet....Stephen Frazier, NBC News, Tripoli." They continue going over the tape and inserting pictures of friends of the victims in Korea and a close-up of the engine. "Where the fuck is 5?" growls the editor, as he hunts for the cassette his boss wants that contains a shot of the nose cone. When they're finished, Shanbacker looks up at the clock and notes with relief that it's only 6:28.

He picks up the phone. "Hi. We'll make it. It's 1:33, but we'd like to add some things for the second show. Maybe we can open it up a little bit with the people crying and weeping and a few other little things."

The word comes back over the line: They've beaten the other team, Bernard and Catalano. Shanbacker cries, "You're kidding! Did we?" He can hardly believe it. "And those guys were plan A." He's exultant. "Fantastic!" he says, "Fan-*tas*-tic!"

"Now," Shanbacker says, "we've got to go back and see what we can do to make it better." For the 7:00 show, he and Gibney open the story up by dropping in pictures of the pilot in his hospital bed, the firemen with their hoses, and a snippet from Seoul showing the Koreans weeping for the more than seventy passengers who died. Later, while watching the beginning of the second feed, Shanbacker gets a message of congratulations from Dave Miller, the newly appointed NBC deputy for foreign news. "We were the only network with a reporter on the scene," he tells Gibney. They look at one another and exchange smiles. Somehow you don't feel quite so tired when you crash and don't burn.

Clearly, Shanbacker and Gibney, two NBC pros, had busted their peacock tails in order to give Tom Brokaw's "Nightly News" and its millions of viewers something better than the competition offered. But what in fact did Steve Frazier's presence in Tripoli actually add to our knowledge of the Korean plane crash?

Alas, the answer is very little. Frazier never even got to the crash site. Except for his nineteen seconds in front of the control tower, all the pictures finally used in the Libya story had been sent to New York much earlier in the day by Eurovision. Had there not been big hopes for fresh video from the crash site, Stan Bernard could have had his story finished in plenty of time to make the evening newscast. As it turned out, the Bernard piece—though finished and perfectly fine— was never aired.

Network news has always been a wasteful business, and it inevitably remains so even under the new belt-tightening, Argus-eyed management of GE, Cap Cities and Tisch. In an instance such as the Tripoli crash of the Korean DC-10, it was essential that NBC, if it had any desire to be taken seriously as a major newsgathering organization, dispatch a correspondent and camera crew to Libya as soon as it learned of the event. Unfortunately, all it could count on in doing so was a hefty bill for expenses. If not for the outstanding teamwork of Frank Shanbacker and Tim Gibney, that would have been all NBC got.

Call it a pyrrhic victory then for this season's also-rans in the network news derby, an odd sort of success in the competition born of the ratings game. For even though absolutely nothing came of Frazier's North African excursion in the way of hard news, he was, as Dave Miller proudly noted, "the only...reporter on the scene."

RATINGS: Week ending July 28th

1st.   Rather   ("CBS Evening News")—9.0/20 [8,136,000]

2nd. Jennings (ABC's "World News Tonight")—8.8/19 [7,955,200]

3rd.   Brokaw   ("NBC Nightly News")—8.6/19 [7,774,400]

CHAPTER FIFTEEN

What's Wrong with the News?

For all NBC's satisfaction, what Stephen Frazier's fleeting presence in Tripoli had actually produced was not newsgathering at all. It was the illusion of newsgathering—the illusion of having a hard-working reporter collecting information on the scene, when in fact he was only doing the briefest of cameos. Over the past two or three years, the distinction between news and the illusion of news has been getting more and more muddled. And this confusion is just one of the many flaws of network news.

The very idea of trying to cram the entire world into twenty-two minutes is a little ludicrous. TV news is, after all, like a newspaper that has only one page—the front page. Unquestionably, the newscasts would be better if they were twice as long, but according to everyone in the industry, the chance of getting another half hour, at least in the forseeable future, is somewhere between nil and never. The affiliates are less likely to give up thirty minutes of their lucrative time than Israel's Likkud Party is to part with the West Bank. And the networks themselves, of course, are not likely to sacrifice a valuable swatch of their primetime either.

Given the little time they do have, the three broadcasts manage to do a lot. Somehow, five nights a week, the "CBS Evening News," the "NBC

Nightly News," and ABC's "World News Tonight" succeed in covering a good chunk of the globe. Their ability to get information, and to broadcast it to the public quickly, is impressive indeed. And as for the sheer technological stunt they pull off every night, linking far-flung corners of the planet—often with live coverage—it's absolutely astounding.

Each of the networks prides itself on its investigative reporting, and it has every right to do so. On more than one occasion in the past year, major morning papers had to acknowledge that their source for a particular breaking story was the previous evening's TV news. Among the recent stories broken by the networks were the Felix Bloch spy case, the use of foreign mercenaries in the drug war in Colombia, and the Iraqi attempt to acquire nuclear "triggers."

Then too, when a very big story breaks anywhere in the world, nothing takes you there like television, with the immediacy, the emotional impact, the vividness of its pictures. The saturation coverage of such events—news plus sidebars (or "bounce pieces" as they're called) on political, cultural, economic life—prove both valuable and eye-opening.

But when sixty-four percent of Americans get *most* of their information from television, according to a recent Roper survey, our TV news is just not good enough. Skewed and limited, network news is only fulfilling a small part of its important reponsibility. Even the anchors themelves admit that their newscasts are insufficient to thoroughly inform the public. Peering attentively at the screen, the American couch potato sees the world through a glass darkly.

Lord Marmaduke, head of England's BBC, has to scoff when he looks at American TV news. He shakes his head at the thirst for bad news, especially spectacular bad news, and the penchant for flash over substance: "Body-bag journalism" is what he calls it, and "the bimbo factor." Some of his criticisms apply most accurately to local news, but the shoe fits on national news as well.

The ratings war has placed great pressure on the networks to jazz up their offerings, to be sexy in order to woo viewers. Large audiences, after all, are what bring in the advertising dollars. But the audience for news has recently begun to dwindle away and now, according to Nielsen, hovers just below sixty percent of the viewing households. And yet, at the same time, a mutant hybrid is on the rise—TV tabloid journalism.

Barbara Nevins, a reporter for CBS's local New York affiliate, WCBS, says, "It's a confused picture today. The ratings of traditional news are falling off, but all this 'reality-based programming' ["A Current Affair," "Hard Copy," "Inside Edition"] is booming. For viewers, the question is, 'What's news? What's entertainment?'"

The news executive faced with a shrinking viewership, and the rise of flash and trash tabloid-style journalism, might well wonder, "How can I get those ratings? Maybe I should borrow an element or two from the tabloids?"

Former CBS News president Van Gordon Sauter was, ironically, a little ahead of his time, helping to blur the distinction between news and entertainment with his emphasis on tearjerker scenes that he called "moments." Moments were small, emotion-filled epiphanies, like a starving mother cradling her dead daughter or a farmer looking at his bankrupt farm with tears in his eyes. Moments meant: Facts are fine, but let's have some recognizable "little" people experiencing real emotions. Let's have some of those striking visuals that work so well on TV. To put the point simply: Let's make the news more entertaining. It was Sauter's view that one unshaven guy with his head in his hands was worth fifty unemployment graphs.

"Van keeps saying that we need stories that reach out and touch people," Dan Rather explained to reporter Ron Rosenbaum back in the mid-1980s. In choosing between the war in the Falklands, the decimation of refugee camps in Beirut, and the Princess of Wales having a new baby as the day's lead, guess which story won? "I decided we had to go with the royal baby. On the back-fence principle."

The back-fence principle? "The back-fence principle," Rather said, "is, well, you imagine two neighbor ladies leaning over a back fence at the end of the day and one is asking the other what happened today and you figure out which of your stories they'd most want to know about....today it's going to be what happened with the princess...."

The back-fence principle doesn't sound too different from the "Hey Martha" principle (stories that make a reader say, "Hey Martha, did you hear...?"), which just happens to be the guiding credo of the *National Inquirer*. Irritated with these show-biz imperatives, Charles Kuralt not too long ago lashed out in a speech against the recent "unseemly emphasis on image and flash and tricks of electronics as substitutes for hard fact."

But even when it comes to facts, it's amazing how much the networks routinely *don't* cover. Whole chunks of the globe, whole areas of human life are ghettos into which the network news fears to wander. Dean Joan Konner of the Columbia School of Journalism claims, "that the network news has a very, *very* narrow agenda." She is clearly right.

Most of the peoples of the world are not discussed on the evening news. Name one thing that's happened recently in Scandanavia, or Australia, or India, or anywhere in the entire continent of Africa, *except* white South Africa. Once NBC and ABC had bureaus in Nairobi, Kenya, but both networks abandoned them due to their frustration in getting around the politically and geographically inhospitable continent, and because of the supposed lack of viewer interest. How about the entire Pacific Rim? Aside from a trade dispute or two, we're told surprisingly little about vitally important Japan. Much of the globe is a black hole on TV news.

Many subjects, too, are untouchables. One almost never hears stories from the cultural world: movies or books or plays or music, rock or classical. The visual arts are scarcely mentioned unless a painting has been auctioned off for $82.5 million or stolen. Photography doesn't make the news unless it's labeled obscene. The entire field of science, so crucial in shaping our future and our children's future, is meagerly covered, and only when someone discovers a vaccine, or a worldwide epidemic breaks out, or a rocket blasts off into space with a multibillion dollar telescope. And how about economics, the dollars and cents issues that affect every viewer's pocket money? Sure, there'll be a brief squib on this month's inflation rate, but what about the big questions? What's the story with our national debt? Why did the Savings and Loans industry bite the dust? What exactly is going on with Social Security? It's pretty hard to tell from watching TV.

Perhaps the most significant flaw of all is the networks' inability to handle ideas. The news broadcasts successfully cover facts, like wars and elections. But what about beliefs, values, religions, ways of living and thinking? What about broad trends that affect us all: the way crime is getting worse and worse, the way traffic is getting more and more congested, the way public schools are failing, the increasing disparity between the haves and have nots? "TV is worst," says CBS economics correspondent Robert Krulwich, "at dealing with words and exploring ideas that you can't see."

Perhaps for this reason, the networks have defined TV news not as ideas, but as a series of facts and events. But what shapes those events? No one's giving us the big picture. In this regard, we need more commentary on the news. As of now, only NBC's John Chancellor is fulfilling that function on the evening news, and only three nights a week at best.

Network news has a hard time getting beyond the facts. And the facts presented are shockingly lacking in context: historical, geographical, ideological. We're told that events have occurred: the who, what, when, and where. But what about the why? Why were Iran and Iraq fighting a war for years? What is America's peace plan for the Middle East? And why, exactly, doesn't our criminal justice system work?

It's not that the anchors themselves are unaware of the problem. Dan Rather states: "We do some things marvelously well—we take you there. But television always has trouble with depth. It has trouble with context and perspective, particularly in news programs."

The networks have attempted to broaden their areas of concern. In ABC's "American Agenda," in NBC's "Assignment America" and "Assignment Earth," the broadcasts have been striving to present general issues rather than specific events: how sex education is taught around the world, what drugs do to a small town, how industrial development can lead to pollution. This kind of coverage is an important change for the better, but there's still a long way to go.

Even the stories that are covered are rarely followed up. All too often a piece is reported, only to disappear into the void. What, for example, ever happened to cold fusion? After all the tragedy, what's going on now in Beijing?

One such story that cries out for revisiting is the American invasion of Panama. Our own government no longer controls the news as it initially did with its small pool of approved correspondents. Print journalists have begun to atone for the failure of TV to give a true account of what actually occurred there. If as claimed in the *Los Angeles Times*, four times as many Panamanian civilians were killed as Panamanian soldiers in the course of our invasion, some by alleged misconduct of the U.S. military, then a serious reevaluation of events cannot come too soon. No more appropriate place exists than the evening network news which is seen by millions of viewers.

With so much news going unreported, it's surprising that at 6:30 PM on any given busy news day, the three networks will probably be covering exactly the same stories, and often at exactly the same time. No wonder viewers think all three look the same. They do. At all the networks, editorial decisions are made by people with relatively similar professional backgrounds, and relatively similar definitions of TV news. Washington politics is news. Developing trends across the country are not. There's just no time to cover them.

Time is always seen as the real villain. Just how much can you cram into twenty-two minutes? Stories are jammed down to fit into tiny one and two minute slots. There's only time for seven real stories, and even the biggest will only occasionally exceed three minutes. But how can a newscaster talk seriously about the AIDS epidemic, or America falling behind Japan, or anything really important for that matter, in three minutes? And when the networks consistently use sound bites that are less than ten seconds (during the 1988 election campaign, the bites actually averaged 9.8 seconds, as opposed to over forty seconds in 1968), how can anyone understand certain issues at all? The entire newscast ends up as a rapid-fire barrage that leaves viewers feeling dazed, bewildered and vaguely dissatisfied. They have the illusion of being informed, but all they've really learned is some random assortment of factoids.

Recently, Robert MacNeil had occasion to look at a tape of a Huntley-Brinkley broadcast from the mid-1960s. He found it hard to believe how slow and thoughtful it seemed. According to MacNeil, there were, "no gimmicks, no graphics, no captions to speak of, and the commercials lasted a minute for Salem cigarettes. On and on and on for an entire minute. Nowadays, it seems like a complete movie of someone's life." The individual stories were fewer, and much longer.

MacNeil makes the interesting speculation that in order to get a larger audience and sell more advertising, the networks strove to satisfy the average viewer's allegedly shortened attention span with constant variety and lots of distractions, including the distraction of four commercial breaks. "It's clear to me," he says, "that the whole aesthetic is driven by the length of the commercials, because as commercial time got more valuable, and they squeezed commercials from a minute to thirty seconds to twenty seconds to fifteen, the whole thing speeded up and, of course, the news had to be speeded up too, because it would look slow by comparison with these new commercials."

Despite this speed-up, the continuing limitation of time is still the TV newsman's main enemy. The abiding question: How to pack everything in? With all the stories they don't have time for, with all the stories that could really use an extra minute or two for explanation, with the whole huge range of stories that are *never* covered at all, it comes as a real surprise that the networks choose some of the material they do.

On Thursday, April 20, 1989, for example, the "CBS Evening News" presented one of a seemingly endless number of pieces that they, and their competitors, ran on baseball's Pete Rose. This one was simply a rehash of previously reported information on Rose's gambling, with a new CBS/*New York Times* poll about what the public thought of Rose tacked on. The climax was a clip of the late baseball commissioner, Bart Giamatti, saying "No comment."

CBS ran the piece because they were stuck with the poll, and tried to build something around it. Actually, even for baseball fans, the whole story was a bore. "We got ourselves trapped. We really considered killing the whole thing," CBS executive producer Tom Bettag had to admit. "That Pete Rose thing was a piece of shit." On the same night that this non-story took up time, other pieces—like Jordan's President Hussein dining at the White House with President Reagan, while a bloody riot racked his country back home—couldn't make it onto the air.

Even more puzzling is the way the three networks routinely dedicate fifteen percent of their evening news to square dancers, ventriloquists, ghost towns, and adorable gorillas. The last segment of all three newscasts seems to be designed to send the audience out into the night feeling good, capped by the anchor's smile and "gee whiz." Call them "sayonara" pieces. Soufflé-light, they routinely occupy one-seventh of the entire broadcast.

For several nights running last year, NBC News devoted large segments of its twenty-two minutes of evening news time to the story of a paraplegic mountain climber inching his way up to the top of El Capitan. The multiple segments must have been irresistible to Brokaw, linking as they did his love of climbing with his sentimental attachment to "inspirational" tales. Each evening, "Nightly News" viewers saw the crippled climber in his special harness climb a few more slow, painfully laborious feet closer to the peak. What a news story.

Brokaw talks of himself and his broadcast as "user friendly," a scary phrase at best when applied to the evening news. To be fair to NBC, the other two networks have more than their share of fluff too. And Brokaw and Rather and Jennings all continue to be pushed even further in this direction, because of the entertainment imperative, the misguided belief that these kinds of pieces bring in viewers. They don't seem to realize that most of those who watch the evening news don't watch for this kind of human interest story, and that those who might be attracted by it are not the same audience that turns on the news in the first place.

The pressure to be entertaining is increased under the new corporate ownership. The bean counters are in the saddle, and money is now the name of the game. At journalism's recent duPont Awards Seminar, the three current network news presidents were in perfect harmony about one thing. They were in business to make money. "There's nothing wrong with that," moderator Dean Konner concluded warily, "except when business interests come into conflict with the public interest."

To be in the public interest, the evening news must provide its viewers with accurate and up-to-the-minute information. In doing so, it can be thoughtful, disturbing, provocative, even exciting. The one thing it can't be is entertainment.

Fortunately, there are still some executives like ABC's Roone Arledge who recognize that "there has been a de facto arrangement for a long time that, in return for the use of the public airwaves, the networks would provide programming of a certain quality. The role that the networks have traditionally played in news and public affairs programming is a part of our public responsibility."

But it's obvious that under the new regimes not every network news president feels the same responsibility. NBC's Michael Gartner stated, "I happen to think 'Cheers' serves the public interest in a way, just as 'Nightly News' does and as the Super Bowl does."

At that rate, so does a commercial for 2,000 Flushes.

RATINGS: Week ending August 11th

1st.   Rather   ("CBS Evening News")—9.0/20 [8,136,000]

2nd. Jennings (ABC's "World News Tonight")—8.7/19 [7,864,800]

3rd.   Brokaw   ("NBC Nightly News")—8.3/19 [7,503,200]

CHAPTER SIXTEEN

Rather as Anchor

Dan Rather was nervous. His whole career had been building to this point—the moment when, on March 9, 1981, he would finally walk onto Walter Cronkite's set, sit in Walter Cronkite's chair, and become the anchorman for the "CBS Evening News." But if it was the realization of a dream, if Dan Rather was bursting with pride, he was, on this Monday, much too anxious to savor his triumph.

The question he asked himself—the question that dogged everyone from the senior producers to the desk assistants—was: How do you replace Walter Cronkite, America's most trusted man? How do you take over for the ratings demi-god who has a lock on first place? How do you sit in Uncle Walter's seat?

Dan Rather couldn't bring himself to do it. All weekend long he had been practicing his delivery with a team of producers, but no matter how often he tried it, he was stiff. Now Rather, as he himself will admit, is too tightly wound to be a natural smiler, but he was an experienced professional, with more than three decades of announcing experience, and at least ten years of weekend and substitute anchoring. Yet whether he tried standing up or sitting down that day, he was just plain uncomfortable.

So that night, his first night as anchor, Rather didn't sit. He didn't stand either, exactly. Instead, he perched one hip on Cronkite's desk, and leaned forward in an uneasy half-standing, half-sitting posture, an awkward bid for his own identity.

It was a tough time for Rather. The brash young journalist had crashed TV news's Olympus, and now he was trying to prove that he belonged. He had to convince his critics and, at some level, himself. As always, Rather compared the situation to a fight: "I was glad to have that first broadcast over with. It was tremendously scary. I really wanted to do well. But it's not something anyone else can do for you. You have to do it yourself. You know, I spent some time as a boxer—I boxed in high school, and college, and even some golden gloves—and I always remember how your trainer and everybody else whispers in your ear, but when the bell rings, and the stool goes out from underneath you, it's just you, not anybody else."

In fact, for Rather even to be in this championship bout was something of a long shot. Early on, everyone from vice president Bud Benjamin to Charles Kuralt had assumed that Cronkite's successor would be Roger Mudd, the patrician Washington-based correspondent (and descendant of Harvey Mudd, the doctor who treated John Wilkes Booth, giving rise to the expression "his name is Mudd"). An astute Washington insider, Mudd was everything Rather was not: slow and deliberate where Rather was fast; a writer where Rather was a doer; an East Coast-educated thinker with a Masters Degree where Rather was a Texas scrapper. And while both men had been groomed to mount the CBS ladder, Mudd was considered a shoo-in by many. He had the wit, the academic historical training, the unyielding, unbending devotion to the CBS brand of news. CBS at the time was still thought of as "the church" of hard news, and Mudd had the right amount of piety to become Pope.

It wasn't that Rather hadn't proved his dedication and courage time after time, from civil rights riots to Vietnam, where Mudd had refused to go, citing his Washington expertise, and his disgust with "macho" journalism. Rather just seemed a little too loud, too flashy, too outsized. Dan Rather wasn't discreet—he kept calling attention to himself. He was, well, frankly, too *nouveau*. Everywhere he went, he stirred up a fuss, especially in the careful halls of Washington.

What few CBS insiders quite realized was that in a TV age, an ability to stir up a fuss is money in the bank. And Rather had been bringing in the bucks. The season he joined "60 Minutes," the show reached an unprecedented high in the ratings, and by his second season there, "60 Minutes" pulled a 36 share (that is, 36 percent of the viewing audience), probably the first time in the history of television that news was routinely outdrawing entertainment. As a result, CBS News turned a profit for the first time in its history.

Even if the CBS management seemed a little slow to realize Dan Rather's potential, ABC wasn't. Roone Arledge, the flamboyant ginger-haired chief of ABC News, knew a ratings draw when he saw one. Arledge not only had a fondness for flashy women and jewelry, he also had a flair for TV. As the head of ABC Sports, he was the man who oversaw the development of slow motion sports coverage, instant replays and the "honey" shot (showing cute girls in the stands), not to mention ABC's trademark phrase, "the thrill of victory, the agony of defeat." By 1977, Arledge had become the head of ABC News, and he wanted the thrill of victory for his news team. With an aggressive insistence, he set about raiding CBS for talent, producers, correspondents. Like George Steinbrenner, Arledge was out to get the best team money could buy, offering double and triple the going salaries. In the end, so many CBS producers and correspondents jumped ship to ABC that a sign was posted in the CBS Washington bureau: "Will the last person to leave for ABC please turn out the lights?"

Above all, Arledge needed a captain for his team, a central presence, and that's what he saw in Dan Rather. In order to get him, he put an amazing offer on the table: "World News Tonight" would expand to an hour, and Rather would be the center of it. He could anchor from the field, wherever the big stories took him. Should he want to, he could also anchor everything from "20/20" to live events to documentaries. Not only that, Rather would have a management role as well. He would have a voice as to which stories were covered, and how, even who would be hired and fired. Dan Rather would be the ABC News franchise. And the pay was astronomical. At a time when even Walter Cronkite was earning $650,000 a year, Dan Rather would make nearly $2 million. Those were movie star numbers.

The negotiations dragged on over several months, as described in great detail in Barbara Matusow's *The Evening Stars*. Bill Leonard, the CBS News president, had been hoping to hang onto both Rather and Mudd, and institute some sort of co-anchor system, a new Huntley-Brinkley team. Although Rather had originally been willing, if grudgingly, Mudd had not been thrilled with the idea. Both men believed Mudd had the upper hand.

But the ABC offer changed everything. Leonard suddenly realized that—uncertain as he was about the flashy Rather as sole anchor—he just couldn't afford to let any other network get this ratings winner. He came back with a staggering offer: $22 million over ten years, with a five year "window" at which either side could renegotiate, as well as management powers similar to those ABC had offered Rather as "managing editor." Through all this, Mudd kept aloof, as if unwilling to sully his hands in such proceedings. So Rather, with the help of his agent, Richard Leibner, negotiated himself into the enviable position of being able to choose between the anchor slot at CBS, or ABC, whichever he wanted.

In making the decision, Rather felt tortured. ABC's final sweetened offer had come to nearly $3 million a year with extra promises to hire a crack staff of producers. Also, it was a place to start over, to build a new empire away from Cronkite's shadow. On the other hand, CBS was his home. He owed his career to CBS, and Dan Rather valued loyalty. Even his closest advisors were split. While his agent Leibner pushed for a new start at ABC, his wife Jean, after initially favoring ABC, came down on the side of loyalty and CBS.

Over some eight months, Rather vacillated back and forth, asking old friends like Bill Johnston and colleagues at CBS for advice. "I was stunned at the number of people he went to, asking what he should do," says longtime colleague Peter Herford. "I was one of a hundred. I felt if there was ever a time to jump to ABC, this was it. But then, there had been stories about Arledge making promises he never fulfilled. Dan must have changed his mind at least eight or ten times. He just wasn't sure who he was, what he wanted to be. In the end, Jean came down firmly for CBS, and in day-to-day decisions, I think he relies heavily on her common sense."

Rather recalls: "A number of people said go to ABC, because the first person to replace Cronkite is going to get his head blown off." But for Rather, loyalty tipped the scales towards CBS. Then too, there was another reason. CBS was "the church," the place Rather had always worshipped. The brash side of him liked the idea of leading a hot new ABC team to glory. But an even deeper part of him, the Sam Houston grad in an Ivy League world, preferred to be the standard bearer for CBS News. That was tradition. And although in the long run, he probably would have been happier at ABC with a clean slate, he never could have passed up that pivotal moment when he stood at the podium with Walter Cronkite.

As the flash bulbs popped to capture this royal transfer of power, the expression on Dan Rather's face confirmed that he felt his life's mission had been achieved. On the countenance of this "non-smiler" was a smile so charged that it threatened to leap off his face and dance with glee. Dan Rather, as he himself might say, was in tall cotton.

But not Roger Mudd. Only two hours before the Rather announcement, Bill Leonard came to the CBS Washington office to tell Mudd the news. It was a bitter meeting. And as Rather was being crowned, Mudd released a statement full of tight-lipped venom: "The Management of CBS and CBS News has made its decision on Walter Cronkite's successor according to its current values and standards. From the beginning, I've regarded myself as a news reporter and not a newsmaker or celebrity." Within months, Mudd would slam the door behind him and storm off for NBC.

But some bitter seeds had been left behind, and when Rather took over the anchor position, there were still some at CBS who felt that Roger Mudd was the man for the job and not him. And though Rather boasted that he and CBS would show the competition their "tail lights," in the first few weeks and months he was floundering. As the ratings dropped one and a half points—and CBS relinquished its long-held ratings lead to a three-way tie—the critics became more vociferous.

"I knew there'd be a lot of people on the outside who wanted to see me fail," Rather recalls, "but I believed that almost everybody inside CBS would be pulling for me. Even when it was glaringly apparent that they weren't, I refused to believe it. When I finally realized that not everybody inside this building was supporting me, it staggered me. It hurt. It was intended to hurt and it did. I believed that almost anybody here would say, 'Well, he earned it.' I mean, there's a vicious side to this business. We're all big boys. It's a tough world out there. But I didn't think that anyone would be actively working to see me fail."

And so came a period that Rather calls "the march of the long knives," when he felt that he was under siege. "I remember one day the door outside my office was open," Rather says, "and I heard people outside—the coterie, the camp followers [of Mudd]—saying loudly, 'That Dan Rather, he's doing terribly. He's going to be out of here in five weeks.' They said it loudly. They wanted me to hear."

"Well, that stunned me," Rather recalls. "But in some ways it probably saved me. That's when I said, 'It's up to me.'"

If Rather is anything, he's competitive, and when it seemed that a battle was shaping up on his doorstep, he wasn't about to walk away.

"I'm slow to get in it," he says, "but if I'm in it, I want to win it. I believe in the Cortez philosophy. When you get there, burn the boats. When Cortez got to Mexico, he burned his boats. Once I'm in, I have to feel that I'm all in."

Rather approached this battle like all the others in his life, with a homespun philosophy at once hokey and heartfelt, a two-fisted Texas can-do spirit. "I feel this very strongly. Keep your head up, have a polar star out there, a navigational star. What happens off to the side barely matters, what's behind you doesn't matter at all. It's kind of a peasant stamina. Put one foot in front of the other. Just keep going. You're going to get knocked down, even with the best training, the fiercest determination. Even with your relatives and God's help, you're still gonna have those times when you're staggered, when you're lucky if you don't get knocked down. I've been knocked down a lot of times, but that's when you really have to be determined to get up, get your bearings, keep going on."

At CBS, the battle often centered on a bureaucratic system known as "net first." News divisions have several shows—CBS's stable included "60 Minutes" and "Sunday Morning," as well as the "Evening News"—and net first meant they would all pitch in as equal partners to cover joint stories, and share the results based on whatever show was up next in the day, not unlike the news desk system that NBC recently established. This method of operating may sound very egalitarian, but for Rather it meant that the network's flagship, the "Evening News," forced to use a pickup staff, was sinking fast.

He said, "The 'Evening News' is the most important broadcast we do day in and day out, and it was getting third and fourth choice producers and cameramen. If I'm in a fight, I can't win it for us unless I get the best people and resources. The whole health of the broadcast, my own health depended on cracking through and carrying that point."

If Rather didn't feel that he was getting the most out of his CBS team, he was partially right. The net-first bureaucracy had become unwieldy. But the tension of a new job and lowered ratings may have exaggerated his fears. He was a crusader, fighting to make the

"Evening News" the best it could be. Yet in some ways, he may have been fighting shadows, a Dan Quixote, taking on windmills.

"Dan felt that the organization wasn't behind him," says Peter Sturtevant, then national news editor. "It infuriated him. When things went wrong, when we didn't cover stories as well as we should have, he felt it was a consequence of people not trying hard enough. That wasn't true. I remember one time when 'Evening News' didn't get an adequate piece and 'Morning News' did. Dan came into my office, closed the door, and started yelling about our coverage. 'If I were Walter Cronkite,' he shouted, 'you wouldn't have done that.' I was so struck by that. We weren't doing *anything* differently. But I suddenly understood what was driving Dan Rather. I suddenly understood what had created his insecurity."

Uncle Walter was certainly a father figure for Rather. He talks of "worshipping" him, and in quiet moments will admit that, well into his anchor years, he still felt a strong desire to please Cronkite, to live up to him, coupled with an equally strong need to break free of his shadow.

But the Mudd followers had already sent warning shots across his bow. So it was small wonder that Dan "acted like nobody was on his side," in the words of one colleague. Some may have felt that "it was pure paranoia on his part." Well, maybe it was paranoia, but that didn't mean that there weren't several on the CBS staff who were in fact out to get him. Under siege, fighting two simultaneous battles—a ratings war against the other networks and an internal dispute within his own organization—Rather sought to consolidate his clout, taking certain decision-making power, like which stories to cover and who should cover them, from net-first executives like Sturtevant and consolidating them in his office and the offices of his "Evening News" producers.

Of course, none of this could have happened if the CBS News president at that time hadn't let it. Arriving in late 1981, the professorial-looking Van Gordon Sauter, sported a pipe, a beard and a comfortable paunch. As the story is meticulously detailed in Peter Boyer's *Who Killed CBS?*, Sauter felt his number-one priority was to keep his bonus baby, Rather, happy, and so he turned over the reins of power to his anchor. And Rather, both for positive and negative reasons—to help the show regain its prominence and to insulate himself from his enemies—absorbed all the power he could get. His contract had awarded him the title of managing editor. Sauter slipped him the keys to the kingdom.

"They didn't hire a secretary, they didn't move a paper clip, without Dan Rather's approval," recalls former CBS producer Richard Cohen. Cronkite had always had a role in the show. He had been famous among his staff for showing up in midafternoon, chatting a little about sailing, then rearranging the entire story lineup. He was renowned for his autocratic "WW" commands, "Walter wants" this story done. But no one had ever seen anything like the sway that Rather held by the end of 1982. As one of Cronkite's executive producers, Russ Bensley, said, "No one had ever wielded that kind of power."

Together, Sauter and Rather shook up the news division, remolded it, restructured it. The staff was divided into "yesterday" people and "today" people, old guard Cronkite followers and the new wave of Rather faithful. Partially because he believed CBS needed a spring cleaning and because he himself wanted to start with a new slate, Rather became instrumental in casting out the old guard, like Cronkite executive producer Sandy Socolow and correspondent Morton Dean. Lists were drawn up of "A" correspondents and "B" correspondents. Rather reportedly told one correspondent, "Look, it's like a play. Some people get to play the lead, and some are spear carriers. You're just a spear carrier."

Rather jealously guarded the personnel he wanted in his fierce desire to improve the "Evening News," hoarding them even from other CBS News shows. The former executive producer of "Sunday Morning," Robert "Shad" Northshield, recalls, "They got chewed out if they were ever seen even going into our building."

Together, Sauter and Rather also instituted a new CBS News philosophy. It was a philosophy that said news had become too much Washington and not enough heartland, too much about minor congressional legislation and not enough about real folks. At its core was the affective principle previously mentioned, known as "moments." And so CBS reporters, and Rather himself from time to time, tromped across the heartland—knee-deep in cow flop—in search of moments, and good ratings.

This audience-driven news proved tremendously popular. From 1982 through 1983, Rather and his team opened up a huge lead over the competition. All the worrying and the tension eased away for Rather, as CBS ran off more than two hundred straight weeks on top. The ratings that had panicked him earlier now soothed and encouraged him. "200" buttons were printed up and worn around the newsroom. With the aid of Sauter, Rather had found his way back to the tall cotton. "Sometimes at the end of the day," Rather would say at the time, "we'll put our feet up on his desk and swig on a beer and say, 'Hey, man, this is fine, ain't it?'"

But beneath the surface, all was not happy at CBS, and when the ratings began to fall off by the mid-1980s, the cracks beneath the surface began to show. The notion of moments had offended many of the hard-news oriented CBS staff. For them it was heresy in the church. Others were equally offended by the way they and their friends, longtime CBS staffers, had been carelessly cast aside by the Sauter-Rather regime.

When the pressure inside was compounded by pressure outside— attempts by everyone from Ted Turner to Jesse Helms to take over CBS, even an attempted inside buy-out of the network by Rather, Mike Wallace and Don Hewitt—things got really touchy. And in mid-1986, as an internal power play was being orchestrated by board member Larry Tisch, a *Newsweek* cover summed up the mood: "Civil War at CBS." The gloomy black magazine cover, with its cracked CBS "eye," bore the subhead: "The Struggle for the Soul of a Legendary Network."

Then came a series of firings—including the mass layoff of more than two hundred staffers—that decimated morale. "It was like the French Revolution here for two years," recalls Shad Northshield. "Those carts kept going back and forth with headless bodies."

In the newsroom, Rather caught his staff by surprise one night when he signed off the broadcast using the word "courage." No one knew quite what it meant, but night after night, for a week, the broadcast ended with "courage." Perhaps it was an attempt to bolster morale at CBS, a general's "keep your chin up" speech to the troops. Perhaps it was just a bit of Rather flash. But then, just as abruptly as the anchor's exhortation to bravery had appeared, it disappeared.

In a way, the whole "courage" episode was like the situation at CBS News. No one was quite sure what was going on, but rumors abounded. And in another way it would be emblematic of Dan Rather's decade-long tenure as anchor—a strange incident that could be interpreted dozens of ways, full of good intentions but a little bit off.

From his earliest days as anchorman, there were many at CBS who didn't know what to make of the complex character of Dan Rather. Or more aptly, everyone had his or her own interpretation, and no two were the same. It's as if there's something about Rather's reserved, tightly-wound personality that just makes people inside and outside CBS want to play junior psychologist.

Bring up the subject of Dan Rather and you're sure to hear about his generosity, the loyalty of his friendship. "If you've gone a certain number of miles with Dan, he's tremendously loyal," says "48 Hours" executive producer Andrew Heyward. It's characteristic of Rather to pick up his phone after a broadcast and call reporters in the field to congratulate them. For a correspondent like Richard Threlkeld, sleeping on a floor in Panama, or Bernard Goldberg, stuck covering a jet crash in the Everglades during the Christmas season, that call means a lot. "There are people you go out and do things for," Goldberg says, "cause they would have done it themselves."

For Goldberg, one incident of Rather's loyalty sticks in his mind, because it struck close to home. "I went into Ed Joyce [then president of CBS News], and I said I thought I should become a national correspondent. He told me to deal with the 'Evening News' staff. It's their decision. So I spoke to the producers and to Dan Rather, and they listened, and Dan said, 'It's done.' And the next time I did a piece, he said, 'national correspondent Bernard Goldberg.' Well, Ed Joyce called down right after the show and yelled at Lane [Venardos, then executive producer] and Dan. 'What's this?!' he demanded. 'Don't do it again.' You see, Joyce had been lying to me. He didn't want me to be a national correspondent.

"But the very next piece I did, Dan went on the air and introduced me as national correspondent Bernard Goldberg again. You want to put out for that guy. He cares. Well, Joyce called him in, gave him shit, and Rather smiled and said okay. But the day after Joyce left CBS, Dan called me and said, 'Bernie, remember that national correspondent thing? You're it.'"

Rather brought to the anchor job a small-town Texas charm, a team spirit and a solicitousness for his staff. In contrast with his electric image, he could be one of the most gracious and downright polite men in a business that checks its pockets when threatened by too much courteousness. Rather became known for sending flowers, lots of flowers, huge extravagant bouquets at the slightest provocation. Reporter Betsy Aaron recalls the time back in the mid-1970s when her leg got badly broken covering a Ku Klux Klan rally in Georgia. Although she barely knew Rather, she remembers, "Dan was terrific. He wrote. He called. It was a little overwhelming, actually." And when three CBS technicians were brutally shot and killed at a parking lot at 57th Street and 12th Avenue, Rather was extravagant in his support and sympathy to the widows.

This Dan Rather was a sentimental, old-fashioned kind of guy. Sure he was ambitious. Of course he wanted to get ahead. But he was also a Texan who just wanted to fit in and be liked at the home office. A percentage of the CBS employees, however, accustomed to life in the complicated rabbit warren of offices at West 57th Street, were suspicious of his charm. They thought he was trying *too* hard. They believed he was two-faced.

One day, soon after Rather had taken over the anchor role, a group of producers stood around the newsroom talking about the day's show, when they heard a voice behind them: "How do you take your coffee, cream, sugar?" It was Dan Rather with a pad, the anchor taking orders for coffee from everyone in the room. No one knew quite what to make of it. He thought he was just trying to be gracious, one of the guys. They thought it was weird and that he was up to something.

Richard Cohen, once Rather's producer, now alienated from him, tells a story about Rather's early days as an anchor. "Dan was uncertain, unsure. He would ask me, 'What would Walter have done?' For example, to his credit, Dan used to know everyone's name, the name of every desk assistant. Walter never knew anyone's name. When someone told Dan that one day, he came to me and asked, 'Am I making a mistake? Should I be more aloof?'"

Vulnerable and not quite sure of himself in his new role, Rather sent off signals that others interpreted as disingenuous. He desperately wanted to do the right thing. But then, with his small-town politeness, he had difficulty criticizing people to their faces. So stories of Dan's doublespeak began to spring up. More than one CBS producer talked of having run-ins with management. Then Rather would stop by and tell them, "You've no problem with Dan Rather."

"Uh-oh," they would say, "It's the kiss of death."

Actually, even friends kid him about his euphemisms. Long-time CBS producer and friend Andrew Heyward gives Rather some good-natured ribbing about the language of "Dannish." He jokes about the times Rather came into the newsroom fuming and said, "I'm in a holiday mood, *but*..." Of course, the point was the "but."

"I kid Dan about it," says Heyward. "The best example ever was when we were in Geneva, after the Shultz-Shevardnadze summit. All the anchors were there, and we all had to race back to Washington, where Reagan was making a major speech, in time for the evening news. Well Rather had asked, 'What if we don't make it in time? Maybe we should stay and do the show from Geneva?' But we convinced him, and we took a charter from Switzerland to London, where we got on the Concorde.

"Well, as it turned out, Brokaw, Jennings and Rather were all on that Concorde. And forty-five minutes out over the Atlantic, the Captain comes on and he says, 'Ladies and Gentlemen, there's this small red light on. We're going to have to dump our fuel and return to Heathrow.' It was scary. We might not make it back in time for the broadcast. We might not make it back at all. I went back in the airplane, and there Dan was, glowering in his seat. All he said was, 'I blame myself.'"

For Heyward, this was quintessential Rather. It spoke to his competitiveness, and something else besides. "It could be seen on so many levels," Heyward says. "'I blame myself' really means he blames us. Then on the other hand, he has to blame himself, because his motto has always been, 'If it's gonna be, it's up to me.'"

This complex character, so ambitious, so hard-charging, so full of self-doubt, so driven by contradictory emotions, has always seemed more intense, more passionate than either of his competitors, Jennings and Brokaw. Dan Rather has always appeared a little larger than life. Any small event about him is news. Whether he wears a sweater or not, whether he stands or sits, the event gets reported. This person-ality—with his demons and his many accomplishments—often seems bigger than the small screen. That's Dan Rather's power, his draw. It's also his undoing. He's a high-voltage personality, on and off the tube. This is what people in the industry mean when they talk about Rather as a "lightning rod." He's the kind of guy who braves a hurricane, who gets slugged at a political convention—who makes things happen around him. He's also the kind who often travels with a bodyguard, ex-secret service man Toby Chandler, and keeps a shotgun in his house.

Take the infamous cab ride in Chicago. On his way to visit writer Studs Terkel for a "60 Minutes" story, Rather got in a cab at O'Hare International Airport. As the cab driver meandered around Chicago, it became clear to Rather that the cabbie either didn't know where he was going, or was giving him the runaround. So Rather asked the driver to stop. But afraid that he would lose his $12.50 fare, the driver stepped on the gas. As the cab hurtled through the streets of the city, Rather stuck his head out the window and yelled for help. It was a messy incident that got splashed all over the papers, with Rather threatening to sue, and the driver complaining about damage to his reputation. It was a silly episode, but for old friend Bill Johnston there was a larger lesson.

"I was once visiting Dan in New York, and I had to take the shuttle from LaGuardia to Boston. He told me, 'Be sure they take you to the Eastern shuttle building, not the Eastern terminal. It's a favorite trick of theirs to add four dollars on to the fare. It just infuriates me,' he said, 'to be taken as so naive.' You see, it wasn't a matter of the four dollar fare, it was a matter of principle. He wouldn't let anyone take advantage of him. That's what drives him."

Certainly the most famous of the "lightning rod" incidents took place late one Saturday night in October of 1986. On his way home strolling down Park Avenue on a particularly pleasant October night, Rather was stopped by a man in his thirties, who allegedly asked, "Kenneth, what's the frequency?" Rather protested that he didn't know what the man was talking about, that he had the wrong guy. That's when this well-dressed white man, 6'1", and over two hundred pounds, lit into Rather, punching him in the jaw and the body.

Rather ran down the block, ducking into the lobby at 1075 Park Avenue. The assailant and an accomplice chased Rather into the building, punching him, knocking him to the floor, then kicking him in the ribs. All the while, they allegedly continued to ask, "Kenneth, what's the frequency?" It was only when the building's superintendent rushed out that the two men dashed off, leaving Rather bruised and the whole side of his face red and swollen.

Neither assailant has ever been caught, and the mystery remains unsolved. But interestingly enough, almost no one at CBS seems to believe the story the way Rather tells it. Although his best friend David Buksbaum insists that Rather was on his way home from a convivial evening of spaghetti and watching one of his favorite movies, *Patton*, at Buksbaum's Park Avenue apartment, many at CBS speculate that there was a woman involved and that Rather was getting roughed up as a message from a jealous husband or a boyfriend. This *Peyton Place* scenario is only a rumor, but many CBS staffers are absolutely convinced it's true. To this day, when Rather is cranky about having to stay late to cover a plane crash, staffers will joke about Dan having to break a date.

There have been other incidents, equally bizarre but less well known. Making his way through a crowded Kennedy Airport terminal, Rather was once attacked by a man who walked up to him and, without a word, knocked him to the floor. And as Peter Boyer recounts, Rather was ambling along San Francisco's Nob Hill at an affiliates convention, when a crazed man suddenly leaped at the anchor, yelling and screaming what he would do to him. Later, the same man came to New York, checked into the New York Hilton, and called CBS with a message. He was going to kill Dan Rather. The man was arrested. The anchor was shaken up.

If all of these incidents speak to Rather's ability to stir up a whirlwind—to generate extreme emotions—none involved his performance as an anchor. These were things that happened around Rather, not things he did. Until the six black minutes in Miami.

On September 11, 1987, Dan Rather and the "CBS Evening News" team were in Miami covering the visit of Pope John Paul II. The lead-in program, the U.S. Open Tennis tournament, ran slightly over its allotted time. When it finished at 6:32:50, the network cut to the "Evening News." Absolutely nothing came on. Across America, television screens tuned to CBS went black. For six minutes and six seconds.

"It was the single most embarrassing moment at CBS," says former CBS News producer Marty Koughan. "When you're in journalism school, you're taught there is only one crime in television, and that's going black. Anything else is better, even putting up color bars. And here's the most professional news organization in the world going black."

The official explanation that came from the CBS organization the next day was as follows. Dan Rather, Tom Bettag and their team were concerned that the tennis tournament was running into their time. Rather went off to find a telephone and lodge a complaint with CBS News president Howard Stringer. While he was away, the tournament finished, and the network cut to Miami, but Rather couldn't be found. Minutes went by. When he was finally located, he rushed back to the anchor chair, and the broadcast started. A bad mistake, but just a mistake. So ran the company line. The CBS explanation was a lie from start to finish.

The only element of truth in the whole story was Rather's frame of mind. He was mad; he was absolutely pissed off. His evening news broadcast—more than just a program to him, a sacred trust—was being amputated by some stupid tennis match. "The *semi-finals* of a tennis match," Rather still notes with dark sarcasm, even today. "News is important. It should be reliable, dependable fare....CBS News is not just another division of another corporation. We have a past, a responsibility, and nobody but nobody takes this lightly. They shouldn't want me in this job if I didn't feel it was the most important thing every day."

Yes, Rather was shocked when he learned the tennis match would eat into his broadcast. He thought the whole issue had been resolved earlier. And yes, he had gone off to call Howard Stringer and complain. But for most of the time the screen was black, Rather was not missing in action.

"They told us they couldn't find Dan," says one CBS producer who was in the New York control room at the time. "They couldn't find Dan, my ass! The place was filled with reporters and news people. And no one can find the anchor?"

Actually, several sources confirm, Dan Rather was out on the balcony staring over Miami, fuming mad. Perhaps he originally thought that Sports would keep filling time with a post-match wrap-up. But soon enough, he knew they weren't. He knew exactly what was going on. He was still mad as hell, and he wasn't going to take it sitting down in the anchor chair. He had staged a deliberate walkout.

"Even if you want to be Mother Teresa, and give him the benefit of the doubt," says one CBS staffer who was in Miami, "even if you thought there was a misunderstanding, at some point Dan knew he was in black. He had to know."

But, the staffer also notes, "Whether Dan was right or wrong, he thought the news was more important than a tennis match. The thing I find fascinating is how many other people were there—I counted seven or eight—and not one of them stopped it. Not one of them said, 'Dan I care for you too much. I can't let it happen. Dan, you're gonna have to step over me, cause if you don't they'll be making jokes about you on Letterman on Monday and Carson on Tuesday. Dan, get your ass back in the chair.' How could they have all let it happen? Simply put, they were all afraid. They were all chicken."

"It's a flaw in the structure," says ex-CBS producer Marty Koughan. "The anchor's boss is the executive producer. But the executive producer's boss is the managing editor, which is Dan. When

Tom Bettag went running out after Dan, he was also looking at his boss. He didn't have the authority to bring him back. He didn't dare."

As it turned out, two veteran reporters, Richard Roth and Bernard Goldberg, were both on the scene, only about one hundred and fifty feet away, across the building, in the room that was functioning as the Miami bureau. Either of them could have filled in. "Nobody asked me," Goldberg admits.

Later that night at a dinner gathering, according to the story that circulated around CBS, Goldberg was asked if he would have filled in. Goldberg responded with a mixture of healthy respect and genuine affection for the anchor. "Oh no," he said. "Dan Rather's gonna have to have a heart attack first."

The question was then put to Richard Roth: "Oh no," Roth responded. "Bernie Goldberg's gonna have to have a heart attack first."

There was an extra twist that evening in Miami. The entire beginning of the program had already been recorded. The introduction ("This is the 'CBS Evening News.' Dan Rather reporting from Miami..."), as well as the first piece were all on tape, ready to roll. There were at least three minutes on tape, which combined with some two minutes of commercials would have bought the network almost all the time it needed. So how come no one said, "Roll tape"?

"Someone should have made that decision," said one CBS staffer in Miami that day. "But no one was willing to be a hero."

Finally, some five and a half minutes later—an extremely brief time in a heated, confused situation, but an eternity on a blank screen—Dan Rather strolled back into the room, put on his jacket, and started the broadcast, six minutes and six seconds late.

Some would later see the incident as a morality play, and blame Tom Bettag, saying he was too close to Rather—"joined at the hip" is the industry phrase—too blinded by loyalty to a man to be loyal to the job, the team, the organization. Others would use the morality play to lay blame on the structure itself, pointing out how the anchors had become such "anchor monsters" that no one could dare contradict them, even when they had made a terrible blunder.

In part, both of those notions are true, but whatever happened in Miami happened in haste, in confusion, in the mix-up of a Friday evening. The worst part of the whole affair happened three days later, on Monday, after a weekend of deliberation.

As the bureaus from all around the country hooked up in the daily national conference call at 10:00 AM Monday, CBS staffers were dying to hear what would be said about the events of the past Friday evening. "Tom offered up an explanation," says Marty Koughan, who was one of the producers in on the conference. "He gave us the company line, that Dan had gone out to call, that they couldn't find him. Well, I was sitting in that control room on Friday. I saw Dan saunter back in with this pout on his face, looking all put out. And Tom's telling us Dan rushed back? That's what we're all supposed to believe?"

Several producers listening in on the call started chuckling. Some even laughed outright. Others slammed their phones down in disgust. "We were offended, it was so dishonest," says one CBS producer. "I hung up," recalls another. "I felt you can con the outside world, Okay, but don't try to pull that shit on *us*."

The $64,000 question was asked by several CBS reporters after the call: "Why didn't they just say, 'We made a mistake?' Why did they have to say, 'Okay, Dan, we'll protect you, we'll cover for you'?"

After all, Rather, and perhaps Bettag, had made a decision of principle. It was gallant, if wrongheaded, a symbolic gesture to uphold the importance of news. Maybe it wasn't the right move, but it was made for the right reason. It had a certain Dan Quixote charm to it. Why be ashamed of it? "Why not just say," a CBS reporter asked, "'Look, we thought it was right, but in retrospect it was a mistake'?"

In fact, there was no dishonor in such a statement, only in the attempt to cover up the facts out of embarrassment. It still seems surprising, even today, that a reporter like Rather and a producer like Bettag, who both spent years in Washington exposing lies—that these two, like their old enemy Tricky Dick, would be caught "stonewalling." Even today, Rather will admit, "It wasn't a good day." He sighs and stares out the window. "I feel terrible about it."

Ironically, because of the cover-up, because of the decision by Bettag and Rather and CBS to downplay the incident, instead of allowing Rather to be seen as a champion of the news, the public began to get an increasingly strange impression about the anchorman. With all the weirdness that was swirling around him, they started to view him as some outrageous Hunter Thompson character, off on the edge.

Newspapers like the London *Times* asked, "Is Dan Rather, bishop of the nation's news business, losing his marbles?"

Novelist Stephen King said, "I've got a sneaky admiration for Dan Rather because I'm never sure when he's going to go bonkers on you. He always looks like he's gonna just stop and say, 'All right, motherfuckers, here it comes. We've got the bodies in hangar 18, the government has been lying to you....' And then they're going to drag him off."

Certainly the most creative explanation came when Rance Crain, in the staid *Crain's New York Business*, broke the following surreal story. "Dan Rather remains in the grip of alien beings from another world....The exchange of Mr. Rather for an alien double took place when the anchorman claimed he was kidnapped by a Chicago cabbie for refusing to pay his fare. Apparently the alien's code name is Kenneth, because shortly thereafter he was beaten by two men asking, 'What's the frequency, Kenneth?'

"They were obviously two fellow aliens trying to find out on which frequency they should broadcast communications between their planet and Earth. And Mr. Rather's (really Kenneth's) short-lived sign-off, 'Courage,' was undoubtedly a signal to his fellow interstellar travelers.

"...The six-minute period of blank airtime that resulted when 'Dan' walked off the set was actually a carefully contrived opportunity for his fellow aliens to beam down vital instructions, using CBS' powerful signal capacity...."

Then came yet another lightning rod incident, this time nine supercharged minutes on the air. It was a Monday evening in January 1988, and Dan Rather was interviewing presidential candidate George Bush on the "CBS Evening News," live. The New York-Washington hookup started as a normal question and answer session. It quickly erupted into something else altogether.

"You have said," Rather began, "that if you had known that this was an arms-for-hostages swap you would have opposed it. You also said—"

"Exactly," jumped in Bush. "May I answer that?"

"That wasn't a question," Rather said. "It was a statement."

"It was a statement and I'll answer it," Bush replied abruptly, leaning forward in his leather chair.

"Let me ask the question if I may first."

"The President had created this program," Bush steamrolled, his forefinger wagging, "as stated publicly he did not think it was arms for hostages—"

"That's the President, Mr. Vice-President..."

After a few more back and forths, Rather said, "...I don't want to be argumentative, Mr. Vice President."

"Yes you do, Dan," Bush shot back. Rather laughed at Bush's sally.

Then Bush turned up the heat. "It's not fair to judge my whole career by a rehash on Iran. How would you like it if I judged your career by those seven minutes when you walked off the set in New York? [sic] Would you like that?"

A stunned silence, as Rather's jaw locked in disbelief at the low blow. He was momentarily speechless. "I have respect for you," Bush continued, "but I don't have respect for what you're doing here tonight."

As a shocked nation watched in astonishment, an historic bit of television was played out, one of those powerful live TV moments when a packaged presentation suddenly lurches out of control, and raw emotions explode off the small screen.

"I want to be judged on my whole record," Bush said.

Rather bore in, "I'm just trying to set the record straight. You sat in a meeting with George Shultz, and he got apoplectic when he found out—"

"He didn't get apoplectic!"

As time ran out, and the last seconds were being counted down in Rather's earpiece, he asked a final question: "Are you willing to go to a news conference before the Iowa caucuses, answer questions from all—"

Bush interjected, "I've been to eighty-six news conferences since March—"

"I gather the answer is no," Rather cut him off. "Thank you very much for being with us, Mr. Vice-President."

The tense session ended as abruptly as it had begun. Bush unhooked his earpiece, and stormed around the vice-presidential suite. "That bastard didn't lay a glove on me," he fumed. "Tell your goddamn network that if they want to talk to me, they can raise their hands at a press conference."

At first, the story seemed clear: A liberal newsman had tried to ambush the Republican Vice-President, and had gotten his come-uppance. The CBS team had asked for a general straightforward interview, but then tried to pull off a sneak attack by focusing solely on the Iran-Contra issue. Bush had fought back and won. Or so it seemed.

Actually, it was the Bush team that had mounted the sneak attack.

Both executive producer Tom Bettag and senior political producer Richard Cohen had sent clear signals to Bush's staff that this would be a "tough" interview. Far from surprised, Republican media advisor Roger Ailes saw such an interview as the perfect opportunity for Bush to shake his "wimp" image. George would come out swinging, and the rich, East Coast, namby-pamby Vice-President would be transformed into a macho guy, the perfect heir to Ronald Reagan. "It was the most amazing bit of Ailes black magic I ever saw," said Marty Koughan, the CBS producer who crafted the Bush profile that led into the Q & A session.

While George Bush claimed all along that he had been set up—"a misrepresentation on the part of CBS"—that he had come in expecting a straight-ahead interview and been suddenly forced to fight for his life, in fact it was CBS and Rather that were bushwacked. "George Bush," says Bettag, "was lying through his teeth."

The clues add up. First, CBS had promoted the interview during "60 Minutes," the day before, as being about Iran-Contra. No sneak attack there. Second, the White House itself notified reporters early that afternoon that the interview would be adversarial. Finally, minutes before the interview, CBS producer Koughan was called by someone within the Bush camp and warned that Bush was preparing to throw in the seven (actually six)-black-minutes crack at the first available opportunity.

The White House's pre-planning was evident throughout the interview. Roger Ailes, just behind the camera in Washington, was popping up and down like a boxing coach in the corner, egging his man on, holding up a pad of paper with key phrases for Bush to remember. Phrases like "my career...yours," a reminder about the six minutes in Miami. Bush was a man looking for a fight, looking to be champ, and who better to take on than a heavyweight like Dan Rather? Seen in this light, the interview itself appears quite different. Rather can now be seen as trying hard to get some real answers, perhaps a little more aggressively than is customary, but not much, and Bush, bobbing and weaving and ducking the Iran-Contra issue, is the one who is trying to stir up as much of a brouhaha as he can.

All in all, George Bush made some real political hay at Dan Rather's expense. Talking about "combat pay" and "Tension City," the candidate milked the event at campaign appearances during the next

The anchor as sales tool: A Peter Jennings bus shelter advertisement on New York's Upper West Side, and . . .

Dan Rather promoting his documentary "The Moon Above, The Earth Below" with TV critics (co-author Robert Goldberg among them) over lunch at the 21 Club.

Rather in Tiananmen Square, Beijing, China—the only anchor on the scene when the democracy movement began (May 1989). (Courtesy Erica Lansner/Photoreporters)

Rather at the Berlin Wall, the second day of mass demonstrations. The Brandenburg Gate is in the background (November 1989). (Courtesy CBS)

Brokaw at the Berlin Wall on the night East Germany first permitted free travel to the West. The overcoat was borrowed from NBC European correspondent Mike Boettcher (November 9, 1989). (Courtesy NBC)

Jennings on the scene at the San Francisco earthquake (October 1989). The collapsed Nimitz Freeway is behind him. (Courtesy Stu Schutzman)

Jennings sledding with his wife, Kati Marton, and children Elizabeth and Christopher. (Courtesy Evelyn Floret/People Weekly © Time Inc.)

Brokaw climbing in the Tetons near Jackson Hole, Wyoming (1982). (Courtesy Tom Brokaw)

Tom and Meredith Brokaw on a visit to Kyoto, Japan in 1987. (Courtesy Tom Brokaw)

Rather with his wife Jean two days after the "What's the frequency, Kenneth?" attack (October 1986). (© Paul Adao: *New York Post*)

(Courtesy Paul Schirnhofer)

The three anchors in their improvised newsrooms at Malta
(December 1989).

Brokaw in the Barrakka Gardens, Malta, waiting for his cue (December 1989). (Courtesy Paul Schirnhofer)

Jennings delivering the news from his stand-up location at Msida Bay, Malta (December 1989). (Courtesy Paul Schirnhofer)

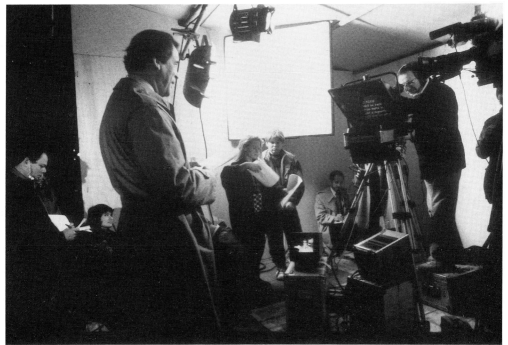

Anchors Peter Jennings, Dan Rather, Tom Brokaw and CNN's Bernard Shaw toasting their distinguished predecessor, Walter Cronkite. (Courtesy John Chiasson/Gamma-Liaison)

few days. The non-wimp was on his way to the presidency. And Dan Rather?

"I tried to do my job as a reporter," he would later say. "The job of a reporter is to ask questions and to keep on asking questions...."

As he would later tell his old friend Bill Johnston, "When Bush didn't answer, I didn't back down."

That, said Johnston, "is how Dan gets into confrontations."

Dan Rather has been saying that he will step down as anchor when his contract runs out in 1994. Some at CBS say they wouldn't be surprised if it happened even sooner than that. They say he is wearying of his job, after a decade in the anchor role. In many ways, Rather is at the peak of his personal and professional life, at about $4 million a year, the highest paid newsman ever, with a loving wife, Jean, and two grown kids, Robin and Dan Jr. But there is one question that puzzles even Rather's admirers, and probably the anchor himself.

"The real enigma," says one CBS producer who counts himself among Rather's friends, "is why Dan hasn't enjoyed himself more. He does great stories. He has a great salary, fame and power. He's at the top of his profession. If all that doesn't make him happy, what will?"

No one knows the answer to that question, but it may be why so many at CBS talk of Rather as a kind of "tragic" figure. According to one former CBS executive, "As a correspondent, he was so hard-driving, so ambitious to get to the top. But when he made it, when he became anchor, well....Do you know the final scene from the movie *The Candidate*? Redford has won the election, and his people are celebrating, and he comes into the room with this blank expression on his face. And he asks, 'What do I do now?' That's Dan Rather. He got exactly what he always wanted. But what does he do now?"

The analogy seems apt. Rather did fight his way to the top, only to find that the top wasn't as sweet as he thought. There are just too many responsibilities, too many roles to fill and too many backstabbers for any anchor to be completely at home. Then too, for all the power he has, Rather is today stuck behind an anchor desk, when, classic reporter that he is, he would probably be much happier and much better suited to his original correspondent's role. That's why these CBS staffers talk of Rather as doomed by his own success.

But such a characterization misses something important about Dan

Rather, the fighter. Even though an air of tension always seems to reign at CBS News, even though Rather is such a potentially volatile figure that he ends up distancing some would-be allies, for all that, you have to respect his toughness: the way he was willing to fight to get to China, and to stay there, the way he battled for a long thematic series on "The Changing Face of Communism" (the most spectacular called shot since Babe Ruth pointed at the center field bleachers and banged the ball into the seats), the way when his ratings numbers slowly started to sink in late 1989 and early 1990, he was more than willing to take his show on the road to Moscow.

And, despite all the needless flailing about that he does, you have to admire his damn-the-torpedoes attitude, his readiness to fight, to scrap, to make the news better, to advance the "church" of CBS. And just when his critics start to count him out, you know Dan Rather will still be good for a few more rounds.

RATINGS: Week ending August 25th

1st. Rather   ("CBS Evening News")—9.7/21 [8,768,800]

2nd. Jennings (ABC's "World News Tonight")—8.5/19 [7,684,000]

3rd. Brokaw   ("NBC Nightly News")—8.0/18 [7,232,000]

CHAPTER SEVENTEEN

On the Set with Rather

"Captain on the bridge!" The call goes up as Dan Rather makes his way onto the floor of the CBS newsroom. "Captain on the bridge!" Rather gives a small smile. It's 5:40 on a September afternoon, and as he strolls across the newsroom floor in his blue pinstripes, he carries an undeniable presence, the solidity of a senior banker or a top politico.

With a small sigh, he removes his jacket, hangs it on the back of the anchor chair. Settling into the chair, he takes off his glasses, and awkwardly starts to put in his contacts, peering into a big white magnifying mirror on his desk. On a screen over Rather's head, one can see the face of Walter Cronkite looking down, beaming benevolently like the ghost of Christmas past. A middle-aged woman in a tan pantsuit makes her way across to him. She looks like a housewife, straight off the Mall, but she's actually one of the best makeup artists in the business, Frances Arvold. All three anchors rely on makeup to overcome the ravages of time. Since Rather is seven years older than Jennings and nine older than Brokaw, he needs a few more minutes than the competition for makeup artistry.

Brush in hand, Frances dabs at the area under Rather's eyes. Then, with a small toothbrush implement, she arranges his eyebrows. The anchor leans back and shoots the breeze with Lee Townsend, his editor. They're talking baseball, the National League East, the race

244

between the Cubs, the Expos and the Mets. "If you like a late inning reliefer...," Lee is saying. But Rather's got his mind on another sporting event, the Graf-Sabatini match that CBS is covering live, which might just run over into the news.

"Where's the tennis match?" he calls.

"It's almost over," comes the answer. Rather relaxes as Frances pads in the final flesh tones. Then, attaching his microphone and ear-piece—"bring the volume down a third," he calls—Rather settles in to look over what he's about to read. It's the promotional copy that's used to tease the national news on local stations.

"Quiet please!" calls the floor manager. "Dan Rather headlines for affiliates! Five seconds. Four. Quiet!" With the cue, Rather starts reading "...all that and more coming up soon, so stay with us." Then it's a three-second ID: "Drugs—One Nation Under Siege—Tomorrow." "Drugs—One Nation Under Siege—Tonight." "Drugs—One Nation Under Siege—All This Week." He nails each one on the first take.

For Rather, at 6:07 PM, just before the evening news, this is the culmination of a long day. Most mornings he'll be up before six o'clock. In fact, a light sleeper, Rather has been known to call into CBS's news desk for updates at 2:00 AM, 3:00 AM, any hour of the night. Some mornings, Rather says, he'll go out jogging just as the sun comes up. Almost every morning he'll pick up the *Times*, the *Post*, the *Journal*, then switch on CBS's morning news while he shaves and showers. By contrast, Peter Jennings is a morning fan of BBC radio and National Public Radio.

Though he's not in early as often as he used to be, on most days Rather will be striding in the front door of the CBS News building on West 57th Street by 9:30 AM, past the Edward R. Murrow plaque in the lobby and down the corridors. This large white structure is sometimes called "the Dairy" because it was once the site of the Sheffield Farms Milk Company, but today it's hard to imagine anything remotely pastoral going on in such a squat, windowless bunker of a building. Inside, the tiny corridors meander with Kafkaesque vagueness and the white walls are so close you can almost touch both at once.

When Rather arrives, he'll be handed a xeroxed sheet. "Good Morning," it says conversationally, and then proceeds to list such things as the main stories of the day, and which reporters are assigned where. Rather and Tom Bettag will huddle several times informally, discussing which stories are in the can, which are on assignment, which have yet to be generated.

Usually, Rather will not attend the 10:00 AM call, nor the 10:30 call, as foreign and domestic bureaus present their menus of stories for the day. Even with the title of managing editor, Rather does not shoulder the primary story assignment responsibility. He is not a detail person. Like a senior executive, he'll poke his head into a meeting and check up on overall status from time to time, but only infrequently will he get involved with micro-management, when a major story or a foreign trip is being planned.

"At about eleven o'clock," Rather says, "we begin to play the game. That's what Tom Bettag calls it. The game is: If we had to put together the news right now, what would we do?" Over the next four hours, Rather will wander in and out of the newsroom, stopping off sporadically to play the game with Bettag, or chat with senior producers like Bill Crawford or Susan Zirinsky, before returning to his office.

His office is unquestionably the executive suite. One floor above the newsroom, he can look down on the producers below like Caesar contemplating the gladiators. It's a two-part layout, an outer and an inner sanctum, and before you get to either you have to pass not one but two secretaries out front. This suite used to belong to the president of CBS News. Today, Rather resides there. As polished and decorated as an elegant stage set, the outer office includes a large freshwater fish tank, an ornate, old-fashioned wood bureau, with an old manual typewriter on one side, and a computer on the other. Inside, a large Bible lies open on a book stand.

As part of his job, Rather is called on to fill many roles. He is the most visible representative of CBS News—the living logo of CBS itself—and as such on many afternoons, he is frequently required to play the combined role of network figure head and salesman. He'll shake hands with affiliate managers or local news directors passing through town, record TV promos, do photographs for a print ad campaign, emcee a retirement luncheon, host a presentation of a new show for the national TV critics. Then there are phone calls to make, contacts and sources to stay in touch with, and producers to keep an eye on.

He says, "I want to spend some of the day as a reporter, to make phone calls, and some as managing editor. We have a family of people who work on the broadcast and I like to see them, talk to them, encourage them, sometimes chastise them and discipline them." Finally, although "Evening News" is what Rather calls his first, second and third top priority, there are the other shows he appears on: the weekly primetime "48 Hours," and "Dan Rather Reporting," the daily radio show, for which Rather sketches out ideas, later drafted by a writer, then delivers the report. In short, like all anchors, Dan Rather is, as he puts it, "a man who wears many hats."

You know this to be so as soon as you enter his office. They're all there, hanging in the closet, a large rack of hats. There's everything from a New York Mets baseball cap to a taxi driver's cloth cap. Some are disguises, which the superstar anchor uses when he walks the streets of New York, to keep from being recognized.

But then there are other hats that are pure Rather. There's the soft, tweedy hat of the angler, the fishing addict who, in the words of his longtime friend Bill Johnston, is "never happier than when he has a hook in the water." Rather often goes off on weekends or vacations to his fishing cabin in the Catskills, or his country home above Austin, Texas, on the Highland Lakes.

And then there is the Stetson. It may say the most about Rather, a man who still has a Texas temper and a Texas graciousness, an old-fashioned, down home "yes sir" and "no ma'am" style. Framed on the wall of the anchor's office is a poster that reads "Gene Autry's Ten Rules of the Cowboy Code." It goes from number one—"A cowboy never takes advantage—even of an enemy"—to number ten—"A cowboy is a patriot." It may be cornball, it may be an unlikely anachronism, especially at the end of the 20th century in a city like New York, but Dan Rather still believes in the cowboy code.

Executive producer Tom Bettag's office is downstairs. A narrow, windowless pie-shaped wedge, the space is decorated with Japanese posters and TV monitors. Most of the time, though, he's in "The Fishbowl," the glassed-in office that looks out on, and serves as the command post for, the CBS newsroom. The Fishbowl always seems to be full of senior producers banging on computers, talking into telephones, or shaking their heads over some piece they're screening. At 2:45 though, it's absolutely packed. Rather comes downstairs from his office, Bettag steps over from his, and the lineup, the official run-down of stories to appear that night, gets hammered out.

They talk easily, jovially, Rather and his executive producer. In the volatile world of TV, theirs is a special relationship, with a special closeness. Some suggest that Bettag, who lost his dad at an early age, sees Rather as the father he never had. Others describe an older brother-younger brother relationship. Clearly, the two speak of each other with a mutual admiration. Bettag glowingly details the anchor's long history in the news business, from the JFK assassination to Tiananmen Square, and his "golden gut" for news hunches.

But there are reporters and producers, both inside and outside CBS, who suggest that perhaps the relationship is a little too close. Perhaps Bettag is a little too deferential, too protective. Perhaps it isn't healthy.

"It's sycophantic," says one CBS reporter. "Tom is running around, trying to shield Dan, as if he needs shielding. Dan isn't so fragile. But if Dan comes over to talk to you, Bettag will stand behind him and make gestures, like 'Don't say something to upset him,' as if you would. Tom wants to keep people away, to be the intermediary, and in the end that hurts Dan Rather more than it helps him."

As Rather and Bettag stand together in the Fishbowl, sorting through the day's stories, it's intriguing to wonder how these two characters found each other. Pale and wiry, the midwestern Bettag is boyish looking for the father of two college kids. He rides his bike to work each day from the Upper West Side. Yet despite the boyishness, his critics claim that Bettag is a clever in-house politician, almost Machiavellian in his ability to play subordinates off against each other. There are some who say that he's "able to walk three sides of a two-sided street."

But one thing everyone agrees on, as "60 Minutes" producer David Gelber says: "I don't know anybody as thoughtful about the news as Tom Bettag." Behind his glasses and his slow, rambling, interminable sentences is a keen mind, deeply concerned about the shape of the news. With a low-key intelligence, he talks about not reinventing TV, not "putting dents in the box, but doing pirouettes inside the box."

Rather, who stands looking over Bettag's shoulder, can be prickly and tightly-wound, something of a lonesome cowboy. Even those who count themselves among his allies say that he believes he has few friends, perhaps fewer than he really does, and that he frequently subjects his colleagues to "loyalty tests." But he is fiercely protective of those he counts as friends, which is perhaps why Rather has publicly said that as long as he is anchor, he will never have an executive producer other than Bettag.

At heart, the midwestern Catholic and the Texas Baptist are kindred spirits. They share a passion for the news, an enthusiasm for what

Bettag calls "the world's greatest job," and a commitment to preserving the CBS tradition as the "Tiffany" among the network news divisions, even as the luster is starting to fade. Rather says, "I never thought I'd meet anybody who works as hard as I do, who cares as much as I do. Tom Bettag is the heart of the 'Evening News.' "

At 6:11 PM, Rather is sitting at his anchor desk running through the evening's copy. Pen in one hand, a cup of coffee in the other, he's cutting a word here, adding a phrase there. "Dan's a tinkerer," Bettag says. "He doesn't like being reined in. He'll change words just to not feel constrained. Dan is a master of doing unpredictable things just to say 'you're not going to control every aspect of my life.' "

As he sits at the anchor desk quietly scanning his copy, while desk assistants and editors rush by with last-minute changes in the material, Dan Rather seems to be at the exact center of the CBS newsroom. In fact, that's precisely the way it was designed. Imagine a series of concentric rings, radiating out from the anchor desk like ripples on a pond. On the outer edge, beyond the circles, are the control room and the satellite transmissions center, Room 34, where, under a sign that reads, "And your mother always said watching TV won't get you anywhere," harried technicians are taking in feeds from around the world.

The outermost circle contains the offices of the "Evening News" foreign editor, national editor, and the Fishbowl, all with large glass windows looking inward. The next two rings in are the foreign desk, the national desk, the writers' desk, where intense figures in shirt-sleeves pound away at humming computers, the screens amber and green. Finally, at the heart of the matter, is the anchor desk.

In all the glassed-in surrounding offices, the fluorescent ceiling lights are lined up on a radius from the center, that is, Dan's chair. He is clearly, by design, at the core of everything. In this anchor-centric vision, a stream of facts flows into him, and news flows out. Which is exactly how set designer Hugh Raisky conceived it.

"I wanted the 'Evening News' set to be a world news center," the dapper Raisky acknowledges. "Everything would feed into the studio. I wanted everybody outside the circle—the people in the surrounding offices—to feed into the anchorman and he'd be the center, the end of the process. There were technical problems in having the anchor in the center, but it was worth it symbolically."

6:13 PM, and in the inner ring, editor Lee Townsend, the bespectacled veteran who sits at Rather's right hand through the broadcast, is talking with Tom Bettag. "So we're killing the piece from Colombia?" he asks. "Right," says Bettag. "We're putting in gypsy moths."

Rather gets up, and walks around the ring to Bettag. "Tonight gonna be an easy one?" he asks.

"Well," says Bettag, "it's a Friday, and it's a full moon."

Over in the corner of the studio, beyond the rings, stands a lonely blue podium, four feet tall. It's Rather's solution to a problem that's nagged him since the post-Cronkite era. When the podium is installed in a matter of days, Rather will be able to deliver the news standing. In a way it makes sense, for unlike Charles Kuralt, a writer's announcer, Rather is an action announcer, and as Kuralt says, "I think with the ends of my fingertips. Dan thinks on his feet."

As Rather walks back toward his anchor desk, he has to admit that he prefers standing: "The podium came out of the China trip. Burke said, 'The stuff you did on your feet is better.' That's true for almost anyone. People speak better on their feet. The voice resonates more. That's why the priest or the rabbi speaks on his feet." (But despite the lengthy rationale, Rather used the podium for only six months in 1989, and by early 1990, he was once more back in his anchor's chair. The change was indicative of a certain basic uncertainty at CBS News, a recent tendency to grasp at straws.)

Behind the podium is a massive ten-foot screen, a double Sony rear projection unit that Rather uses for charts and graphs. "Yeah," says a technician hurrying by, "I'd sure like to have me one of those sets in my basement." CBS staffers jokingly call the unit "Mister Map."

"Five minutes to air," comes the call. "Five minutes." Rather is huddled with Bettag and Townsend. "We're gonna try to keep the bumper," Bettag says. "The second section goes 'Crash,' then Braver." Near the writers' desk a printer spews out the last revisions, in triplicate. "A federal judge in Atlanta has just issued a gag order on Martinez," shouts a writer. "Do you care?"

"Three minutes." Rather walks back to the anchor desk, pats down his hair, and puts on his jacket. Assistants are dashing around the newsroom, grabbing the latest copy and running off to the control room. "Two minutes." A stack of papers arrives on Dan's desk. "This is what you haven't seen yet."

"One minute." Bettag runs over for a literal last-minute huddle with Rather. At thirty seconds, the anchor takes a last sip of coffee, puts down his glasses, adjusts his tie, neatens the stack of papers, and ...

"*This* is the CBS Evening News, Dan Rather reporting. Former President Ronald Reagan will undergo skull surgery tonight...." Rather throws to correspondent Phil Jones in the field. As the red light over camera one goes out, he turns to ask for more coffee. Tom Bettag comes over to the anchor desk to update Rather. He reports that they're expecting more information on Reagan any minute.

"Fifteen seconds!" Bettag hurries back to the Fishbowl, and Rather starts in on the stories about President Bush on drugs, and assault weapons. "Lesley Stahl begins our coverage..."

Out in the control room, the commands come quick and sharp: "Ready one. Roll...Dissolve...Take two, my cue. Slowly, David. Roll track... Matte...Lose the matte, please. 34 standby, please. Cue, Mike. Cue! Okay, unless the phone rings, we have Braver, then a bumper." The phone rings, and everyone laughs. "Ready to black. Black." And so the show runs: from the handicapped, to the New York mayoral race, to Jim and Tammy Bakker, to Mother Teresa, with just a few commercials thrown in: "Oil of Olay—age looks so much better on a man."

At 6:53, with a commercial running, Tom Bettag hurries out of the Fishbowl, and a routine night shifts into overdrive. "Reagan may have just been operated on," he yells. "We'll let you know." Rather nods, and he's back on camera. "We end the week on a bittersweet note...." In the Fishbowl, Bettag is standing up, the phone cradled on his left shoulder. He hurries out and stands over writer Paul Fischer's shoulder as he types rapidly.

6:57:45. "And that's a part of our world tonight," Rather closes. And then it's time for the second feed, which is often just a taped replay of the first, but not tonight.

6:59. "We have no confirmation," yells Bettag. "We have no confirmation." The phone rings, and he rushes back to the Fishbowl to grab it. He listens and slams down the receiver. "We got it!" he shouts.

"Lee," Rather yells, "are we starting on tape?"

"Yes," Tom says. "No, start live! Just throw it up live! GO! GO!" He dashes out of camera range.

"Lee, is it on the teleprompter?" Rather asks. "I'll do it off the page." He grabs the copy that an assistant throws him, and in one motion, like a shortstop completing a double play, he turns smoothly to camera and begins "This is the CBS Evening News, Dan Rather reporting. Former President of the United States, Ronald Reagan, has undergone skull surgery to relieve pressure on his brain...."

Bettag pokes his head out of the Fishbowl. "Okay," he calls. "Nice. We may have a tag." The Reagan tape piece is running. Seconds tick by. "What?" Bettag says into the phone. "Right." He yells to Rather: "The tag: resting comfortably after routine surgery. Believed to be a success."

The Reagan piece is seconds from finishing. "I'll just ad-lib it," he yells. The red light over camera one goes on. Rather looks into the lens and smiles. "We are happy to report that CBS News has been told that the President is resting comfortably after what doctors insist was routine surgery. The surgery was called a success."

As they go back to tape, everyone around the newsroom lets out a collective sigh. "Phew!" says Bettag. "The trick is that Susan Zirinsky in Washington had the tip that the announcement would be coming out of the White House. Otherwise, you couldn't get it through the system fast enough." He gives a little grin, and rubs the back of his head. "You can mess up in those situations real bad."

"Did anyone else get the story?" Rather calls. Naturally, it's the first question that the competitive anchor would ask. The others did get the story, but not quite as quickly.

It's 7:09, and all the excitement is over, a squall that subsided as quickly as it blew up. The rest of the second feed is on autopilot, on tape. But Rather has one more thing yet to do, a brief update for the West Coast: "Former President of the United States, Ronald Reagan, is said to be resting comfortably...."

When the update is finished, it's time to turn out the lights and call it a day. Getting up from his anchor desk, Rather looks about at the editors and producers still on duty in the rings around him, and nods his head with satisfaction. "Okay," he calls, "let's get these troops out of the sun."

RATINGS: Week ending September 15th

1st. Rather   ("CBS Evening News")—9.4/20 [8,657,400]

2nd. Brokaw   ("NBC Nightly News")—9.0/20 [8,289,000]

3rd. Jennings (ABC's "World News Tonight")—8.9/19 [8,196,900]

(In September, the Nielsen Company changed one point = 904,000 households to one point = 921,000 households.)

CHAPTER EIGHTEEN

Berlin: The Wall

In the back of the newsroom at NBC, in one of the partitioned booths that resemble college library study carrels, the foreign producer of the "Nightly News," Marc Kusnetz, was banging out a memo to a correspondent. The words flashed across the screen on his Digital VT 320 monitor as he typed: "I'd love to see more of that heavy historical stuff in the spot."

It was Tuesday, November 7, a big news day, and Kusnetz looked a little harried. There was political unrest in East Berlin. Hundreds of thousands of demonstrators were marching in the streets of Leipzig. And in the U.S., it was Election Day. To top it all off, Kusnetz had to play host to his two kids home from school for the day.

Nicky, his youngest, was squirming on his lap when the wire report came up on the monitor. "Hey folks!" he cried out. "Folks!"

Tom Brokaw, who happened to be in the newsroom just then, hurried across to the producer's desk. Peering over Kusnetz's shoulder, he read the bulletin. The entire East German cabinet had just resigned. Within minutes, Brokaw was on the air, reporting the latest development from behind the Iron Curtain. Eager to avoid any delay, he didn't bother to write anything down before breaking into regular programming with his Special Report. Only three weeks earlier, Brokaw had taken a critical pasting for NBC's delayed coverage of the San Francisco earthquake, and he was damned if he'd be left in the starting blocks again.

As the anchor finished his report and came off the set, Jerry Lamprecht—NBC senior producer for future planning—was standing there. He told Brokaw, "You gotta go tonight."

Plans to go to Berlin had been in the works for weeks. On the 18th of the previous month when Egon Krenz replaced Erich Honecker as Secretary General of the East German Communist Party, executive producer Bill Wheatley had almost immediately attempted to arrange an interview with him. "We were exploring with the East Germans the possibility of broadcasting live from there," Kusnetz recalled. Soon stories were assigned, correspondents moved into place. Then on October 23 and 30, more than 300,000 East Germans demonstrated in the streets of Leipzig, demanding *democracy now*! Though the original plan was to go to Berlin the week before the Bush-Gorbachev meeting in Malta, which was scheduled for December 2 and 3, events in Eastern Europe were moving so rapidly that Brokaw began to feel nervous about holding off until then. And now Lamprecht was anxious too.

The two of them were soon joined by Don Browne, the executive news director, and Dave Miller, the foreign news director. The question was: To go or not to go? Brokaw was trying to think ahead. "Listen," he said, "I've got a couple of things in Washington that we've already set in motion."

Corazon Aquino was visiting the United States, and Brokaw had arranged an interview with her the next night in Washington. As it turned out, it would have been a good time for such an interview. Within the next few weeks, Aquino would suffer the sixth, and most serious, coup attempt against her Presidency. The four of them stood there ventilating the pros and cons of leaving immediately, but because of the Aquino meeting, Brokaw still wasn't sure what to do when he left for lunch. On the way out, he stopped by his executive producer's office and told Bill Wheatley, "I probably ought to go to West Germany tonight." Wheatley nodded. He had been thinking the same thing.

By chance, Brokaw's lunch that day happened to be with a high-powered group of people who had, in his words, "been around the world of geo-politics." It included Paul Nitze—once the U.S. representative at Geneva in disarmament negotiations with the Russians—and Richard Holbrook, formerly of the Rand Corporation and active in defense research. Brokaw told them about the news from East

Germany. They were stunned. The entire luncheon was spent discussing the astonishing changes going on behind the Iron Curtain. By the time Brokaw returned to NBC it was well after 2:00 PM. Walking into Wheatley's office, Brokaw noted that both the executive producer and Jerry Lamprecht were looking somber. "We think you ought to go," Wheatley said.

"I understand," Brokaw replied. But as he always does in this sort of situation, he pointed out that if he went, it was going to alter the entire newscast. "And what if I get there," he said, "and Czechoslovakia goes instead?"

"Yeah," said Lamprecht. "Well, let's all just take the chance."

When his baby-sitter arrived to pick up his kids, Kusnetz walked them down the hallway to the elevator. Suddenly he heard someone calling him. It was Cheryl Gould, the senior producer, and she was clearly excited about something. "I'll be right back," he told her. "I'm just bringing my kids to the elevator."

"It's *important*," she shouted. "Come *now!*"

Kusnetz kissed his kids goodbye and hurried back to Bill Wheatley's office where Cheryl and Jerry Lamprecht and Don Browne were talking with Wheatley. Turning to Kusnetz, the executive producer asked, "Is there any reason you can't leave tonight?"

The new plan was to take off for Germany right after the evening newscast. Kusnetz spent a good part of the afternoon mapping out logistics and making sure that they had the right people in place over there. When the anchor moves into the field, a whole new team has to be assembled. With the help of the people on the foreign assignment desk, Kusnetz arranged to move correspondent Jim Bittermann from Paris to Frankfurt to cover the border, and Martin Fletcher from Israel. Frankfurt bureau chief Suzette Knittl was sent to Berlin. Mike Silver, the head of the Jordan bureau, traveled from Amman to Frankfurt, and Rick Davis also shifted to Frankfurt. Mike Boettcher went to Berlin, and later so too did Arthur Kent. This movement of correspondents is like a zone defense in basketball, where defenders shift their positions as a unit to cover the ball, but like a zone defense, it can be defeated simply by bad mismatches. A bureau chief based in Jordan, for example, is not necessarily the best source of information about events in Eastern Europe.

That afternoon, Brokaw worked the phones hard. He was already generally familiar with the political situation in East Germany, but for an important trip like this one, he needed more information: "I called an old friend of mine at the Harriman Institute at Columbia, Bob Legvold. I called Bill Hyland at the Council of Foreign Relations. I called some people in Washington."

Then he raced uptown to his Park Avenue apartment to get his traveling bag. The apartment, which was being remodeled, happened to be locked, and as luck would have it, he didn't have a key. "So I had to grab what I could. One of the things I do is take carry-on baggage. I always travel light and fast," says Brokaw, the same way he likes to move when hiking or mountain climbing.

He obtained another bag, packed it, checked to make sure he had his passport, and picked up his plane and hotel reservations from unit manager Maralyn Gelefsky, who had succeeded in booking them at the last minute. And in his spare time that Tuesday afternoon, he also got ready to go on the air at 6:30 PM to bring millions of viewers their "Nightly News."

By nine o'clock that night, Brokaw was at JFK Airport ready to board Lufthansa's 9:35 PM flight to Frankfurt. With him were an NBC production assistant, a computer technician and Marc Kusnetz, his longtime producer, whom Brokaw considered "really plugged in on what had been going on in Germany." Both Brokaw and Kusnetz brought big clipping files on board with them, and even before they were in the air, they had begun going through the material. Airborne, they discussed story ideas. They wanted to do something on the new East German opposition alliance. They planned to talk to its members when they got there. But what they really tried to do was sleep. They both knew there would be little time for rest once they arrived in Berlin.

Sitting next to one another on the plane, Brokaw and Kusnetz, though about the same age, seemed an odd pair. Kusnetz, wearing rimless glasses, was bearded, professorial, grayhound thin, with maybe a hint of urban nervous energy just beneath the surface. Brokaw was calm, fair skinned, at home in the world, Waspy. But they were, in fact, close friends. When Kusnetz's wife was dying of cancer, Brokaw pulled out all the stops for her. He contacted a specialist he knew at the University of Minnesota. He loaned the couple his house in Connecticut. He did everything he could to help.

To Kusnetz, "Tom has been much more than a colleague to me. He's been like a brother."

Now the widower had left his two kids behind, after a whole lot of hugging, and was on his way to Europe with no definite idea of what he and Brokaw would find there or when they'd be back.

The flight seemed quick to the travelers, and after making their connection in Frankfurt, they arrived in West Berlin on Wednesday, November 8, in the early afternoon. They went straight to the Schweizerhof hotel, just off the glittering Kurfürstendamm, Berlin's Fifth Avenue, where a temporary base of operations had already been set up. Kusnetz says, "My bag of clothes sat there all day. I didn't get around to even checking into my room that day."

Brokaw quickly learned that Egon Krenz was attempting to reorganize the Politburo. The East German leader had asked Hans Modrow to form a new government. In the face of the mass migrations and demonstrations, the Communist Party was clearly on the run. Brokaw had supposed that this would be his story when he left New York. In order to cover it, he had asked for permission to bring his cameras into East Berlin.

About 1:15 PM (7:15 AM Eastern Time), he called his executive producer back in New York. "The story's taking shape," he told Wheatley. "Now they're saying that they're going to recognize opposition parties. They're even talking about elections. We've gotten permission to shoot tonight in East Berlin, so we'll do our taping there."

Crossing at Checkpoint Charlie, Brokaw felt the arctic chill of the expressionless armed guards, as grim as ever. It was hard to be patient as he suffered their exasperatingly time-consuming interrogation and search. His story lay on the other side, and in the line of traffic, their car seemed to be moving forward an inch at a time. As they sat there, Kusnetz was struck by the irony: Mind-boggling developments were sweeping the Eastern Bloc, but some things never seemed to change.

It took Brokaw and Kusnetz well over an hour to get across. The one hundred meter no-man's land between the wall and the streets of East Berlin was heavily patrolled by army units with automatic weapons and dogs. The two of them quickly drove over to the Brandenburg Gate—once the heart of an undivided Berlin and a unified Germany—where they pre-taped the opening of that night's broadcast.

"Good evening from the Brandenburg Gate in East Berlin," Brokaw began. "East Germany remains a country in turmoil tonight, and no one knows for sure how or when calm can be restored." The anchor reported that in the past twenty-four hours still more Communist Party hardliners had been "thrown overboard in an effort by the party to stay afloat." Later in the program, Jim Bittermann from Bonn had Chancellor Kohl declaring, "The Berlin Wall cannot endure." And Wheatley closed the broadcast with an interview Brokaw had done earlier that day with three young East Germans who had fled to the West.

It was not a particularly inspired performance by the anchor. Perhaps he was still suffering from jet lag when he asked them such predictably boring questions as, "One year ago did you think that you'd be standing here today?" (This from a man who prides himself on never tossing a lob!)

The answer to the final question that he asked, however, was of more than routine interest. "Do you think it will come down?" he inquired of the young man who had lived beside the Berlin Wall for eight years. The young man hardly paused before answering quite matter-of-factly, "Yes, of course. It *is* down." To him it was already a *fait accompli*.

Brokaw would say after the broadcast, "I gather that at the New York end there was a fair amount of second guessing on the part of our competitors. They were saying, 'Well, what's he doing there?' This was the day after the elections in America. But we were already making the judgment that the elections contained no major surprises."

In the U.S., Douglas Wilder, the grandson of slaves, was elected governor of Virginia—the first black governor ever in American history. In New York, another black man, David Dinkins, had been elected the first black mayor of the city in an unexpectedly tight race. But as far as Brokaw and NBC were concerned, that news had apparently gone stale very fast.

"It was a good story," the anchor acknowledged, "but everybody knew they were going to win. From eleven o'clock the night before they had been on the air. So we were feeling secure in what we'd done. And everything was looking good."

One thing that was looking especially good was the story that Brokaw had already begun to prepare about some members of the opposition New Forum group. In conjunction with this report, he was hoping to arrange a meeting with Günter Schabowski, the East Berlin Communist Party leader and spokesman. Brokaw had never met the man, but today American anchors are surprisingly well-known abroad. Perhaps this is a result of more Europeans visiting our country, or the anchors' appearances on Armed Forces Radio, or rebroadcasts on European TV of their interviews with leading European statesmen, like Brokaw's of Gorbachev, or the presence of CNN in European hotels.

Brokaw, who has noted the change, says, "Almost everywhere in the world they now know who we are. And *that*," he points out, "means access." Together with Michelle Neubert—an NBC Production Assistant in Germany—Brokaw had earlier attended a news conference for Schabowski. Approaching the Party leader, the NBC anchor told him that he wanted to do an interview with him. Schabowski, who speaks English, said no. He couldn't do it. *But*, he added abruptly, perhaps tomorrow night.

The next morning, Thursday, the 9th of November, Brokaw was up by 7:30 after only about five hours sleep. The first thing he did was go back across the border to talk with the New Forum group in order to get a better understanding of their objectives. That morning he and his producer also learned that the East German Politburo had met and were continuing to fire people. "So we knew that we had a strong story going on that day, and we continued to cobble together that and other elements," Brokaw said.

Around midday at the West Berlin side of the Brandenburg Gate, Brokaw and Kusnetz ran into Jerry Lamprecht who had followed them to Germany. Lamprecht wanted to know if they would be needing the satellite uplink facility that NBC had on the west side of the Brandenburg Gate. The famous landmark is the one obvious location for such a live broadcasting facility. The Wall and the Gate make for a spectacular background.

"I think you'd better keep it up," Brokaw replied, "but I don't know if there's going to be anything so fluid that we'll need it. If we can continue to tape in East Berlin, let's do that, because nobody has seen that much of it." Besides, as they both knew, it was always easier to tape than go live.

Again, Brokaw returned to East Berlin for the news conference being given that evening by the New Forum, and afterwards he taped interviews with some of the artists and intellectuals who make up the group. Kurt Masur, who would subsequently be appointed conductor of the New York Philharmonic, was among their leaders.

Later that evening at the press ministry, Schabowski appeared before about three hundred journalists to spell out the government's new political concessions and to announce a Party conference in December. He spoke of the need for a free press. He spoke of the need for more women in positions of authority. He said the economy should reward performance. But in every instance, he was vague on details.

As far as Kusnetz was concerned, the news conference was a bore. "It was ponderous. It went on and on. I was feeling all these developments are interesting, but it's all so disparate. How can I make it into a coherent story of the day?" Restless, Kusnetz took off the earpiece he was wearing for translation and wandered out of the room.

"And then," as Brokaw recalls the scene, "with just five minutes left in the scheduled time, as reporters and cameramen were preparing to pack up, Mr. Schabowski began to describe a new travel policy recommended by the Politburo that day. It came in stacatto bursts from the English translator. 'The regulation for permanent exit...we consider this to be an impossible situation, when this movement is carried out through a friendly state [Czechoslovakia]. For this reason we have decided...a regulation...possible for every citizen to exit the border crossings of the GDR [East Germany].' "

"Immediately?" shouted one reporter.

Putting on his glasses and pulling a document from an inside pocket, the East German party leader began to read. "Private travel...can be applied for without prerequisite travel permission...the permit will be issued promptly."

By now, the reporters in the room began to look at one another to see if they had all heard the same translation.

"Does that include West Berlin?" asked one of them.

Schabowski nodded. "Yes, yes...permanent exit can take place through all border crossings of the GDR, to the Federal Republic of Germany or West Berlin."

Just then Kusnetz returned to the room. Immediately he noticed the stricken look on Brokaw's face.

"Did you hear *that*?" Brokaw asked.

"What?"

"I think he said that the border is open."

"What?" Kusnetz looked to see if he was joking. "As of when?"

"I think he said immediately."

An astonished British journalist came up to them. "Did you hear what he said?"

Everybody stood milling around and talking at once, not yet sure that they could believe what they heard. It was a mob scene. "Just don't lose sight of Schabowski," Kusnetz warned his camera crew as they ran after him. The Communist spokesman had promised to talk with them, and Kusnetz would be damned if he'd let him slip away now.

The interview with Schabowski was held in a twelve-by-twelve room two floors up in the press ministry, a spartan office with only a few chairs and a sofa. In the room with the anchor, his producer and their camera crew were Schabowski and two assistants. What Brokaw wanted to do, as any reporter would, was nail down the new policy in plain language in order to be sure that he had understood it correctly. So he began by walking him through it. "Let me just understand this here.... Mr. Schabowski," he said, and then read slowly from the notes he had taken at the press conference. "Do I understand correctly...citizens of the GDR can leave through any checkpoint that they choose for personal reasons? They no longer have to go through a third country?"

Schabowski listened carefully, his hand on his chin. A heavy set, fleshy man with gray hair combed straight back, he sported a Party membership pin in his lapel. "Yes, yes," he nodded. "They are not further forced to leave GDR by transit to another country."

"It is possible for them to go through the wall?" Brokaw asked, attempting to pin him down.

"It is possible for them to go through the wall," Schabowski repeated.

"Freedom to travel?"

"Yes, of course."

As Kusnetz watched, he was amazed at the impromptu nature of Schabowski's responses. "I had the distinct impression that the decision had just been reached," Kusnetz recalled. "It all had an ad hoc quality. The guys were passing him sheets of paper during the interview. At one point, Brokaw asked a question, and Schabowski had to check the papers for the answer. He was so tentative. It was absolutely surreal."

No sooner was the interview over than Brokaw bolted out of the room, and ran down the stairs. On the way, he met a group of Western reporters standing around reading the new policy. After twenty-eight years of the rigidly enforced, repressive old rules, they were understandably looking for the loopholes.

"It's true!" Brokaw said. "They're going to let them through!"

"Did he say—?"

"I asked him *specifically*. It's true! I've got it on tape. The passport business will be taken care of immediately beginning tomorrow morning."

There was no more time to waste answering questions. Brokaw hurried out of the building. Looking back at that moment, Kusnetz smiles in wonder. "Well, when things go right, they *really* go right." Their rented Mercedes stood just outside the door of the press ministry. And by some incredible stroke of luck, the car just happened to have a "really solid" Telefunken cellular phone. In minutes, Brokaw was speaking to NBC in New York. Patched into a special bulletin with Garrick Utley at 7:40 PM (1:40 PM New York time), he reported to America on the dramatic new East German policy while sitting in the front seat of a Mercedes.

Although Rather and Jennings were probably already on their way, Brokaw had been the first to break the news. He felt that he had a big jump on the competition, and there were still about five hours left before that evening's broadcast. The Schabowski press conference had been broadcast live, so word spread swiftly. As they crossed back into West Berlin through Checkpoint Charlie, Brokaw asked the guard, "What do you think of the new travel policy?"

"I have no opinion," the guard said stiffly. This time, however, the check of their car trunk was only casual. Just before waving them through, the guard beamed a smile and said, "My opinion is the official opinion."

Back at the Schweizerhof hotel, Brokaw began writing up his account of the press conference for that evening's newscast on one of the NBC computers. He also spent time looking over the tape of the Schabowski interview. There were now about eighty people crowded into the temporary bureau that had been set up in the wing of rooms just off the hotel lobby. Soon, correspondents were dispatched to the various checkpoints where the East Germans might be coming across.

It was between 11:00 and 11:30 that night—an hour before their newscast in New York—when Suzette Knittl came running into the room where Brokaw was finishing up his piece. She was wide eyed.

She had just heard that huge crowds were gathering on the west side of the Brandenburg Gate, right next to the NBC live remote unit.

"I think we're going to have to get security so that you can do the program tonight," Knittl said.

"Wait a minute, Suzette," Brokaw stopped her. The events were so extraordinary that the Frankfurt bureau chief didn't get it: This wasn't a crowd attracted by a TV news team's presence, he explained. It was a crowd attracted by historic events, landmark events, events even bigger than TV. When she realized what was going on, the two of them started to laugh.

Brokaw left immediately for the Brandenburg Gate, leaving Kusnetz behind to supervise the operation. At the Schweizerhof, pieces began coming in from Frankfurt, from Moscow. From London, Peter Kent was reporting on German reunification. Up and down the corridors of the hotel, it was bedlam. Talking to Wheatley in New York on a "co-ord box," a contraption resembling a combination speaker phone and taxi dispatch box, Kusnetz described his situation: he had a first piece, a second piece, a third piece. What he still needed was a "cold open."

For about two months, "Nightly" had been using cold opens— beginning its program not with an NBC logo or even Brokaw's face, but starting right in with news footage and a voice-over—in a not always successful attempt at drama. Talking with Wheatley, Kusnetz laid out the problem: He couldn't find a picture that even came close to capturing the remarkable events that were going on in Berlin.

"I was dying a thousand little deaths," he said. "I was looking at all the pix coming in, and they didn't make it. We had pictures from the news conference, but that was just a guy at a news conference. And minutes were passing."

With only twenty-five minutes to airtime, Kusnetz got back on the box with Wheatley. He still didn't have anything good. "Can we make this work?" Kusnetz asked, his voice displaying his lack of enthusiasm for the option he had presented.

Just then, Peter Samsun, one of NBC's cameramen, came running in waving a cassette in his hand. Samsun was attempting to stay cool but his eyes were on fire.

"They're thousands..." he blurted out. "Thousands of East Germans coming across at the checkpoints. Thousands...."

And Samsun had the footage in his hand to prove it. There wasn't even time to look at the pictures. Without seeing what he had, Kusnetz sent him flying out of the hotel to their live feed point at the Brandenburg Gate, to send the video on to Wheatley via satellite. A few minutes later as the new footage came into New York, Kusnetz was listening on the earpiece. He could hear Wheatley's voice saying, "Just look at these pictures!"

About fifteen minutes to air time, Brokaw was standing on a small platform near the Gate ready to be photographed. The area was jammed with West Germans. It was a cold night, and he had borrowed correspondent Mike Boettcher's heavy overcoat because his own green parka—an L.L. Bean special—was just too light for the temperature. Without warning, the West German police showed up and urged everybody to go home. "Oh God!" Brokaw thought. "They're all going to be gone by the time we come on the air."

It was about that time that the crowd in front of the Gate came surging forward. They began to climb up on the wall. From the other side, the East German military police opened up full blast with their water cannons, trying to knock them off. And just then Brokaw could dimly hear in his earphone the countdown for the broadcast to begin. "Look," he said to New York, "I don't know where this is going to go, but just stay with us." There was so much shouting all around him that it was hard to hear anything.

On the monitor, the cold open revealed a small army of young East German men and women marching inexorably forward on their way to a narrow bridge. Accompanying the picture, Brokaw's disembodied voice declared, "A historic moment tonight! The Berlin Wall can no longer contain the East German people. Thousands pouring across at the Bornholmer Bridge."

Then Brokaw appeared on the screen in a dark overcoat that looked at least one size too large for him, holding a hand to his earphone in order to hear New York better. In the background, a few young men gamboled on top of the wall, one holding a brown umbrella as the East German soldiers bombarded them with water cannons.

"Good evening," said the anchor. "*Live* from the Berlin Wall on the most historic night in this wall's history. What you see behind me is a celebration of this new policy announced today by the East German government that *now*, for the first time since the wall was erected in 1961, people will be able to move through freely."

Segments from the news conference at the press ministry followed, and then came the Schabowski interview. Then it was back to Brokaw live. "The party continues," the anchor reported, as the camera rose to the top of the wall where a couple of revelers were being drenched with water. "The police are not even able to discourage those two men even with water cannons."

Then came Jim Bittermann's piece from Bonn on the reaction of the West German parliament to news from the East. It contained a startling moment of patriotic euphoria when the entire parliament spontaneously sprang to their feet and sang their nation's national anthem. To Americans watching the telecast, it seemed as if it could have been choreographed in Hollywood. About halfway through the broadcast during a commercial break, senior producer Cheryl Gould in New York told Brokaw, "You're not going to believe this, but we've just had a plane crash in Atlanta tonight."

"How bad is it?" he asked.

"We don't know yet. There are lots of flames. But we'll work it out."

It turned out to be a Navy A7 jet fighter that had crashed into an apartment complex just north of Atlanta. What next! thought Brokaw. The crowds at the wall kept growing and the story kept building. According to the anchor, "At the end of the first show, I could hear them in the control room in New York, and they were saying we've got to turn right around and do this again. And I said be prepared to come back to us because it's really going crazy here."

It was shortly after 1:00 in the morning Berlin time (from 7:00 PM, ET, the beginning of the newscast's second feed in New York) that a roar went up from the noisy merrymakers surrounding Brokaw. Though there was no checkpoint at the Brandenburg Gate, a crowd of East Germans could be seen dashing toward the wall across the no-man's land on the other side.

"The first to reach the wall," as Brokaw later recounted the scene, "was a young man in a brown jacket. He seemed to land on top of it in a single bound. The crowd parted and cheered as he raised his arms in triumph and danced along the concrete slab that hours before had imprisoned him." Brokaw motioned frantically for the camera to come back to him live.

Cutting short Garrick Utley's updated account of the plane crash near Atlanta, Brokaw began, "What you're watching live on television is a historic moment. A moment that will live forever. You're seeing the destruction of the Berlin Wall, the dividing line between East and West Germany. On the other side of the wall, young East Germans have rushed through the Brandenburg Gate undeterred by water cannons fired at them by East German police. They have been pulled up on this wall by other young West Germans who have come there from this side on this day when the announcement went forward that there would be no more checking from East to West and West to East...They said they would allow them to go through checkpoints, but now it's clear. They have effectively taken down the wall."

Despite the glitches—calling West Germany's Chancellor, Helmut Schmitt instead of Helmut Kohl; the awkward switching from New York to Berlin that brought up a stock market graph rather than Brokaw—the entire broadcast had gone off well, given the nature of the events and the technical problems.

"You know," Brokaw would say afterwards, "it's the broadcasting equivalent of being a thousand feet in the air without a net. It's a real adrenaline pump. It's not playtime. These are important events, and you didn't want to be there at this historic moment and get it wrong. You didn't want to say something that was going to be embarrassing. The event spoke for itself in a way, and what you wanted to do was supplement what you were seeing with, you hope, some observations that would give it some context, some perspective. And that was what I was trying to do."

That night in Berlin, Marc Kusnetz told the people in New York to put the phone near a TV monitor, so that he could hear the broadcast. He sat there in the small hotel room listening to the newscast and feeling the strangeness of being so very close to the story, yet getting it via New York. In the final segment, there were excerpts from President Kennedy's *"Ich bin ein Berliner"* speech, and the broadcast closed on the cheers of the crowd. Above that sound and drowning it out, Kusnetz heard the entire newsroom in New York break into applause. "It gave me chills," he said. After the dismal year that NBC News had had, it was great to finally come up with a winner.

Later that evening, Kusnetz went out with a cameraman to get additional material for the news special that NBC planned to do on the historic developments in Germany. On top of the wall, which is six to eight feet thick, there were now throngs of people. "Does anyone up there speak English?" he shouted.

Directly above their heads, a redheaded woman with a hammer and chisel was banging away at the wall. Without stopping, she said, "I speak English." As she hammered away exuberantly at the cement, chips flying off in all directions like acetylene sparks, the producer conducted his interview.

The next morning, back in his room at the Schweizerhof, Kusnetz, feeling better after a few hours sleep, showered early. Washing his hair, he found tiny pebbles. He glanced down at the tub, and saw that it was littered with pebbles going down the drain. Puzzled for a second, he suddenly realized what they were and smiled. "That's the Berlin Wall!" he thought.

RATINGS: Week ending November 10th

Despite Brokaw's "scoop," the score card that week read:

1st. Jennings (ABC's "World News Tonight")—11.1/20 [10,223,100]

2nd. Rather   ("CBS Evening News")—10.3/19 [9,486,300]

3rd. Brokaw   ("NBC Nightly News")—10.0/19 [9,210,000]

CHAPTER NINETEEN

Jennings as Anchor

In July of 1983, Peter Jennings returned to the ABC Washington bureau to fill in for the ailing Frank Reynolds. Reynolds had been in and out of hospitals since March, and Jennings had been asked to take over the anchor chair for a couple of months until he recovered. No one was sure exactly what was wrong with Reynolds, and the intensely private anchor wanted to keep it that way.

But only a few days after arriving in the U.S., Jennings was invited to Reynolds' house for lunch, the first business visitor Reynolds had received in months. Jennings thought he looked thin and weak. But as they sat down to eat, Reynolds packed away his food with gusto, and when the conversation turned to the future, the color came back to his cheeks as Reynolds talked enthusiastically about returning to his job in the fall.

Less than a week later, on July 20, Frank Reynolds was dead. He had been suffering from cancer, and had concealed the fact from his colleagues. The sudden death of the sixty-year-old anchorman sent ABC into shock. Reynolds was the first anchor to die on the job. ABC not only had a terrible tragedy to cope with, but they also had a gaping void to fill: How could they replace their principal anchor, their most respected journalist?

For Roone Arledge and his management team, the first decision was to get rid of their multiple anchor format. It had been only partially successful. Many still felt it was gimmicky and awkward to hop from anchor to anchor around the globe, and there were some who believed that Max Robinson wasn't pulling his weight. The second choice was harder: If there was to be just one anchor, who would it be?

Ted Koppel and Peter Jennings were the two logical candidates. Koppel, despite his Alfred E. Newman-meets-Howdy Doody features, was almost universally respected. Former colleague Richard Threlkeld was one of many who thought of Koppel as "the smartest man on television." But Koppel had established a strong identity on his own program, the 11:30 PM "Nightline," and he was reluctant to give that up. Also, he wasn't sure that he wanted to enter the high-stakes, high-pressure world of evening news anchordom. He wasn't even sure that he was the best man for the job. The conversations between Arledge and Koppel never got past a few phone calls.

Peter Jennings was the obvious choice. He had previous experience as an anchor. He had the looks, the charm. And he now had the credibility as well, an education gathered over sixteen years on the road. There was only one problem for Arledge. Jennings didn't want the job either.

His sister Sarah Jennings remembers, "At various points in his years abroad, Peter had wanted to go back to the United States, but after his third marriage, he had a good life in Britain. He had a great job, and anonymity, which most TV reporters don't have. He had a wonderful large Edwardian brick house in Hampstead, a great place for his kids. He wasn't terribly enamored of New York, especially for his small children."

Jennings and his wife, Kati Marton, loved England. They did *not* want to leave. Jennings recalls this period as "a terrible, *terrible* time of great tension between me and my boss. My boss thought, 'God, look here I'm going to offer this young man the so-called ultimate job in television.' I didn't want the job. I had what I regarded as the best job in television news at the time. I was both anchorman and chief foreign correspondent. The triumvirate, which I sometimes think we should go back to, enabled me the complete freedom to travel to virtually every major story of importance for years without being a slave to the daily broadcast. Because anchor people are slaves to the daily broadcast. Very high-priced slaves, I grant you. But slaves. So I was very much opposed to the job."

Jennings and his wife rented a cottage in East Hampton that

belonged to the local school superintendent, and spent hours hashing over the pros and cons of the job offer. "I'll never forget it," he says. "We sat there night after night after night saying we don't want to do this. We just don't want to do this."

As he thought back over sixteen years as a foreign correspondent, Jennings recalled with great fondness his days on the road, hopping on and off planes, barging in and out of countries from Nigeria to Pakistan, commandeering army jeeps, barreling down back roads, even working under the surveillance of frightened teenage soldiers carrying automatic weapons. One of the most important, and most terrifying stories he had covered had occurred only the year before, when the Israeli army, under General Ariel Sharon, had launched an invasion into Lebanon to drive the PLO out of Beirut.

Flying into Damascus in the summer of 1982, Jennings had teamed up with his old ABC colleague John Cooley. Together they drove from Syria, through winding mountain roads in the dead of night. They arrived in East Beirut just in time for one of the biggest Israeli bombardments. Holing up in the Alexander Hotel, they decided to make a break across the Green Line to West Beirut. Under heavy airborne shelling, they hired a cab, and though the driver was well paid, he would only take them part way. As shells exploded around them, fragments piercing the air, they managed to grab another cabbie, and offer him a very large fee to take them to the Commodore Hotel in West Beirut.

As Jennings would later say on the air, every war usually ends up having its hotel, the one where all the journalists band together, and in Lebanon, it was the Commodore. As the bombing became particularly severe in early August, with Israel pounding Beirut, intent on expelling Yassir Arafat, the correspondents huddled in the Commodore's basement, only venturing out sporadically, like groundhogs sniffing the air.

But ABC producers Jeff Gralnick and Rick Kaplan wanted their correspondent to get back to East Beirut, where it was possible, in Jennings words, "to watch the battle like theater." They gave him his marching orders. "Driving across the Green Line was always hairy," Jennings says. "You never knew what was going to happen." This time, as Jennings walked through the door of the Alexander Hotel and into the lobby to check in, a car bomb went off outside the hotel.

"It blew the shit out of the entire front of the hotel," Jennings recalls. "Pieces of the car ended up on the hotel roof. I phoned New York, and I screamed at them, 'You fuckers, I'm going back to the West!'"

From West Beirut, Jennings chronicled the Israeli attack. Working the phones, making the rounds, Jennings called on all his old sources, from the Italian ambassador to PLO officials to find out if and when Yassir Arafat would cave in to Israel's demands and leave Lebanon. In late August, when Arafat capitulated, Jennings got the story, and Arafat. But the experience had shaken him: "The Israelis had cut the food, vegetables, fruit, even water to Lebanon. Here were the Israelis, who we were raised to look up to, carrying out this terrible siege."

In fact, the siege was only a prelude to a greater tragedy, the attack on the Palestinian refugee camps known as Sabra and Shatila. In mid-September, two weeks after Arafat had sailed from Lebanon in defeat, Israeli forces surrounded the camps and opened the doors to allow Lebanese Phalangists to carry out a "mopping up" operation, killing off hundreds, even thousands of innocent, already destitute refugees. Jennings and his ABC team, who had left the Middle East only two weeks earlier, found themselves back on a return flight.

"At 7:00 PM, we caught a British Airways flight to Paris," recalls ABC producer Tom Yellin, who would later become a close friend of Jennings. "At 11:00, a TWA Paris to Tel Aviv flight. We're sitting with all the news people, and everyone's trying to catch some sleep, because when we get there, we'll be going for days without sleep. Everyone has their eyeshades on and the lights out, except Peter. He looks like he's studying for an exam, like he's cramming, trying to learn it all in one night. He's got books, back issues of magazines. He's got articles that he's razored out of newspapers, and he's going over them, with a yellow highlighter. I woke up and I said, 'It's going on 3:00 AM. What are you doing? You lived in Beirut, you've been to Israel 2,000 times.' And he said, 'I just don't want to miss anything.'"

As Jennings sat in the rented house in East Hampton, mulling Arledge's offer, he knew he didn't want to give up those days. In the end, though, it was Kati Marton who, both as Jennings' wife and a former ABC staffer, convinced the newsman that he had to take the anchor position. She told him, "If they offer you this job, it's basically simple—you can't say no."

The hidden threat, never stated by ABC, was that if Jennings turned the anchor job down, he would not be allowed to return to his old London position, because it wouldn't exist anymore, at least not in its old freewheeling form. "They would have radically altered my career," Jennings acknowleges.

Stressing the positive, his wife urged, "If this job does represent one of the brass rings, you might as well not throw it on the floor. You might as well see what you can do with it."

And so Jennings, with much trepidation, reported to ABC's New York headquarters in September of 1983 as the new anchor. "He was terribly nervous," Tom Yellin recalls. "He had had the job before and failed, and that's a scar that will never go away."

If there was a criticsm of the new and improved Peter Jennings, it was his lack of understanding of the U.S. Growing up in Canada, reporting from Europe and the Middle East, he had an international perspective unique among America's journalists. The advertisements during his first year as anchor heralded: "We bring you something you can't get anywhere else. Peter Jennings. From the Middle East to the Olympics, he's been there."

He just didn't know America. "When I came back from overseas...I hadn't covered domestic politics in about twenty years," Jennings recalls. "I was a bit apprehensive. I had heard that Brinkley and Koppel and Barbara Walters had been asked some questions about Jennings, sort of a promotional campaign which, I thank God, never got on the air. Someone said to Brinkley, 'What does Jennings know about Egypt?' He said, 'Everything there is to know.' 'What does he know about Africa?' 'Everything there is to know.' 'How about Eastern Europe?' 'He knows more about Eastern Europe than any other correspondent.' 'What does he know about domestic politics?' 'Not a goddamn thing.'"

Through the 1984 election-year coverage, Jennings would stumble more than once in his reporting, his grasp of the American political horizon considered "shaky" at best by his colleagues. But he would spend hours studying the notebooks researchers had prepared for him, and by election night, November 6, when the flashy computer-generated ABC logo "The '84 Vote" came flipping and twisting onto the screen, Jennings looked quite comfortable as he introduced the acerbic, dapper, white-haired former anchor sitting to his left as "my distinguished colleague David Brinkley." Then in short order, Jennings was reeling off the voting statistics with nonchalant ease, as Ronald Reagan racked up twelve electoral votes in Florida, nine in Alabama, on his way to a landslide.

The new anchor also had the necessary minutiae well in hand, like Strom Thurmond taking to the campaign trail with family recipes. Best of all was the easygoing banter between Jennings and Brinkley, as the ironic former anchor and the newly crowned ABC anchor blended into a team.

"You know," said Brinkley, "Jesse Helms started out doing radio commentary, and he became so popular doing it that he wound up in the Senate." He gave Jennings a deadpan glance, the smile just creeping in at the corners, and the anchor started to laugh. "Not a favorite path for all of us," he guffawed. "I'm sorry, I just had to say that."

If the 1984 election proved that Jennings had begun to settle into his new job, certainly surpassing his callow, unpolished performance as a twenty-six-year-old, it was the events of the next two years that would prove he had arrived as a legitimate anchor.

First, in June of 1985, came the hijacking of TWA flight 847 in Greece. As the hostage drama played out over seventeen days of terror and boredom and tension, Jennings was continually on and off the air. "When such a thing as this hijacking occurs, we realize how little we know of people like those in Amal and their grievances," Jennings stated. But the anchor and his ABC news team clearly had a good grasp of the Mideast picture, and while Tom Brokaw was off on vacation, and Dan Rather was doing a creditable job, Jennings' years as a Beirut native clearly gave him the edge. He knew about Shiite Moslems. He knew Nabih Berri, and understood what he was trying to achieve as a negotiator. He had interviewed Syria's President Hassad, who brought the thirty-nine American hostages over the winding mountain roads to Damascus. And he was able to get the entire drama in perspective.

"Not everyone in Lebanon carries a gun," he said, "but there are probably more guns per capita there than almost anywhere else in the world."

And so the images of TWA 847—the pilot speaking out the cockpit window with a gun to his ear, the hijackers with strange bags over their heads, giving a press conference—came to us bearing the stamp of ABC and Jennings. Through it all, Jennings kept the cool, crisp, semi-detached demeanor for which he was known, and yet he, too, was wracked by the same emotions most Westerners felt.

As ABC News president Roone Arledge came down to the studio to hear Jennings sign-off at the end of a primetime special on the hijacking, the anchor ad-libbed "Good night, and keep your fingers crossed." And then he started crying. "It wasn't a very substantial thing to say," Jennings recalls, "but it triggered something in me, and as we went to black, I fell apart."

The next year would bring similar events, live and harrowing, the kind of crucible in which anchors are forged. The Iceland summit between Reagan and Gorbachev was one such moment. Ad-libbing on his feet in the driving rain and sleet, Jennings turned in a performance that even competitors praised for sheer physical stamina. From the waist down, he was absolutely drenched, soaking in the wind and rain for an hour. CBS executive producer Tom Bettag termed it "an extraordinary feat of human endurance."

But it was the coverage of the 1986 Challenger disaster that took perhaps the greatest emotional toll on Jennings and yielded the greatest praise. ABC had not covered the lift-off. In fact, only CNN was reporting the story live when the shuttle exploded at 11:39 AM. Jennings recalls that he, along with a number of other senior reporters, had gone to the White House that morning, getting a preview of President Reagan's State of the Union address. "As we waited for the President to come into the dining room, a message was handed to Don Regan. It said 'Shuttle exploded—details to follow.' Of course, we all fled from the room."

Within less than an hour, Jennings was on the air, and he would provide continuing broadcasts over the next eleven hours. It was an inspired performance, at once informed and elegiac, and capped off by an hour-long special report.

"The flags are at half-staff tonight, here in the nation's capital and across the country, and this is why," Jennings said, as he recounted the story of the tragic explosion. "The picture is now etched in our minds, but still horrifying: the disastrous end of the twenty-fifth shuttle mission, the sudden death of seven astronauts, Americans once again reaching for the stars, and this time, the first time, not making it."

If Jennings had the facts—2,000 miles an hour, one minute after takeoff—he also, and more importantly, had the context. He asked the right questions. After the 1967 Apollo fire, he noted, it took NASA twenty-two months to recover. What would happen now? He asked about the role of manned versus unmanned missions in space.

Finally, Jennings stopped and looked straight into the camera. As the smoke from one of the countless Export A King cigarettes on which he had been puffing (off-screen during the taped segments) curled into the picture, he wrapped up his report:

"We invested a large part of our national psyche in the space program. This is a catastrophe, and it will surely set the program back. But America will stay in space. That's where America belongs. I'm Peter Jennings. Thank you for joining us."

If disasters can be turning points for newsmen—like the Kennedy assassination for Rather—then the Challenger explosion was widely perceived as just such a moment for Jennings, the moment when he finally came into his own. Some felt that at the same time as internal troubles were wracking CBS, the next great anchor was being born at ABC. One thing is certain. After the Challenger disaster, thousands of letters poured into ABC from viewers who thanked Jennings for his sensitivity and intelligence in covering this national tragedy.

Since 1986, Jennings' credibility, both internally at ABC and with the American public, has continued to grow. Hosting "Capital to Capital," the first live hookup between citizens and leaders of the U.S. and the U.S.S.R., in 1987; delivering questions that skewered both Bush and Dukakis in the 1988 presidential debates (to the technocrat Dukakis: Do you have "the passion and leadership that sometimes a President needs?"; to the sentimental Bush, who declared himself "haunted" by the lives of inner-city kids: "If it haunts you so, why over the eight years of the Reagan-Bush administration have so many programs designed to help the inner cities been eliminated or cut?"); covering Eastern Europe in 1989; launching the new series "Peter Jennings Reporting" in 1990. As a consequence of his performance, Jennings has slowly and steadily risen to the top.

With success has come something new for the journalist, celebrity. Since growing up in his parents' house, Jennings had always traveled with ease among the movers and shakers, the rich and famous and powerful. To a certain degree, that's an anchor's job, and Jennings was born into it. But unlike his reporting days overseas, where he was more or less unknown, in New York he is now a highly visible figure. His face is plastered all over sidewalk bus shelters. And, encouraged by his wife Kati's social inclinations, he lives the celebrity life.

There are the foray's into the city's fashionable social scene, with friends like movie director Alan J. Pakula (*Klute, All the President's Men*), writer Peter Maas (*Serpico*) and public relations executive John Scanlon. And then there is country life in the exclusive Hamptons, the upscale romping ground for media figures, well-heeled artists and assorted deal-makers.

Every New Year's Eve, at their newly constructed home in Bridgehampton, Kati and Peter throw a party packed with the literati and the glitterati, and Jennings hosts it, decked out in a kilt. Summers are packed with sailing, tennis, even croquet and bocci. On occasion, Jennings will join the clubby Sag Harbor softball game, and step up to the plate against pitcher Mort Zuckerman, owner of the *Atlantic* and *U.S. News and World Report*, and field grounders from the likes of Carl Bernstein.

But with fame, of course, comes the dark side of celebrity, the loss of privacy. Although New York is more blasé about celebrity than most places, there are still plenty of people who take a famous face as an invitation.

"I'm always getting stopped on the street," Jennings says. "I must say that very few people are, by and large, antagonistic. But there are enough who are antagonistic enough that you are always a little bit on edge in public. My wife doesn't take to it very much."

Jennings himself likes the interchange. He often chooses to walk to work along Manhattan's West Side, or to take the bus. He enjoys rubbing up against people. In one instance, he even found a great source of political information in Greece from a New York bus driver who had been born there.

"By nature," Jennings says, "I'm a street corner talker. If we're walking down the street and somebody asks me a question, I'm probably going to ask them five back. My wife finds that somewhat unbearable."

Of course, the most difficult part of fame, especially for the family, is the feeling that they are always being scrutinized. "You are careful about your behavior all the time," Jennings admits. "You should never drink too much in public. And other things besides. I remember years and years ago, when my father came to visit me in New York, I had a small old Porsche that my sister and her husband had lent me for a while. I remember driving down Columbus Avenue with my father and

Walter Cronkite sitting in the back seat screaming at the top of their lungs. I would no more do that today than fly to the moon."

The danger, of course, is that he is being watched, even when he's shopping. "I was in the grocery store with my son once, and he was acting like a beast. He's a wonderful, angelic little boy, a great character. But he was acting like a beast, so I gave him a kick in the pants. The next day on Page Six in the *New York Post*: ANCHORMAN BEATS CHILD IN PUBLIC. People write about your private life. It's awful."

Brokaw, Rather and Jennings have *all* suffered this embarrassing intrusiveness. In some way, since the public makes them famous, they become public property. This sense of ownership, unquestionably, has its wacky side. Once, three elderly ladies trapped Jennings and his family in the revolving door of the New York toy store, F.A.O. Schwartz, and smiling and pointing, they refused to let them out. Then there are the loonies who write to him, like the woman in San Francisco, who has been sending letters for some twenty years. She believes that she is Peter Jennings' wife. She also believes that Jennings has removed her brain, and replaced it with the brain of a parrot.

Not all the incidents are funny. Some are genuinely scary. Like the time he was threatened by one of those unnamed, elusive religious groups, and told, "You have until midnight to live." Or when an armed intruder, angrily waving his gun around, broke into the ABC set in Washington looking for Jennings. The anchor was in fact in the capital that day, and for several very long, tense minutes, the gunman grasped his weapon and stalked through ABC's bureau office, until he was distracted by a security guard and eventually overpowered by the police.

In 1987, just as Jennings was beginning to rise to the top as an anchor, things went sour on other fronts. Some reporters at ABC felt he was getting a little too big for his anchor chair, continually meddling with their copy and demanding changes. Some of them felt that he was a swift pain. The biggest brouhaha at ABC, though, was Jennings' clash with his executive producer Bill Lord.

Lord had been brought in from "Nightline" in 1984 to replace Bob Frye, who had lasted only a few months with Jennings. At the beginning, Jennings and Lord had worked well together, although the disquieting thought did flash across Jennings' mind that perhaps Lord had been brought in to clear a path for Ted Koppel as his replacement. But with the "World News Tonight" successes of 1985 and 1986, Jennings and Lord settled into a comfortable professional relationship.

It was not until 1987 that the relationship began to deteriorate. Staffers recall long, heated arguments between the two behind closed doors over which stories to run, how long to run them, what order to run them in, which story to pick for the lead, in short almost every significant aspect of the newscast. "Peter didn't think that Bill was creative," says one senior ABC producer. "And Bill thought Peter a bit of a loose cannon."

For Jennings, most of their disputes came down to a conflict of styles. "Well," he said, "some of it was temperament. I think you have that in jobs at times. And I think we got ourselves into more of a wrestling match than we should have about authority. I am sure almost anyone will tell you, I am boundlessly enthusiastic. I think that Bill wanted to restrain that enthusiasm to a greater degree than he should have. It seems to me that the secret of good leadership is to channel enthusiasm."

In several instances, their disagreements focused on who had the final decision. Jennings, with the title "senior editor," unlike Rather and Brokaw's "managing editor" role, was technically subordinate to Lord, but the truth was much fuzzier. Power on paper, of course, isn't the same as real power. And if there is a point at which someone has to employ that power, to pull rank instead of reaching a consensus, something about the relationship isn't working right anyway.

As one former ABC correspondent remembers it, "Peter couldn't take it, and finally said, 'It's my show.' Lord said, 'Fuck you.' So Jennings pushed Lord against the wall.'" The anchor had a solid footing with his boss, Roone Arledge. More than once he went over Lord's head to the ABC News president, and his VP, David Burke, to help sort matters out. The friction between Jennings and Lord grew.

Reporter David Blum of *New York* magazine was on hand one day in October 1987, when the relationship bottomed out. He told the story of watching the two men lock horns over a show closer. Lord wanted a piece from London on the royal family, the marriage problems of Charles and Di. Jennings insisted that the story wasn't news. It was gossip. Getting testy, Lord pulled rank and told the anchor that he had made the decision, and his decision was final. The executive producer sent Jennings off to write an introduction to the London piece.

Near the end of the news that night, Jennings looked into the camera and read his introduction, as downstairs, Bill Lord watched a monitor in the control room. "And finally this evening," Jennings read, "gossip at the highest level. We're never quite certain whether it's because the British press is having a quiet week or because they know it sells newspapers...."

Down in the control room, the quiet hum was shattered by an angry voice. It was Bill Lord, his nose as red as a stop light, yelling at the screen: "Or maybe it's because it's the *truth*! Did you ever think of *that*, Peter?!"

"...but once again," Jennings read on upstairs, oblivious of Lord's outburst, "what's called the popular press and sometimes called the downmarket press is fascinated with Prince Charles and the Princess of Wales, Diana. ABC's John Laurence is in London."

As soon as Laurence's videotaped piece had played out, Lord stood up and announced, "*That* is a perfect illustration of why it's important that the anchorman should not be the managing editor." His hands punctuated the air for emphasis. "That piece is on all the network news shows tonight. It belonged there. It was news. We were right to put it on."

A few days later, Jennings would comment, "Any anchorman who thinks he is always right is a fool. Any executive producer who thinks he is always right is a fool...for a shorter period of time." Within a matter of weeks, Bill Lord had been removed from his post.

The new executive producer was Paul Friedman, a former Columbia School of Journalism student under Fred Friendly, in the same class with CBS's Tom Bettag and NBC's Marc Kusnetz. Friedman had served as former ABC London bureau chief, where he had formed a solid, even jovial, working relationship with Jennings. The anchor had lobbied hard to bring Friedman to New York. Apparently, Friedman had also done himself a lot of good in the eyes of management at an ABC think-tank seminar he attended in 1987 in Westchester.

Flying in from Europe with other bureau managers, Friedman had designed a series of proposals to reshape the news, derived in part from his days as a local executive producer in New York. He was one of the few executives to show up with concrete suggestions, and Roone Arledge was impressed by his ideas. Friedman was given the inside track, and when Lord was moved out, he was moved in. Since then, he and Jennings have had, by all accounts, a remarkably smooth relationship.

"Paul is very smart," one ex-ABC staffer noted. "He has the ability to make sure everyone gets along. He will not go head to head with Peter, but most of the time you don't have to, to get what you want."

Indeed, their rapport is such that on most afternoons Jennings and Friedman will be found seated side by side working on a story, teasing each other mercilessly or playfully punching each other in the arm.

In mid-1987, just as Jennings' relationship with executive producer Bill Lord was falling apart at work, his relationship with his wife began falling apart at home. Jennings was putting in extra-long days anchoring the Iran-Contra hearings.

Meanwhile, Kati, his wife, had carved out a niche of her own, having become, in just a few years, the author of a celebrated biography of Raoul Wallenberg, and a novel, *An American Woman*, loosely based on her own experience as the daughter of Hungarian journalists who fled Soviet occupation.

In her own way, she was just as ambitious as her husband, and she reveled in the social life of New York and Washington. Family friends noted that Kati was determined not to get lost in Peter's shadow. Their marriage, Marton would later say, was "on automatic pilot." It was in early June that Jennings found out she was having an affair with Richard Cohen, a columnist at *The Washington Post* (not the former CBS producer).

If Jennings suffered, that was nothing compared to the misery he felt when the press got wind of the story. *USA Today* tantalized readers with a front page headline on the rocky state of his marriage. And in mid-July, Liz Smith announced to New York in the *Daily News*:

"BAD NEWS: Peter Jennings, the ABC ace news anchor, and his wife, Kati Marton, the distinguished author, are separating after eight years of marriage and two children. I recently extolled them in this column as the perfect couple. Well, I still think so. All their friends hope this is just a temporary situation." The gossip had really hit the fan.

All around New York and Washington, tongues wagged. Jennings had got what he deserved, said some: After two discarded marriages, the noted Don Juan was finally getting a taste of his own medicine. But many felt that having the pain of private wounds spilled all over the papers was too brutal an indignity for anyone. And friends rallied around, trying to patch up the wounds, heal the hurt.

Jennings, who certainly felt humiliated and betrayed, rarely let those emotions creep into his work. With the exception of one shattering moment when old friend and colleague Charlie Glass was kidnapped in the Middle East, Jennings was, each night, as crisp and collected as always, soldiering through his unhappiness.

But he was also doing some serious thinking, and one thing was clear to him. His top priority was getting his wife back and keeping his family together. After all sorts of phone calls, Peter Jennings and Kati Marton were tentatively reunited. They are still together, but Jennings hasn't forgotten the pain.

"It's no secret," he'll say today, "My wife and I went through some difficulties, and it was on the front pages of the goddamm newspapers. It was horrible. Worst thing that ever happened to me." He shakes his head. "Worst thing that ever happened to me."

Today, all too aware of how fragile relationships can become, Jennings constantly tends his marriage, pruning it like a well-kept garden. He is ultra-attentive to Marton, quite clearly not taking her for granted. He'll talk with her on the phone several times a day, and when, on occasion, she shows up at his office after the evening news is over, his hand lightly dances attendance on her shoulder or her back, as if afraid to let her get beyond his reach.

While some women at the office may still claim that even if Jennings can't remember their names, he continues to flirt with them "to the point of being obnoxious," it is absolutely clear that for Peter Jennings, his home life comes first. When his wife talks of him as a ladies' man, she says, "That's behind him now. He's like a reformed alcoholic."

As Sarah Jennings explains, "Annie, Peter's second wife, provided a warm social environment, a context in which to talk about ideas with people. But Kati, she actually talks about the ideas. She provokes Peter. She argues with him about ideas. And the fact that she actually writes books, Peter's in awe of that. In a way, he thinks that's more real work than what he does."

Get Jennings started about his wife and he will ramble on and on, beaming with pride: "My wife has just done an absolutely sensational book! It's called *Murder in Salonika Bay*, and it's the true story of who murdered George Polk, the CBS correspondent, during the Greek

Civil War. The true story has never been written, and she's blown it right out of the water!"

Today, Jennings and Marton will collaborate on many projects. He edits her books. "I'm a pretty good editor. But it's very hard, trying to edit your wife. It took me three books to learn." And, when he journeyed to Hungary last year to cover the reburial of Imre Nagy, one of the first signs of the lifting of the Iron Curtain, he brought Marton with him. Hungarian-born, she still remembered her native tongue. She was eager to see the political changes in her homeland.

"I had taken her because she knows the story much better than I do," Jennings recalls. "We got up whatever the morning was, and turned on the television set—the great thing was that Hungarian TV was carrying this from start to finish—and she took one look and burst into tears. Actually, it was a bit disconcerting. My editor was an emotional basket case."

Kati had lived through the 1956 Hungarian uprising. "Her parents were both in prison for two and a half years. They were pardoned just before the revolution. Kati was farmed out to one of those families that take care of political prisoners' children, she and her sister. Then a year after the revolution, in 1957, when things began to harden down again, they got a call in the middle of the night that said, 'Time to go.' Woosh, under the fence of the Austrian border the next day. But an elegant family. They took champagne with them."

For Jennings—as for most fathers—the only thing that gets him more excited than talking about his wife is his kids. He positively gleams with delight when describing Elizabeth, his competitive daughter, and Christopher, his sweet-natured son. He'll chime in proudly about what a skiing demon Lizzie is, how she'll stick right to his tail as Jennings, an advanced downhiller, plunges across the slopes. He'll ramble on fondly about taking his children for a little "rough riding" vacation in Turkey on the "Stambul Express" and down to the Bosporus. He'll mention how he watches over the two carefully, severely limiting their TV viewing during the week.

Tom Yellin, his friend and colleague, says, "Peter is intensely committed to his family life." Yellin describes a scene at the airport in Crakow when he and Peter were waiting for a plane, and Jennings gave him a ten-minute lecture on kids. "If you don't have kids, you're missing something. They pay you back in ways you can't imagine."

There are times when the witty and acerbic anchor sounds as meltingly tender-hearted as one of Dickens' gentle souls. On days when Jennings gets home after the children have gone to sleep, he'll sometimes try to wake them up, or crawl into bed right alongside them. His children are, Marton once said, "his ultimate emotional release."

Striding down West 67th Street on a crisp January night, Peter Jennings turns the corner and walks purposefully uptown. It's well after his evening newscast, and he is in fact just heading off to a dinner, but he never simply strolls anywhere. He's always off at a brisk clip, charging ahead down some street or into some project.

Jennings likes to describe himself as an enthusiast, a full speed ahead kind of guy. "I'm someone who is ignited by ideas," he says breathlessly. "Just *ignited* by ideas. I drive people crazy around here. I come in the door having discovered the latest idea and beat everybody into submission until they listen to it."

Sometimes it's the poetry of Elizabeth Bishop or the short stories of his Bridgehampton neighbor, Peter Matthiessen. Other times it's the need for young journalists to have a sense of history, of context, for overseas stories. Whatever it is, he's *passionate* about it. Whatever hobby horse he's mounted that day, he'll ride it right into the ground. The sentences come tumbling out, the words leaping one ahead of the next.

Jennings is not just that way at work. He's that way on vacation too. Tom Yellin's family has shared several trips with the Jennings clan, to places like Vail and Sun Valley.

"Some people are intense doers," he says. "With Peter, it's boating one minute, swimming the next. Then he's working on making a fire, and at the end of the day, he's trying really hard to go to sleep." Although Jennings is quite an accomplished skier, he'll spend his vacations taking lessons.

"The way he relaxes is trying to improve," says Yellin. "He'll work on technical things—handling moguls, where his body weight is through a turn. It's like his work. What makes it fun for him is concentrating on getting better."

When Roone Arledge first labeled him "the anchor for the nineties," it appeared to be a wishful marketing ploy. But as the 1980s ended and the 1990s began, Jennings had been named best network TV anchor by the prestigious *Washington Journalism Review* for four years running.

On top or not, Jennings is no less driven. He's never actually satisfied, never content. "I always tend to look at the program in terms of how many nights I can be proud of," he is often quoted as saying. The top score is rarely more than two and a half a week. "Never close to four."

He turns those critical standards on everyone at ABC News. Jennings is constantly fussing with everyone's work, even the correspondents he admires most, complaining that this copy is too dry, that that piece doesn't have enough historical context.

Jennings is no different on the home front. He corrects his son when he says "Yeah" instead of "Yes." He wants his wife to be extra-special. "He wants me to be more European, elegant, but it should be seamless, effortless," she says. All Jennings wants from his wife is that she "always excel and be smarter than anybody." His high standards are clearly, at times, exasperating. Even his sister admits that he can be "a pain."

But to give Peter Jennings credit, he's harder on no one more than himself. When he's told that the broadcast was good on a given night, he'll reply, "Except for yours truly." Right in the middle of a broadcast, during a commercial break, he has been heard complaining that he's "terrible" or "no good."

"Peter," his executive producer Paul Friedman has to coax him, "you're being too hard on yourself."

"Peter tends to criticize his own work more than he should," Tom Yellin says. "He should be on top of the world. He's about as successful as you can be in this work. But he doesn't feel like it. He's not capable of enjoying his success as much as he should. Even when we're skiing, on vacation. Instead of saying, 'It's going great,' he worries about what isn't going well. That's the most frustrating thing about Peter."

If Jennings is perhaps more self-critical than most, if he's troubled with self-doubt, the root may lie in some long-time insecurities. After half a lifetime of trying to cover up for his lack of formal education, he may still have some lingering doubts about whether he really is as good as the next guy, especially in an ultra-competitive business like TV news.

In fact, he is probably better-read than most. He is certainly a more voracious reader. Everyone who's ever worked with him talks of Jennings lugging around copies of *Foreign Affairs* magazine, briefing books on U.S.-USSR relations, stacks of local newspapers. But like many self-taught people, he tends to doubt his teacher.

"He's never quite gotten over it," says more than one ABC staffer. "Maybe he never will."

Jack Laurence, an ABC correspondent based in London, provides a description of Jennings that one hears from many other colleagues as well: "Peter is very insecure about his abilities as an analyst, an intellectual, when he shouldn't be. He *is* a thinking journalist. But Peter will admit in his most private moments how deep those insecurities run. I'm convinced that's what makes him work harder. Those old insecurities keep driving him."

But perhaps Jennings isn't only a classic case of overcompensation. Perhaps he's also trying to live up to an ideal, a tough ideal to match, the memory of his father. After all, Charles Jennings was the voice of Canada for the first half of his career, and CBC's arbiter of taste for the second half, overseeing all the programming for both radio and TV. As his son says, he was a huge presence in both the family and the business at large. And during the years when Charles Jennings was at his peak, his son was lazy, spoiled, in many ways a disappointment. Though Charles Jennings died more than fifteen years ago, Peter may still be trying to prove himself to his dad: "He does indulge in father worship," says his wife Kati.

The old clipping up on the wall stares down over Jennings' desk. It describes Charles Jennings as "an imperialist," back in the days in Canada when that was a high compliment.

"I think," Peter Jennings says, "I still—to a very great measure— want to impress my father."

When Peter and his sister Sarah speak of their father, they talk of him as almost saint-like, a paragon: "a very good person," "a man of impeccable morals." Part of Charles Jennings' legacy for his son is a certain standard of public service. Perhaps that's why Peter Jennings frequently gives speeches for causes he believes in, why he—alone of all the anchors—also does work for public television, narrating specials and documentaries like "The AIDS Quarterly Report." And that's why, though he doesn't like to talk about it, he heads downtown to work with the homeless in a soup kitchen.

"It's a part of his Canadian Protestant character," friends have said, "the noblesse oblige. If you have a lot, you have to give something back."

To this day, growing up in Canada shapes Peter Jennings in his values and interests. And to this day, he is still a Canadian citizen. Although he may talk about "we," he is no more American than any green-card holder, no more American than Morley Safer, Barrie Dunsmore or Robert MacNeil. It's MacNeil who tells the story about the time Jennings returned to the U.S. from London, and was invited to a black-tie reception at the Canadian Embassy in Washington. The ambassador made a speech about what a great day it was for Canadians with a native son ascending to the ABC anchor desk.

MacNeil noted the Ambassador's outspoken wife, Sondra Gottlieb, standing with a drink in her hand and eying Jennings like warmed-over Brussel sprouts. All at once, she asked loudly, "Then why are you thinking about giving up your Canadian citizenship?"

Jennings laughed uncomfortably and said, "Well, if Robin [Mac-Neil] can get away with it all these years, I suppose I can too."

In fact, Jennings' boss, Roone Arledge, had pressured the anchor to become an American citizen. "After he decided he wanted me to do this job, he suddenly got this bee in his bonnet about whether it would be okay to be Canadian. So he said something publicly, and a lot of people began to challenge me: 'When are you going to become an American?'

"And I didn't know how to deal with it. Because it never occurred to me at that point to become a U.S. citizen. I had only lived here for five years back in the 1960s. But it became one of those things where people began to poke me with a stick, to the degree where I finally said to my boss and a couple of other people, 'Did it ever occur to you that this is a personal choice? Not a business decision. And I'll come to this in my own due time.'

"Then I went through this whole thought process....If I'm going to live in America the rest of my life, do I want to become a U.S. citizen? My children are American. My wife is American. And I talked about this at one point, and I got this *very very* passionate letter from my mother saying, 'My boy, you're at the end of a long line. You must think seriously about this. You have roots.'"

Jennings says that as long as his mother is alive, and perhaps after, he will remain a Canadian.

Being a foreigner is Jennings' strength—and his weakness. "It makes a difference in the way I look at the world," he admits. Despite his many years of living in the U.S., he is much more of an outsider than either Brokaw or Rather, and he approaches the news as an outsider, a skeptic. With Jennings, the eyebrow is always raised, literally and figuratively. He examines the news with a keenly measured sense of distance and balance, a cool, ironic detachment, unlike either the hot-blooded Rather, or Brokaw, the boy next door. Peter Jennings is from the country next door.

Jennings' wife speaks of him as rootless, "a nomad." It is true that he has never voted anywhere, in any country he's lived in, *ever*. It is also true that he created this nomad life for himself, that his years on the road were his formation, the period when he transformed a handsome but limited high school dropout into a sophisticated foreign correspondent. Though for the past seven years comfortably anchored at ABC in New York, Jennings is still, in some ways, spiritually out of place, dissatisfied, a man constantly trying to make himself (and others) measure up.

RATINGS: Week ending November 17th

1st.   Jennings   (ABC's "World News Tonight")—11.2/21 [10,315,200]

2nd.   Rather   ("CBS Evening News")—10.7/20 [9,854,700]

3rd.   Brokaw   ("NBC Nightly News")—10.1/19 [9,302,100]

CHAPTER TWENTY

On the Set with Jennings

5:05 on a Thursday afternoon, and Jennings stares intently at the computer screen in front of him. "Oh *Scheiss*!" he exclaims. He peers in at the electro-green characters, the flickering cursor, and then starts banging away at the keyboard, his two index fingers flying in a staccato hunt-and-peck.

Over Jennings' shoulder are two signs pasted to the wall. THE PERSON WHO SAID NO NEWS IS GOOD NEWS WAS DRASTICALLY MISINFORMED reads one. TV MADE ME WHAT I AM TODAY announces the other.

This is "The Rim," the main workspace where "World News Tonight" gets assembled. Around the large, dark blue semi-circular desk that gives the Rim its name, the senior producers for ABC's evening news are gathered. To Jennings' left is Milt Weiss—bald, bearded and bespectacled—the anchor's main writer. To Jennings' right, executive producer Paul Friedman, whose mustache and glasses and eyes twinkling with deviltry may remind some of Groucho Marx. And across the table, the show's other main producers, Bob Roy and Dennis Dunlavey.

In ABC's high-tech but eccentrically arranged skyscraper, the Rim is two floors above the control room, three floors above the tape rooms, and one floor below the newsroom-studio known as "The Bubble." Although the "World News" empire is spread out, it is here, at the Rim, that the hub lies, where the phones ring and the questions get answered.

Just off the Rim, Peter Jennings has an office, a comfortable affair with a solid desk, large windows, family photos, sofa, globe, Eskimo prints, stacks of books and magazines, and a wall rack near the door in which the day's newspapers, from the New York *Daily News* to *The Wall Street Journal* are neatly tucked away. But much of the day, Jennings sits in a chair on the Rim, his shirtsleeves rolled up, his tie loosened, his grandfather glasses perched precariously on the edge of his nose.

"It's Laurie," Bob Roy calls across the desk to Jennings. "Gerasimov has said that Moscow drafted a law that might allow the republics to have independence." Jennings picks up the phone to listen to Jim Laurie's conference call about the first stirrings of revolt in Lithuania.

"Just give me a sense of what it's all about," he says. "Uh-huh." He leans back and looks up at the TVs mounted above the Rim, polished chrome monitors for ABC, CBS, CNN and a small black and white set for NBC.

"I think Peter has to incorporate some of this in his lead," Bob Roy chimes in.

Jennings listens to Laurie, 5,000 miles away, and comments, "Maybe the thing to say is we really don't know what to make of it...Uh-huh...But there's nothing in Gorbachev's history...If a law really has been passed, it's an enormous change in policy...."

On most mornings, Peter Jennings will not attend the regular 10:00 AM meeting, the one held in the conference room behind the big map that serves as the anchor's backdrop for each broadcast. On most mornings, Jennings does not join Paul Friedman and Bob Murphy, vice president of TV news coverage, as they talk to the domestic and foreign bureaus, and make the story assignments for the day. But when it comes to the copy, to the shaping of stories as they flow into the New York office from reporters around the world, Peter Jennings is perhaps the most hands-on of any of the anchors. All afternoon long, he's on the phone with correspondents.

"I think that's less important..." he says to Laurie. "I think the thing to guard against...Okay, how about saying 'Neither Lithuanians nor foreign correspondents have the vaguest idea of what Moscow is talking about.'"

Jennings likes working with correspondents. He prides himself on being a good story editor, and spends a large part of his day editing his colleagues' stories.

"I grew up in an era when you didn't have producers," he says. "When I was on the road all those years, you produced your own stuff....So the shaping of pieces, giving them impact, letting them breathe, trying to convince people there's no sense having bites which are only four or five seconds long, trying to keep the great range of statistics out of pieces—I work with correspondents on that all the time.

"The longest time I spent yesterday was with our correspondent in Nicaragua, Peter Collins, an old friend, and a very intelligent man. He's doing a piece, and from top to bottom it came in dry. We spent about an hour on the phone getting him to talk it to me. A lot of us in this racket talk better than we write. So I said, 'Well now, Peter, can we transfer that to the script?' A sort of massaging so that what he really feels and thinks about Nicaragua gets transferred on the tape. I do a lot of that. And I like that a lot. There's *nothing* better. The anchor person gets so much credit just automatically because of this highly visible job, but there's nothing more gratifying to me than to see a broadcast come in with three or four good pieces."

The correspondents who work with Jennings often talk about his willingness to share ideas, advice, a good contact in Budapest or Amman. He'll often take time to work with reporters, trying to "soften" Rebecca Chase, sitting for hours in front of a microphone with Todd Carrel or Beth Nissen, coaching them on their delivery.

But there are those at ABC who complain that Jennings is sometimes a little *too* willing to share his thoughts. They feel somewhat badgered, beleaguered even, by his constant stream of suggestions and orders. It's hard enough satisfying executive producer Friedman, let alone Friedman plus Jennings. And Jennings is so persnickety, some of them say, that he can send them up the wall. Even the anchor himself will admit to driving reporters crazy.

"I think the thing to guard against..." Jennings is saying to Laurie. "Uh-huh. Until they hear what Gorby says...Let's use those shots of the crowd to explain it....Okay, and Jimmy? Two things: You say, 'says Gerasimov.' Can you say, 'Gerasimov says'? And can you find a better phrase than 'hard line'?" Jennings signs off on the conference call, and Bob Roy says, "Okay London, you're on."

Around the ABC organization, Peter Jennings doesn't pull any punches. For all his on-screen polish, Jennings is not much of a diplomat. He acknowledges that he works better "in a position of some antagonism with management." Up or down the line, he has no trouble expressing his criticisms. Surprisingly, it's Dan Rather who, despite his pugnacious side, is more of a diplomat. Rather prides himself on politeness and graciousness.

At ABC, it's not unusual to see a flare-up, like Jennings and a producer hotly debating whether one hundred percent of the babies with AIDS will die or not. At CBS, that kind of explosion is much more rare. And yet, at CBS, there's always a low-level tension in the air. "Peter's not bashful about criticism," says colleague Stu Schutzman. "But there's a lot less behind-the-scenes innuendo here than at CBS."

"I don't think people know precisely what you mean by a surplus." Jennings is back on the phone, talking with Brit Hume in Washington this time. "Does that mean more money is in the Social Security fund?...Well, where is the money?!" He hangs up the phone with an emphatic crash, and turns to Paul Friedman. "I have no desire to spar with him," Jennings says, "but he's using that word 'surplus' twice....Especially in this year of Gramm/Rudman."

At the Rim, several producers are trying to define exactly what is meant by a Social Security surplus. It's a question that has baffled everyone from Senator Daniel Patrick Moynihan to the President, and no one at ABC is getting any closer. The discussion is boisterous, collegial, like an undergraduate B.S. session.

"Look," pipes up one producer, "the contributions to the Social Security fund are counted as revenue in the Federal Budget, which has the effect of reducing the overall Federal Budget deficit." Jennings stares at Hume's piece on his computer. "In other words," he says, "they move it around as paper money?" He types in a few words, then mumbles aloud as he reads through the copy. "How about 'Social Security has more money in the fund than it currently needs'?"

The telephone rings. It's his wife, Kati. "Hi babe," he says. "Sure, we'll see *Henry V* if you want to. You organize it." All around the Rim, his colleagues offer their suggestions. What about *My Left Foot*? What about *sex, lies and videotape*? They're all planning the anchor's spare time. "Don't go to see *sex, lies...* says Paul Friedman. "Since you only go to see one film a year, it shouldn't be *sex, lies....*"

Jennings turns back to the phone. "Okay," he says, "come and pick me up at 7:30."

As he hangs up, his longtime assistant, the calm, efficient Gretchen Babarovic, breezes by. The anchor snags her on the fly. "Tell them to invite Havel's brother to have coffee with us next week," he says. Turning back to his computer, he moves on to the next piece, the show's closer. "Who is deemed to have the best arm in football?" he asks the room, obviously a lot less comfortable with gridiron heroes than with Czech politicians.

"Well," says Milt Weiss, "Joe Montana if you talk about accuracy, but others have stronger arms...." Jennings starts typing in a lead, then stops and deletes it. Then he types again. "Finally, this evening, the best arm in football. No, it is not our intention ..."

Around ABC, staffers like to talk about Jennings' distinctive writing style. It's clearly cooler than either Rather's or Brokaw's. But more intriguing, Peter Jennings likes to reverse the order of a traditional news story, putting the punch line ahead of the joke, the why ahead of the who what when and where, a broad tease before the facts. ("We begin with a harsh reminder that secrecy sells.") The majority of his work, though, is rewriting rather than writing.

What Jennings believes is most important is the ability to go *live*, to ad-lib—like the recent time he was in Paris for the Bicentennial, and the broadcast came up fifty-five seconds short. As the crew in the control room started chewing on their fingernails, the producer asked, "Can we go to French TV?" And so they started feeding the French TV signal, footage Jennings had never seen before, and the anchor launched into an off-the-cuff commentary about the French Revolution to fill the hole.

Jennings sees this ability as one of the key functions of today's anchor: "I try to convince people...to understand how technology has changed us. I'm here for a good twelve hours every day, and at some point in those twelve hours, I may be asked to go on the air and talk about or lead a discussion about *anything*. I don't want to overstate my ability to do that, but it's all wrapped up with network news divisions trying to redefine their role, trying to retain their dominance in the marketplace [vis-a-vis CNN], trying to keep technology at bay, and yet being forced to behave in a much different way because of technology. I call it 'videoflow.'

"All of these local stations all across the country have videoflow—

pictures streaming in. You can have a little hut in the middle of North Dakota as a television station, and the stuff is just pouring out of the sky. What they don't have is the experience to provide context or history. So any time of the day or night, whether it's for the crash of an airplane or the crash of the stock market or a Presidential arrival or a murder or whatever my management decided they're going to put on the air live, I've got to go up and talk about it."

Jennings looks at his screen and shakes his head. "And to think," he says. "I could have been a dentist." It's 6:00 PM, and the revisions aren't even close to being finished. Jennings is scrolling through an A.P. wire story from the U.S.S.R. "The A.P. says that Gorbachev told the Lithuanians, 'I am for self-determination—all the way up to secession.'"

He looks over at Friedman. "I suggested to Laurie that we be rather cautious with this."

Friedman peers down at Laurie's copy. He's satisfied. Turning back to Jennings, he says with a chuckle, "Between you and me, the Lithuanians are already independent."

Jennings, typing away on another story, nods and says, "This is flim-flam, boys, flim-flam."

Friedman smiles, "You want to be independent? Poof! You're independent."

The executive producer and the anchor have an easygoing relationship, and enjoy horsing around together. "It's like that senator from New Hampshire—what was his name?" Jennings says. "The one who said the way to get out of Vietnam: declare you've won and go home."

On one of the monitors, Jim Laurie's footage from Lithuania begins to come in. Crowds in the street, throngs in the square carrying placards. "Oh this goddamn thing," Jennings exclaims, pounding on his keyboard. As the footage finishes, Friedman wants to know who they have for their "Person of the Week" feature tomorrow. "We have two good candidates," the anchor says. "Art Buchwald and Douglas Wilder."

"You certainly don't want to do Buchwald," Bob Roy says. The feeling around the Rim is that the columnist may have won his plagiarism case against Eddie Murphy, but that he's still a shameless self-promoter. "Well, we did do Qaddafi," says Friedman.

Jennings turns with a rueful smile to his visitor. "Did you see that PBS special last night?" he asks. "The one where they followed

Rather around? We thought we'd behave like that for you. Then we thought, Aaah, we'll give him reality instead."

"Whatever you say, boss," Friedman chimes in ironically.

It's 6:10. They're crashing for the deadline and everyone's getting a little hyper. Bob Roy is on the phone trying to squeeze a piece on alternative fuels out of Jim Wooten. "Mr. Wooten," he says sarcastically, "don't you want to wait another twenty minutes to finish?"

Paul Friedman gets on the line. "Would you read us your drivel, please?" He laughs and listens as Wooten runs it by him.

"That is pure fucking poetry, you know that? And it's on a subject of *such* importance." They laugh and hang up.

Across the Rim, Mike Stein, an editor is asking Jennings, "Can I make a suggestion on Social Security? How 'bout instead of 'cautious step' you say..." Jennings listens thoughtfully, nodding. "Yeah, that's good," he says. "Much beter." He types the words in, collects his pages, and heads up towards the studio. "Ain't nobody gonna get that Social Security piece anyway," he sighs.

It's 7:30, the broadcast is over, and Jennings is striding down 67th Street with his wife Kati and his friend and ABC colleague Tom Yellin. Peter and Kati are heading off to the movies, but before they do, there's one last piece of work he still has to finish, the conclusion of a documentary on guns. They troop up to the second floor of another ABC building on Columbus Avenue, to a small musty room full of discarded equipment, dials and wires. There, in the corner, is a tiny soundproof chamber, not much bigger than a telephone booth.

Jennings steps inside, puts on earphones and Alex, a wrinkled old soundman, flips on the giant reel-to-reel recording and checks the sound levels. He nods to Jennings. The anchor begins reading: "Perhaps Americans are simply *willing* to accept the present level of violence."

He tries again: "Perhaps Americans are simply willing to *accept* the present level of violence."

Jennings runs through five takes, with Yellin offering direction, and on the fifth, everyone agrees. "That's it!" they all say, smiling. Jennings takes off the headphones, comes out of the booth and listens. "Nah," he shakes his head, "it's too sing-songy." He heads back for the booth. "Recording to pictures is so much easier for me."

Earphones in place, Jennings goes for two more takes. "Perhaps

Americans are simply willing to accept the violence," he abbreviates. Finally, he stands up contentedly and comes out. His brow furrows as he concentrates on the replay. "That is *it*," he says. He puts on his raincoat and smiles at Kati, and together they head for the door. Suddenly, he hesitates.

"You know," he says, before he can quite make it out into the hall, "if you don't mind...." He turns around and goes back into the booth one last time.

Kati, chicly attired in a beige pants suit and scarf, smiles indulgently. She's seen this before. "It's not often we make a movie," she says, her tone a little wistful as the minutes tick by.

Finally, the last line in place, the anchor and his wife head off into the night. Watching them go, Tom Yellin shakes his head. "Peter *always* does that," he says with a mixture of affection and chagrin. "Retakes once. Retakes twice." His voice trails off. "He's just never satisfied."

RATINGS: Week ending November 24th

1st.   Jennings (ABC's "World News Tonight")—10.0/20 [9,210,000]

2nd. Rather   ("CBS Evening News")—10.0/19 [9,210,000]

3rd. Brokaw   ("NBC Nightly News")—9.3/19 [8,565,300]

CHAPTER TWENTY-ONE

Brokaw as Anchor

In 1976, NBC president Herb Schlosser and NBC News head Dick Wald went behind closed doors to consider who might succeed John Chancellor, their struggling anchor. Since his debut in 1971, Chancellor had been coming in second in the ratings to Cronkite, and although he occasionally whipped him in convention coverage, NBC was simply not happy with Chancellor's performance.

Tom Brokaw's name came up as a possible replacement. But Schlosser wasn't sure their White House correspondent was the man for the job. Now semi-retired, Schlosser the shrewd, calculating power-player is still evident behind his quiet manner and dull red tie. "We thought the 'Today' show was where his career should go," Schlosser remembers. NBC management was looking for "a kind of genial traffic cop" to run "Today." He adds, "The reason we thought of Tom for that was that he was attractive, he was articulate, he knew his way around, he was ambitious, and we thought he could do it well."

If the thirty-six-year-old Brokaw was marginally in the running for the anchor post, a stronger prospect was Tom Snyder, his colorful compatriot from the old days back at KNBC in Los Angeles. "When I first met him in '68 or '69 in Los Angeles," Brokaw said, "I was terrified. I thought if this is the future, that's not why I got into this business."

Brokaw had never met anyone quite like Snyder. He was "a pure broadcaster." All he cared about was being in front of a camera. To Brokaw, it seemed that when the little red light above the camera went on, Snyder's life came on.

"In addition to anchoring the 11:00 news, I did political reporting on his 6:00 show. I used to say, 'Well, Tom, as you know...' which would break him up. He just didn't care about the stuff. He loved being on the air, being a catalyst, keeping things going, and he was awfully good at it."

Coincidentally, the two Toms had the same agent at that time, the Los Angeles-based Ed Hookstratten. Hookstratten, seeing the lucrative prospect of placing *both* his clients on the "Nightly News" as co-anchors, said to Brokaw, "What would you think if you went to Washington and Tom did New York?" Brokaw wanted no part of such an arrangement. "I told him I just didn't think it was going to work."

Leaning forward, Schlosser says, "Let me make this point because it was controversial. I would meet with the news division once a week as I met with each of the divisions. And in these meetings various things would come up. Tom Brokaw going on the 'Today' show. Jane Pauley going on the 'Today' show. Both of which happened during my presidency. And we were considering a number of candidates who might go on after Chancellor, and Snyder was one of them. There were very strong forces in the *news* division who thought that Snyder might be a good anchor."

It's crystal clear that Schlosser doesn't want it to be thought that Tom Snyder was his idea alone. But equally clear, according to Lawrence Grossman, who became president of NBC News in 1984, is that "Herb Schlosser *very much* wanted him to be anchor."

After Los Angeles, Snyder had come East to anchor "News Center 4," the network's local New York news program, and had done well. He also became host of a late-night talk show called "Tomorrow." "If the world were to be divided between the boring and the never boring," wrote Tom Shales, *The Washington Post* television critic, "Snyder would be among the latter." Shales viewed the unpredictable Snyder as blazing across the TV sky, "a comet, something to behold with awe and fear."

Though unpredictability is lively and dramatic—and best of all, as far as management is concerned, glues a viewer to the TV screen—it's not a quality high on the list of qualifications for "anchordom." On the other hand, one of the qualities that an anchor *must* have, in Schlosser's opinion, is "weight."

"He must be responsible. He must be experienced. You want the feeling that there's stability there. You'd love to feel that there's some wisdom there, some depth. But," he adds, "let's face it, what we're also looking for in an anchor man—and if anyone tells you that they're not looking for it they're crazy—are performance qualities."

Chancellor knew he was vulnerable not because of his "weight" but because of his ratings. "What the bosses want are numbers," says the former anchor, with a cynicism born of long experience in the business. "I had somebody in management say to me once—he looked at the ceiling and had this thousand-yard look—and he said, 'Tom Snyder's never been on a program that he hasn't improved the numbers.' They *love* that!"

As far as Schlosser was concerned, Snyder's numbers *were* impressive. But under the pressure of the ratings war, NBC eventually opted not for Tom Snyder, but an older hand, David Brinkley, as Chancellor's co-anchor. The new "Nightly" team made its debut on June 7, 1976. And, after a year-and-a-half of unimpressive results, Brinkley was out, and Chancellor was back on the throne alone, *solus rex*.

Brokaw and Chancellor liked each other. "I often sought his advice," Brokaw recalls, "and he would come to me in confidence and talk about things."

If Chancellor had serious doubts about Snyder's qualifications for the job of anchor, he had no such qualms about Brokaw. Tom, at least, hoped that was so. He knew how to play the game, and friends and mentors in high places were essential. They had helped him at every step in his career: from Bob Mulholland at KMTV in Omaha and later KNBC in Burbank, to Dick Wald whom he met for the first time in Los Angeles, to John Chancellor at network headquarters in New York. Despite his other competitors within the house, Brokaw could see that he now had a real chance of being in line for the gold ring. What he couldn't see was CBS's Roger Mudd.

When on February 18, 1980, Dan Rather signed his new ten-year, twenty-two million dollar contract with CBS, Roger Mudd knew he had lost his battle to succeed Walter Cronkite. After a meeting that CBS News president Bill Leonard termed "short and ugly," Mudd was determined to leave CBS.

Further downtown at 30 Rock, presidents of the NBC News division had been coming and going during this period with the frequency of commuters. Dick Wald and Les Crystal had (collectively) been presidents for no more than five years. The president *du jour*, as one NBC wag labeled him, was Bill Small. When Mudd indicated his desire to jump ship, Small, a CBS alumnus, snatched him up. As part of their deal, Mudd was guaranteed Chancellor's anchor post as soon as he gave it up.

Following the CBS signing of Rather, Brokaw guessed what was coming next. "No, I wasn't surprised when Roger came to NBC. I knew Bill Small's connection to CBS." Having worked for NBC his entire professional life since college days, Brokaw had naturally assumed that NBC was his future as well. In the spring and summer of 1981, he began casting his eyes elsewhere. His five-year contract was running out, and with his success at "Today," he was clearly a hot property.

It was CBS that approached him first. "Bill Leonard and John Lane came to me and Bill said, 'Listen, we'd be interested in talking to you about coming to work here at CBS. One of the things we'd be interested in talking to you about would be '60 Minutes.'" Brokaw was seriously interested, and he and Meredith had dinner with Leonard and his news deputy, Bud Benjamin, and their wives. After that night, "it was fairly clear to me that they hadn't run all this by Hewitt [Don Hewitt, the executive producer of '60 Minutes']."

Though a bit disappointed, Brokaw continued to talk with them about other CBS roles he might play. It was then that Dick Wald, now over at ABC, heard about their discussions. "Hey," he informed Tom, "if you're looking around, we'd like to talk with you." And that, according to Brokaw, "is when Roone called me and said we've got to start talking."

Roone Arledge was another of Brokaw's well-placed friends. Since Arledge's appointment in 1977 as president of ABC News, he had— with an impressive combination of vision, daring and money— been developing a news division at ABC that for the first time ever was offering a real challenge to the undisputed hegemony of the two network powers. Arledge wanted Brokaw. After having lost Rather to CBS following lengthy nail-biting negotiations, he wanted Brokaw badly.

"So," Brokaw said, "we went through a fairly intense courtship. And it went on—gosh, I guess it must have been a couple of months. We'd have lunch together. I'd go by his house and we'd talk some more. Then it got down to fairly serious discussions about what I might do. And ABC was offering me a lot of things. But money was never discussed. I made Hookstratten stay in California, stay out of it. I was doing all the talking. I was interested in job definition. That's what I wanted to get settled. Then we'd make the money."

Chancellor and others at NBC, fearing the handwriting on the wall, made an effort to convince Brokaw to stay. Had there been more continuity at the top, perhaps there would have been less danger of losing him. There were some insiders who even felt that Small, with his preference for Mudd, would not have been too grieved to see Brokaw walk. But at this time, as chance would have it, another Brokaw friend, Thornton Bradshaw, was suddenly named chairman of RCA, NBC's parent company.

"Brokaw had cultivated Bradshaw in Los Angeles when Bradshaw was president of Arco," Reuven Frank said. "He's pretty good at that kind of stuff." Bradshaw gave Small his orders. Brokaw was to be kept at all costs.

Brokaw, who admired Roone Arledge, "had no doubt that he was going to deliver on all the promises he was making, which were incredible. And I got all the right calls from their people. I came very close to taking the ABC offer. At one point I made up my mind I was going to take it. It was a Friday afternoon and I said to myself it makes sense. It's a fresh start. It's an exciting organization. I like the people over there. Some of my friends had already gone over there. Dick Wald, Paul Friedman, others. Then I went home that night after dinner, and I sat by myself and reflected on where I had been in my life and what I wanted to do and where I wanted to end up. And I decided I can't leave NBC. This is where I belong. These are my friends. And so I went over and said I've decided. I'm going to stay here if we can work it out."

When he had first learned of Rather's multimillion dollar contract, Brokaw was doing a political reporting job on the primaries down in Florida. Spring training had already begun there. A baseball fan, he went out to the Yankee training camp, and Reggie Jackson came rushing over to him.

"Reggie said to me, 'My God! Are you going to get a contract like

Rather's?' It was the first thing he thought about. I laughed and said, 'Everybody wants that kind of a contract, Reggie, but there aren't many of those around.' We both had a big laugh about it. That's what Reggie understood about television news. You could suddenly make the kind of money he was making. He was very aware of it. I honestly never thought that those kinds of numbers were going to be available to me at some point in my life."

Small's "solution" to his problem was to get Mudd to agree to Brokaw as his co-anchor, but it was easier said than done. Small was well aware that the difficult Mudd had already refused one co-anchor. He might easily turn down a second. But much to his surprise, Mudd proved to be amenable. Whether he felt that half an anchor desk was better than none—realizing that his all-or-nothing approach was more appropriate for children in sandboxes than grown-ups in the corporate world—or simply found Brokaw more palatable than Rather, Mudd made no objections. In fact, unknown to most, he actively worked to solidify the arrangement. In the middle of all the negotiations, Brokaw's phone rang and it was Mudd calling from Washington. He announced he was coming to New York and said, "We've got to have lunch."

"We had lunch at the Four Seasons," Brokaw recalled. "And he said, 'Don't leave. If it's "Nightly News" you're worried about, I'm willing to share it with you. I'll stay in Washington. You can be in New York. I think it's very important that you not leave the organization.' And that meant a lot to me." For Mudd, the proposed arrangement would allow him to remain in Washington where he and his family were firmly rooted.

Prodded by Small, Chancellor finally set a date for his departure, agreeing to step down from his anchor post in April 1982. Now having put together the essential parts of the succession, Small went into the nuts-and-bolts phase of his operation, negotiating Brokaw's contract with his agent, Ed Hookstratten.

A hard bargainer, Hookstratten knew he was dealing from strength. The contract—inflated by one of Brokaw's friends' desire to woo him and another's eagerness to prevent his leaving—went beyond even Brokaw's wish-list. He was reportedly given a seven year, $18 million deal, plus approval of the "Nightly News" producer, director and set design, as well as the naming of a successor should Mudd leave the newscast. He was also given the right of consultation in matters pertaining to the operation of the news division *as a whole*. Small even dangled the prospect of the broadcast becoming an hour in length at some point down the line. In short, he all but gave him the store.

It was Walter Cronkite who said that to be an anchor, you have to be adept at organizational politics. Brokaw is certainly that. If NBC pulled out all the stops to hold onto him because it had the impression that he was being offered the anchor desk at ABC, Brokaw wasn't going to do anything to correct that impression.

"We always assumed it was to anchor," Reuven Frank said, "but it was *not*. It was a lot of money but, if you believe ABC, it was to be some kind of star reporter." Brokaw recently confirmed this. "No, it was not to be an anchor. I was not to replace Frank Reynolds. It was to work *toward* an anchor job. My guess, and it's *only* a guess, is that they had Peter and me in mind as a kind of twin operation of some sort."

The contract was signed on July 1, 1981. "The money came as a huge surprise," contends Brokaw. "When Ed came to me that last day of negotiations and said, 'You're not going to believe this,' I didn't. The best story that sums it all up is that news of the stuff started leaking out around the edges, and my father read about it and called me. He asked is this true, and I kept saying why? You've never asked me about this before. Why are you asking me about it now? And there'd be another story, and he'd call me again and say is this true? Finally, he called me after *Time* magazine printed the story and he said, 'Well, I see where *Time* magazine has it.' So I said, 'Why do you *keep* asking me about this?' 'Well,' he said, 'you know as long as Mom and I have known you you've always come up a little short at the end of the year, and we're here doing our budget, and we want to be certain that we leave a little pad just to make sure you've got enough to cover you.'"

The new anchor team of Brokaw and Mudd went on the air for the first time on April 7, 1982. Brokaw had known Mudd six years earlier when Brokaw was working at the White House, and they had stayed in touch. "When he came here to substitute for Cronkite, Roger came over to our house—once or maybe twice—to have dinner in the kitchen with us and the kids."

Brokaw was sure he could work with him. As politic as ever, he paved the way for a smooth transition in his relationship with his new co-anchor by going public about his enthusiasm for Mudd in *TV*

Guide. He described his new partner as a first-rate journalist, a great guy. If Mudd had problems at CBS, he had been more sinned against than sinning.

The executive producer of their new program was Paul Greenberg. A bright, thin-faced, watchful man with a short beard and glasses, Greenberg had been the executive producer for the previous anchor, John Chancellor, as well. In Greenberg's estimation, and he minces no words about it, "Chancellor was moved out *essentially* by Brokaw."

Though a Chancellor loyalist, Greenberg found Brokaw "very smart, very energetic and with tremendous curiosity." He was not hard to get along with, and Mudd was tucked away in Washington. "We had a good relationship as far as power is concerned," Greenberg says. Essentially, Greenberg ran the program, and Brokaw and Mudd had input. But Greenberg was flexible with his stars, realizing as he wisely did, that it's hard to replace an anchor but producers, if not exactly a dime a dozen, are at least two for five. "In the time we worked together," he said, speaking of Brokaw, "maybe once a month we'd have a test of wills [on story selection, etc.]. It really came up no more than once a month."

While Cronkite, with whom he worked at CBS, and Chancellor were both managing editors, Greenberg regards Brokaw as the most hands-on, the most involved anchor he's ever worked with. "Tom Brokaw is a *very* active managing editor. I'll tell you he's more active than Walter ever was....You discuss the day's events, discuss the approaches to stories. He has his opionions about everything. About the way the program is directed, the way graphic art looks, the way the studio is set up, the way the computers are working. He has opinions about *everything*. And he makes them known! Who's working on the program? Who's working with him? Who's writing? Who's directing? Who's the associate director? Who's the P.A.? Who're the people answering the phones?"

Jack Chesnutt, a "Nightly" producer who's worked for both Chancellor and Brokaw, agrees with Greenberg. "It's been a much more hands-on management under Tom. John Chancellor it wasn't. Tom is *very much* consulted on the choice of a bureau chief somewhere. He doesn't want the last word, but he's consulted."

With his new contract securely in hand, the forty-two-year-old anchor wasn't shy about using his new power, insisting upon having his say about every aspect of the broadcast from top to bottom.

Brokaw may have thought he was the same sweet innocent guy he had been in those halcyon days when he was romping around the high school hardwood in his fleecy warmups, but he was now making tough-minded decisions that affected the lives of a lot of grownups and not everyone was inclined to like them, or him. When he was on the "Today" show, he had few critics within the house. Betsy Aaron, who worked at NBC at the time, recalls that, "Nobody had a bad thing to say about him. It was unreal."

But as a hands-on anchor, he wasn't likely to endear himself to everybody. If he happened to tell a reporter in jest that "I want to be on the air all the time. That's what drives me," there was sure to be someone who would label him an "air hog." As anchor, he was just too big a target to miss. "The guy thinks he's the greatest journalist in the world," said one disgruntled member of his staff. "A lisping mediocrity," sneered another.

What's most interesting in Brokaw's role change from host to anchor is his own reaction. Though he enjoys flexing his power—indeed seems to think of it as part of his leadership responsibility in the job— he still wants to be regarded as one of the boys, still wants his people to like him.

"I was not prepared for the anchor syndrome," he frankly admits. "You are suddenly thrust into a different category. Friends no longer look at you as a working reporter—they feel you're above that. It's difficult to deal with and to understand."

Shortly after his anchor career began, it almost came to a sudden end. A week and a half before the Brokaw-Mudd team took to the air for the first time, Reuven Frank replaced Small as president of the news division. Frank quickly decided that he didn't care for the new anchor team, but waited to give them more time to jell. "It was almost a year before I did something about it. Not till the summer of '83. The show wasn't working. I looked at it and I said that's a dead show." He concluded that the problem was the dual anchors.

Behind the scenes, the two of them were squabbling about who got the lead stories, who got the most air time. Though they probably didn't actually have a stopwatch on one another, as some claim, there was a basic underlying disagreement between them about which news was most significant, which deserved the most time.

Brokaw describes it as a "tug of war that would go on between Washington and New York about what was more important that day.

Roger saw the world much more through a Washington prism than I did. He would not be much interested in a story about popular culture, for example, and the impact it had. He didn't care at all about foreign news to speak of. His whole life was spent as a Washington correspondent. That's what his interest was. That's what drove him. I think it confined his scope of vision."

The Brokaw-Mudd show had been early blessed by those eager and susceptible hearts in NBC's publicity department for recapturing the chemistry of Huntley-Brinkley. But as Reuven Frank early noted, the chemistry wasn't working. Brokaw realized it too. At one point after they had been at it for almost a year, and the show was losing a lot of money and the affiliates were complaining, Brokaw told Mudd, "We're not doing well in the ratings. We've *got* to think about it. But he didn't see the urgency."

Brokaw was frankly worried. It seemed clear to him that one of them was going to go. "And I didn't know whether it was going to be Roger or me." He feared that his co-anchor might be in a stronger position contractually.

For Reuven Frank, the key question was: Which one had to go? "I thought about that long and hard," he readily acknowledges. Mudd was an excellent news reader. In addition to that, Frank regarded him as a "pretty good writer." He also had a "fair presence" on the air.

Brokaw, on the other hand, was a "wonderful ad-libber. He's a television creature. There are better, but not many. He's the kind of person we never had in the very early days. I guess Brinkley was the first. The guy really knew television. Cronkite knew how to talk, but he didn't know how to shut up. Brokaw is very good at that. I believe that Brokaw is better at that than as a newscaster."

Then, too, Frank foresaw a problem in getting Mudd out of Washington to cover a story. "He hates it. Brokaw goes anywhere. You know that kind of Joel McCrea in a trench coat. He loves that stuff."

But in the end, the reason he got rid of Mudd had nothing to do with the news. "We were coming up to an election year. Mudd can't ad-lib. The prospect of Mudd in the booth alone for two conventions—particularly two conventions where you knew nothing was going to happen—just terrified me."

Remembering back to that summer of '83 when he spoke to Mudd, Frank makes a noise like the Goodyear Blimp springing a leak. "That was some damn day!"

Though he knew that Mudd had already got the news from his agent, Frank felt that it was his job to meet Mudd personally and tell him his decision. That morning he had to be in Washington anyway to appear at a House subcommittee meeting. With the election only a year away, the subcommitte was looking into the subject of the networks' early projections while the West Coast was still voting.

"I spent the morning having my ass chewed out by Congressmen Tim Wirth and Al Swift," Frank says.

If that wasn't enough to kill Frank's appetite, what he had to do next was sure to do it. Instead of having lunch, he called Mudd and arranged to meet him on K Street, where in anticipation of difficulties, he had borrowed an office from one of the NBC lobbyists. If there was going to be a scene, he wanted it to happen as far away from the NBC Washington Bureau as possible. They faced off, the big rugged-looking Mudd and the donnish Frank, with his thick glasses and thinning white hair.

"He was very angry," Frank recalls. "He insisted on an explanation. I gave him an explanation. He said that's not enough. He said this is a blank-and-blank joke. I forget the adjectives, but they weren't flattering. What can you do? The thing just wasn't working. He's entitled to be disappointed. I told him it wasn't personal, but what can you do?"

Late that afternoon back in New York, Frank called Brokaw into his office and said, "I've just told Roger."

When Brokaw took over as solo anchor in August 1983, not everyone seemed to be as enthusiastic about him as Frank was. The critics carved him up as if he were rump roast. "I went through a very bad passage," he says feelingly, the memory still remarkably fresh in his mind. "The press reaction to me getting the job and not Roger was *very* negative. The good cop lost his job, and the young kid got it. There was a lot of very tough stuff written."

But Brokaw was so harried trying to get the show on every evening that he had little time for self-pity. Overcoming obstacles is something that holds a curious appeal for him, witness his taste for rock climbing and inspirational stories. "I really tried to put my head down and just do my work, because there was so much speculation that the wrong guy had gotten the job. A lot of people were complaining. And Roger had a constituency."

All through this period of turnover at NBC, the news division was in disarray. There was confusion in assignments, and stories inevitably were missed. "Nightly" under Brokaw slipped to third place in the ratings. Reuven Frank, who had the confidence of NBC newsmen and managers alike, had been brought back for a second term as president simply as a stopgap measure and to help stem the tide. But by 1984, the news division at NBC had lost $75 million. "That was the low point for us," says Natalie Hunter, a former NBC News comptroller. "1984 was an election year and, of course, that affected it."

Alluding to this period of turmoil at NBC, Dick Wald said, "Tom Brokaw had an enormous amount of power then, but that was because of a vacuum." Brokaw wanted better equipment, more aggressive news coverage, a new set: "I thought our production values weren't very good at all." Though the anchor had confidence in Paul Greenberg, his executive producer, he had strong views on what they should be doing on "Nightly" and what correspondents should be doing it, and he emphatically made them known.

"What I tried to do is say these are the things I think we ought to be covering and the direction we ought to be going," Brokaw remembers.

About their equipment, Greenberg agreed with him. "Equipment was a big problem at NBC," Greenberg recalls. "But it improved immensely toward the end of Reuven's regime. It was midway into the eighties before we came up to our competition. Whether it was cameras, graphic arts, editing equipment, we weren't keeping up with the changes."

And in addition to these problems, even Brokaw recognized that part of the responsibility for "Nightly's" low ratings might be the anchor himself, or at least the public's perception of him. Alma Varvaro, an image consultant employed by many broadcast journalists, describes Brokaw as having universal appeal. "By universal appeal— and this is not at all meant to downgrade him—I mean if Walt Disney were doing a movie on broadcast news, it'd be with somebody like Brokaw, somebody you always want to like."

Though he dresses conservatively, she feels that he has a "slightly younger quality" than the other two anchors. Perhaps it's this attractive, youthful quality that made some viewers regard him as an intellectual flyweight. Or despite the occasional serious journalism that he did on the "Today" show, it may have been his five years in the role of its charming host—his bantering with weatherman Willard Scott and being smooched by the likes of singer Eydie Gorme. Whatever the cause, Brokaw was convinced that he had to do something to change the image he had of being "just a pretty face."

His decision to grant an interview to *Mother Jones*, the politically left San Francisco-based publication, was, from one point of view, understandable. Brokaw has given much thought to political issues. He is knowledgable about them, and has firmly held independent liberal convictions. From another point of view, however, the interview proved a disaster. Anchors, after all, are not supposed to have strong political opinions. "There is nothing more white bread than an anchor," says Jane Pauley, his erstwhile sidekick on the "Today" show, and she should certainly know.

In the interview, Brokaw criticized Reagan as "simplistic and old-fashioned," described El Salvador as "controlled by a handful of people, a right-wing oligarchy that takes most of the money out of the country," and characterized himself as pro-feminist, anti-death penalty and pro-choice. Then, just to top things off, he leveled a blast at his network masters: "Salespeople run the TV networks. They don't have any real interest in what we do, except when it's commercially successful."

No wonder NBC management wasn't thrilled. Nor, for that matter, was the press. Colman McCarthy in *The Washington Post* wrote, "Anchor jobs are reportorial. Airtight objectivity is impossible for any newsperson, but Brokaw's outburst is a scattershot venting that can't help eating into the public trust of the media. The suspicion is now raised that whenever Brokaw reports a critical story about the Reagan administration, he is on a personal mission."

Somewhat further right of center, columnists couldn't decide whether he was a "limousine liberal" or a "chauffeur-driven populist." Even before all the dust had settled, Brokaw, who has always prided himself on his journalistic, if not personal, objectivity, considered the interview a mistake.

In looking to bring new energy, ideas and stability to the news division, NBC took the unusual step of going outside the three major networks to select Lawrence Grossman from the Public Broadcasting System to replace news president Reuven Frank. Though a respected figure in public television, Grossman, as one "Nightly" staffer summed him up, "knew nothing about the news." There were some who felt that he was way over his head in the job.

Grossman is a tall man with a neat gray beard and an easy manner. He looks attentively out at the world from under heavy gray eyebrows that cantilever out from his forehead like an upstairs balcony.

"He was not the most charismatic guy," says "Nightly" producer Jack Chesnutt. "But he started 'Sunrise' and 'Sunday Today.' He did *good* specials. I guess a president is always an asshole while he's in power. Then in hindsight he doesn't look so bad."

Summing up what he himself regarded as his major achievements as president, Grossman says in a quiet voice, "Taking a news division that was dead from the neck up and moving it to the number one spot. And," scratching his beard thoughtfully, "keeping Geraldo Rivera out of the news division and sending him to entertainment."

When Grossman took over the operation of NBC News in March of 1984, the division had the reputation among many in the industry of being "the morgue." Its correspondents always seemed to arrive late in the field. "They came late and stayed late," is the way one NBC producer described the sorry situation that existed there in the early eighties. The new president was determined to turn the division around, and within two years he had.

"I had been warned," said Grossman, remembering a friend's advice when he first accepted the job, "that NBC News was notorious for being a very difficult organization where everybody was out for himself, and there was no sense of loyalty. But it was understandable because they had five presidents in seven years, so that there was no direction or stability. Once we had some success, then it was wonderful. You had the normal battles, but the lines of authority were clear, the support from Grant Tinker [the president of the company], who brought me in, was *very* clear, so people played their roles the way they should."

By late 1985, Brokaw's "Nightly News" had risen from the basement of the Nielsen ratings to take first place.

Brokaw seemed to get on well with Grossman initially, and he still regards his ex-boss as "a decent and honorable man." But right from the beginning—the election year of '84—there were problems. "One of the first decisions that Larry made was that we would not report election results until after we'd seen the first tabulation results."

Brokaw still finds that hard to believe, shaking his head in amazement.

"Geez! It put us in a terrible competitive position. We ran through it all that night long, and it didn't make any sense to anybody, except that he felt there was a kind of lobby out there saying that the networks are wrong."

Reflecting on the role that Grossman adopted, Brokaw says, "I think Larry decided that he was going to be a kind of public ombudsman as president of the news division. I said to him there're just some times when that's in conflict with what we do." And *this*, Brokaw felt, was plainly one of them.

There were other disagreements as well and blunt private exchanges between the two men. Though these discussions helped to ventilate problems, they no doubt also left scars. "Brokaw," in Grossman's view, "tends to be very stubborn and dominant in many ways." On the surface, their relationship appeared relatively smooth, but there were serious seismic faults just below. Those closest to the two reported major disagreements about which correspondents or bureau chiefs were assigned which stories, and about the amount of rehearsal time the anchor needed to devote to his script-reading, so that it didn't look like the teleprompter was running ahead of him.

Then, too, the NBC News president didn't like the frequency with which Brokaw's name appeared in society columns. He was, after all, the prime representative of the news division, and his image had to be serious. If he attended a private party at Mortimer's, a fashionable restaurant on Manhattan's Upper East Side, for the wife of a friend— say, for example, the former Health, Education and Welfare Secretary, Joseph Califano, Jr.—that was, of course, his business, but how did it look when NBC's "living logo" was photographed talking to the ex-governor of New York with his fist cocked and the caption read, "Tom Brokaw shows Hugh Carey how he punishes himself when the ratings dip"?

Brokaw was hardly unreasonable. He understood the importance of his image, of being taken seriously. If Grossman wanted him to write more, to publish more articles in newspapers about who he was, that was fine with him. It made sense to Brokaw because he knew that there was still this "perception problem about me and whether or not I had the credentials to do this job." What didn't make sense to him was

Grossman's flagrant eagerness to placate others rather than defend both him and NBC News.

"I guess my one major disagreement with Larry over the course of his tenure was that he was not out there on the cutting edge holding the line in behalf of us. He was," according to Brokaw, "too inclined to see things from an apologist's point of view, too quick to make compromises. Sometimes it's tough to be in this business. It may not be popular, but sometimes you've got to stand up and say wait a minute. We've done the right thing here."

On one occasion, for example, "I got into a flap with the Chinese government while reporting on Tibet, and he was not supportive." Then there was the storm that blew up with the Israeli government when NBC News aired "Six Days Plus 20 Years: A Dream Is Dying"—a documentary critical of Israel's twenty-year occupation of the West Bank and Gaza Strip—which was condemned by Israel as "a shocking example of one-sided TV journalism." For a time thereafter, NBC News found it difficult to gain access to top Israeli officials.

"At that point, Larry and I had some discussions about this," Brokaw recalls. "He didn't fold or anything, but he sent emissaries over there in a way that I didn't think was necessary to do."

Adding to the tension between them was the overall pressure for change in the way the division functioned. Under Grossman, NBC News continued to make tremendous technological changes in its operation as videotape and satellite and computers came in. The new technology increased their capacity to get out of the studio and broadcast live. "So we really opened up our operation," Grossman said. "Put the 'Today' show on the road. Took the 'Nightly News' out of the studio."

Then in an attempt to improve the efficiency of the division, Grossman brought in McKinsey & Company, a consulting firm, to see what could be done to save money. Some feared that they might lose their jobs.

Others took the company's attempts to quantify the news as a joke. "They never really mastered what was going on," said one producer, reflecting the attitude of most. Like Dickens' Thomas Gradgrind with his "rule and a pair of scales, and the multiplication table always in his pocket, sir, ready to weigh and measure any parcel of human nature, and tell you exactly what it comes to," they summed up everything about the news but its essence. One result of their survey was a story indexing system to help allocate expenses, but NBC has recently thrown it out.

Then Grossman called in set designer Frank Lopez to build him a working newsroom for the "Nightly News." He wanted it to be an environment in which people actually worked and not look like a stage set. The viewer would see Brokaw backed by rows of desks with staffers busy at their phones and TV monitors and computers.

According to Lopez, "Usually most presidents of news have one pet project that they want to get going, and this was Larry Grossman's. Needless to say by then both CBS and ABC had what's known as 'working newsrooms.' NBC was the only one that did not. I think it's clear that they wanted to get on the bandwagon also."

The basic contradiction faced by the talented Lopez in realizing Grossman's *grand projet* was to make the anchor look good while at the same time locating him in a twenty-four hour functioning newsroom. (Hugh Raisky and Roger Goodman, in designing their respective newsrooms at CBS and ABC, had the same problem.)

Lopez acknowledges, "I was trying to do this balancing act of giving them something truly elegant and still have the feeling of a working place where people come in every day and work." After he had finished, NBC management basically liked what they saw.

But if Grossman seemed satisfied, Brokaw was not. The original decision was to have a "warm gray" as the dominant color. The plan was to distinguish the "Nightly News" visually from its competitors by color, an instant recognition factor as viewers scanned their channels in search of the evening news. The other two networks used blue, so blue was out, even though it's generally regarded as one of the few "safe" colors.

"Other than blue," says Lopez, "neutrals are the only colors that many wouldn't have some prejudice against. Reds are too intense. Lavenders are offensive. Greens just don't look good."

But Tom was not keen about the way he looked in "warm gray." He wanted it changed. He thought he looked better in blue. Brokaw flexed a few muscles, and blue it became!

Lopez—a short, soft-spoken guy with a friendly manner—sighs over what might have been. "When we took this job, I *said* that Tom Brokaw should be consulted. In essence, I was told he would sit wherever we told him to sit. In essence, they said, 'we are responsible for doing the set and he is "talent."' But of course when push came to shove, that was not the case at all."

As Lopez found out, you just don't tell the gorilla where to sit if you know what's good for you, or try to shove warm-gray down his mouth, unless you don't mind ending up black and blue. "I suppose management wanted to keep the number of people involved down to a handful," Lopez speculates, and that's why they never consulted him. "But *goodness* knows, Tom Brokaw!"

If Grossman's relationship with his chief anchor did not run a totally smooth course under the old dispensation, it became positively wrinkled in 1986 under the stress of the GE buyout of the network. "I think that almost from day one, " Brokaw says, "—based upon what I was able to hear and what I was told—Larry did not have the confidence of his new masters from GE. [Robert C.] Wright and [Jack] Welch and others. That was my *very* strong impression. From day one. I think as well that he'd lost the confidence of a lot of people around the organization." Brokaw cites Steve Friedman, who was then executive producer of the "Today" show, as one of those unhappy with Grossman.

Despite early fears of wholesale layoffs comparable to those that had already taken place at CBS and ABC, NBC's new owners seemed to be in no hurry to make changes at first, preferring to study their new toy before taking it apart. But few doubted that the cuts were coming. After all, GE's president, Jack Welch wasn't called "Neutron Jack"— he leaves the structures standing and wipes out the troops—for nothing.

And then in June 1987, to compound the uncertainty, NABET— NBC's union of news writers, cameramen, editors, sound technicians, graphic artists and researchers—went out on strike. The strike lasted seventeen weeks. It was an especially bitter time on the peacock farm, and there were many walking the picket line outside Rockefeller Center who, according to one striking writer, felt that Grossman was doing little to help.

But some praised Brokaw. "I really felt," another writer-producer said, "that Brokaw was working to help the situation on the inside. He came to several of our writers' group meetings."

John Clark, the head of Local 11 of NABET, confirms Brokaw's behind-the-scenes constructive role during the strike. "I felt that he did *all* that he could under the circumstances. I know that he had a lot of private meetings with a lot of people during the strike. He even called up and spoke with our chief spokesman, Tom Kennedy, who's network coordinator in NABET. I think he also had a discussion with the president of the company, Bob Wright, but there wasn't all that much he could do. I think he tried to do as much as he could."

Brokaw acknowledges that he spoke to Wright—NBC's chief executive officer and Welch's handpicked man at the network—on more than one occasion, trying to bring the two sides together, but he didn't broadcast the fact. It's just something that he believed went with the territory of being the anchor of the "Nightly News," the leader of the team.

Brokaw has been called "the ultimate insider." During the strike, for example, Connie Chung openly sided with the strikers, attending their picnic in Central Park. Brokaw absented himself, preferring a different role.

"I felt *very* strongly about the strike," he stresses. "And I thought I could be an honest broker in it. I chose not to play it out in a public way. I chose to keep it very private and go in confidence to members of the rank and file here and to members of management here. I don't pretend to be a key party in all of this, but there were times when they were missing each other in the night, and I was always trying to make sure they were talking to each other."

There were several times, in fact, that he felt as if he were dealing "with two separate solar systems."

Recently, when Chung left NBC for CBS, there were many who faulted Brokaw for not doing more to keep her, regarding his apparent apathy as symptomatic of either his fear of claimants to his throne or his lack of sympathy for female correspondents. In this case, neither could be further from the truth. Typically, Brokaw was working quietly, diligently and out of camera range, to keep her at NBC. Chung herself has revealed that, "He paid the greatest daily attention to my negotiations—so much so he became a broker of sorts. He kept calling me at the office and at home trying to persuade me to stay. He even sent computer messages to me in the office."

The same month that the strike began Brokaw was named chief of correspondents in addition to being managing editor. "It was not a good idea," Brokaw says in retrospect, "and I said so at the time. In fact, I turned it down, but the consultants [McKinsey] thought there ought to be a place where correspondents might go [for help with management] because they didn't have one. Then Larry Grossman came back and said everybody continues to think it's a good idea."

Though Brokaw may have said he took the job reluctantly, he also said some other things at the time. He spoke of his new position as "a watershed move," a far-reaching step in "the institutional future of network news." The announcement of Brokaw's appointment came as a blow to network correspondents. Morale sagged. How could they complain to their new chief about not getting more air time when he was the cause? Even Grossman came to reject the idea.

"In retrospect," he admitted, "it enforced everyone's perception that this was a 1,000-pound gorilla who now had additional powers." Today, Brokaw claims that his chief of correspondents title "no longer has standing."

It was in the fall of '87 when Brokaw scored a newscasting hat trick. In a single week, he was seen in high-profile primetime interviewing Mikhail Gorbachev in the Kremlin and Ronald Reagan in the White House, and moderating a debate with the leading presidential candidates. NBC News, after two and a half years of relative stability under Grossman, seemed to be on the uptick. In the ratings, "Nightly" had edged out Dan Rather's "CBS Evening News" for first place. Smiles brightened the carpeted third-floor corridors at NBC.

"There is no fixed formula for ratings success," said Brokaw philosophically. "I've been down, and I've been up." But up was clearly better. Today, Grossman waxes nostalgic over those halcyon days. For him, that was the great good time. "When NBC News was moving to the top and restoring its tarnished image and becoming a much more successful and better organization, everybody was working together and there was a real sense of accomplishment and teamwork and sacrifice for the common good."

But the friction between Brokaw and Grossman was growing. And then in September 1987, the Nielsen Company in an attempt to improve their ratings system shifted from diary entries to its pushbutton People Meter, and the consequences for NBC proved traumatic. Shot out of the sky like a dead duck, the "Nightly News" plummeted to third. When that happened, according to Grossman, "when the atmosphere turned and soured and there were clearly problems at the top, it went back to the every-man-for-himself syndrome."

From Brokaw's point of view, it probably seemed as if Grossman's leadership had become enfeebled under their new owners, with potentially dire consequences for the news division and perhaps even his own career. Going over Grossman's head, he put out feelers to the GE men, Wright and Welch. Though he laughs now when people write about him as Jack Welch's pal—not having seen Welch since that Sunday a year ago when Bob Wright had his party for Grossman's eventual successor—Brokaw does admit to receiving Welch's Christmas card. And there is no doubt that he had earlier received Welch's confidence.

Brokaw remembers "one time in particular that I went to Jack Welch—it was late '87 after the strike and GE wanted to send down a dictum that we had to make these cuts, and we were to do it from the bottom up on the seniority list. Just cut this number of people. And Larry knew that that was wrong, but he didn't have much leverage over there.

"So I went as an emissary, and I said to Jack, 'Listen, I understand your concerns about costs, but you've got to give us a chance to get these things under control. You can *not* allow this to happen in the meantime.' I knew it would be destructive. I said, 'You're not making a judgment based on the quality of the people. You're making a judgment based upon when they were hired.' And he said okay. He saw the strength of that argument."

Brokaw couldn't hold back the tide any more than Canute, but he did manage to make the firings less destructive. NBC's former comptroller, Natalie Hunter, says, "I think we tried very hard to keep whatever turmoil there was off the front pages, and from that standpoint we never had the kind of publicity that CBS had at the very beginning where everybody got fired overnight."

Nevertheless, in a relatively short period of time in late 1987, NBC's work force was reduced to seventy percent of what it had been when Larry Grossman first took over in 1984. By means of severance packages, early retirement programs, buyouts of contracts and two rounds of layoffs, NBC culled four hundred out of the herd, leaving a somewhat bewildered and demoralized work force of one thousand.

Desk assistants and news and feature assistants were simply fired, their positions to be filled in, when necessary, by less experienced freelancers and part-timers. Two-man crews that consisted of a cameraman and a sound man became, in some instances, one-man bands. The Houston bureau was closed. Though it's obvious that waste existed in the organization in that former golden time when, as Brokaw wryly says, revenue came in over the transom, under the doors, through the windows and "there was a lot of guilt money being thrown around by the networks," it is also true that NBC's ability to cover the news had to be affected by these "new realities," as the cutbacks were called.

In this rather bleak, lean and very mean period at NBC News when "Nightly" was consistently a poor third in the ratings, the relationship between Brokaw and Grossman was inevitably strained. Grossman noted that "Tom gravitated toward management." Others in the organization had only an inkling of what was going on. And then came the quake. It was only a tiny one on the Richter scale, but given Brokaw's impressive self-control and eagerness to keep things smooth, it certainly caught the attention of staffers like Jack Chesnutt:

"The tension between Grossman and Tom, that was very subtle. Till four months before he left, there was nothing. Then, one night, Grossman didn't like a story, and he phoned down after the news to tell Tom. Tom took the message, slammed down the phone, and said Larry didn't like the story. The translation was Larry didn't like the story, *and he doesn't know what he's talking about.*"

After that, Grossman's days were numbered. It was clear that things were rapidly deteriorating between him and Welch and Wright, but only later did Grossman realize Brokaw's role in his exit. "Jack Welch and I were operating at different—at cross purposes. There were major battles. And Tom played a role in my case." It was Tom, Grossman now recognizes, who was "in part" responsible for the hiring of Michael Gartner.

The way Brokaw tells it, one day Wright casually said to him, "We're looking around for some people. He didn't even say anything about Grossman's job," Brokaw insists. "He said we need to get some new people into the mix around here in the news business."

Brokaw could guess the kind of people they were looking for because he was reasonably certain that he knew the priorities of Wright's boss Welch. One through ten, Welch's priorities were to get control of the news division, to stop what he regarded as its financial hemorrhaging. And if that were indeed the case, Brokaw wanted to make sure that they were seeing people who could talk to them not only about things financial, but on the editorial side as well.

Brokaw admits, "There was a certain terror on my part that they were going to go out and hire an accountant to run this place. Or a lawyer."

So most of the names he submitted to Wright were people who had management responsibilities somewhere in journalism. Then he arranged lunches for him. In some instances, Wright seemed just to be seeking information from knowledgeable outsiders as to exactly what NBC News was doing.

Brokaw adds, "Then one day I was talking to Gordon Manning [a vice-president for special projects at NBC News] about this and asked him to think about it. And Manning came back and said, 'Michael Gartner,' and I said, 'Hey, that's a good idea!'"

Though Gartner was not a friend, Brokaw had met him on at least four occasions, the first one in Iowa in 1980. "I remember I met him briefly at a luncheon in downtown Des Moines to which Chancellor and I were asked to come on behalf of the station. And Michael was one of the movers and shakers of the Des Moines establishment."

Brokaw, who has a lot of pals in the newspaper business, had already heard about the former president of the *Des Moines Register*, who had become a Gannett executive. After all, Meredith Brokaw serves on the Gannett board of directors. "Some people," Brokaw says, "believe that I reached out and got my friend from the Midwest and put him in this job, which is just *not so.*" What is so is that he functioned as matchmaker.

Brokaw sent Gartner's name up to Wright with the message, "'Here's a guy from the Midwest who's been a publisher and an editor and gets very high marks from everyone. If you're talking to people, you ought to talk to him.' And he called me back and said, 'Listen, he's way out in the Middle West, and it doesn't seem to make a lot of sense.' I said, 'Fine, but I'm just telling you he's got good *bona fides.*' That's the last I heard of it until it got close to the 1988 Democratic convention. Wright said to me then, almost in a glancing way, 'Hey, your friend Gartner, we like him.' I saw Michael in Atlanta at the convention. I went to find him. I said, 'Are they talking to you?' and he said, 'Well, yes, but it can't mean much.' I said, 'It means more than you realize.' And within twenty-four hours, they offered him the job."

Grossman's ouster was announced in New York on July 27, 1988. He was, at the time, busy attending a business conference 3,000 miles away.

Gartner, the bright-eyed fiftyish ex-newspaperman, affects perky bow ties and suspenders that look about as quaint and out-of-place in the NBC president's office at 30 Rockefeller Plaza as the dinky green mailbox hanging outside it that says, *"The Daily Tribune*, Mid-Iowa's Daily Newspaper."* Despite his folksiness and the gray hair and kindly look, he seems to have somehow managed—with a rapidity bordering on genius—to alienate a large number of longtime NBC News people who consider him "rigid," "cold" and "arrogant."

Others just laugh at his cloyingly upbeat memos every Friday. And those fearing still more cuts at the hands of GE's new man dubbed him "Mike the Knife." In short order he succeeded in eliminating, either by design or fecklessness, such important correspondents as Chris Wallace, Connie Chung and Ken Bode. The Wallace case was especially messy and ended in heated words.

"Everybody sees Gartner as screwing that up," reports one "Nightly News" staffer. "We can't figure out if he was just stupid and didn't realize Chris would go, or whether he wanted to show us that any one of us was expendable."

The firing in May of Bill Chesleigh, executive producer of the weekend "Nightly News," resulted in a protest letter signed by over one hundred NBC employees. "Right now," said one insider at the height of the troubles, "it's a fearful and unhappy shop."

Gartner's often-stated and much publicized disdain for television during appearances on "Nightline" could hardly endear him to the troops. To judge from those who know him even casually, "He fundamentally believes in the superiority of print. He thinks TV is all shlock."

It also must be pointed out that not only did Gartner dislike television when he was hired, but he was also a relative ignoramus as far as his knowledge of the medium was concerned. But this didn't bother Brokaw. Gartner had editorial and managerial skills, and besides there were plenty of people at NBC who knew how to do television.

Others at NBC, however, were troubled. One senior correspondent said, "Of the top four news management people at NBC [Tim Russert, Tom Ross, Joe Angotti and Michael Gartner] only one of them understands television and that's Angotti. Michael Gartner certainly doesn't understand television."

A recent incident makes the point. Excited by Brokaw's good fortune at the Berlin Wall, Gartner gathered a group of senior news executives together immediately after the broadcast, and told them he wanted a one-hour retrospective special on the entire history of the

Wall, by 10:00 PM that night. The newsmen looked at their boss, their jaws dropping in dismay. Gartner didn't realize that he was asking them to do three weeks of photo archive work in three hours. Finally, one newsman gently explained to Gartner that it couldn't be done.

Right from the beginning of his tenure, perhaps fearing embarrassment, Gartner held himself aloof, apparently trying to play catch-up on television news heuristically rather than be tutored by experts. One senior producer offered to take the boss through a day, have him pull up a chair, sit in on the roll call of bureaus and see how it's done. He's still waiting for an answer. The learning process for Gartner appears to be a clandestine one, and slow. And it hardly seems to be helped by his regular weekending in Iowa.

"From my conversations with him," says a NABET representative, "I don't really think he knows what's going on at NBC News. I met him earlier this year. He didn't know certain things about his employees. He's not that familiar with broadcasting. I think he's a stopgap. I don't really think he's going to be there that long. I think he was brought in just to make cuts."

Since Gartner's appointment, NBC News has been taking its lumps in the press with articles about internal bickering, stories being muffed, correspondents leaving and sinking morale. Many European bureaus were frankly surprised that after a year they still hadn't been visited by their new president, which, according to one foreign correspondent of long standing, was highly unusual, and bound to have a leaden effect on the overseas staff. Then, too, there were raised eyebrows in the industry when newspapers announced Gartner's closing of NBC's Paris bureau as an economy measure after more than three decades of continuous operation.

It seemed as if every day there was another horror story in the papers about the peacock's unhappy crew replete with sour captions: Gartner Irate! Brokaw Puzzled! Gumbel Miffed! Toward the end of 1989, a troubled Brokaw—feeling that NBC had become like chum in the water for the print-journalist sharks—called an unusual meeting of about ten of "Nightly's" special-segment producers.

It was held at 7:30 PM, right after the show. Brokaw told them that the leaks to the press had to stop. If they had complaints, they should talk to him or Bill Wheatley. The way it looked to him, the place was damn near hitting rock bottom. Gartner was beleaguered. "We have to work from the inside," Brokaw advised them, in his typical fashion. If they kept leaking stories to the press, they were only going to alienate Gartner and make things worse.

Brokaw mentioned nothing about the criticism of himself, but that went without saying. Of late he was showing a surprisingly thin skin. His attitude may have had something to do with the fact that "Nightly" had been finishing last in the ratings for much of 1989. Third place was not very cheerful to contemplate for someone as competitive as Tom Brokaw.

Had he been feeling the stress every Tuesday of the past year when the Nielsen results came in? "I never feel it when we're ahead," he tosses off flippantly. "I only feel it when we're behind."

In off moments, with his gray hair disheveled and his tie askew, it's easy to see he's been feeling it. There may have been an Edenic time when he had no idea what his ratings were, but he admits that's never been the case since he became "Nightly's" anchor.

Under the pressure of adverse ratings and publicity, Brokaw even suffered a rubber-tipped arrow in his hometown *Yankton Daily Press and Dakotan* (circulation 3,610) as painfully as if it had been "Little Boy," dropped on him in *Time* or *Newsweek*. On the July 26, 1989 op-ed page of the *Yankton Daily* in a column entitled "Notes from Indian Country," Native American Tim Giago, after walloping South Dakotans Al Neuhart (retired chairman of the Gannett Newspaper Group) and TV sportscaster Pat Ryan for their "good-deed" of helping to raise money to preserve Mt. Rushmore, faulted Brokaw in passing, too, for "having the nerve to form a company called 'Tom-Tom Productions'" and thereby obtain a minority loan to start his country and western radio station in Rapid City, South Dakota.

It's not hard to think of Brokaw owning a country and western station, but it is hard to conceive of him needing a minority loan to do it. It's harder still to think of him taking the time to write a rather lengthy and tortuous response to the charge: "What is it in your experience that led you to the conclusion that I act as if I have a skeleton in my closet when asked about the Sioux? Just one example, please?"

But when he gets to the point, he makes it emphatically, denying that he ever received a minority loan. "As for my 'nerve,' as you describe it, to name my radio company Tom-Tom Broadcasting, it may interest you to know the name grew out of the first names of the principals, Tom Brokaw and Tom Krens. Is there a copyright on tom-tom of which I am unaware?"

Giago's was just one more attack, and a fairly silly one, but in 1989, Brokaw, feeling himself under siege, was in no shape to laugh it off.

Year One of the Gartner presidency proved to be more trying than anyone might have suspected. Another year like it might be disastrous. Brokaw, who thrives on challenges, had to look to the out of doors to find a suitably rigorous image to describe what had happened. "In kayaking," he explained, "there are various degrees of water. Class 1 water. Class 2 water. Michael's been through a *loooong* ride on Class 4 water, which is *very* rough white water. And he's been upended a couple of times. And he's had to do the Eskimo roll a couple of times. He's gotten wet. And he's even been out of the boat! And now he's back in the boat, and now he's emerged into a period of some calm water."

This may only be wishful thinking on Brokaw's part, but perhaps the new decade does hold better things for Gartner and NBC News. In 1990, the "NBC Nightly News with Tom Brokaw" has inched up out of the cellar and, on occasion, taken second place in the ratings by a narrow margin. As for Gartner, with a fresh mandate from his GE masters to stay on for a while longer, he has decided to publish a new image of himself, the "Good Mike," acknowledging in the press that he probably has "irked some people" and promising to "reach out" to them. But after a year of the "Bad Mike," it's not surprising that many of NBC's disaffected employees are shrinking back in suspicion and guarding their jugulars.

The new decade has also brought with it other changes at NBC. On February 6, for example, "Nightly's" anchor turned fifty. Brokaw wasn't especially impressed with thirty or forty, but fifty has gotten his full attention. "I didn't have much trouble with forty or a couple of the others. Hell, there's plenty of time.... But suddenly with fifty you're dealing with a ticking clock. It's not one you take lightly. You begin to think long thoughts." Then he smiles, and sounding like a character from a Beckett play, he says, "I'll go forward."

The birthday plans had been six months in the making by Meredith and his three daughters. They would be taking over the trendy downtown eaterie Sounds of Brazil, which has, according to one restaurant guide, "the worst food since high school." But who goes there to eat? It's the place to go to drink, to dance, and to listen to the wildest Brazilian music you're likely to hear anywhere north of Rio— ideal for a fiftieth birthday party. Friends and family were coming from all over the country.

"This was the one time I decided I just had to honor a personal commitment," Brokaw said. "I have a long string of broken family vacations, commitments, whatever, and I just said to everybody I'm going to stay for this one."

But what about the historic Central Committee Plenum going on in Moscow at that very minute, with Rather already there and Jennings on his way? What about the battle of the anchors, the ratings war?

Brokaw snapped impatiently, "But that's kind of what's happened in this business. There's this kind of frantic tone that has overtaken us. Anytime one or the other of us goes across the street, the other two have to follow. That's crazy!"

So that night, millions of Americans on the "Nightly News" saw Garrick Utley in front of St. Basil's in Moscow and asked themselves, "Where was Tom Brokaw?"

At the Sounds of Brazil, of course! Celebrating his fiftieth birthday thoroughly, he kicked up his heels with friends and family to a Latin beat. "I just said in this case you can only go so many places so many times and leave so many members of your family scattered behind." Despite the big bucks, it's obviously *very* expensive in human currency to be an anchorman and a family man at the same time.

But on the whole Brokaw seems more than willing to pay the price. "Who wouldn't like this job?" he says emphatically. The eyes in his tired face start to light up like the eyes in some billboard advertisement. "I went down to Bogota on Friday. Had dinner with the mayor and a group of journalists in the city who gave me a complete read on their views about what's going on in the drug war. The next morning, I'm up early and off in the streets of Bogota with the head of the Colombian FBI. Then I go to see the President of Colombia. He walks me around the president's palace, and we have a long talk about how the drug war is going on. Then I'm on a plane coming back. Now tomorrow night I'm going off to South Africa for a couple of days or maybe a week."

Stopping to catch his breath, he shakes his head and grins the way he does at the end of his program when somebody with no arms or legs has just managed to climb Mt. Rushmore. "You know," he says, "it's an *exhilarating* existence." He leans forward. "And I'm paid well for it," he insists, his voice running out of steam. "And I can pick up the phone and generally get to the person I want to talk to about what's going on."

Brokaw sinks back into his chair. "Adrenaline?...Oh, sure," he says softly, wearily.

RATINGS: Week ending December 1st

1st. Jennings (ABC's "World News Tonight")—11.5/21 [10,591,500]

2nd. Rather   ("CBS Evening News")—10.3/18 [9,486,300]

3rd. Brokaw   ("NBC Nightly News")—10.2/19 [9,394,200]

CHAPTER TWENTY-TWO

Anchor Monsters

There is a Zen Buddhist story about a monk contemplating a mountain. As a novice, he looks at the mountain, and sees a mountain. After meditating on it for months, he realizes it is no longer a mountain at all. Then, one day, his education complete, he looks at the mountain, and sees a mountain.

On the television screen, today's anchors Brokaw, Jennings and Rather are in many ways indistinguishable—all handsome, male, white Anglo-Saxon Protestants in their fifties. Get to know them a little, and you realize just how different they really are: Rather, the two-fisted can-do Texas scrapper; Brokaw, the smooth charmer, the Gatsby, the deft behind-the-scenes operator; Jennings, the urbane self-taught enthusiast, schooled on the road.

But fundamentally, they are, in fact, surprisingly similar, these three men who all got their start as radio disk jockeys talking to tiny audiences, and wound up addressing the nation. Ambition is a whetstone that they've honed themselves on for years. All three have a strong sense of power, of who they are, what they want, and how to get it, whether by charm or enthusiasm, raw energy or brute strength.

"They are a different species of human being," says one producer. "Men on stage, a career on stage. They walk into meetings and tell jokes, and everyone laughs whether they're funny or not."

Most important, all three have, in a way, created themselves, fighting to overcome limitations of education or class or geography.

Dan Rather, a natural reporter, worked hard to make himself into an anchor; Peter Jennings, a natural anchor, worked hard to turn himself into a reporter; Tom Brokaw, a natural charmer, worked hard to turn himself into both. All three have molded what they are today.

Perhaps because of that, each has surprising insecurities. "It never ceases to amaze me, as long as I've been in this business, how fragile the egos are," says one executive producer. "And the bigger they get, the more fragile the egos are. You'd think the longer they've been in the business, the more self-confident they'd be. But the anchors need enormous amounts of positive reinforcement."

Solidly ensconced in TV journalism's top job, they are nonetheless all still trying to prove themselves week after week. "They all want to prove they're good reporters," says CBS correspondent Dick Threlkeld. "They don't want to be perceived as Ted Baxter. They want to be seen as news editors, reporters, producers."

Over the years, as the anchor position has evolved from news reader to celebrity, as marketing concerns have made the anchor a bigger and bigger presence, the job holders have branched out into many roles, and assumed more and more executive powers in almost every facet of the network news organization. With the clout they have as living logos, mixed with the demands of a fragile ego...When logo meets ego, something a little scary is born.

Call it gorilla inflation. Around the news business, anchors for years have been referred to as "800-pound gorillas." Walter Cronkite was the original 800-pound gorilla. But when Rather, Jennings and Brokaw arrived on the scene, they acquired a different order of magnitude. Former CBS "Evening News" producer Richard Cohen says, "I remember a conversation I had with Dan back in 1980, on a plane home from Ohio, about his impending ascent to power. I said, 'Walter is an 800-pound gorilla; I hope you never take it so seriously.' He laughed, and assured me that it would never happen. Now he's an 1,800-pound gorilla. And when he thunders through the forest ..."

Even the most loyal staffers have to grumble a little that so much power and airtime is being gobbled up by this voracious new breed that they've taken to calling "the anchor monster." On really bad days, when things are getting a little out of control, they'll talk about "bigfoot"— either a noun or a verb, as in "I just got bigfooted."

Paul Duke, the moderator of "Washington Week in Review" on PBS, says, "It's the age of the superanchorman. When I was at NBC, I always thought they had a strong team. If a big story broke, there were any number of people who could move into the studio and anchor programs and do specials—Newman, McGee, Chancellor, in addition to Huntley and Brinkley. Today, the superanchorman does everything. It's as if [a newspaper] had one reporter who wrote the lead story in the paper every day. It just doesn't make any sense. They're putting all their financial marbles into one guy, and the rest of the staff are kind of like drones to serve him."

Peter Jennings argues that this is an overstatement, that television news is by nature collective, and doesn't allow for hierarchies. "We do not have a particularly vertical structure," he says. "We have a sort of Guggenheim structure. You know, I have a lot of muscle around here because I'm the anchor person. But I have a lot of influence because I've been around a long time. And I have a measure of power because I'm good at what I do. You could interchange all those things. So if I think that correspondent A will do a story particularly well, because I have a pretty good eye, the shop will listen."

If everything Jennings says is true, it is only part of the story, because it leaves out how much more muscle he and the other anchors have than their predecessors—the power to choose who gets on the air and who doesn't, what stories will be covered, and even who works with them on the broadcast. The anchorman was never one of the boys, but now his job has a management side as well.

Take Tom Brokaw who, with his political finesse, even managed to help ease out one boss and select his replacement, the very president of the division for which he works. And for those who work under him? One NBC correspondent who left was quoted as saying, "Tom is like a giant redwood tree. He casts such a huge shadow that nothing but stunted saplings can grow."

Dan Rather, especially in the earlier years under Van Gordon Sauter, certainly absorbed a lot of management responsibility, moving out longtime correspondents, and promoting his own cadre. "Dan was like a spoiled child who ran amok," says one unhappy producer who was fired.

Rather apparently felt that part of his new anchor role was to be on top of every facet of the news business, including the job of story editor. This eagerness, according to one CBS staffer, would lead to some humorous consequences:

"When he first began as managing editor, he'd go to all the

screenings of the pieces. One of the first times, when a piece finished, there was silence in the room, and everyone looked at Dan, out of deference. He thought he had to say something. So he made something up: 'I think we should cut forty-five seconds out.' There was a long pause. Then he said, 'Of course, you can talk me out of it.' "

Of the three, Jennings has marginally the least managerial power (although he still wants to have veto power over everyone who may be hired, even the lowliest researcher), but he's involved more closely than the others in the hands-on day-to-day rewrite and reediting of stories. This, of course, is bound to annoy correspondents, who already have to please several other editors. Even friends like John McWethy are sometimes put out. "He's all over my copy," McWethy sighs. In the past, some correspondents complained that Jennings would take interesting writing or ideas from reporters, and use them for himself, simply seizing them by the anchor's law of eminent domain. ABC correspondents say that no longer happens: "Peter used to steal lines. Then he realized how demoralizing it is, and he stopped."

Of course the most common criticism you'll hear leveled at the anchors is that they are air-hogs. This is old news, but today the anchors each take up between five and a half and six minutes a night, about a fourth of the broadcast. Understandably, all of the anchormen have on occasion been approached by distraught correspondents asking for more air time. The complaints most often come when a big story breaks, and the anchor goes on the road to cover it. "The concern of the guys in the field is, you cover an issue until it gets good enough, then wham-o, it gets taken away," says John McWethy.

The anchor monster issue can be summed up in one phrase, a phrase that could apply equally well to all three network broadcasts. As one former CBS staffer put it, "It's ceased to be a news show. It's now the Dan Rather show, featuring Dan Rather, with Dan Rather, also starring Dan Rather." That many of the negative quotes in this book about Jennings, Rather and Brokaw are without attribution is a small indication of the anchors' power. "Look," said one reporter, "No one is going to say anything on the record about these three anchors if you still want to have a career. They're just too powerful."

But for all their power, there is a sad irony to the anchor's lot. It's a newsman's Peter Principle at work. The very abilities that thrust them to the top aren't necessarily so crucial in their new role. Good, even first-rate, reporters out in the field, they are now chained to anchor desks. Jennings, Rather and Brokaw always talk with a little regret about not being out in the trenches covering stories.

It's Peter Jennings who speaks of being "a slave to the broadcast." And as for Dan Rather, former colleague Marty Koughan says, "I feel sorry for Dan. He was a terrific reporter. Now he's one of the most important people in the Western World. For all the millions he makes, there's no satisfaction in it. He comes in, reads the teleprompter, looks serious in bumpers. He's a prisoner of the throne he occupies. Which is too bad, cause Dan's the kind of guy, when the gun goes off, he'll chew his leg off to get to a story. To sit back and be a general—I don't believe for a second Dan is fulfilled in his job."

Which is, of course, why the anchors like it so much when the big stories take them abroad—to China, East Germany, Malta. It's a taste of freedom, a reminder of their former reporting days. Instantly, the old correspondents' black book comes out, full of sources and phone numbers, and for a little while, even if much of the legwork is done in advance for them, they get to bird-dog a story.

Critics complain that the downside of "anchors away" is that all the rest of the coverage gets slighted. No less an authority than former anchor John Chancellor complained that major foreign coverage has become simply a foot race to see who can get their anchors to the scene first. But just because the anchor wins the foot race, doesn't mean he'll know anything when he gets there. Ex-NBC correspondent Ken Bode asks, "How can you expect a Tom Brokaw to be at 30 Rock on Thursday morning and in China on Thursday night, and to know what's going on?"

The problem is very real. In an era of corporate cutbacks, with more and more major events happening in far-flung corners of the world, network coverage is getting stretched very thin indeed. The news teams have gone to their zone defenses, shifting reporters and anchors to cover the globe. But when events happen on the fringes, in places like China and Romania and Ethiopia (not even considering the Syrias and Albanias that totally bar all foreign cameras), the zone defense usually gets trounced.

"In China," says Ken Bode, "we all thought the government would fall. We thought the democracy movement was too strong. We missed the story. No one had any sources in the Chinese government. No one knew anything more than what was happening behind the stand-uppers in Tiananmen Square." Bode argues that that's the fault of the shifting coverage, sending the anchors and other reporters to different locations all around the globe. "The networks," he says, "are going all over the world, putting up Potemkin villages. But they don't have any reporters, any bureaus to back them up."

There are many worthwhile TV reasons to send anchors out on the road, all described previously, the most fundamental being that it draws the public's attention to the big story. Robert MacNeil observes that "It dramatizes for the American viewer the importance of the story. It says, hey gee, something important is going on here. It's a different order of story than the normal routine thing. And also because you send the anchor, it's like you send the President somewhere. You send a whole train of other things, and you devote time and resources and energy."

But when it comes to better coverage around the world, there is no substitute for reporters in place, correspondents who know the territory, who know the major players, who understand what's likely to happen next and why. What's needed, in short, is someone with detailed knowledge, a correspondent who can work in tandem with the generally experienced anchor. It's self-evident that for serious coverage the bureaus are the single most important resource for the networks. Money expended on them is money well spent. It also enhances the value of the anchor.

Quite recently, the anchor's role shifted again. Perhaps as a backlash to the popular perception of the anchor monster, the three anchormen themselves started downplaying their "bigfoot" roles. "Neither Peter Jennings, Dan Rather nor Tom Brokaw has as much power as people think," Brokaw asserted. "We're not innocent bystanders, nor do I believe that the anchor should be someone who walks in and reads the script. After all, I do have a fair amount of tenure and experience in this business. But I know my place. People around here will tell you I'm not playing the part of the 800-pound gorilla."

More significantly, the network news divisions started reining in the anchors. Within the labyrinthine world of CBS News, where malevolent gossip is a high art form quite unrivaled since the days of the de'Medici court, the arrival of David Burke as CBS News president in late 1988 was seen as a direct challenge to Dan Rather's hegemony over the news division.

"Burke was brought in to tame Rather," is generally how the new president's appointment was viewed. It certainly seemed as if that were true when management marched into the newsroom to announce Burke's impending arrival, and Rather was standing among the surprised staffers, and not, as he used to, on the management side. And when Burke fired first vice-president Joan Richman, a friend of Rather's, and then special events director David Buksbaum, perhaps Rather's closest friend at CBS (dubbed "VP of Dan" by insiders), the message seemed clear indeed.

Perhaps it was just a clash of styles between the abrasive Buksbaum and Burke, the reserved executive known as "the Ice Prince." But no matter what Burke claimed, it was obviously a double-barreled blast, making it plain that Rather didn't have the power he once had.

At NBC, the arrival in 1989 of the new, strong news-desk system under Don Browne, beyond simply improving NBC's coverage capabilities, also eroded Tom Brokaw's power. The anchor's "Nightly News" would now be pooling correspondents and camera crews with the other NBC News divisions not directly under the anchor's sway.

Yet if the three anchors have had their clout somewhat reduced, there is no question that each of them can still exercise a lot of control when he wants to. One network executive producer candidly admits: "Hey listen, as an executive producer with a powerful anchor, you don't have to be a brain surgeon to realize that his survivability is more than mine. More guys do what I do than what he does. He wields the power. Each day is a compromise. You figure out what you can go to the mat on. You never go to the mat over something you can't win. You can't go to the mat over every single issue, what story will lead every night. You can't get in a fight every single day with their annointed guy. C'mon. When push comes to shove, *you* get sacrificed."

It's a strange role these anchors have today. Gorillas, Monsters, Bigfeet, Abominable Snowmen—whatever you want to call them, it's clear that when they growl, people listen. And they have earned their domain by being simply among the best on-air reporters that TV has produced. Maybe they're not great as writers, and maybe they're uneven story editors, but all three are terrific ad-libbers, visually charged, factually trustworthy, and all have years of reporting experience around the globe.

Nevertheless, the question remains: Should any anchor have quite the authority that these three do? It is, after all, only a fluke of capitalism that they have so much visibility. Or, as Sarah Jennings says, her crisp Canadian syllables articulating a healthy skepticism for the anchor's sanctified role in the Lower Forty-eight:

"The notion that these people are some vehicle for truth, with a capital T, is complete and utter nonsense. Compare it to the disembodied, dispassionate voice of the BBC or the CBC, that lets the listeners evaluate the facts for themselves. The glamour of the anchor is only the result of the drive of the commercial world for stars to sell a product."

RATINGS: Week ending December 8th

1st.   Jennings (ABC's "World News Tonight")—11.2/21 [10,315,200]

2nd. Rather   ("CBS Evening News")—10.2/19 [9,394,200]

3rd. Brokaw   ("NBC Nightly News)—9.9/18 [9,117,900]

CHAPTER TWENTY-THREE

The Future of Network News

W hen people in the TV news business start talking about the future, they always get around to the bus question. Generally, it's phrased this way: If Roone Arledge were hit by a bus tomorrow, who would run ABC News? If Dan Rather were hit by a bus, would Tom Bettag still have a job as executive producer? Or, most frequently: If Peter Jennings (or Brokaw or Rather) were sitting in a bus decimated by terrorist mortar fire next week, who would take his place?

At all three networks, the answer is not clear. These days, correspondents are less frequently being groomed for the top. The notion of a successor to one of the big three anchors is something that befuddles the network brass. These executives have spent so much time building up Rather and Jennings and Brokaw that they have a huge emotional and monetary investment in the three and can't quite bring themselves to imagine who could replace them, even when the ratings take a dive. "They don't have the foggiest idea for replacements," CBS News correspondent Richard Threlkeld says. "They think the anchors will be there forever, and then they're surprised and dismayed when they aren't."

The situation today is unlike the time when Cronkite prepared to step down, and both Rather and Mudd waited in the wings, or when Chancellor was squeezed out by a combination of Brokaw and Mudd, or even when Frank Reynolds died suddenly and Peter Jennings and Ted Koppel were the logical choices to replace him. Today, it's hard to find two good alternatives at each network. In some instances, there's barely one.

Part of the reason is that when anyone takes over the anchor chair now, he or she has to be not only a seasoned journalist, but also a ready-made star. Which may be why one name often mentioned as Tom Brokaw's eventual replacement is Bryant Gumbel. Even though Gumbel has zero hard-news experience, and the only thing he has covered is part of a sofa on the "Today" show, and even though Brokaw and Gumbel go on at great length about how Mr. Today has no interest in the "Nightly News" anchor chair, the rumors still persist. And only because Gumbel is a star. When Brokaw talks about taking a summer vacation and Gumbel is discussed as a fill-in, and when Gumbel's friend Dick Ebersol is brought over from NBC Sports as the number two for NBC News, and considered quite seriously as Michael Gartner's replacement, such developments only fuel the rumors.

The most likely Brokaw successor—or co-anchor—is Jane Pauley, the former "Today" star, who often fills in when Brokaw is on vacation, or sub-anchors when he's on the road. Like Gumbel, Pauley is low on news experience. She hasn't done pure news since her local TV days, more than a decade ago. Once again, the reason she's considered is her star appeal, the wonderfully low-key rapport the Midwestern Pauley has with the camera. The affiliates have recently been demanding to know why she isn't installed at once as Brokaw's co-anchor. She has charm. She has intelligence. She has charisma. She has everything but twenty years of reporting the news.

NBC's lack of successors may be due to the network's weak "bench" strength, its lack of an impressive lineup of reporters. The traditional rap against NBC News has been that "it's a network of guys named Irving." In fact, NBC does have plenty of solid reporters, from Andrea Mitchell at the White House to Mike Boettcher in Europe. It just doesn't have stars.

What's true at NBC is, in some ways, true at the other networks as well. While some stars are born, most of them are made. Exposure makes a star. Marketing makes a star. And the real breeding ground for anchors within the current news framework is clearly the weekend anchoring slot.

Some allege that the current anchors, perhaps fearing a fast-rising

competitor, have exerted their power in selecting weekend or replacement anchors, although the anchors themselves deny the charge. But it
is a strange coincidence that these weekend slots are all filled today
with faithful "deputy dogs," like CBS's Bob Schieffer and ABC's
Carole Simpson, skilled journalists certainly, but no star-quality threat
to the reigning anchors.

At ABC, the potential anchor replacements are Ted Koppel and Diane
Sawyer (and eventually perhaps Chris Wallace). Although each has
territory of his and her own in "Nightline" and "Primetime Live," either
Koppel or Sawyer might leap into the breach if Peter Jennings left. Ted
Koppel is certainly the most universally respected newsman, especially
inside the television news business. His successful interview show just
celebrated its tenth anniversary. Though in one memorable "Nightline"
appearance, George Bush may have erred in calling Ted "Dan," the
President clearly knows anchor quality when he sees it. (As this book
went to press, one rumor even had Koppel being offered Dan Rather's
anchor spot at CBS.)

Within CBS, Connie Chung is mentioned as an anchor candidate. She
is one of the best newsreaders in the business, and has honed her craft
both at NBC and CBS. However, she is widely known to be a mediocre
ad-libber, and her news experience has thus far been limited to
documentaries on such subjects as weight loss ("Life in the Fat Lane").
The outside favorite in the CBS anchor race is Ed Bradley; though not
noted for being a hard worker, Bradley does have a strong news
background. Also, his beard, his glasses, his low-key manner and his
newsreading skill all add up to an avuncular presence that may remind
CBS of the days of Uncle Walter.

But assuming Rather, Jennings and Brokaw look both ways before
crossing streets and are able to dodge New York's fearsome taxis and
notorious bike messengers, the more important bus question for the next
few years may well be: What if TV news itself gets hit by a bus? Or
perhaps more to the point: Has TV news already been hit? Is it already
crumpled on the asphalt?

Professional skeptics like ex-CBS News president Fred Friendly and
NBC's ex, Reuven Frank, say that it is. "There's not going to be any
national news," Friendly states categorically. "The business of running
news night after night, they will figure, is not in their interest." Some
insiders like Jack Chesnutt, NBC producer for domestic news, have

doubts as well: "We wonder if we're taking the last ride on the dinosaur." And Robert MacNeil asks, "Are you sure the animal you are studying will not be extinct by the time the book comes out?"

Even the vice-presidents, the presidents—the pin-striped suits that run network television—have to be worried about the continually diminishing audience, a worry that hits them right in the pocketbook. The percentage of viewers watching the three network newscasts just keeps going down, sinking well below sixty percent of houses with TVs.

Prognosticators like David Poltrack, CBS vice president of research, say that there is good news for news ahead. Poltrack notes that news watchers are traditionally the older segments of the population, and as the huge baby boom group gets older, with the graying of America, news should experience a great comeback.

Sounds wonderful for the future, but right now executives are nervously pacing their corporate suites and desperately sifting through Nielsen tea leaves, searching for a hidden message and finding none. The numbers have been so bad that the networks recently started attacking the Nielsen Company. They demanded that their lost audience be found, and the Nielsen people, eager to oblige, conducted their own surveys and conveniently discovered hundreds of thousands of "secret" viewers, clandestinely watching their favorite shows at work, in college dormitories, in hotels and bars. But none of the network bosses was quite sure how to explain the sudden, inexplicably precipitous drop for the first quarter of 1990, a loss amounting to almost eight percent of the total audience.

Given their corporate orientation, these network executives will try to solve their problem with corporate decisions, with more marketing, with a change in news division structure, with still more cost-cutting to balance the budget. One ill-fated notion revolved around CBS's quickly abandoned plan to move the London bureau out to Acton, which is comparable to moving the network's New York headquarters to Secaucus. Mini-mergers between one-time archrivals, CBS and cable's CNN, have even been proposed to split the costs of international coverage, and are currently under discussion. At best, these various solutions cut some costs; at worst, they are merely cosmetic. Either way, they will not bring back the dwindling television audience.

The scariest prospect currently floating around as a rumor at all the networks is that one of the news divisions will be forced to close up shop altogether. Some producers, executives and reporters have already read the obituary. It's inevitable, they contend, when you have three networks all doing the same thing at the same time that at least one will go. As Dan Rather himself confided: "I think the chances are very strong."

Through most of 1989, as NBC languished in third place, the most likely victim appeared to be the Peacock Network. Trapped in a record-breaking losing run, surpassed only by Columbia University's football team, NBC was having internal problems under the unsteady hand of newspaperman-turned-reluctant-TV-newsman Michael Gartner, as well as external problems with its corporate masters at General Electric, who did not take kindly to losing. At the lightbulb company, an often-stated corporate aim is never to be in a business if you aren't number one. Perhaps they could accept number two. But number three? All sorts of stories began flying around "NBC Nightly News."

One tale that was most persistent, a story both Gartner and GE head Jack Welch ended up confirming, was that NBC was experimenting with new ways of delivering the news.

"It's got to change," said NBC News head of finance, Natalie Hunter. "If I were going to project, I'd say that you won't know this organization in five years. We have a factory that's building a product that doesn't meet the needs of the public. Not that it's a bad product. It's not a frequently usable product. It's too expensive, and for news to appear early in the morning and in the middle of the evening only, and not late at night because that's local news, doesn't make any sense. I think we've got to think about the whole day, when network and local news or a mix of both of them appear on the air, and it ought to be frequent and it ought to be routine and it ought to be a mix of network and local product regardless of who produces it, whether it's us or our affiliates or somebody else."

The alternative most often discussed was that NBC might leave the "Nightly News" business, and instead serve as a newsgathering operation for all the local NBC stations, a kind of video wire service to which the local affiliates would subscribe. Under that plan each local station would take whatever reports it wanted, combine them with their local stories, and structure their own broadcasts—*voilà*, a do-it-yourself news program.

NBC reportedly has also experimented with a speeded-up news broadcast, putting together each night for several weeks a fast-paced, hard-charging program in which almost all the stories were in the minute to minute-and-a-half range, rather than the more typical two to three minute range.

Although NBC's quickie news did not make the air, the first proposal—for the video wire service—apparently still has adherents among the NBC and GE brass, much to the chagrin of Tom Brokaw and his staff of reporters and producers. Certainly, the local affiliates continue to have a lopsided amount of power in today's market. After a lot of grumbling about NBC's San Francisco earthquake "fiasco," the affiliates needed to be appeased; so at the Berlin Wall, Tom Brokaw and other reporters were on the air round the clock with special tie-ins to local stations—"Hi Chuck, I'm here at the Wall"—in addition to all their other chores. Dan Rather had to do the same thing for the CBS affiliates from Tiananmen Square, and Jennings performed similarly from Eastern Europe. If any of the three network news divisions folds, which at this point still seems a long shot, the most likely scenario is that it will turn itself into a video news wire format for the locals.

That would be a significant loss. And a bungled opportunity. Although executives are searching for the answers to their dwindling audience problem with these kinds of executive-type quick fixes, the best solution is not corporate but editorial.

The networks' basic dilemma is that except for the most hardened news junkies, viewers are fundamentally unable to tell the three news programs apart. Only the three anchors differentiate the broadcasts in the eyes of most of the TV audience across America. Plainly their corporate bosses are well aware of this, and that's why Jennings, Rather and Brokaw make as much money as they do. Send the three anchors on vacation for a week, and nine out of ten viewers couldn't tell one program from the other. Even an old news hand like Morley Safer admits that he has trouble distinguishing among the three programs. But what if even one of them showed a little imagination? What if it changed its format?

These days, news goes by so fast—it's so fragmented, that it's often difficult to absorb. With only a handful of minutes to deliver the leading stories of the day, the networks rush to cram everything in. "I personally think all the evening news programs move along a little too fast," Charles Kuralt says. "All you have is twenty-two minutes of stuff to squeeze in. And there are at least half a dozen people sitting in the Fishbowl with stopwatches and computers figuring out whether we're two seconds over or three seconds under. If I were the producer of the evening news programs, they'd be a little slower, a little more thoughtful."

Recently, the network newscasts have become faster than ever because of the influence of two cable upstarts, CNN and MTV. As the percentage of TV homes with cable rose from twenty-one to fifty-six percent through the 1980s, the aesthetics of both MTV and CNN altered—even warped—our sense of time. The hyperactive MTV has made five seconds without a cut feel like forever. And with its twenty-four-hour coverage, CNN makes anything less than instantaneous availability of breaking news seem as if it's hopelessly out-of-date. As Tom Brokaw recently said, "When we come on at the end of the day, a lot of the news is already old." Today, "live" is the byword, and CNN's round-the-clock coverage has consigned network news to roughly the same position to which TV first relegated newspapers. Either network news revises its methods or risks becoming obsolete.

Given a 22-minute news hole, the solution is not to speed things up, as NBC tried to do, not to cut the program into "headline" tidbits or fast-paced featurettes about animals or roller coasters or kids fishing, but to slow things down. Instead of further fragmenting and accelerating the news, a different approach is called for. It's an approach suggested by the coverage that CBS, and to a lesser degree ABC, achieved while covering the funeral of Hirohito in Japan. It's the direction hinted at by ABC's "American Agenda," and NBC's "Assignment America."

The best path for the future may well be increased thematic coverage. The first third of the show could provide the same type of reports as the newscasts do now, covering a wide range of the most important stories of the day, and presenting them as headlines or short takes. But then the rest of a revamped evening news could be devoted to one or more of these headline stories and provide expanded coverage from a variety of angles, as was done in Japan. Using the anchor as the pivotal figure, this type of treatment would focus the public's perceptions on a significant problem, or trend, or geographic area.

The sort of newscast being proposed here would present not simply the facts of an important story but the facts behind the facts—that is, the background of the problem, the principal players involved and the major issues at stake. Such coverage would offer a much needed shift in emphasis from straight news to contextual news and news analysis.

As presently structured, the evening news has, for example, failed miserably in trying to convey to the American people the dimensions of the Savings and Loan debacle. Certainly a series of events that have been described as "a coordinated wave of white-collar crime unlike anything in history," involving the theft of billions of dollars—and that will result in making each taxpayer at least $2,500 poorer—should be of some little interest to its audience. By means of a group of interrelated stories on the subject perhaps viewers would finally be able to make some sense of it.

The basic idea is cluster coverage. Totaling five to ten minutes, this expanded portion of the newscast could be more videogenic than static, more like "60 Minutes" than "MacNeil-Lehrer."

With the Savings and Loan story, for instance, the segments might include a background piece with pictures juxtaposing the angry crowds seething in front of the failed Bank of the United States in 1930 and the docile customers in 1985 waiting patiently in line to collect their FSLIC insured money in the face of the collapse of the Molitor Savings and Loan in Cincinnati. This might be followed by an account of the principal wheeler-dealers involved in the scandal, and their bought-and-paid-for political allies in the Congress. Then finally a piece on the role of the S & L examiners and the current state of their investigation, with pictures of one of the many FSLIC auctions.

This contextual plan would not only make world news more meaningful to the viewers, but also more accessible and engrossing. With an in-depth approach such as this one, the networks might have treated the revolutionary changes sweeping Eastern Europe in 1989 very differently. Instead of repeatedly dwelling on the apparently obligatory shots of mass demonstrations (as if an East German crowd were fundamentally different from one in Czechoslovakia or Romania), they might have shown what life is really like in Poland today, or why ugly nationalist hatreds are suddenly popping up in the Soviet Union and Czechoslovakia, or how Romania is struggling to discover what democracy is.

Instead of watching brief newsflashes, the viewer would see and come to understand how a single family is coping, how one worker is making his way, how one mother is trying to afford food and clothing for her kids. In addition to the Robert MacNeil factor—the discussion of issues—the evening news could also contain this personal dimension. Call it the Charles Kuralt factor, the human factor. Properly linked to an important news story, this cluster of so-called "bounce" pieces (the term used in the industry for secondary or tertiary features), could make for a strong combination, a winning combination.

Regardless of what plan the networks finally decide to adopt, they desperately need a new and innovative approach. Without one, they run the risk of getting flattened by the busloads of TV viewers fleeing their newscasts.

RATINGS: Week ending December 15th

1st. Jennings (ABC's "World News Tonight")—11.0/20 [10,131,000]

2nd. Rather   ("CBS Evening News")—10.4/19 [9,578,400]

3rd. Brokaw   ("NBC Nightly News")—10.2/19 [9,394,200]

CHAPTER TWENTY-FOUR

Malta: The Summit

Thursday Night

On the cavernous third floor of the old Gerolamo Cassar Building Trade School in Valletta, the capital of Malta, just upstairs from a faded sign that reads PUBLIC HEALTH LABORATORY—BACTERIOLOGY SECTION, five or six harassed people are screaming into telephones and walkie-talkies:

"Msida Bay? Msida Bay?!"

"A new bible just came out from the White House...."

"I've got the registration number on that crane...."

"What do you mean he's coming in Friday?!"

It's the ABC News team, and it sounds as if they're mounting an invasion. Which, in some respects, they are.

When George Bush and Mikhail Gorbachev capped the most amazing news year in recent history by announcing that they would meet for a summit—or rather, a non-summit summit—in Malta, the news world started making plans to attend. This Thursday evening, they are showing up in force.

The tiny island of Malta has withstood Napoleon and Suleiman the Magnificent, but the arrival of the international press corps is still an eye opener. Two thousand five hundred very aggressive men and women have descended on this small hunk of rock, one-tenth the size of Rhode Island. Over this one long weekend at the beginning of December, more than a quarter of the population of Malta's ancient and well-ordered capital are journalists.

348

For centuries this Mediterranean island has been a sleepy backwater of scraggly olive trees and two and three-story limestone buildings. None of these slowly yellowing structures with balconies and rounded arches would seem out of place in the deserts of North Africa or in southern Italy. On this particular weekend, in honor of the major-league event about to take place, they are all festooned with U.S. and Soviet flags, and welcoming signs that read: LAQGHA BUSH-GOR-BACHEV 2-3 TA' DICEMBRU, 1989.

The TV networks have come to Malta for the story, of course, but they are also here to show the flag. If CBS and CNN won China, ABC the San Francisco earthquake and NBC the Berlin Wall, no one wants to lose this summit. "Everyone's got the fever," a CBS producer says. "Plans are getting bigger and bigger. Everybody's getting more and more ambitious."

The difficulties in putting together this kind of extravaganza are staggering. Each network will spend at least $1 million. ABC, NBC and CNN are bringing sixty to seventy people; CBS has over one hundred and twenty, counting some twenty-five pool personnel. Around the island are nine huge "flyaway" portable satellite dishes, and more than forty microwave "hops," or relays, to funnel the signal from the Russian cruiser Slava and the USS Belknap anchored in Marsaxlokk Bay to a relay in the harbor, up to a church tower, and across the island to the newsrooms in Valletta.

"Everything about that Marsaxlokk Bay is wrong," says one annoyed member of the ABC team. "It's the least picturesque part of the island. It's got an oil rig right in the middle of it. Why did they put the boats there? It's the wrong place. At night the boats have no glory lighting, and they're too far off to throw light from the shore."

In order for the networks to relay their images from the bay, the priest at the Ghaxaq church has graciously given them permission to use the church's lofty bell tower. Later he will graciously give them his bill—a shopping list of electronic equipment he wants them to donate to his church, complete with model numbers, and including a twenty-eight-inch color monitor and a photocopying machine. "Anything else?" the networks asked dryly. "How about a ground-station?"

"On the day the summit was announced, within one hour I had booked one hundred rooms," ABC's location producer Paul Tilsley says. Tilsley is a tall, pale Brit with a skinny ponytail. "And twenty-six cars with drivers."

Cramming the hallways of this large, old-fashioned municipal structure ordinarily devoted to the building trades are great quantities of ABC's most sophisticated electronic equipment. In the jerry-rigged control room, gleaming monitors are stacked one on top of the other, in a four-by-four pile. Small taped-on signs read "Bird," "Msida Bay," "Tight 1," "Tight pool 2." Wires and cables snake in and out of the control room—phone lines, power lines, a huge plate of giant electronic spaghetti.

"This building," ABC's Tilsley explains as he looks around, amazed at what they've accomplished in so short a time, "is a television station that's been built in a week."

In the main newsroom, the machinery is humming: fax machines and squawk boxes and telephones. On the wall are two clocks, labeled "Here" and "There," reading 11:25 AM (for Malta) and 5:25 AM (for New York). The walls are covered with large white signs containing long lists of telephone numbers: Here/New York/Washington/CBS/ CNN/ White House/Hilton/Phoenecia/Belknap/Press Centre/Camera position at Msida Bay. Number after number. "What's our best communication line with the theater at the Press Centre?" a senior producer shouts. "What? Oh Christ—all that technology, and we can't get through....Okay, send a runner."

Communication—instant communication—is clearly the lifeblood of this industry. As CNN's Washington correspondent Charles Bierbauer says, "This business is ninety percent logistics, five percent journalism and five percent whimsy."

Neither Bush nor Gorbachev has arrived yet, nor has Rather, Jennings or Brokaw. The three anchors are in Rome, covering the Gorbachev-Pope religious summit. ABC News director Charlie Heinz comes into the newsroom and announces, "Some group in Manila is staging a coup. They've taken over the airport and one of the broadcast facilities." It's the sixth attempt to bring down the Philippine president, Cory Aquino, and another huge story in the making. A third clock goes up in the newsroom: "Here," "There" and "Manila."

Friday, 11:30 AM

In the ad hoc "World News Tonight" newsroom at the Trade School, Peter Jennings is seated at the central desk going through the London papers. His ruler out, he's tearing articles from the *Times*, the

Independent. The whine of a modem hookup resonates through the quiet room, the buzz-click of the fax machine.

Steve Tello, the London-based senior producer who handles much of ABC's logistics on the road, wanders into the room and sees Jennings hard at it. "Oh Peter...." He shakes his head at ABC's workaholic anchor. "We got in at three this morning to our hotel, and Peter got us up at ten."

Tello sighs. "When we were on the plane coming over, he was reading, going through the research notebooks. When I was trying to nod off, he was still reading. I had to tell him, 'Peter, turn the light out.'"

Friday, 1:30 PM

Across the road from ABC, up on the second floor of the Mediterranean Conference Centre—a former hospital of the Knights of Malta that is serving as the general press center—NBC has taken over one huge hall. Inside the large, high-vaulted, well-lit room are tables for correspondents, for specials, for the "Today" show. There's a dispatch desk, stacks of technical equipment, and of course lots of computer terminals. Near the front door one can see a large, makeshift control room.

The "Today" show director is in the first row of this improvised studio. "Where are the guards?" he asks with annoyance. "There's nobody there! We're supposed to have guards!" On the monitor, Bryant Gumbel is standing against a wall next to a suit of armor. "Bryant, can you hear me?" calls the director. Gumbel seems to be adjusting his pants. "Bryant? Bryant?!" All over America viewers catch a fleeting glimpse of "Today" show host Gumbel with his back to the camera.

By now the director is on his feet screaming, "Cue Bryant! Cue Bryant!" But the cue has come and gone, and Jane Pauley has taken over in New York. Not everything runs smoothly when newscasters venture into the field.

Joseph Angotti, the silver-haired vice-president of NBC News in a black windbreaker, winces at the glitch. But when he turns back, he glances around the enormous hall with pleasure at all the different NBC News programs together under one roof. Angotti says, "Three years ago each program would operate as a separate entity. It was a very wasteful process. Lots of duplication."

No doubt by pooling its coverage NBC is more cost-efficient. But what gets lost in the process? "Well," Angotti acknowledges, "perhaps some quality control is missing. Because each program doesn't shape the report from beginning to end. I mean, it used to be an unshaped lump of clay that was shaped by each program. Now the lump of clay [the common footage] is fashioned a little to begin with. But," he insists, "this way is efficient, and effective."

This is Angotti's prelude to an aria on the frugality of NBC News entitled, "We can be cheaper than they are." Actually, on Malta, all three of the networks are singing the same song. The refrain is identical—half-fact, half-exaggeration—and all designed to make the corporate bosses feel good. In this era of corporate takeovers, every news division wants to be seen as leaner and meaner than its competition.

Angotti is eager to report, "I hear CBS is going crazy. They've brought all sorts of people. They rented out the *whole* Excelsior Hotel! They've bought out an *entire* lighting company, and lit the *whole* front of a mountain!" He positively chortles over their alleged extravagance.

Tom Brokaw is due in by mid-afternoon from Rome. In the meantime, Philip Alongi, a producer for NBC News Specials, has gone up to the Lower Barrakka Gardens to check on the spot nearby where Brokaw will do his newscast. It's a lovely, palm-filled setting overlooking a spectacular expanse of bay. But loveliest of all, for Alongi and Angotti and the entire NBC News team, it's cheap.

Pointing down the hill to their newsroom at the press center, Alongi says, "For us, this is just a cable run. We've saved on the microwave. Our set-up time is less, and this location works on both the AM and PM shows. We're able to get more out of our dollar."

Friday, 3:00 PM

"Good Morning America" correspondent Steve Fox has just thrown on his coat and is walking out the door. "Okay," he says, "see you in Romania in two weeks."

"Hear that?" says Steve Tello. "That's it. The technology has improved so greatly that now all you need are a couple of fax machines, some phone lines, some editing equipment.... You can get your anchor on the air with ten to twelve people from anywhere."

Tello looks across at Peter Jennings who comes over to join the conversation. "I remember one time we were in Mexico," Jennings says, "and standing in the middle of an empty parking lot. They wired us up, and two minutes later we were talking to Ted Koppel on 'Nightline.'"

The thin-faced, mustached executive producer of "World News Tonight," Paul Friedman, says that he loves being on the road. "The broadcast is better for it. But it's not easy to keep your perspective. Last night, for example, we were going to play the Philippines story much lower in the broadcast, but our senior producers back in New York said, 'You're wrong. It's important.' Well, we had it, and CBS buried it."

Jennings turns back to his typewriter, a small black electronic Canon Typestar 6, under a little yellow lamp. He's going over the lead-off piece that he and producer Stu Schutzman are putting together, a discussion of how badly Gorbachev needs relief, any kind of plum from this summit. The anchor also has another piece hanging over his head. "I've got to write a forty-second closer on Malta." He grimaces. "Lots of people don't know where it is, what it is."

Friday, 10:00 PM

Seated side by side, Jennings and Friedman are revising the "pages" written for the anchor by the staff. Jennings is wearing a blue cashmere sweater, Friedman a red one. To Jennings' right sits his travel-battered briefcase open on a chair, revealing a comb, pens, some loose pages. "By the time President Aquino decided she could use the help..." Jennings is reading into the phone. "Hang on. Prior to Zelnick's piece, we never mentioned that we offered her help. He has her pleading for help. Not only does that not sound like Cory to me....Oh...Okey dokey." He hangs up, and putting a sheet in the typewriter, starts typing furiously, a two-fingered attack on the keyboard.

"Did President Bush never talk to Cory?" he asks.

"Quayle was the hand-holder," Friedman shoots back.

"Oh..." Jennings rips the paper out of the typewriter and tosses it at the trashcan.

In the corner of the "World News Tonight" Malta newsroom, Bob Legvold, the pale Sovietologist, is being made up by Charlotte Taylor. "I'm doing what I call the 'dependent clause interview," he says. "I only have three to four sentences. I won't be able to say much of anything at all. A full answer would take five to ten minutes. But in spots like this, they don't want you to give too many ideas. They don't want you to overwhelm the audience. I try to just get across one idea. That works best."

Jennings walks over to the makeup table. He sits down and starts putting in his contacts. "I hate doing this," he says.

For convenience, ABC will be pre-taping this evening's broadcast by about an hour, and Jennings is reminded of what happened the night before. "CBS got caught badly last night going with tape. Dan likes to go around town and visit spots. But on the first roll of last night's program, they didn't have the story of the Philippines coup attempt till later."

Friday, 10:53 PM

Jennings and two of his producers jump into a van. They are headed out to Msida Bay, to the anchor stand-up location where they will tape the program. It's a scenic spot, but ironically, even further from Bush and Gorbachev's vessels than the ABC newsroom. The van peels off into the night.

"How long to Msida?" one of the producers yells up front to Jennings, who is seated next to the driver.

"He says ten minutes, but we're negotiating seven," Jennings yells back. The van screeches around the corner. *"Insh'Allah,"* Jennings adds under his breath, invoking the deity in Arabic to make it happen. The van hugs the road along the base of Malta's centuries-old fortifications, past the guards who have blocked off the road, and along the coastline, where the castle fortifications are all illuminated.

Jennings turns to the driver. "Where does Malta get its electric power?" he wants to know.

The driver mumbles and shrugs as the van negotiates another curve, blasting by a little church. "How many churches are there on this island?" Jennings asks. "Is it three hundred?"

"Three hundred and sixty-five," he's told, one for every day of the year.

"*Prego*," says Jennings, who clearly likes to pepper his speech with foreign phrases.

Friday, 11:30 PM

Jennings is on location inside a hastily constructed shack along Msida Bay. But the audience will never see the shelter. They will only see the spectacular background, a near-perfect night shot. It's a brilliantly illuminated church that ABC has paid to light up, outlined like a Christmas tree in the background, and neatly painted fishing boats rocking gently in the foreground, where they are docked. "I think it's very pretty, Steve," Jennings congratulates Tello, the ABC site producer.

"This shot says everything we want to say about Malta," says Tello. "Religion, fishing, surrounded by water."

As Jennings steps up in front of the two cameras, lit up by the four lights within the little hut, his makeup assistant, Charlotte Taylor, whips out a can of hairspray and starts spraying his hair.

"I could do without eight hundred pounds of hairspray," Jennings says with a wry smile. "You know, there's this joke in the news business about Dan Rather being down in Florida, in the middle of this horrendous storm, trees are falling down all around him, and his hair stays perfectly in place."

A warm breeze wafts through the hut. "It seems ridiculous to be wearing raincoats," Jennings says. He stops, and listens to his earpiece, hooked up to the control room in Valletta. "Mr. Friedman says keep the raincoat on. Okay...." He listens. "We're up against some time pressure. We'll roll tape and try to pretape as much as we can. If there are any last-minute changes, we'll have to go live."

They start rolling, Jennings running through the arrival of Bush and Gorbachev. "After a night of stormy weather, they'll get started..." he says, then stops and looks around at the peaceful bay. "I know," he says to the voice in his earpiece, and laughs. "Okay, after a night of the stormy weather that's been promised by the weathermen...Oh, that's rubbish—take it out altogether." He fiddles with the script in his hands, then turns back to the camera. "Here's our White House correspondent, Brit Hume."

They run through the rest of the pages: "Mr. Gorbachev, up to his hammer and sickle in trouble....Here in front of one of Malta's three hundred and sixty-five churches...." Then he wraps up. "Finally, this evening, where we are. A fortress island nation about fifty miles south of Italy in the Mediterranean...twice battered by major wars, and never broken. Fitting, perhaps, that Malta should host a summit to discuss the diminishing threat of global war...."

Jennings finishes up, and taking out his earpiece, he looks around. "This is quite an amazing place," he says. He points across the water to the low buildings, bristling with TV antennas, an incongruous field of metal on top of the limestone buildings. "It's the contrast. That's why you notice it," he says. "Do you know Jerusalem?" he asks. "It's like what you see looking back from the Damascus Gate."

After Jennings leaves, a photographer who had been taking pictures of him shakes his head, and says, "You know, they're taping here, but the boats, Bush and Gorby, they're on the other side of the island. All these anchors say, 'I was there for the action,' but they aren't exactly. It's like 'I was there, but I wasn't....I was nearby.'"

Saturday, 12:45 AM

Only a few minutes later, Tom Brokaw is in the Lower Barrakka Gardens, delivering the news live back to the U.S. In the NBC control area, Brokaw's image, in a blue overcoat, is replicated in monitor after monitor. On every one, he is saying, "The White House was willing to help before Aquino was willing to ask...."

Executive producer Bill Wheatley and VP Joe Angotti are in the second tier of seats in the control room area. Brokaw's earpiece is hooked in to them, but he's also getting Cheryl Gould, in the New York control room. Brokaw is conducting a live interview—called a two-way—with correspondent Fred Francis, halfway around the world in Manila: "Fred, this is the sixth attempted coup. How long can the U.S. keep helping her?"

The wind begins picking up, whipping through his hair, as the program cuts to a commercial. "This teleprompter keeps going in and out. I can't see it," says Brokaw. "Ten seconds," comes the call, and he goes into an introduction for a Nadia Comaneci piece.

When the taped segment starts rolling, he turns to the cameraman. "This teleprompter is just terrible," he says irritably. "Every time it runs it turns to white. Can we reverse the polarity [change the color of the letters from white to black]?" From New York, Cheryl Gould's voice says in his ear: "Why don't we fix it when we go to the break, Tom?"

Later when a commercial starts up, Brokaw turns to the technicians: "Is that a reflection or what?" he asks, as they frantically fiddle with the teleprompter. "How are we for time on the show?" he wants to know. "Okay, what is that behind me? I'm going to take a second to say what it is." A few grumbles come over the wire. Brokaw dismisses them. "People will want to know," he insists.

"Five seconds," comes the call, and Brokaw is back on: "Behind me," he says, "that's a tribute to the British who drove out Napoleon."

Saturday, 1:00 AM

Brokaw has finished the show. But he still has the pick-ups, the small corrections for the second feed, to do for the stations that run "Nightly" at 7:00 PM Eastern time. Rain starts to come down. Brokaw looks into the camera. "I think we better get out of here," he says to the producers sitting inside. A gust of wind hits him head on, whips through his hair, jostles him a little. "Do you want me to do one quick one?" he asks hurriedly. "Do you?"

Brokaw hunches up his shoulders against the wind and rain. "We better get out of here," he says, looking at all the electrical equipment getting soaked. Inside, the producers are talking with New York, a giant conference call going on in Brokaw's ear. A blast of wind and rain slams into him. "Jeeezus," he says, "we better get out of here."

The monitor is still playing the rest of the half-hour news when Brokaw hurries in, his coat speckled with rain, his hair disheveled. He sticks out his tongue and raises his eyebrows. "Oh boy!"he says.

Saturday 1:30 AM

As the program finishes, the Malta annex of the NBC newsroom takes on a convivial, after-hours feeling. The guy running the sound board turns on some music. It's jazz, a trumpet wailing. Executive producer Bill Wheatley, a beer in hand, tells Brokaw: "CBS really croaked on that Philippines stuff." In their navy blazers, Wheatley and Brokaw look as if they're on the same team.

Saturday, 11:45 AM

At the Excelsior, a faded grande dame of a hotel overlooking the water, and not far from the competition's temporary headquarters, the CBS team is in high gear. Although, like NBC, they didn't finish broadcasting until 1:30 that morning, events on Malta had begun by 9:00 AM local time. Technicians are still shaking their heads about the sudden squall during the night when they were driven indoors by the weather. Laughing, one techie explains, "It was our second feed. It was raining so hard, we had everybody run downstairs from the balcony, our anchor position. They had six minutes to do it. They had to run to our inside position, pop the [removable] windows out, get everything set up. By mistake, we hooked up the teleprompter upside down!"

CBS has taken over much, but not all, of the Excelsior, and has parked its huge white satellite dish proprietarily outside the front door of the old limestone structure. Up on the fourth floor, the white hallway is littered with large silver boxes—trunk-sized equipment packing crates—turning the corridor into a giant closet. Room's have been transformed into editing studios, with beds removed, and electronic gear stacked incongruously among frills and curtains and carpet.

Downstairs, a huge dining room has been converted—potted palms, chandeliers and all—into a giant newsroom. Across the room are six sets of tables, with signs that read "48 Hours," "Morning News" and "Special Events." It's a mega-operation, a huge hub with activity in all the corners. At the long table in the center, Susan Zirinsky is on the telephone, playing the dispatcher. In a corner, Stephen Cohen, Princeton professor and CBS Soviet expert, is talking to correspondent Lesley Stahl as she types into her computer terminal.

"When Gorbachev came to power, those were not his people," Cohen says. "Eighty-five percent were put there by Brezhnev, fifteen percent by Andropov." In the far corner, technicians are hanging a curtain, and popping out the windows to create the anchor position, an indoor space with the illusion of being outdoors, the dining room overlooking a spectacularly scenic stretch of bay in one direction, limestone fortifications in the other.

Dan Rather wanders in, looking very sporty in jeans, buttoned-down shirt and sneakers. He says, "Hello," to correspondent Wyatt

Andrews, then goes over to pour himself the first of many cups of coffee. "I need to get jump-started," he says.

Coffee in hand, Rather walks over to join his executive producer Tom Bettag and waxes philosophical: "This is news by handout."

"There's no way you can really cover these things," Bettag says. "The real story isn't the pool coverage of smiles and handshakes. It's a classic case of 'it all happens behind closed doors.' You only know what they want you to know."

"Yup," Rather agrees. "It's a series of photo opportunities... 24-karat photo ops, but photo ops."

Rather takes a sip from his coffee. "They called this a 'feet up, back porch, shoot-the-breeze' get-together, not a summit. I didn't believe it for a second, especially after the cataclysmic events in Eastern Europe."

When asked about his own politics, Rather says, "I'm for a strong defense and clean water, whatever that makes me."

"A Texas Democrat?" someone suggests.

"More a Texas maverick," Rather offers, with an uncomfortable smile.

"You know," he says, trying to change the subject, "I'm the only one of the anchors who was ever in Malta before. I did a '60 Minutes' piece here."

The conversation shifts to the way each network is showing Malta, and where the anchor is being photographed. Rather says, "Well, that's a little bit 'inside baseball.' You have to watch for a long time before you see it. But ABC, they believe in the 'Wow Factor.' They believe in the importance of your first shot, using one shot to say it all. At CBS, we want the viewer to get a sense of the whole of Malta, so we use a series of postcard shots from all over the island, rather than put all our eggs in one basket."

Tom Bettag comes over with a schedule in hand. "Okay," he says, "we're waiting for America to wake up. At 8:00 AM [2:00 PM Malta time], we'll do a fifteen-minute special report."

"All right," Rather replies. "I need to go up and get changed."

The bad weather blowing since last night has picked up, rocking the U.S. and Soviet cruisers Belknap and Slava at anchor in Marsaxlokk Bay, and throwing a crimp into the summit planning. "I find it all rather delightful," Bettag says. "What was to be a well-orchestrated show of naval might is now a different story. Man's frailty against forces he can't control. The White House and the Soviet press officers have lost control over their photo opportunities. They're scrambling. And if they're scrambling, there's more chance we might get some news."

Saturday, 1:55 PM

Six Arri Daylight lamps light the corner of the dining room where the windows have been popped out and Rather will do his special report. Lane Venardos, in charge of special events, is running the show from the control room upstairs on the fourth floor, while Bettag is orchestrating operations on the scene.

Fresh, composed, resplendent in an immaculate navy suit, Dan Rather walks to his position next to correspondent Wyatt Andrews, a position marked by a small piece of metallic tape on the floor next to the open window. Vivian, a young production assistant, hands him his IFB earpiece, and runs the wire down his back, under his jacket. Bettag listens to the voice coming over his blue headphones. "Thirty seconds to air," he calls. "Vivian out."

Vivian, fumbling with the IFB hookup, finally attaches it to Rather's belt, and scrambles off. "Standby," calls Bettag, counting down to air time. And then, just as Bettag cues him, Rather's IFB hookup falls from his belt and hits the floor with a thud.

"Hello from Malta," Rather begins, his face betraying no emotion as Bettag dives across the floor to the fallen IFB unit. Out of camera sight, Bettag curls around Rather's feet and frantically hooks up the wire on the floor with the wire that runs up Rather's back to his earpiece. "But it didn't happen as planned," Rather is saying, as Bettag suddenly realizes that he's stuck. If he lets go of the IFB unit, it will become disconnected or pull out of Rather's ear. So he stays curled at Rather's feet as the anchor reads the rest of his copy: "....owes as much to the Marx Brothers as Marx...."

"Quickly please. Standby," Bettag calls to the two Soviet experts. "Ready to zoom to a three-shot." Noticing that Stephen Cohen is casting a shadow on Rather, he gestures him back. And then the three-way interview starts.

"They're coming from different points," says the Russian Sovietologist. "George Bush is more comfortable with the old rules of international diplomacy...."

Rather turns to Cohen. "I have a sense," says Cohen, taking the cue, "of events shaping men more than men shaping events." Cohen likes to turn phrases.

Bettag, still at Rather's feet, starts quickly scribbling on a card, outlining the upcoming shows of the day. He holds it up for Rather to read. "We'll be on the air from time to time today," says Rather smoothly. He passes on the schedule to the viewers.

As the special finishes, Bettag uncurls himself, stands up, and congratulates the trio. "By the way," he adds with obvious glee, "ABC was on at the same time, but they were forced to go with an indoor shot."

"Is that good or bad?" asks Cohen, a TV neophyte.

"That's good. Jennings has an outdoor/indoor [the shack at Msida Bay]. It couldn't withstand the storm," he chuckles. "A storm is only a story if you can show the storm."

Saturday, 3:00 PM

"Raisa is on the move," shouts Susan Zirinsky, who's running the CBS operations desk. She picks up a walkie-talkie, and barks into it. "Follow her."

Tom Bettag, in the lull before the next storm, is discussing just how much it costs to mount an invasion armada like the one CBS has in Malta for the weekend. "You're always juggling figures for all of this. For example, the White House contingent always travels with the President. Do you count them in the cost of the weekend? How about the bureaus? The bureaus have their own budgets [because they provide news for all the various news programs]. But when Larry Tisch wants to give us a hard time, he says that all the bureaus are on the 'Evening News' budget.

"I think you'd have to say that for any of the networks, the floor is about a million per operation. But if Larry was to say, 'I understand you spent a million for the weekend,' that would be bullshit, because we got a week's worth of programming. We went to Czechoslovakia and to Rome, too, this week. We amortized it. For the price of the hotel rooms, we got a week's worth of good programming.

"Our need, these days," Bettag continues, "is to prove how efficient and cost-conscious we are, to show that that's our top priority. Which is a lie anyway."

Saturday, 3:30 PM

The weather, which has been cold and windy and wet right along, is starting to turn ugly. Winds are gusting up to sixty miles an hour. In the bay, towering waves are crashing against the Belknap and the Slava.

In CBS's newsroom at the Excelsior, the noise level suddenly dies off. Technicians, producers, even veteran reporters are all clustered around the television monitors, staring at the images. President Bush's small launch, returning from the Slava to the Belknap, is being tossed up and down on the heavy seas. "The boat can't dock! They can't lash on! These are great shots!" All around the newsroom, no one is working. They are all simply staring. They all know good television when they see it.

The great twist on that stormy Saturday—as the story went from the summit to the weather—is that a terribly important news story that wasn't very good TV became a not-too-important story, but great TV. The wind howling, the waves crashing, the brave little launch circling and circling.

As the launch comes back around on its fourth attempt, Lesley Stahl, perched on a desk, pipes up, "I'm definitely going to use this in my piece."

Tom Bettag says, "Oh no! That's for Dan." Stahl grimaces. "Look, Lesley," Bettag says. "There's no dishonor in being bigfooted by Dan."

"There's no dishonor," Stahl agrees, "but there's a lot of pain and suffering."

Saturday, 3:40 PM

Dan Rather is once again standing in the anchor position, in the corner of the dining room, by the popped-out windows, waiting to go on the air. With him is Lesley Stahl. "Are we sure that was the President's boat?" Rather wants to know. "Are we sure Bush was on it?"

"We couldn't see Bush," Stahl reports, "but that was his boat."

"Can we go with it?" queries Rather.

"We're close to getting the navy to confirm it," Bettag says. "Here's what we know. The President is back on the Belknap. We saw the boat. We saw the President's Secret Service men on the boat."

"WE HAVE A CONFIRMATION!" yells Susan Zirinsky, one ear still attached to the phone. "The White House Press Office says that was Bush."

"Let's go!" Bettag shouts. "Dan, we have two separate pieces of tape. We can bring Bill Plante in over the tape. All right, we're going to go in forty-five seconds. Lesley, your role is to ooh and ahh."

Bettag cues Rather, and he's off. "The weather played havoc with the plans...." And suddenly the teleprompter's script becomes stuck. "The plans" remains fixed on the screen. Rather smoothly segues into an ad lib as the taped images of the President's launch begin rolling. "The boat is loaded with Secret Service men," he ad-libs. "Look how low it is in the water...."

Finally, Bettag holds up crossed arms to indicate time to wrap up, and Rather concludes with, "This is Dan Rather, reporting from Malta."

Saturday, 4:30 PM

Outside the Sea Breeze Hotel on Marsaxlokk Bay, where the two cruisers are anchored, the wind is roaring. It's strong enough to knock a man off his feet. Even inside the sheltered bay, the waves are rising to five feet, and beyond the breakwater, where the Belknap and Slava are anchored, they're huge, up to twelve feet high.

Inside the resort hotel, deserted except for the CBS crew, the wind is a howling, mournful presence. In room 214, CBS Special Events producer Anne Reingold is talking on two phones at once—one phone cradled on each shoulder, a CBS cap cocked on her head, a cigarette in her mouth, and typing messages on the computer terminal in front of her. From time to time, she looks up at the five monitors along the wall.

Reingold and a roomful of technicians are staked out in this small makeshift control room waiting for George Bush to reappear and ride back over to the Soviet liner Maxim Gorky for the evening's events. "Guys," she says, "your mission is to go on the air as soon as we see him."

Later, a member of the U.S. Sixth Fleet stops by to brief Reingold on the weather. "It's more than a storm," he says. "It's a depression. It should last through ten o'clock tonight. The boats are rolling ten to twelve degrees." Reingold is taking notes as he talks, typing them directly into the Newstar computer system, then "mailing" the notes to everyone on the system, the crew back at the Excelsior, even the staff back in New York. "A year ago," she says, "we used to fight over clipboards. Now if we don't have a computer terminal...." These days, the name of the game is instant communication.

A message comes in on the telephone on her left shoulder: "They're going on the air from the Excelsior," she reports. "The White House has announced it's too dangerous to leave the Belknap for the next session."

Saturday, 6:30 PM

Inside the Press Centre in Valletta, NBC's Joe Angotti has sent Tom Brokaw downstairs to the briefing room. In addition to the afternoon's session being cancelled, it now looks as if the planned Bush-Gorbachev dinner is off too, as well as all the rest of the evening's activities. "I want to get Brokaw on the air with an interrupt the minute they confirm it," he says. "I'm hoping we get on the air with the information before anyone else."

Brokaw materializes downstairs in front of the camera. Hooked into the control room via his earpiece, he talks with Angotti. "I don't have the announcement," he says. "I don't go on the air without the announcement."

Standing in position near a doorway at the top of the briefing amphitheater, Brokaw is poised for the announcement as the crowd files in. It's a quarter to seven. Then ten of.

In the control area, Angotti is fretting. "What'll almost certainly happen is extra meetings tomorrow," he speculates. "Maybe we ought to go back to 'Sunday Today' from 8:00 to 10:30 AM. For the last two weeks, we've been talking to our affiliates. We put out this thick advisory book. Now *this*....We have to call them all, and go back to our regular schedule."

It's five to seven. Seated, Brokaw is chatting quietly with his floor producer downstairs. "My father was named Anthony too," Brokaw says. "I only had daughters, but if I had had a son, I would have named him Anthony."

Suddenly, the word comes via walkie-talkie to the producers in the control area. "It's off. No dinner." Angotti grabs for the microphone: "Tom, it's off. Let's go!" He looks around. "Okay, we're coming up on a window in one-minute. We have fifteen seconds intro music. Cue! Cue!"

And downstairs, Brokaw begins: "This is the first time in memory that a summit has been called because of weather...."

Saturday, 8:35 PM

ABC producer Paul Tilsley, in olive drab rain gear, his ponytail pulled through the back of his baseball cap, comes inside out of the howling wind, and shakes off the rain. "We've got two engineers, one hundred feet up in a church tower, clinging onto microwave dishes, literally holding ABC on the air."

Steve Tello stops by to talk. "We're three hours and fifty-five minutes from airtime, and we don't know where the evening news will be coming from." He shrugs. "I've got to go off to Msida, and see if we can broadcast from there."

Executive producer Paul Friedman walks over. "The story is the weather today," he says emphatically. "We have to go from the outside if we can." Tello hurries off. "I got this far in the business," Friedman shakes his head in wonder, "and I'm back doing weather stories."

Peter Jennings comes by, talking with a striking-looking young woman who is clearly Maltese. "Griegal, you said?"

"G-R-I-E-G-A-L," she spells it for him.

"Griegal," he repeats with a smile. "That's what they call this wind. It's a Nor'easter...." He throws on his trenchcoat, adjusts the collar and heads up the stairs to the roof. On the roof, a light drizzle falls, and a wind, warm but strong, is gusting.

Huddled under the lights are a skeleton crew: soundman, camera-man and Tilsley as director. Jennings marches over and almost immediately launches into a special report for half-time of the Saturday ABC basketball game. "Good afternoon. It was a short day in Malta—short, and windy, and wet."

The wind picks up, begins to howl, and on a roof across the street, the bending metal shrieks as an old air vent is ripped apart by the furious gusts.

"They call this wind the Griegal—"

A ferocious blast interrupts him. Adjusting his collar, Jennings prepares to start from where he left off. The producers want to start from the beginning.

"We are in the middle of a voice-over, guys," Jennings reminds his producers, who are comfortable and warm in the control room downstairs. "You don't need to go from the top. Just do a pick-up."

He turns to Tilsley. "Why is this taking so long?" Jennings plainly wants to get back inside.

Microwave receivers across the roof start to wiggle in the wind, even though they're weighted down with heavy concrete blocks. The rain begins to come down in driving sheets. "It's *really* raining on this roof, guys," Jennings says with more than a touch of sarcasm. "We could never do the whole broadcast from up here," he says. "It's crazy."

Tilsley finally gives him the go-ahead.

"Take a look at President Bush," the anchor begins, describing the videotape, "trying to get back from shore...." Suddenly, a powerful gust hits Jennings from behind, lifting him off his feet, and knocking him into the camera.

Jennings laughs as he straightens up. The weather has gotten so bad, it's funny. He shrugs his shoulders. "Let's do a pickup," he says.

He speeds through the rest of the voice-over and closes wryly. "...On Malta, they tell us, most of the time it shines."

Saturday, 9:30 PM

Meanwhile, across town at CBS, everyone is nice and dry inside the Excelsior. "I think this is a great morality play," Tom Bettag is saying. "The two world leaders and they can't even get together. The weather is a great leveler."

Susan Zirinsky, her hand clamped over a receiver, shouts, "This is *urgent*. I'm getting some real news right here from the White House people." She starts typing furiously on her computer: "U.S. approves observer status. Urges Soviet market system...."

What Zirinsky is taking down is the substantial sixteen-point proposal that the Bush administration has brought to Malta as a starting point for discussions. It's Bush's attempt to upstage the charismatic Gorby, but it's been lost in the bad weather. The White House staffers are desperately calling all the networks to ensure that the Bush-Baker plan makes that evening's news in the U.S. Looking at the material that Zirinsky has noted down, Stahl and Barry Petersen head for their computers and begin typing away, the amber characters flashing across the screen.

Saturday, 11:15 PM

"Open the windows," the CBS director calls, as he prepares to pre-tape an hour early. The technicians pop the glass out, and the wind and the rain blow in. Lesley Stahl's neatly-coiffed platinum hair whips forward and back, as she desperately tries to pat it down.

"Lesley, can you move more to your right?" calls the director, framing the picture. "Even closer to Dan."

Stahl snuggles in right next to Rather, who smiles and gallantly throws his arms around her in a broad stage hug. Stahl gives him a big smooch on the cheek.

"Not so close!" chuckles the director.

"They don't want us doing that, Dan," Stahl says flirtatiously.

"We're still getting a shadow on Lesley's face," calls down the director. "Dan?"

"It's the anchorman's big head," Rather quips.

Up in the control room, executive producer of special events Lane Venardos is sitting at the back of the room. "In just a few hours, we'll be able to pull down those nice wet sheets and go to bed," he says. "Every night, it's as if someone sprayed them with a fine mist."

"Take two," the director orders. "Ready one."

"Are you sure my hair is okay?" Stahl asks.

Saturday, 11:45 PM

"Okay," the director calls. "This is a two-way, Dan and Bob. Make sure Dan is framed in the window there." As the cameraman frames the shot, Bob Schieffer in New York talks to Rather on his earpiece: "Dan? Hi, it's Bob...."

Rather looks into the camera. "Hi....You get the picture, Bob. They're trapped on that boat for the night. I'm sure that well-known seafarer, Marlin Fitzwater, is feeling terrific."

"Dan," Schieffer says, as they begin taping, "you made your name covering the weather. Is there any chance the weather might swamp this thing?"

"There is a chance," says Rather, checking his crystal ball. "This is a vicious storm—a storm that might drive Sinbad the Sailor or Lord Nelson to take cover...."

Downstairs, after the feed, Tom Bettag has a cat-that-ate-the-canary grin on his face. "ABC and CNN lost their satellites," he reports.

Sunday

And then the rains subsided.

Today, everyone is back and it's business as usual. ABC, CBS, CNN and NBC are all covering the very first press conference ever given jointly by the U.S. and Soviet Presidents. The leaders take the occasion to make the following memorable announcement: "The world leaves one epoch of Cold War, and enters another epoch." Important? Naturally. Historic? Of course. But most of the U.S. TV audience is waiting impatiently for the start of that afternoon's pro football game.

In the end, as the Malta summit draws to a close, there's hardly an American viewer who can tell which news organization did a better job in covering this historic superpower meeting. After all the breathless and costly competition between the networks and their anchors, most of the audience would call the coverage a draw.

Inside the Mediterranean Conference Centre, CNN's Charles Bier-bauer is preparing himself for a final summing-up two-minute commentary.

"Should I stand or should I sit?" he asks his cameraman. "Oh, what does it matter," he says, not waiting for an answer. "No one will remember in fifty years. Hell, no one will remember in fifty minutes."

Bierbauer places himself in exactly the same spot where Bryant Gumbel had interviewed the Prime Minister of Malta, in exactly the same spot where earlier an American reporter watched a French TV crew filming an American TV crew interviewing a Soviet journalist.

"You know," he says, "I went out to the Belknap with the reporter's pool on Friday, and we couldn't even see the President when he landed. Then he came on deck. We asked him about the situation in the Philippines. He said he didn't know. Then he went back inside."

"Okay," Bierbauer says, "It's dumb. But the circus comes to town, and you've got to pitch your tent. You've got to get in there and do your two minutes on the trapeze. Then it's over, and you move off to the next town."

RATINGS: Week ending December 29th

1st. Jennings (ABC's "World News Tonight")—11.4/21 [10,499,400]

2nd. Brokaw   ("NBC Nightly News")—10.3/20 [9,486,300]

3rd. Rather   ("CBS Evening News")—10.1/20 [9,302,100]

CHAPTER TWENTY-FIVE

Coda: Winners and Losers

On Wednesday, January 3, 1990, reporters, executives, producers, technicians all crammed into the second floor newsroom at ABC known as the Rim. Champagne was carted in, and soon the wine began to flow. ABC News had, for the first time in the history of the network, won first place in the year's ratings.

Standing along the far end of the room, Roone Arledge raised a glass. Then he started reading a list of names: "...Bob Siegenthaler, Av Westin, Jeff Gralnick, Bob Frye, Bill Lord, Paul Friedman..." The crowd, at first confused, finally caught on by the end of the list. Arledge was reading off the names of every executive producer who had ever worked at "World News Tonight." All around the room, people were laughing and cheering as he finished. "I want to tell you guys something," Arledge said. "All of you should be *really* proud. Everyone who has worked at 'World News Tonight' since the beginning...."

Paul Friedman said a quick thank you, and the attention focused on Peter Jennings. "I've been at a lot of these events," the anchor said. "I've heard Roone make a lot of speeches, but this is something special." He turned to Arledge with a slight choke in his voice. "You really mean it this time, don't you? It really means a lot to you."

Jennings took a sip of champagne, then held up his glass. "You know, the first time we won in the ratings for a week, Roone sent

370

champagne, but I sent it back because it wasn't vintage. This time, it's vintage champagne." The crowd laughed and applauded their approval.

Finally, Thomas Murphy, head of ABC's parent company, Capital Cities, stepped up to speak. He talked about being happy to let ABC News run itself, to stay out of the way, to let them do their own thing. "I still get chills up my spine when I hear that announcement, 'More people get their news from ABC than any other source,'" Murphy said. "You know, the key to any network is to have a great news division. CBS used to have that reputation. Now you guys do."

Ten blocks downtown, at the former dairy building that houses CBS News, the mood was less sanguine. The fall from the top position had been painful. It was taken especially hard by the CBS staff because for a few weeks they had actually plummeted to number three in the ratings. Dan Rather, Tom Bettag and others were reported as being depressed, even despondent, about their ratings position. After all, Rather had been the only regular anchor to present the news during Christmas week, and CBS had still come in third. CBS News had once again becoame a tense and edgy place to work, with all sorts of rumors floating around. Tom Bettag was in trouble, news vice-presidents Don DeCesare and Joe Peyronin were in trouble, CBS News president David Burke himself was in trouble. "Everyone's real demoralized," said one CBS staffer. "No matter how hard Dan works, he's not number one. Who's gonna take the fall?"

But Rather picked himself up and set off for Moscow, where CBS scored a real beat reporting on the growing democratization and the new multi-party system in the USSR. Then without a rest, he was on to South Africa to cover the release of Nelson Mandela. "It's hard at fifty-eight to run around the world," said a CBS producer. "But Dan keeps going. He keeps running. He keeps fighting."

At NBC, the mood was cautious optimism, *very* cautious, a "been down so long it looks like up to us" feeling. Now at last they were in contention for second place, not irrevocably doomed to third. And there was the year-end mega-meeting in Princeton, New Jersey. Called a "work-out" session, it was attended by some seventy-five NBC News staffers, from cameramen and reporters to executive producers. Surprisingly enough, even after a year of doubts and naysaying about the new management, the hard-nosed group thought that executives

Michael Gartner and Bob Wright acquitted themselves quite well, and many left with a new sense of optimism.

"I don't want to sound like a Moonie," was the phrase most often heard around NBC, "but I think this is really going to work." Staffers felt the critics were tired of shooting at NBC, and now it was CBS's turn to take the heat. Tom Brokaw and NBC were no longer alone at the bottom.

But halfway into 1990, NBC was still at the bottom of the barrel. Taking the fall for their failure, executive producer Bill Wheatley was abruptly replaced by Steve Friedman, Brokaw's old executive producer from the "Today" show. The talk about Jane Pauley as a co-anchor continued to grow.

As for ABC, the victory they were celebrating amounted to this: on the last week of 1989, ABC's "World News Tonight" scored just well enough in the ratings to eke out a win over the "CBS Evening News" for the calendar year. The 1989 results read:

ABC   10.14/20

CBS   10.09/20

NBC   9.44/19

In other words, ABC won the ratings war for 1989 not by a percentage point, not by a tenth of a percentage point, but by five one-hundredths of a percentage point—less than 50,000 people in a nation of 240 million.

If it was a close victory, no one could explain why it had happened. "Recently a lot of news that is important has been international," suggested Alan Wurtzel, ABC's head of research and marketing, "and Peter Jennings is uniquely qualified in that area." Others suggested that it had something to do with demographics, with Jennings' reputed popularity among younger urban viewers, a growing population, whereas Rather's success was among older Midwestern viewers, figuratively and literally a dying breed.

The truth is, no one had a clue. No one has *ever* had a clue when it comes to the Nielsens. They're like some mystic mumbo-jumbo, currently more mystical than ever with the Nielsen Company first finding hundreds of thousands of uncounted viewers in early 1990, and then in subsequent months acknowledging that they had suddenly "lost" up to eight percent of the TV viewing audience.

And even if the ratings are a yardstick of anything, they are today a yardstick that is being used to measure micro-millimeter differences. CBS's Morley Safer says, "These days, when it comes to news, we're down to Olympic timings, one-hundredths of a second. Frankly, it's effectively a tie. It has been for a few years now." And yet the TV industry still believes in the Nielsens, still acts as if they really mean something. (Just as this book goes to press, the networks have finally begun to acknowledge the problems with the Nielsens, and to develop a new system for charging advertisers.)

Even Peter Jennings, the latest big Nielsen winner, has to admit, "I don't know why we're in first place in the ratings. I didn't know why we were in third place when we were, and I don't know why we're in first place now. People keep asking me, and I can't tell them."

While ABC celebrates and CBS anguishes over the latest ratings, while all three networks are keeping an extraordinarily keen eye on the slightest fluctuations in the weekly Nielsens, they continue to ignore the other numbers. Those are the big numbers, the figures that say that the overall audience for evening network news is inexorably shrinking.

Ironically, the subtle difference in weekly ratings that elicits such strong reactions from the networks may in the end prove to be irrelevant—like the difference between those who are dancing on the deck, and those who are riding steerage on the Titanic. Whether they're first class or third, the ship is still going down.

"Everyone's worried about being number one or number two," said CBS's Bernard Goldberg (back when CBS was still on top). "It's crazy. Today's number one would have been number three, ten years ago. Everybody's losing. We better start thinking about making the news more important to people. The reason we're losing viewers is because of what we've defined as important. We're always looking at cable and VCRs as the reason we're losing our audience, but maybe we're not as interesting as we ought to be."

As Goldberg suggests, as senior producer Sally Holm (head of ABC's "American Agenda") suggests, as Charles Kuralt suggests and as we suggested earlier, the answer may well be a new role for the evening newscast: an expansion of its treatment of trends/ideas/achievements, and a new rhythm that slows the news down and gives it both more depth and a human face.

Despite the current bad news, while the audience for the traditional 6:30 and 7:00 PM national evening newscasts on ABC, CBS and NBC is dwindling, TV news as a whole is in fact burgeoning. The spectrum of televised news programs is broader than ever before. Like so many American businesses today, news is simply getting more fragmented, more specialized, as both the public and the product get more sophisticated.

People are watching special reports during the day. They're watching local news, primetime news hours, Ted Koppel's "Nightline." They're looking at CNN around the clock. (Small wonder, with all this viewing during the day, that the evening news feels old by 6:30 PM.) Viewing habits may be different, but if all the figures are added up, more people are actually watching some kind of TV news than ever before.

As radio once did, today it is TV that brings us the world. With the new portable, state-of-the-art equipment, when major events erupt, as they did last year, from San Francisco to Malta, TV delivers the news to our living room with breathtaking speed and immediacy. From one corner of the globe to the other, TV news is now the electronic tie that binds.

In fact, in almost every way, during the eighties the small screen got bigger. Much bigger. By the end of 1989, American households were watching an average *seven hours* a day (news, entertainment, sports, etc.), and TV became more significant than any other single factor in shaping the way most of us view our world. More than newspapers. More than books. More than films or records or radio. Welcome to the age of the couch potato.

Because of those great numbers of Americans glued to the tube, something mysterious started to happen recently: Slowly and subtly, the line between "reality" and television began to blur. It was no longer simple to tell the two apart. Events were reshaped to make for better television. Both the Democrats and the Republicans, for example, asked the networks how they should run their conventions.

Some events were reshaped *even as they were happening*. President George Bush himself was responsible for luring a drug dealer to the park across the street from the White House, solely for the purpose of heightening the drug problem in a nationally televised speech.

Then too, in this extraordinary age of satellite technology, the time lag between the news happening and the reporting of that news began to grow much shorter. In the past, when wars occurred, historians eventually wrote about them. Today, in these dazzlingly self-conscious times, TV allows us not only to watch our wars as they are being fought (or our stock market as it crashes), but to be acutely aware that we're actually sitting in on history in the making.

These days, it's harder and harder to differentiate between news, and the coverage of news. At the Malta summit, CNN was fed out to the ships where Bush and Gorbachev were talking. As the two superpower presidents shaped the future, they were actually able to watch themselves "live," and see how they and their statements were being played, and to adjust accordingly.

It's a new era, an era of video feedback. Today, the global village has become the global living room—one small room where everything is happening and everything is being watched, all at the same time. And in the center, both as observers and participants, are the anchors. At pivotal moments, in times of crisis or uncertainty, people turn to them for information and insight. In some ways, they are more trusted than our elected officials.

Take this story from Panama. American businessmen, hiding inside the Marriott Hotel during the recent invasion, were being interviewed on the phone by Tom Brokaw and Bryant Gumbel. From minute to minute, the businessmen gave live updates on their situation. "It feels real dangerous here," one reported to Brokaw and Gumbel. Then in the next breath, he asked the New York-based anchors, thousands of miles away, "Do you think it's safe to go down to the lobby?"

Veteran newsman John Chancellor, sitting next to Brokaw and Gumbel, commented on this bizarre hall-of-mirrors phenomenon. "They're watching American TV in those hotels, and they have people [there] working for NBC and other networks reporting on TV that they were trapped in this hotel, presumably being watched by the people who have trapped them....We live in a strange world."

What does all this mean for the nineties, for the future of news on the small screen? What does it mean for the future of the anchors? As TV news evolves into increasingly frequent live hookups from around the world, the anchors will not only be reporting major stories more often from wherever they are happening, but, by their sheer presence, influence them as well. It's not easy to imagine the May uprising in China without television coverage. As for the subsequent events in Eastern Europe, the speed with which they occurred would have been unthinkable in an electronically less sophisticated age.

Made increasingly mobile by technology, the anchors will no doubt continue in hot worldwide pursuit of one another in their competitive quest for the "freshest" news. As to their impact on that news? It can only be guessed, but as the last decade ended and this one began, we were given a parable for the future of TV journalism:

The people of Romania rose up and, overthrowing the dictatorial Ceausescu, installed a new provisional government. Of all the buildings in all of Bucharest from which their new leaders might have chosen to run the country, they picked a TV station.

Acknowledgments

Our special thanks to the three anchors themselves—Dan Rather, Peter Jennings and Tom Brokaw—who, despite appointment calendars heavy with other tasks and obligations, generously gave us their time and cooperation.

In addition, we'd also like to thank the following current or former staff members at the three networks, ABC, CBS and NBC:

Betsy Aaron, Bob Abernethy, William Abrams, Elise Adde, Robert Albertson, Philip Alongi, Joseph Angotti, Jeff Apodock, Roone Arledge, Karen Beckers, Annie Benjamin, Alejandro Benes, Russ Bensley, Tom Bettag, Jim Bittermann, Bill Blakemore, Ken Bode, Mark Brender, David Buksbaum, Katie Carpenter, William Catalano, John Chancellor, John Chesnutt, John Clark, Michael Clemente, Richard Cohen, Stephen Cohen, Ann Compton, John Cooley, Lester Crystal, Donna Dees, Edward Deitch, Don DeCesare, Katherine Dillon, Carroll Dougherty, Jon Entine, Karen Farris, Andrew Fies, Ed Fouhy, Reuven Frank, Stephen Frazier, Larry Fried, Paul Friedman, Fred Friendly, Nancy Gabriner, David Gelber, Tim Gibney, Bernard Goldberg, Roger Goodman, Tom Goodman, Cheryl Gould, Renate Gozlan, Jeff Gralnick, Paul Greenberg, Lawrence K. Grossman, C. Harper Heinz, Peter Herford, Steven M. Herman, Andrew Heyward, Sally Holm, Josh Howard, Natalie Hunter, Geri Jansen, Peter Kallisher, Marty Kaplan, Richard Kaplan, Amy Katz, Jeff Kay, Jake Keever, Rick King, Seymour "Sid" Kline, Marty Koughan, Robert Krulwich, Charles Kuralt, Marc Kusnetz, John Lane, John Lawrence, Robert Legvold, David Lewis, Frank Lopez, Elmer Lower, Robert MacNeil, Tony Malara, Morris Mann, Linda Mason, Katherine McQuay, John McWethy, Robert Murphy, Barbara Nevins, Robert "Shad" Northshield, Eric Ober, Rob Pattullo, Bill Plante, David Poltrack, Brooke Porter, Hugh Raisky, Scott Richardson, Brian Ross, Morley Safer, Bill Schechner, Herbert Schlosser, Stu Schutzman, Frank Shanbacker, Paul Slavin, Steve Snyder, Sandy Socolow, Bruce Soloway, Peter Sturtevant,

Charlotte Taylor, Steve Tello, John Terenzio, Richard Threlkeld, Paul Tilsley, Janet Tobias, Garrick Utley, Alma Varvaro, Lane Venardos, Tom Vitale, Richard Wald, Arnot Walker, Milton Weiss, William Wheatley, Lilyan Wilder, Tom Yellin, Susan Zirinsky.

And thanks to the many other helpful contributors who—working in this mercurial and insecure business of network news—preferred not to be listed by name.

The following friends, relatives and associates of the anchors were kind enough to assist us: Don Allan, Dr. Elliott Bowers, Hugh Cunningham, Professor William Farber, Marjorie Gross, Sarah Jennings, Bill Johnston, Norma Dell Jones, Richard Leibner, Darold Loecker, Jack Nichols, Hod Nielsen, Don Rather.

Our thanks also to Jeff James and Jo Laverde at the A. C. Nielsen Company; Dana Rogers and Diane Lewis at the Museum of Broadcasting; Paul Isaacson at Young & Rubicam; John Sisk at J. Walter Thompson; Dean Joan Konner, Columbia University School of Journalism, and Natalie Payne at the Columbia University Center for Media and Society Seminars.

Finally, we would like to express our warm appreciation to those colleagues at *The Wall Street Journal* and UCLA, as well as to the other writers, photographers and TV journalists who so generously offered us information, insights and assistance: Calvin Bedient, Charles Bierbauer, David Blum, Verne Gay, Kevin Goldman, Oliver Herrgesell, Kelly Hertz, Andrei Khoukhrikov, Dennis Kneale, Kevin Lein, Ken Lincoln, Chip Meyers, William Prochnau, Richard Reynolds, Paul Schirnhofer and Joseph M. Tiernan. And merci to our editor, Hillel Black, for his enthusiasm and support.

Bibliography

Our primary sources for *Anchors* were the interviews we conducted with Tom Brokaw, Peter Jennings and Dan Rather throughout 1989-1990 and, of course, their newscasts themselves. Important additional information was supplied to us by the anchors' friends, relatives and colleagues.

The following is a selected listing of publications and other materials consulted in the preparation of our book. Those with asterisks were of particular importance.

Adams, Cindy. "Thugs Drop Anchor." *New York Post* (October 6, 1986), 5 +.

Alter, Jonathan. "Behind the NBC News Blues." *Newsweek* (October 16, 1989), 86 +.

_____."Civil War at CBS." *Newsweek* (September 8, 1986).

_____."Karl Marx, Meet Marshall McLuhan." *Newsweek* (May 29, 1989).

*_____and Bill Powell. "Bottom-Line Larry: Doing What Comes Naturally at CBS." *Manhattan, inc.* (November 1987), 75-85.

Arlen, Michael J. *The Living Room War*. New York: Viking, 1969.

_____."The Prosecutor." *New Yorker*, LIII (November 28, 1977), 166-173.

Bagdikian, Ben. *The Media Monopoly*. Boston: Beacon, 1983.

Barber, James David. "Not the *New York Times*: What Network News Should Be." *Washington Monthly* (September 1979), 14-21.

Barnouw, Erik. *Tube of Plenty*. New York: Oxford University Press, 1975.

Barrett, Marvin. *Rich News, Poor News*. New York: Crowell, 1978.

Bergreen, Laurence. *Look Now, Pay Later: The Rise and Fall of Network Broadcasting*. New York: New American Library, 1980.

Berke, Richard L. "Script for Bush's Drug Deal Yields a Comedy." *New York Times* (December 16, 1989).

Blair, Gwenda. *Almost Golden: Jessica Savitch and the Selling of Television News*. New York: Avon, 1989.

*Blum, David. "Up From 'Club Thirteen': The Rise and Rise of Peter Jennings." *New York* (November 30, 1987), 50-56.

Bode, Ken. "The Backlash Is Starting Against Those Trials by Media." *TV Guide* (October 7, 1989), 21-23.

Bogart, Leo. "Television News as Entertainment." *The Entertainment Functions of Television*. ed. Percy H. Tannenbaum. Hillsdale, N.J.: Laurence Erlbaum Associates, 1980.

Boyer, Peter. "A Baffled Brokaw Sees Ratings Slip." *New York Times* (March 9, 1988).

———. "CBS Explains 'Evening News' Incident." *New York Times* (September 14, 1987).

———. "When News Must Pay Its Way, Expect Trivia." *New York Times* (October 2, 1989), 19.

*———. *Who Killed CBS?* New York: Random House, 1988.

*[Brokaw Radio Interview], American Focus (March 17, 1985).

*[Brokaw Television Interview], "Later with Bob Costas." NBC (August 24, 1989).

Brokaw, Tom. "China: Pictures in My Mind's Eye." *Communicator* (August 1989), 18-19.

———. "A Day in the Life of a White House Correspondent." *Washington Monthly*, XI (December 1975), 138-139.

———. "On the Fate of TV News." *Washington Post* (April 19, 1987), D1 +.

———. "Response to Giago." *Yankton Daily Press & Dakotan* (August 14, 1989), 4.

———. "A Small Town, a Tiny Gym, and a Hero." *New York Times* (April 5, 1987), 12S.

Brooke, Jill. "ABC's Evening Newscast Tops Ratings For 1st Time." *New York Post* (January 4, 1990).

———. "The Rathering Storm: Other Blots on TV News Copybook." *New York Post* (September 29, 1989), 3.

——— and Frank Bruni. "Network May Lose Journalism Award Over Tape Controversy." *New York Post* (September 28, 1989), 3.

Brown, Les. *Television: The Business Behind the Box*. New York: Harcourt Brace Jovanovich, 1971.

Brown, Merrill. "Can Elephants Learn to Waltz?" [An address given in March 1988 and reprinted in], *Media Reader*. ed. Shirley Biagi. Belmont: Wadsworth Publishing Company, 1989.

Browning, Frank. "Tom Brokaw Is Mad as Heck." [An Interview], *Mother Jones* (April 1983), 20 + .

Carcaterra, Lorenzo. "Tom Brokaw, Profile of the Week." *Daily News* (April 21, 1985), 3.

Carter, Bill. "ABC Plans to Impose New TV Rating System." *New York Times* (June 1, 1990), A1 + .

_____. "CBS-ABC Race for 2nd Means Nothing and Everything." *New York Times* (March 13, 1989), D8.

_____. "CBS News Head Denies Fakery Charges." *New York Times* (October 5, 1989).

_____. "CBS Plans New Round of Staff Cuts." *New York Times* (March 30, 1990), D4.

_____. "For NBC, 'Party's Over' at Its Affiliates Meeting." *New York Times* (June 4, 1990), D7.

_____. "NBC News Chief Trying to Smooth 'Rough Spots.'" *New York Times* (August 2, 1989), C22.

_____. "NBC News Decides To Stop Using Dramatizations." *New York Times* (November 21, 1989), B1-B2.

_____. "NBC Show Deletes G.E. Mention." *New York Times* (December 3, 1989).

_____. "Nielsen to Study Changes in Ratings." *New York Times* (May 18, 1990).

_____. "Study Finds Untallied TV Viewers." *New York Times* (May 10, 1990), D21.

*Carter, Hodding. "The Anchor" & "...and so it goes." Inside Story (Program #403 PBS), The Press and the Public Project, Inc. (February 3, 1984).

*_____. "News in the Networks." Inside Story (Program #212 PBS), The Press and the Public Project, Inc. (April 23, 1982).

Castro, Janice. "The Battle in Network News: CBS and NBC Get New Chiefs as the Rating War Escalates." *Time*, CXIX (March 15, 1982), 52-53.

Chomiak Jr., Don. "What TV News Will Be Like In The '90s." *Communicator* (May 1988), 26 +.

*Conant, Jennet, "Michael Gartner: What's Behind the Bow Tie?" *Manhattan, inc.* (March 1989) 51-59.

Crist, Judith. "ABC Anchor Peter Jennings." *TV Guide*, Vol. XXXV, #1 (January 3, 1987).

Crain, Rance. "Now For the Latest Episode in 'Dan, the Alien Anchor.'" *Crain's New York Business* (October 9, 1989).

"Curtain Goes Up on 'NBC Nightly News' Mudd-Brokaw Anchor Team." *Broadcasting*, CII (April 5, 1982), 150.

*Darling, Lynn, "Country Boy Makes Good." *Esquire*, CV (March 1986), 90-93.

Diamond, Edwin. "All in the Family." *New York* (June 25, 1990), 40-44.

*_____. "Anchor Wars." *Rolling Stone* (October 9, 1986), 59-68.

_____. "Attack of the People Meters." *New York* (August 24, 1987), 39-41.

_____. "Behind the Peacock Throne." *New York* (February 13, 1989), 21 +.

_____. *Good News, Bad News.* Cambridge, Mass.: MIT Press, 1978.

_____. "Playing the China Card." *New York* (June 5, 1989), 16-19.

_____. "Power Failure." *New York* (November 6, 1989), 24 +.

_____. "Rather Strange." *New York* (September 28, 1987).

_____. *Sign Off: The Last Days of Television.* Cambridge, Mass.: MIT Press, 1982.

_____. "The Tisching of CBS." *New York* (May 16, 1988), 30-33.

_____ and Paul Noglows. "When Network News Pulls Its Punches." *TV Guide* (June 20, 1987), 3-7.

Donlon, Brian. "Jennings, ABC News Pick Up Steam." *USA Today* (December 14, 1989).

Epstein, Edward Jay. *News from Nowhere: Television and the News.* New York: Random House, 1973.

Francis, Fred. "Get Me to the Invasion on Time." *Communicator* (February 1990), 12 +.

Frank, Reuven. "On Tiananmen Square, Echoes of Chicago in '68." *New York Times* (June 4, 1989).

Friendly, Fred W. *Due to Circumstances Beyond Our Control...* New York: Vintage Books, 1968.

_____. "Network News? 'A National Tragedy' — Local News? 'It's Putrid' — Million Dollar Journalists? 'Obscene.'" *TV Guide*, XXIX (August 1, 1981), 24-29.

_____. "On Television: News, Lies and Videotape." *New York Times* (August 6, 1989), 1 +.

Gans, Herbert. *Deciding What's News*. New York: Pantheon, 1979.

Gates, Gary Paul. *Air Time: The Inside Story of CBS News*. New York: Harper and Row, 1978.

Gay, Verne. "ABC News Nears No. 1." *Newsday* (December 15, 1989).

_____. "Anchors Go To NATO Summit as Three Networks Go All Out." *Variety* (May 31-June 7, 1989), 47 +.

_____. "CBS Recaptures Lead in News." *Variety* (June 7-13, 1989).

_____. "Introspection at NBC: Is No News Good News?" *Variety* (April 5-11, 1989), 1 +.

_____. "Is There Room At The Top For The Women Of TV News?" *Variety* (May 10-16, 1989), 86.

_____. "Mike Gartner Reflects on Hectic 1st Year." [An Interview] *Variety* (August 9-15, 1989), 51 +.

_____. "Peter Jennings Moves Out From Behind Anchor Desk." *Newsday* (January 24, 1990), 2 +.

_____. "Rather Makes War on China; NBC, CNN in Footage Tiff." *Variety* (May 24-30, 1989), 43 +.

_____. "Strong Desk Will Call The Shots; NBC Appoints Exec News Director." *Variety* (May 10-16, 1989), 80.

Gelfman, Judith S. *Women in Television News*. New York: Columbia University Press, 1976.

Gerard, Jeremy. "ABC Surpasses CBS in Evening News Ratings." *New York Times* (November 29, 1989), C22.

_____. "NBC Adds Data Critical of G.E." *New York Times* (December 8, 1989).

_____. "TV Networks Want Nielsen To Change Rating Methods." *New York Times* (December 14, 1989), D1 +.

Giago, Tim. "Rushmore Isn't Everyone's Treasure." (Notes from Indian Country), *Yankton Daily Press and Dakotan* (July 26, 1989), 3.

Gitlin, Todd. "Gauging the Aftershocks of Disaster Coverage." *New York Times* (November 12, 1989).

————. *Inside Prime Time. New York*: Pantheon, 1983.

————, ed. *Watching Television*. New York: Pantheon, 1986.

Goldberg, Robert. "Anchors Away Make Impact at Home." *The Wall Street Journal* (June 19, 1989), A9.

————. "Did the Medium Become the Message?" *The Wall Street Journal* (January 2, 1990), A9.

————. "TV: Up-links and Hi-jinks at the Summit." *The Wall Street Journal* (December 4, 1989), A14.

Goldman, Kevin. "NBC Secretly Fine-Tunes Its Lagging 'Nightly News.'" *The Wall Street Journal* (October 2, 1989), B1.

Goodman, Walter. "For TV Networks at Malta, Big Stars, Great Scenery but 'Anchors Adrift.'" *New York Times* (December 4, 1989).

————. "Network News and the Push To Do Less and Do It Worse." *New York Times* (February 8, 1990), C22.

————. "Professional Judgment vs. Visual Imperatives in TV News." *New York Times* (April 16, 1989), C16.

————. "A Small Flotilla of Unanchored Anchors." *New York Times* (December 17, 1989), 41 +.

————. "TV Watched as History was Made." *New York Times* (December 24, 1989).

Granville, Kari. "CNN Takes on Networks With 'World Today.'" *Los Angeles Times* (October 16, 1989), [Calendar].

Greenfield, Jeff. "Showdown at ABC News." *New York Times Magazine* (February 13, 1977), 32-34 +.

Grula, Richard J. "The Price of Litchfield Living." *On the Avenue* (October 7, 1989) 16-20.

Guider, Elizabeth. "Contrite NBC Appeases Affils in Wake of Quake Coverage." *Variety* (November 1, 1989).

————. "Poll Finds Peter Jennings 'Most Believable' Newsman." *Variety* (November 16, 1989).

————. "Quake Snafu Sends Tremors Thru NBC News Management." *Variety* (October 25-31, 1989), 45-46.

————. "Stations, Networks Ponder Lessons Learned in Quake." *Variety* (October 25-31, 1989), 45 +.

————. "Yank Webs Provide Fanfare As The Iron Curtain Rises." *Variety* (November 15, 1989), 35-36.

Grundberg, Andy. "Blurred and Shaky Images That Burn in the Mind." *New York Times* (January 14, 1990), 35 +.

Halberstam, David. *The Powers that Be*. New York: Alfred A. Knopf, 1979.

Hall, Jane. "The News about 'Broadcast.'" *People Weekly*, XXIX (February 1, 1988), 62-66 +.

Hallin, Daniel. "Network News: We Keep America on Top of the World." In Todd Gitlin's *Watching Television*.

Hanauer, Joan. "Good News for ABC News." UPI (January 3, 1990).

Hickey, Neil. "In ABC's Corner: Peter Jennings." *TV Guide*, XIII (August 14, 1965), 6-9.

Hill, Doug. "How Tom Brokaw Has Built His Power — and Uses It." *TV Guide* (October 24, 1987), 7-11.

"The Houston Hurricane: Dan Rather Is a Country Boy in a Hurry." *Time* (February 25, 1980), 72-75.

Huff, Richard and Charles Paikert. "No More 'Chicken Noodle Network.'" [CNN at 10], *Variety* (April 18, 1990), 49 +.

Ivey, Sue. "Brokaw Remembers Days at YHS." *Yankton Daily Press and Dakotan* (August 21, 1989), 1 +.

Jahr, C. "Dan Rather: Soft Side of a Tough Anchorman." *Ladies' Home Journal*, XCVII (July 1980), 76 +.

Jankowski, Gene. "Better News Shows Can Be Good Business: An Interview." *US News and World Report*, LXXXVIII (June 9, 1980), 61.

*[Jennings Radio Interview], American Focus (May 19, 1985).

*[Jennings Television Interview], "Later with Bob Costas." NBC (August 23, 1989).

[Jennings named Best National TV Anchor], *Washington Journalism Review* (March 1990).

*Jones, Alex S. "The Anchors." *New York Times Magazine* (July 27, 1986), 12-17.

_____. "Black Journalists Seek New Gains in Newsroom." *New York Times* (August 17, 1989).

Joyce, Ed. "Is Network News Getting Better —or Worse?" *TV Guide* (May 13, 1989), 10-12.

_____. *Prime Times, Bad Times*. New York: Doubleday, 1988.

Julian, Alexander. "Dressing Down TV's Anchormen." *GO* (November 1982), 100.

*Kaye, Elizabeth. "Peter Jennings Gets No Self-respect." *Esquire* (September 1989), 158-176.

Kaye, Jeff. "NBC to Drop News Show Re-Creations." *Los Angeles Times* (November 21, 1989), F1.

Kendrick, Alexander. *Prime Time: The Life of Edward R. Murrow*. Boston: Little, Brown, 1969.

*Kenney, Charles. "Top of the News: Why Peter Jennings Is So Good." *Boston Globe Magazine* (November 6, 1988).

Kintner, Robert Edmons. *Broadcasting and the News*. New York: Harper and Row, 1965.

Kissinger, David. "Staff Cuts Put Squeeze on Euro Bureaus; Nets Hussle to Cover Historic Events Despite Cost Cutting." *Variety* (May 2, 1990), 293 +.

Klein, Edward, "Winning Diane." *New York* (March 13, 1989), 36 +.

Kleinfield, N.R. "As Viewers Wander, Networks Scurry After." *New York Times* (February 26, 1989), Section 2, 1+.

Konner, Joan. "Broadcast Journalism: What's Missing?" [A speech delivered to the Cosmopolitan Club], (February 24, 1987).

———. "From Here to Here." [A speech delivered as the Opening Day Remarks], Columbia University, (September 6, 1988).

Kramer, Carol. "The Most Trusted Men in America." *McCall's* (July 1987), 114 +.

*Leonard, Bill. *In the Storm of the Eye; A Lifetime at CBS*. New York: Putnam, 1987.

Lesher, Stephen. *Media Unbound: The Impact of Television Journalism on the Public*. Boston: Houghton Mifflin, 1982.

Levin, Eric. "Are Two Heads Better than One?: Chancellor and Brinkley, NBC's New News Team. " *TV Guide* (December 18, 1976), 6-9.

Lewis, Carolyn Diana. *Reporting for Television*. New York: Columbia University Press, 1984.

Lipman, Joanne. "ABC Rivals Reassess Audience Guarantees." *The Wall Street Journal* (June 4, 1990), B6.

MacNeil, Robert. *The People Machine*. New York: Harper and Row, 1968.

———. *The Right Place at the Right Time*. Boston: Little, Brown, 1982.

Madden, Kathleen. "Peter Jennings." Vogue (June 1985), 271 +.

Matusow, Barbara. "Big Bad Tom." *The Washingtonian* (June 1989), 120 +.

*———. *The Evening Stars*. Boston: Houghton Mifflin, 1983.

Massing, Michael. "CBS: Sauterizing the News." *Columbia Journalism Review* (March-April 1986).

McCabe, Peter. *Bad News at Black Rock: The Sell-Out of CBS News.* New York: Arbor House, 1987.

McCarthy, Colman. "Brokaw: Opinionated And Indiscreet." *The Washington Post* (March 26, 1983), A25.

McFadden, Robert D. "Park Ave. Assault on Rather Leaves Mystery as to Motive." *New York Times* (October 6, 1986), B3.

McGrory, Mary. "Newscasters Have Fine Line on Giving Personal Views." *Albany Times Union* (April 3, 1983), D5.

McLaughlin, Peter and David J. Krajicek. "Mystery of Attack on Rather." *Daily News* (October 6, 1986).

Metz, Robert. *The Today Show: An Inside Look at 25 Tumultuous Years.* Chicago: Playboy Press, 1977.

Miller, Mark Crispin. *Boxed In: The Culture of TV.* Evanston: Northwestern University Press, 1989.

Morse, Margaret. "The Television News Personality and Credibility." In *Studies in Entertainment.* ed. Tania Modleski, Bloomington: Indiana University Press, 1986.

Murphy, Mary. "Tom Snyder: TV's Child Faces the Future." *Esquire* (March 28, 1978), 43-48.

Murphy, Ryan P. "Voted Most Trustworthy of the Anchormen." *The Saturday Evening Post* (November 1988), 42-45 +.

Nash, Alanna. *Golden Girl: The Story of Jessica Savitch.* New York: Signet, 1988.

"NBC News Is Planning to Shut Its Paris Bureau." *New York Times* (August 15, 1989).

Paley, William S. *As It Happened: A Memoir.* New York: Doubleday, 1979.

Paper, Lewis J. *Empire: William S. Paley and the Making of CBS.* New York: St. Martin's Press, 1987.

Petersen, Ross. "YHS Receives Bomb Threat." *Yankton Daily Press and Dakotan* (February 6, 1989), 3.

Pooley, Eric. "Grins, Gore, and Videotape: The Trouble With Local TV News," *New York* (October 9, 1989), 37-44.

Powers, Ron. "Eyewitless News." *Columbia Journalism Review* (May-June 1977), 17-24.

––––––. *The Newscasters.* New York: St. Martin's Press, 1978.

———. "When News Gets Lost in the Stars." *Channels* (June-July 1981), 32.

Puglisi, Rob. "Satellite News Feeds: Many New Sources." *Communicator* (November 1988), 10-17.

*[Rather Radio Interview], American Focus (November 4, 1979).

[Rather Television Interview], "Later with Bob Costas." NBC (August 22, 1989).

Rather, Dan. "Confidence in Washington, Sir?" (Editor's Beat), *The Houstonian* (September 27, 1952).

———. "Democrats Stand on Their Record." (Editor's Beat), *The Houstonian*, 1952.

———. "Ditch Boss is Real Man." (Editor's Beat), *The Houstonian*.

———. "Making Foreign News Less Foreign," [A speech delivered at the Japan House], New York (June 22, 1989).

———. "McCarthy in the Colleges." (Editor's Beat), *The Houstonian*.

———. "New Bible is Writers Guide." (Editor's Beat), *The Houstonian* (October 11, 1952).

———. "'New York, Are You There?'" as part of "In Beijing, a Month of Living Dangerously." *New York Times* (June 25, 1989), 29 +.

———. "The Shot Rod Goes Berserk." (Editor's Beat), *The Houstonian*.

———. "So Far, So Good, Says Dan Rather." *Broadcasting*, C (May 11, 1981), 29-30.

———. "World Needs a Santa Claus." (Editor's Beat), *The Houstonian*.

*——— with Mickey Herskowitz. *The Camera Never Blinks*. New York: Ballantine, 1977.

——— and Gary Paul Gates. *The Palace Guard*. New York: Harper and Row, 1974.

"Rather and Joyce Tiff at CBS Over Staffing on 'Evening News.'" *Variety* (June 19, 1985).

Reasoner, Harry. *Before the Colors Fade*. New York: Alfred A. Knopf, 1981.

Robbins, Jim. "Stars Stake a Piece Of Big Sky Country." *New York Times* (March 21, 1990), C1 +.

Rosenbaum, Ron. "The Man Who Married Dan Rather." *Esquire*, XCVIII (November, 1982), 53-56.

Rosenberg, Howard. "The Berlin Wall: Anchoring the Breaking Story." *Los Angeles Times* (November 13, 1989), F1 +.

Rosenstiel, Thomas B. "News Is Where TV Anchor Is, Study Shows." *Los Angeles Times* (October 3, 1989), Part VI, 1 +.

Roshco, Bernard. *Newsmaking.* Chicago: University of Chicago Press, 1975.

Rothenberg, Fred. "Tom Brokaw: Selling of an Anchorman." *New York Post* (October 23, 1986).

Rothenberg, Randall. "TV Networks See Smaller Audience." *New York Times* (February 8, 1989), D1 +.

Rusher, William. "'Mother Jones' Interview Reveals the Real Brokaw." *Nashville Banner* (July 6, 1983).

Russell, Dick. "Africa." *TV Guide* (December 4-10, 1976).

Sanders, Marlene and Marcia Rock. *Waiting for Prime Time; the Women of Television News.* Urbana: University of Illinois Press, 1988.

Savitch, Jessica. *Anchorwoman.* New York: Putnam, 1982.

Scardino, Albert. "A Debate Heats Up: Is It News or Entertainment?" *New York Times* (January 15, 1989), 29 +.

Schieffer, Bob and Gary Paul Gates. *The Acting President.* New York: Dutton, 1989.

_____. "That Bush-Rather Blowup: A New Twist." *TV Guide* (July 8-14, 1989), 33-36.

Schiller, Herbert. *The Corporate Takeover of Public Expression.* New York: Oxford, September 1989.

Schoenbrun, David. *On and Off the Air: An Informal History of TV News.* New York: Dutton, 1989.

Schwartz, Tony. "Dan On the Run." *New York* (February 3, 1986), 32-38.

Shales, Tom. "Gunga Dan." *Washington Post* (April 7, 1980), B1 +.

_____. "NBC News Losing Its Plumage." *The Washington Post* (March 28, 1989), D1 +.

_____. *On the Air!* New York: Summit Books, 1982.

Sharbutt, Jay. "American Networks Seek Global Audience for U.S. TV Newscasts." *Los Angeles Times* (January 4, 1988), Part IV, 1 +.

*Shaw, David. "TV News: Demise Is Exaggerated." *Los Angeles Times* (December 28, 1986), 1.

Sherman, Stratford P. "Inside the Mind of Jack Welch." *Fortune* (March 27, 1989), 38-50.

Small, William J. *To Kill a Messenger: Television News and the Real World.* New York: Hastings House, 1970.

Smith, Desmond. "Dan Rather in the Hot Seat." *New York*, XIV (November 2, 1981), 33-36.

———. "The Wide World of Roone Arledge." *New York Times Magazine* (February 24, 1980), 37-39 +.

Smith, Sally Bedell. "Dan Rather Heard on TV in Profanity." *New York Times* (September 20, 1983).

Snyder, Tom. "Playboy Interview: Tom Snyder." *Playboy* (February 1981), 63-82 +.

Sobran, Joseph. "The Complex Vision of Tom Brokaw." *Washington Times* (March 21, 1983).

Sperber, Ann M. *Murrow: His Life and Times*. New York: Freundlich Books, 1986.

Steinmetz, Johanna. " 'Mr. Magic' —The TV Newscast Doctor," *New York Times* (October 12, 1975), Section 2; 1 +.

Stengel, Richard. "Bushwhacked!" *Time* (February 8, 1988), 16-20.

Swertlow, Frank. "ABC's Prince: The Most Powerful Man in Television." *New York*, X (October 10, 1977), 39-43.

Thompson, Toby. "The Prince of News: Tom Brokaw." *Rolling Stone* (May 13, 1982), 26-29.

Tivnan, Edward. "The Cronkite Syndrome." *Dial* (November 1980), 44-52.

"Turner's Gutsy New News Service." *Business Week* (January 11, 1982), 42 +.

Vidal, Gore. "Cue the Green God, Ted." *The Nation* (August 7-14, 1989).

Waters, Harry F. "Dan Rather, Anchorman." *Newsweek*, XCV (February 25, 1980), 71-72.

———. "The New Look of TV News." *Newsweek*, LXXXVIII (October 11, 1976), 68-75.

———. "Star Wars in TV News." *Newsweek*, XCIX (April 12, 1982), 72, 75.

Weisman, John. "Is CBS Still the Tiffany of Network News?" *TV Guide* (July 2, 1988), 3-6.

Westin, Av. *Newswatch: How Television Gathers and Delivers the News*. New York: Simon and Schuster, 1982.

Wilson, Janet. "The Afghan Affair: Dan Rather Aired Fake Battles With the Soviets." *New York Post* (September 27, 1989), 5 +.

_____. "Afghaniscam Plot Thickens as Dan and Execs Huddle." *New York Post* (September 28, 1989), 2 +.

_____. "CBS News Stands by Afghan War Film." *New York Post* (October 5, 1989), 5.

"'World Today': Shaw Shines, Crier Controversial, but Ratings Rough." *Variety* (April 18-25, 1990), 54 +.

Yagoda, Ben. "When Leibner Calls, the Networks Listen." *New York Times Magazine* (June 18, 1989), 36 +.

Zoglin, Richard. "Hard Times at a 'Can-Do' Network." *Time* (March 23, 1987), 75.

_____." 'I Was Trained to Ask Questions.'" *Time* (February 8, 1988), 24-26.

_____. "Rather Profile." *Time* (February 8, 1988), 24-26.

_____. "Star Power." *Time* (August 7, 1989), 46-51.

_____. "Star Wars at the Networks." *Time* (April 3, 1989), 70-71.

Index